May 30–June 1, 2013
Cincinnati, Ohio, USA

Association for
Computing Machinery

Advancing Computing as a Science & Profession

SIGMIS-CPR'13

Proceedings of the 2013 ACM Conference on
Computers and People Research

Sponsored by:
SIGMIS

Association for Computing Machinery

Advancing Computing as a Science & Profession

The Association for Computing Machinery
2 Penn Plaza, Suite 701
New York, New York 10121-0701

Notice to Past Authors of ACM-Published Articles
ACM intends to create a complete electronic archive of all articles and/or other material previously published by ACM. If you have written a work that has been previously published by ACM in any journal or conference proceedings prior to 1978, or any SIG Newsletter at any time, and you do NOT want this work to appear in the ACM Digital Library, please inform permissions@acm.org, stating the title of the work, the author(s), and where and when published.

ISBN: 978-1-4503-1975-1

Additional copies may be ordered prepaid from:

ACM Order Department
PO Box 30777
New York, NY 10087-0777, USA

Phone: 1-800-342-6626 (USA and Canada)
+1-212-626-0500 (Global)
Fax: +1-212-944-1318
E-mail: acmhelp@acm.org
Hours of Operation: 8:30 am – 4:30 pm ET

Printed in the USA

Foreword

It is our great pleasure to welcome you to the Annual Computers and People Research Conference - *ACM SIGMIS CPR 2013*. For the past 50 plus years, ACM SIGMIS CPR has engaged the academic and practitioner communities in understanding the issues related to the information technology (IT) workforce. As societies everywhere work to recover from a global economic recession, cities and regions that are particularly challenged are those whose economies have historically depended on 19th and 20th century models of work. Now, the economic sustainability of these societies requires that they reinvent themselves for a 21st century economy that increasingly depends upon innovation and creative uses of information technology. Of concern to the SIGMIS CPR community are the implications for IT workforce career paths in this new economy, the skills and knowledge that will be needed, and human resource strategies in these economically difficult times. As a result, we selected the conference theme of *economic renewal and sustainability through information technology work*.

The papers and panels, within the proceedings, address topics such as IT skill development, diversity and socio-cultural issues in the attraction, recruitment, retention, and development of IT professionals, pedagogical issues and trends which are critical to economic renewal and sustainability. We hope these proceedings serve as a valuable reference for computer and people researchers and practitioners in the coming years.

Putting together the *ACM SIGMIS CPR 2013* conference was made possible by the work of many dedicated individuals. We first thank the authors for providing the program content. We are grateful to the program committee who worked diligently in reviewing papers and providing constructive feedback for authors. In addition, we would like to thank Michelle Kaarst-Brown and Fred Niederman, for organizing this year's doctoral consortium. We also thank Indira Guzman and Susan Yager for their role as Treasurers, and Nita Brooks for publicity. Special thanks go to Lisa Tolles and her team from Sheridan Proceedings Service for their work in processing the proceedings in a timely manner. Finally, we thank our sponsor, ACM SIGMIS, and the leadership of Janice Sipior. We hope that you will find this program beneficial and that the conference will provide you with a valuable opportunity to share ideas with other researchers and practitioners from institutions around the world.

Thomas Ferratt, University of Dayton
Conference Co-Chair

Eileen Trauth, The Pennsylvania State University
Conference Co-Chair

K.D. Joshi, Washington State University
Program Co-Chair

Allison Morgan, Howard University
Program Co-Chair

Kevin Gallagher, Northern Kentucky University
Local Arrangements Co-Chair

Table of Contents

Session 4.1: IT Skills & Education II
Session Chair: Jo Ellen Moore

Session 4.2: IT Workforce Culture
Session Chair: Cindy Riemenschneider

Session 5.1: Panel Session-II

Session 5.2: Trends in the IT Workforce I
Session Chair: Mike Gallivan

Session 6.1: Trends in the IT Workforce II
Session Chair: Jeria Quesenberry

Session 6.2: IT Systems & Teams
Session Chair: Jaime Windeler

Session: Doctoral Consortium Papers

SIGMIS CPR 2013 Conference Organization

General Chairs: Thomas Ferratt, University of Dayton
Eileen Trauth, The Pennsylvania State University

Program Chairs: K.D. Joshi, Washington State University
Allison Morgan, Howard University

Conference Treasurers: Indira Guzman de Galvez, TUI University
Susan Yager, Southern Illinois University, Edwardsville

Doctoral Consortium Chairs: Michelle Kaarst-Brown, Syracuse University
Fred Niederman, St. Louis University

Doctoral Consortium Mentors: Tim Weitzel, University of Bamberg
Andreas Eckhardt, Goethe University Frankfurt
JoEllen Moore, Southern Illinois University, Edwardsville
Harvey Enns, Dayton University
Gaetan Mourmant, President, XLerateur Inc.
Cindy Riemenschneider , Baylor University
Likoebe Maruping, University of Louisville

Local Arrangements Chair: Kevin Gallagher, Northern Kentucky University

Publicity Chair: Nita Brooks, Middle Tennessee State University

Program Committee: Monica Adya, Marquette University
Genevieve Bassellier, McGill University
Tanya Beaulieu, Washington State University
John Benamati, Miami University - Ohio
Bridgett Blodgett, University of Baltimore
Stephan Böhm, Hochschule RheinMain
Kayla Booth, Penn State University
Greg Brierly, United States Army & Syracuse University
Nita Brooks, Middle Tennessee State University
Mari Buche, Michigan Technological University
Curtis Cain, Penn State University
Chris Califf, Washington State University
Lynne Cooper, Jet Propulsion Laboratory - NASA
Andreas Eckhardt, Goethe-University Frankfurt am Main
Mike Gallivan, Georgia State University
Donna Grant, North Carolina Central University
Saurabh Gupta, University of North Florida
Tracy Hall, Brunel University
Andrea Hester, Southern Illinois University Edwardsville
Nathan Johnson, Washington State University
Damien Joseph, Nanyang Technological University
Janet Kourik, Webster University

Program Committee (continued):   Lynette Kvasny, Pennsylvania State University
Sven Laumer, Otto-Friedrich-University Bamberg
Hsun-Ming Lee, Texas State University - San Marcos
Diane Lending, James Madison University
Yibai Li, Washington State University
Bin Mai, Bowie State University
Kent Marett, Mississippi State University
Todd Martin, Washington State University
Jo Ellen Moore, Southern Illinois University Edwardsville
Gaetan Mourmant, Paris Dauphine University
Susanne Niklas, RheinMain University
Stig Nordheim, University of Agder
Lorne Olfman, Claremont Graduate University
Day Orin, RTI International
Brandis Phillips, North Carolina A & T
Norah Power, University of Limerick
Jeria Quesenberry, Carnegie Mellon University
Ijaz A. Qureshi, HITEC University
Adriane Randolph-Davis, Kennesaw State University
Srinivasan Rao, University of Texas at San Antonio
Cindy Riemenschneider, Baylor University
Gail Robin, Baker College Center of Graduate Studies
Sherry Ryan, University of North Texas
Dana Schwieger, Southeast Missouri State University
Nathan Sikes, RTI International
Derek Smith, University of Cape Town
Lone Stub Petersen, Aalborg University
Karthikeyan Umapathy, University of North Florida - School of Computing
Faith-Michael Uzoka, University of Botswana
Liisa Von Hellens, Griffith University
Xinwei Wang, National University of Singapore
Merideth Weiss, University of North Carolina
Donald Wynn, University of Dayton
Xiao Xiao, Washington State University
Susan Yager, Southern Illinois University Edwardsville

Sponsor:

Issues in Managing Information Technology (IT) Professionals

Eric Bishop
VP and GM Enterprise Solutions
Rockfish Interactive
eric.bishop@
rockfishinteractive.com

Larry Buttelwerth
CIO
NewPage Corporation
larry.buttelwerth@
newpagecorp.com

Dan Clark
Chief Administrative Officer
NewPage Corporation
dan.clark@newpagecorp.com

Harvey G. Enns
Dept. of MIS, OM, & DSC
University of Dayton
enns@udayton.edu

Thomas W. Ferratt
Dept. of MIS, OM, & DSC
University of Dayton
ferratt@udayton.edu

Kevin Gallagher
Northern Kentucky University
gallagherk2@nku.edu

Jayesh Prasad
Dept. of MIS, OM, & DSC
University of Dayton
prasad@udayton.edu

Paul Stoddard
CIO
CareSource
paul.stoddard@caresource.com

ABSTRACT

The purpose of our panel is to understand:

- issues that Chief Information Officers (CIOs) are currently facing or expect to be facing in the next few (e.g., 3-5) years with regard to managing people responsible for information systems and technology; e.g., issues could include such traditional human resource (HR) issues as recruiting, retention, and development in light of contemporary phenomena, such as Big Data, Cloud Computing, Mobile Computing, and Enterprise Social Networking or other HR issues, such as job/work design, stress, outsourcing, managing a diverse workforce, or managing change

- how CIOs have addressed, are addressing, or expect to address those issues through
  - practices that have demonstrated or are demonstrating success,
  - practices that they expect to be successful, or
  - challenges that they have experienced (including obstacles or practices that have not worked so well) and what they have done to address those challenges

Categories and Subject Descriptors

K.6.1 [**Management of Computing and Information Systems**]: Project and People Management – *staffing, training*

Keywords

Human resource (HR) management, HR practices, IT managers, recruiting, retention, development, job design, stress, outsourcing, diverse workforce, change management, success stories

1. INTRODUCTION

Why is it important to understand HR issues in the IT arena?

- Studies of key issues for IT executives have included IT HR issues – recruiting, retention, and building business skills in IT (Luftman and Ben-Zvi, 2011)
  - These studies could be more complete (they ask about only a limited set of IT HR issues)
  - They could be more reflective of the changing context or current/future times
  - The percent of time CIOs report spending on HR issues is consistently 7-8% (2007-2011)

- IT human resources are one of three IT-based resources (along with IT infrastructure and intangible IT-enabled resources, such as knowledge assets and customer orientation) that provide IT capabilities for supporting organizational strategy (Bharadwaj, 2000)

2. PANEL STRUCTURE

- Two sets of panelists
  - CIOs
  - Academics

- Process
  - Moderator will introduce purpose of panel, why it is important, and sets of panelists
  - Moderator will ask the CIOs to answer questions for AN issue
    - ✓ Repeat questions until issues exhausted
  - Moderator will ask Academics to answer questions
    - ✓ Questions 1, 2, and 3 will be for Enns, Gallagher, and Ferratt, respectively
  - Moderator will ask panelists and audience to address discussion questions

3. QUESTIONS

3.1 Questions for CIO Panelists

Within the broad context of your responsibilities for information systems and technology, think about the people you are responsible for managing.

1. What is AN issue related to managing these people that you currently face or expect to face in the next 3-5 years?

   You might spend time thinking or worrying about this issue, you might seek assistance with this issue, or it might be an issue that you need to spend your time addressing. Describe the issue and provide enough explanation that we can understand the issue and why it is one you are currently facing.

2. Please elaborate on how you are successfully addressing the issue, expect to address the issue, or have been challenged as you have attempted to address the issue and what you have done to address the challenges.

3.2 Questions for Academic Panelists

1. To place the issues raised by the CIOs in a broader context, would you summarize what prior studies have indicated are a common set of HR issues in IT and practices for addressing them?

2. To place the issue of managing the mix of IT skills (an issue raised at least in a recent CIO study) in a broader context, would you summarize what prior studies have found?

3. To place the issues raised by all the panelists in a broader organizational context, would you explain IT HR strategy and what research has found regarding IT HR strategy and practices?

3.3 Discussion Questions

1. Studies have consistently found that technical, interpersonal, business, and managerial skills are essential for IT professionals. Why do studies keep finding that? Are we not developing IT professionals with those skills? Is there some inherent difficulty in developing such a skill mix?

2. What do you think are elements of IT HR strategy? What roles does organizational strategy play?

4. REFERENCES

[1] Bharadwaj, A S. 2000. A Resource-based perspective on information technology capability and firm performance: An empirical investigation. *MIS Quarterly*, 24, 1, 169-196.

[2] Luftman, J. and Ben-Zvi, T. 2011. Key issues for IT executives 2011: Cautious optimism in uncertain economic times. *MIS Quarterly Executive*, 10, 4, 203-212.

Organizational Commitment of IT Workers:
Leader Support and Differences Across Gender and Race

Jaime B. Windeler
University of Cincinnati
Carl H. Lindner College of Business
Cincinnati, OH 45221
513-556-7140
Jaime.Windeler@uc.edu

Cindy Riemenschneider
Baylor University
Hankamer School of Business
Waco, TX 76798
254-710-4061
c_riemenschneider@baylor.edu

ABSTRACT

The purpose of this study is to determine how psychosocial mentoring, career mentoring and leader-member exchange (LMX) contribute to organizational commitment for IT workers, as well as how these relationships differ according to race and gender. We draw on affective events theory, as well as the literature on IT personnel and leader support to explicate these relationships. We conducted a field study of 289 IT workers in a Fortune 500 company. LMX and career mentoring explained 28% of the variance in organizational commitment. Additionally, we found that the impact of career mentoring on organizational commitment is stronger for women than for men and that career mentoring influences organizational commitment for non-minority races but not minority races. Finally, the influence of LMX on organizational commitment is stronger for minority races than for non-minority races. This study contributes to the body of literature on IT personnel issues by exploring whether and how organizational support mechanisms enhance organizational commitment for private sector IT workers. We also demonstrate that race and gender are important considerations for researchers studying organizational commitment, mentoring, and LMX. Our findings suggest that managers can boost organizational commitment among IT workers by focusing on LMX and career mentoring. Moreover, they may want to place particular emphasis on career mentoring programs for women and on the development of supervisor/employee relationships for their minority race IT workers.

Categories and Subject Descriptors

K.7.1 [Computing Profession]: Occupations

General Terms

Management, Human factors

Keywords

Information technology personnel, Mentoring, Leader-member exchange, Organizational commitment, Gender, Race

1. INTRODUCTION

We live in an economic period marked by tremendous technological evolution and increasing competition from global sources. This market pressure has increased the demand for high-quality information technology (IT) professionals who can help organizations respond to the challenges of a global marketplace. However, attracting and retaining IT workers has long been challenging and has been especially problematic in recent years when the technological capabilities that allow us to respond to global competition have changed the nature of the workplace. Longer work hours, pressure to be connected to one's work 24/7, continuous retooling of skills, increased monitoring of performance, downsizing, and outsourcing are just a few of the challenges that IT workers face [1; 29]. In the IT sector, which arguably bears the brunt of the technological pressure, 71% of managers report concern about employee burnout and turnover [31]. Alarming projections of looming shortages in the supply of skilled IT workers [13; 36] , along with high employee replacement costs [15], make it all the more important that organizations look for ways to provide support so that they can retain qualified IT professionals.

While there are many potential organizational support mechanisms, a large body of established research underscores the importance of the leader-member relationship in influencing an employee's commitment to the organization [e.g., 25]. In fact, a meta-analysis of organizational commitment research finds that variables related to the leader-member relationship are among the strongest correlates of organizational commitment [38]. Additionally, the foundation of Affective Events Theory recognizes that emotional events which occur at work influence employees' affective reactions to their workplace [61]. These reactions in turn may influence either organizational outcomes, employee outcomes, or both. Examples of outcomes include job satisfaction, turnover intention, and organizational commitment [6; 18; 61]. Using Affective Events Theory as a general framework, we focus on leader support in influencing organizational commitment. Specifically, we explore the role of mentoring and leader-member exchange in improving organizational commitment of IT professionals.

Leader-member exchange (LMX) is defined as the value of the relationship between subordinates and supervisors, exhibited through the employee's ability to be included in organizational decisions [30]. High-quality leader-member relationships that are characterized by higher levels of trust are found to result in lower stress [55] and turnover intentions [30], as well as, higher performance [21] and organizational commitment [46]. Mentoring is a type of interpersonal support that has also been linked to reductions in role stress [4; 41; 46], and thus is a natural fit for helping employees cope with the strains of a demanding work environment. Researchers have conceptualized mentoring as consisting of two dimensions: *psychosocial* and *career*. Psychosocial mentoring revolves around providing emotional support, social acceptance, counseling, and cultivating a close relationship between mentor and protégé. Career mentoring, on the other hand, includes functions such as coaching, enhancing opportunities for attaining power and advancement, as well as, increasing the protégé's visibility and access to resources [9; 20; 52].

While there has been some examination of the relationship between LMX, mentoring, and organizational commitment, results have been mixed with respect to the relative influence of these variables on organizational commitment. In some cases, mentoring has not significantly affected organizational commitment in the presence of LMX [46], and in other cases, research shows that psychosocial mentoring can lead to a reduction in subjective stress, while career mentoring leads to an increase in stress [47]. Given these mixed results, there is a need to further our understanding of the drivers of organizational commitment for IT workers. In this research, we explore the influence of LMX and mentoring on organizational commitment among IT workers and look at potential differences due to gender and race. Specifically, we examine differences in the relative strength of the relationship between LMX, mentoring, and organizational commitment among men and women and among minority and non-minority races. We study gender and race differences for two reasons. One, prior work has demonstrated that work values vary according to gender and race [10; 14; 27]. Underrepresented groups, such as women and minority races, have different experiences and thus different expectations and values regarding organizational support. Two, as many organizations look for ways to create a workplace that is diverse and encouraging of participation from underrepresented groups, they will look for ways to support the interests and values of those groups. Thus, it is important for researchers to examine the drivers of organizational commitment so that organizations and managers can proactively and appropriately respond to the needs of a diverse workforce and attract and retain qualified IT professionals. In this pursuit, the objectives of this research are as follows:

1. To explore the influence of psychosocial and career mentoring on the organizational commitment of IT workers

2. To explore the influence of leader-member exchange on the organizational commitment of IT worker

3. To explore the implications of gender and race for mentoring, LMX, and organizational commitment among IT workers

We conducted a field study of 289 IT workers at a Fortune 500 company. By assessing respondents' perceptions of access to career and psychosocial mentoring, as well as, the quality of their relationship with their leaders, we shed light on how these forces shape organizational commitment for men versus women and for minority versus non-minority IT workers. Thus, the current study

contributes to the literature on IT personnel issues by adding further clarity as to what forms of organizational support can enhance IT workers' commitment to their organization and explicates the mechanisms by which they do so. We also contribute to the literature on IT personnel by exploring the implications of gender and race for LMX, mentoring, and organizational commitment. From a practical standpoint, this should allow managers to respond more effectively to the needs of IT workers and engage an appropriate response that will help drive greater organizational commitment. Our research model is shown in Figure 1.

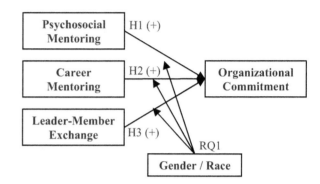

Figure 1. Research Model

2. THEORETICAL BACKGROUND & HYPOTHESES DEVELOPMENT
2.1 Organizational Commitment

Although organizational commitment can be thought of as a multidimensional concept consisting of affective, continuance, and normative commitment [3], in this paper, we focus on the affective dimension of organizational commitment. Affective organizational commitment refers to "employees' emotional attachment to, identification with, and involvement in, the organization" [3]. Porter and colleagues' Organizational Commitment Questionnaire [44] is commonly used and it primarily assesses affective organizational commitment [22]. Using this questionnaire, Porter et al. [44] found that organizational commitment was a stronger predictor of turnover than job satisfaction. Organizational commitment has been consistently found to have a strong inverse relationship with employee turnover [e.g., 2; 28; 48; 54]. Antecedents of organizational commitment include characteristics of the employee (e.g., age), their job (e.g., job scope), the organization (e.g., size), and leader relations (e.g., leader consideration) [38]. As we are interested in affective experiences related to workplace support, we explore the role that leaders play in facilitating organizational commitment through mentoring and LMX.

2.2 Mentoring

Mentoring is, "a deliberate pairing of a more skilled or experienced person with a lesser skilled or experienced one, with the agreed-upon goal of having the lesser skilled person grow and develop specific competencies [39]. In recent years, researchers have further refined the mentoring construct, identifying two distinct types of mentoring. *Psychosocial mentoring* functions include social acceptance, role modeling, counseling, and friendship" [47]. This type of mentoring encourages the discussion of anxiety and concerns, as well as, the sharing of personal experiences, values, and attitudes [20]. *Career mentoring* involves coaching, sponsorship, and protection on behalf of the protégé, which allows for the building of contacts, alliances, visibility, opportunities for career advancement, and access to challenging assignments through which new skills are learned [9].

Mentoring, as a whole, has been found to relieve stress associated with organizational pressure [35]. It acts as a form of social support, which results in increased career and job satisfaction, and decreased turnover [41; 57; 58]. Riemenschneider and her colleagues [47] found that career mentoring actually increased subjective stress for IT workers, while psychosocial mentoring moderated the relationship between perceived workload and subjective stress during a period of transformational change in an organization. They argue that, during a period of transformational change, career mentoring leads to an increase in subjective stress because those who receive career mentoring are exposed to opportunities and situations that create additional pressure and tension in their environment [47]. These findings call into question the assumption that mentoring is, on the whole, a positive support mechanism.

Craig et al. [18] investigated the mediating role of affective organizational commitment between psychosocial mentoring, career mentoring, and turnover intention. Results showed that only psychosocial mentoring influenced affective organizational commitment, indicating the importance of emotional experiences over more objective functions afforded through career mentoring [18]. Despite this progress in understanding the role that mentoring plays in driving organizational commitment, there is a lack of research on the differential effects of the two dimensions of mentoring. Several researchers have recently called for a more nuanced investigation of the different forms of mentoring and how they comparatively influence employee outcomes [32; 43].

Extant literature shows mixed support regarding the differential effects of mentoring on organizational commitment [46]. For example, some researchers have found positive correlations between either psychosocial or career mentoring and organizational commitment [e.g., 45]. A recent study of U.S. Army officers, finds mentoring to be positively related to affective organizational commitment [43]. However, due to the particular questions used to measure the type of mentoring, the researchers were unable to determine whether one dimension of mentoring had a stronger impact on organizational commitment than the other. In another study, Aryee and Chay [5] found that career mentoring was a significant predictor of organizational commitment, but did not examine psychosocial mentoring. Those that have examined both psychosocial and career mentoring have found mixed results regarding their impact on organizational commitment. Scandura [50] found that career mentoring is correlated more strongly with organizational commitment, while Reid et al. [46] found that only psychosocial mentoring was significant in predicting employees' organizational commitment. Reid et al. [46] noted that the significant relationship found between psychosocial mentoring and organizational commitment might have been influenced by the unique context of the study, which was conducted in a state government environment. Additionally, Craig et al., (2012) studied IT workers in state government and found only psychosocial mentoring to be significant in predicting affective organizational commitment. Taken together, these mixed findings in the literature demonstrate

an opportunity for further exploration of the role of mentoring in influencing organizational commitment among IT workers.

We expect that both forms of mentoring will have a positive impact on organizational commitment for three primary reasons that we elaborate on below: (1) mentors enhance protégé integration by encouraging adoption of organizational values; (2) mentors provide support that can reduce protégé stress; and (3) mentors facilitate relationships that can be personally and professionally rewarding for protégés. Affective Events Theory suggests that these experiences should translate into positive moods and emotions that drive attitudes about the organization, thus enhancing commitment [23; 61].

First, mentoring promotes adoption of organizational values [59] thus facilitating identification with the organization. Social and advisory support provided by psychosocial mentoring [20] can demonstrate and reinforce behavioral norms in the organization, while career mentoring involves coaching activities [20] that can attune the protégé to sense and response to expectations governing career advancement. Such activities can help a protégé better understand the organizational climate and be more socially integrated in the organization. Second, mentoring promotes coping strategies that will allow protégés to have more positive experiences at work [50]. Psychosocial mentoring encourages protégés to share their anxiety and concerns with mentors [20]. This provides mentors with opportunities to provide emotional support, feedback, and encouragement to help reduce protégés' stress and anxiety. Career mentoring involves sponsorship and advocacy as well as help building a professional network [20]. These activities can serve to buffer protégés from stressful situations or provide them with resources to help them better cope with stressful situations. In doing so, mentors can contribute to protégés having more positive and pleasant experiences that can engender greater attachment to the organization. Third, mentoring facilitates relationship building that can translate into positive work attitudes and valuable social capital [50]. Psychosocial mentoring involves sharing of personal experiences, values, and attitudes that can lead to interpersonal bonding between mentor and protégé [20]. In a similar fashion, career mentoring facilitates relationship building by way of sponsorship and increasing protégé visibility within the organization, which can introduce the protégé to new contacts and alliances [20]. As protégés build relationships with and through their mentors, they are investing in relationships that can be both personally and professionally rewarding. This should have a positive impact on organizational commitment because it represents valuable social capital that is tied to the work environment. Thus, we hypothesize:

Hypothesis 1: Psychosocial mentoring will have a direct, positive influence on organizational commitment.

Hypothesis 2: Career mentoring will have a direct, positive influence on organizational commitment.

2.3 Leader-Member Exchange

LMX represents the value of the relationship between supervisors and subordinates. Prior studies [37; 42] have shown that the strength of LMX relationships influence organizational commitment. In their meta-analysis, Mathieu and Zajac [38] found strong support for leader-member variables as antecedents to organizational commitment. More recently, studies show a strong relationship between leader–member exchange and affective organizational commitment [33; 46; 62].

As with mentoring, Affective Events Theory suggests that LMX should yield positive moods and emotions that translate into organizational commitment. When the quality of LMX is high, supervisors and subordinates enjoy a relationship of mutual trust and respect that facilitates employee-organization integration and reduces organizational stressors [21]. This should enhance organizational commitment because the subordinate feels supported by their supervisor, which makes for a more positive experience at work. Moreover, supervisors may be viewed as an extension of the organization. They often have longer tenure than subordinates and are in a position of authority, and thus can be seen as a spokesperson or representative of the organization. To the extent that subordinates respect their supervisor and extend these positive feelings to the organization, they should have stronger organizational commitment. In addition to supportiveness, high-quality LMX is characterized by subordinates having greater decision-making authority [26; 51]. Decision making authority enhances task meaningfulness and provides a sense of impact on the organization [37]. This should promote identification and lead to stronger affective commitment because subordinates feel responsible for those activities that influence organizational outcomes. Thus, we hypothesize:

Hypothesis 3: LMX will have a direct, positive influence on organizational commitment.

2.3 Gender and Race Differences

The effect organizational support mechanisms, such as mentoring and LMX, on organizational commitment can be influenced by how much value an employee places on the nature of the support and outcomes associated with it. For example, career mentoring is more tied to instrumental or extrinsic outcomes related to career advancement, while psychosocial mentoring is tied to outcomes related to emotional or social fulfillment and wellbeing [20]. To the extent that a person places more value on a type of work support and its associated outcomes, we expect that support mechanism to have a stronger influence on organizational commitment.

Prior work has demonstrated differences in work values and experiences due to gender and race [e.g., 10]. However, research on gender and racial differences in values related to organizational support are somewhat lacking. Prior research that would support arguments about the direction and strength of the relationship between organizational support and organizational commitment are mixed. For example, Brenner and colleagues [10] found that white women placed more importance on extrinsic outcomes (e.g., income, job security) than white men and that black respondents placed more value on extrinsic outcomes than white respondents. Such findings suggest that women and minorities may value career mentoring more than men and non-minorities because they value the extrinsic outcomes associated with career advancement and place less emphasis on social outcomes. In contrast, research finds that men's sense of self (i.e., self-construal), is independent of others and that they seek to demonstrate their uniqueness and separateness from others in ways that align with extrinsic outcomes [19]. Men place more emphasis on their work role and career objectives [7], promotions

and prestige at work [8]. In contrast, women's self-construal is interdependent or relational, leading them to seek more interconnectedness with others [19]. Their sense of self is tied more to social factors than to extrinsic factors such as success at work, compared to men. In a similar vein, minority races report feeling less social acceptance at work, which leads to lower job satisfaction [27]. Such research suggests that women and minority races may value career mentoring less than men and find social support mechanisms to be much more important. Given these conflicting perspectives regarding work values and orientations toward organizational support in prior literature, we put forth the following research question:

Research Question 1: How does the strength of the relationship between psychosocial mentoring, career mentoring, LMX, and organizational commitment differ between men and women and between minority and non-minority races?

3. METHODOLOGY
To test our research model and explore our research question, we surveyed all 554 IT workers from a large, Fortune 500 company in the food production industry. Participants were sent an email explaining the importance of their participation and an assurance of anonymity in order to encourage open and honest responses about their feelings toward their work. Two follow-up emails were sent, spaced two weeks apart, resulting in 289 complete responses for a 52% response rate. Non-response bias was assessed by comparing incomplete surveys to complete surveys and by comparing early respondents (before follow-up email) to late respondents (after follow-up email). No systematic differences were observed, suggesting an absence of response bias. Of the 289 complete responses, the sample was 21% female and 79% male, with an average job tenure of 9.40 years (s.d.=7.19). The participant pool was 87% White, 5% Hispanic, 2% Asian/Pacific Islander/Indian, 2% Black/Non-Hispanic, 1% Native American/Alaskan Native/Hawaiian Native, and 3% were of another race.

3.1 Measures
3.1.1 Career and psychosocial mentoring
The mentoring scales are taken from Dreher and Ash [20] and measured on a 7-point Likert scale ranging from "not at all" (1) to "to a very large extent" (7). Career mentoring ($\alpha = .94$) consists of 8 items, including "To what extent have you had a mentor who has…'given or recommended you for assignments that have increased your contact with higher level managers' and 'given or recommended you for challenging assignments that present opportunities to learn new skills'". Psychosocial mentoring ($\alpha = .95$) is composed of 11 items, including, "To what extent have you had a mentor who has…'shared personal experiences as an alternative perspective to your problems' and 'provided suggestions concerning problems you have encountered at work'".

3.1.2 Leader-member exchange
Items used to assess LMX ($\alpha = .95$) are taken from Wayne, Shore, and Liden [60] and measured on a 7-point Likert scale ranging from "strongly disagree" (1) to "strongly agree" (7). There are 7 items including, "I usually know where I stand with my manager" and "My working relationship with my manager is effective".

3.1.3 Organizational commitment

The items for organizational commitment (α = .91) are taken from the same source and with the same response format as LMX. There are 7 items in total, including items such as "I talk up employment in this organization to friends as a great place to work" and "I am proud to tell others that I work for this organization". All measures are included in the appendix.

3.1.4 Control variables

In addition to measuring the preceding variables, we also included gender, race, branch location, and organizational tenure in our analysis. Gender, race, and branch location were coded as dichotomous variables. Gender was coded as 1 for females and 2 for males. Given the distribution of race across our sample (i.e. 87% of the sample identified themselves as "White") race was dummy coded as 1 for minority races (all races except for "White") and 2 for non-minority (only "White"). Branch location was coded as 1 for U.S. locations and 2 for non-U.S locations. Organizational tenure was measured as the number of years the respondent had been employed by the organization.

4. RESULTS

We used Partial Least Squares (PLS; SmartPLS, version 2.0.M3) to analyze the data. The approach used to examine the model was consistent with Chin and his colleagues' [16; 17] guidelines for PLS analysis. With PLS, the psychometric properties (i.e. measurement model) of the scales are examined in concert with the structural model being assessed. The measurement model provides an assessment of the reliability and validity of the scales. We assessed the measurement model first to determine which items were not loading highly on their respective factor. These items were systematically dropped until all item loadings were acceptable, with consideration given for ensuring that the dropped items did not fundamentally change the nature of the construct. The loadings for the resulting measurement model are shown in Table 1. Consistent with the guidelines for assessing validity and reliability [16; 17], all internal consistency reliability (ICR) values were greater than .90, providing support for acceptable reliability. All loadings were greater than .70, supporting internal consistency validity. Discriminant validity was supported in the case of LMX and organizational commitment, as all cross-loadings were below .40; however, discriminant validity was a concern in the case of career and psychosocial mentoring, which showed high cross-loadings. For these constructs, a more in-depth examination was employed to assess discriminant validity. We used the method recommended by Fornell and Larcker [24] that compares the square root of the average variance extracted (AVE) to the correlations among the constructs. Discriminant validity is established if the square root of the AVE is larger than the correlations among constructs. As shown in Table 2, the square root of the AVE is larger than the inter-construct correlations, confirming discriminant validity for career and psychosocial mentoring.

Table 2 presents the descriptive statistics, correlations, and reliabilities. From this analysis, we observe some preliminary support for the model. Organizational commitment is significantly and positively correlated with both forms of mentoring, as well as LMX. In addition, we also observe significant correlations between organizational commitment and gender, as well as, race.

Table 1. ICRs, and PLS loadings and cross-loadings

		1	2	3	4
	ICR	**0.95**	**0.96**	**0.94**	**0.96**
1	CMentor_1	**0.87**			0.66
	CMentor_2	**0.91**			0.61
	CMentor_3	**0.91**			0.58
	CMentor_4	**0.93**			0.68
	CMentor_5	**0.83**			0.69
2	LMX_1		**0.87**	0.35	
	LMX_2		**0.90**		
	LMX_3		**0.89**	0.35	
	LMX_4		**0.88**	0.41	
	LMX_5		**0.86**		
	LMX_6		**0.87**	0.41	
	LMX_7		**0.83**		0.41
3	OrgComm_1		0.36	**0.83**	
	OrgComm_2		0.37	**0.91**	
	OrgComm_3		0.37	**0.89**	
	OrgComm_4			**0.82**	
	OrgComm_5		0.37	**0.86**	
4	PMentor_1	0.68			**0.86**
	PMentor_2	0.63			**0.87**
	PMentor_3	0.61			**0.86**
	PMentor_4	0.65	0.36		**0.88**
	PMentor_5	0.51			**0.82**
	PMentor_6	0.58			**0.82**
	PMentor_7	0.53			**0.82**
	PMentor_8	0.61			**0.87**
	PMentor_9	0.64		0.36	**0.82**

Notes: Loadings < .35 are not shown to improve readability. ICR: Internal consistency reliability; CMentor = Career Mentoring; LMX = Leader-Member Exchange; OrgComm = Organizational Commitment; PMentor = Psychosocial Mentoring

Table 3 presents the results of the structural model test for the combined sample (both genders and all races). We employed a bootstrap procedure, using 500 iterations, to generate t-values that would allow us to estimate the corresponding p-values. The results show that psychosocial mentoring does not have a significant effect on organizational commitment. Thus, H1 is not supported. In the case of career mentoring and LMX, we observed significant, positive effects on organizational commitment, thus fully supporting H2 and H3. LMX has the strongest impact on organizational commitment, followed by gender, career mentoring, and race, respectively. The model explains 28% of the variance in organizational commitment. The supported research model is shown in Figure 2.

4.1 RQ 1 Analysis: Gender and Race

To explore differences according to gender and race in the strength of the relationship between mentoring and LMX with organizational commitment, we ran the model using the data for each subgroup and compared the results for men versus women and minority versus non-minority races. Prior research has tended

Table 2. Descriptive Statistics, Correlations, and Reliabilities

		M	SD	1	2	3	4	5	6	7	8
1	Gender	0.81	0.10	NA							
2	Race	0.04	0.15	-.01	NA						
3	Branch Location	0.23	0.34	-.03	-.16**	NA					
4	OrgTenure	9.40	7.19	.05	.06	-.11	NA				
5	Psych-Soc Mentoring	2.38	0.99	.03	-.15*	-.10	-.08	**.85**			
6	Career Mentoring	2.31	1.04	.08	-.19**	-.06	-.07	.72**	**.89**		
7	LMX	4.98	1.32	.01	-.15*	-.04	.06	.38**	.28**	**.87**	
8	Org Commitment	4.95	1.26	-.17**	-.23**	-.03	.04	.31**	.32**	.42**	**.86**

Notes: p< .05; ** p< .01; NA: not applicable; Diagonal elements are the square root of the AVE; off-diagonal elements are the correlation; Gender was dummy-coded as 1 for females and 2 for males; Race was dummy coded as 1 for minority races and 2 for non-minority; Branch Location was coded as 1 for U.S. locations and 2 for non-U.S locations.*

Table 3. Structural model results: Impact on organizational commitment

	β	t-value
Gender	-.21***	4.27
Race	-.15***	2.80
Branch Location	-.03	1.20
OrgTenure	.06	0.87
Psych-Soc Mentoring	.02	0.45
Career Mentoring	.19**	2.55
LMX	.34***	5.74

*Notes:**p< .01; *** p< .001; R2 = .28; Gender was dummy-coded as 1 for females and 2 for males; Race was dummy coded as 1 for minority races and 2 for non-minority; Branch Location was coded as 1 for U.S. locations and 2 for non-U.S locations.*

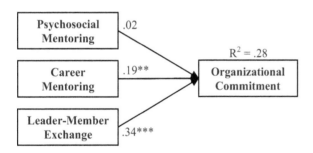

Figure 2. Supported research model

to simply compare the path coefficients of different subsamples to determine differences among groups. Recent work, however, has pointed out that it is necessary to conduct a statistical test to validate differences in the path coefficients. This procedure involves a t-test is conducted using the following formula [34; 49]:

$$t = \frac{\beta_{group1} - \beta_{group2}}{Sp * \sqrt{\frac{1}{m} + \frac{1}{n}}}$$

$$Sp = \sqrt{\frac{(m-1)}{(m+n-2)} * SE_{group1}^2 + \frac{(n-1)}{(m+n-2)} * SE_{group2}^2}$$

This procedure follows a t-distribution with m+n-2 degrees of freedom. The pooled estimator for the variance is given by Sp,

where m and n represent the sample sizes for group1 and group2, respectively. SE is the standard error of the path in the structural model. If the t-test statistic is significant, one can conclude that there is a significant difference between the paths of the two samples.

Table 4 provides the results of this analysis. These results show that men and women do not differ in terms of how strongly LMX impacts organizational commitment. However, they do differ in terms of how strongly career mentoring impacts organizational commitment. The impact of career mentoring on organizational commitment is stronger for women (β=.22, p<.05) than it is for men (β=.19, p<.05). In terms of racial differences, there are differences in the impact of both career mentoring and LMX on organizational commitment. The impact of career mentoring on organizational commitment is stronger for non-minority races (β=.19, p<.05) than minority races (β=.13, ns). Interestingly, career mentoring is not significant in impacting organizational commitment for minorities. Finally, the impact of LMX on organizational commitment is considerably stronger for minority races (β=.65, p<.001), than it is for non-minority races (β=.31, p<.001). The implications of these findings are discussed below.

5. DISCUSSION

Drawing on prior research in information systems and organizational and vocational behavior, we hypothesized three organizational support mechanisms—psychosocial mentoring, career mentoring, and leader-member exchange—as predictors of organizational commitment. Building on Affective Events Theory, we hypothesized that these three support mechanisms would positively influence organizational commitment among IT workers and explored the implications of gender and race for these relationships. We tested the model among 289 IT workers from a Fortune 500 company. The theorized effects were largely supported. Career mentoring and LMX positively influenced organizational commitment, while psychosocial mentoring did not. Moreover, we observed differences according to gender and race in the relative strength of these relationships. The impact of career mentoring on organizational commitment was found to be stronger for women and minorities compared to men and non-minorities, respectively. The impact of LMX of organizational commitment was found to be stronger for minority compared to non-minority races.

Table 4. Multi-group analysis by gender and race

	Gender Comparison					Race Comparison				
	Women n = 68		Men n = 221		Women v. Men	Minority n = 35		Non-Minority n = 254		Minority v. Non-Minority
	β	t-value°	β	t-value°	t-value†	β	t-value°	β	t-value°	t-value†
Psych-Soc Mentoring	-0.06	0.50	0.05	0.90	-	0.06	0.35	0.04	0.75	-
Career Mentoring	0.22**	2.62	0.19**	2.21	2.46**	0.13	0.66	0.19**	2.43	19.78***
LMX	0.36***	2.75	0.35***	5.06	0.99ns	0.65***	4.43	0.31***	5.17	-21.36***
R^2	.18		.29		-	.43		.25		-

Notes:**p< .05; *** p< .001; °t-values generated by bootstrap analysis; †t-values generated by formula for multi-group comparison

5.1 Contributions, Implications, and Future Research

The current study makes several contributions to theory and practice. First, we have applied Affective Events Theory to broaden our understanding of how mentoring and LMX contribute to organizational commitment. In doing so, we shed light on the forms of organizational support that appeal to IT workers and explicate the mechanisms by which organizational commitment is formed. Our research reinforces and extends prior work on organizational commitment. Previous research has examined the impact of the two types of mentoring on affective organizational commitment, finding that, in the presence of LMX, both types of mentoring do not significantly impact the organizational commitment of public-sector IT workers [46]. Other research shows psychosocial mentoring helps to reduce stress and perceived workload among public-sector IT workers [47]. Our analysis reveals that private-sector IT workers do not consider psychosocial mentoring to impact their organizational commitment. Conversely, career mentoring has a significant and positive effect on organizational commitment, in addition to LMX. The current study reinforces prior research by demonstrating that organizational support mechanisms such as mentoring and LMX can have significant implications for organizational commitment. At the same time, we extend prior research by situating our study in the context of private-sector workers and by exploring race and gender differences across these relationships.

A primary difference between our study and prior work is that we sampled IT workers from an organization in the private-sector, while extant research [e.g., 46; 47] has focused on public-sector IT workers. In order to explore the differences in the findings from this study versus those of prior research, further research should be conducted using comparable samples of IT workers from public and private sectors. Buelens and Van den Broeck [11] surveyed 409 public sector employees and 3,314 private sector employees in Belgium and found that public sector employees are less extrinsically motivated. They also establish that "public sector employees are less motivated by money and work challenge and less committed to long working hours than their private sector counterparts" [11]. Their study showed that public sector employees have a stronger motivation to lead a balanced life than private sector employees. These findings provide some support for the differences observed between the current study of

private-sector IT workers and those of public-sector IT workers. However, additional research should be conducted using a mixed sample of private and public sector IT professionals from multiple organizations to determine if there are systematic differences in the impact of mentoring and LMX on organizational commitment. Second, the findings in this study regarding gender and race differences contribute to both theory and practice. We found that career mentoring was more important for women than for men. This finding is consistent with research by Trauth, Quesenberry and Huang [56] who found that mentoring was linked to positive outcomes, especially in the early years of a woman's career. They also found that for women, mentoring is linked to networking and perceptions of support, in general. Our findings are also consistent with the finding that women place more importance on extrinsic outcomes compared to men [10]. The IT field has traditionally been dominated by men. Women in IT may be sensitized to this imbalance and the resulting potential for gender discrimination and their dissimilarity from male managerial hierarchies. Moreover, women lack informal networks for advancement [53] and may identify career mentoring as a means to connect to these networks. Indeed, research shows that mentor sponsoring is not necessary for men to advance in an organization, but it is necessary for women [12]. Going forward, researchers will need to explore these and other potential reasons why women may place more value on career mentoring, compared to men. Moreover, practitioners will want to focus on ensuring career mentoring is accessible to the women IT workers in their organization.

With respect to racial differences, we found that career mentoring was not significantly related to organizational commitment for minority races but it was significant for non-minority races. Conversely, LMX had a stronger impact on organizational commitment for the minority race employees than the non-minority race employees. One potential explanation for these outcomes has to do with the focus of mentoring versus LMX. Research finds that, "by signaling their own acceptance of employees of various backgrounds through the establishment of high-quality relationships with them, leaders can promote norms about equality and inclusion that will facilitate greater power sharing and improve reciprocal exchanges among group members" [40]. While career mentoring may involve fostering protégé visibility, particularly among those in the upper echelons of the organization, mentoring does not serve the function of fostering inclusiveness among peers and thus may be of reduced importance to racial minorities. The inclusiveness fostered by high-quality LMX has been found to decrease the influence of member racial diversity on turnover intention [40] and should have implications for organizational commitment as well. To the extent that minorities experience inclusiveness due to high LMX, they are more likely to see themselves as part of the organization and thus to have higher affective commitment. Future research will be needed to explore these potential explanations for our findings and to examine other reasons why racial minorities place such high value on LMX. Moreover, practitioners can benefit from this study by focusing on the development of strong supervisor/employee relations for their minority race employees.

Finally, our findings provide managers with insight into the drivers of organizational commitment and offers up a potential intervention for impacting this important outcome. Our analysis reveals that career mentoring and LMX increase organizational commitment. To enhance organizational commitment, organizations may want to consider implementing or increasing employees' access to career mentoring and to train leaders with the means to enhance their leadership style and ultimately strengthen the relationship between supervisors and employees.

5.2 Limitations

Though the preceding contributions to the IS personnel and vocational behavior literatures represent important progress toward a clearer understanding of organizational commitment, they should be considered in light of the limitations of our study. First, we only studied one type of worker, IT professionals, in one industry, food production. It is possible that unique qualities of IT work may impact the results observed. Future research should look to other types of work, in various other industries, to determine whether these relationships generalize to a broader sample of workers.

Second, our findings must be considered in light of the fact that our data was collected at a single point in time. Relationships evolve over time and a protégé's relationship with their mentors may evolve. A career mentor may become a psychosocial mentor and vice versa as the needs of the protégé change and their career progresses. Future researchers seeking to broaden our understanding of these forces will want to examine how these relationships and pressures change over time. Therefore, we suggest longitudinal studies be applied to examine mentoring and the changes in leader-member relationships.

Third, due to the constraints of our data collection site, we were unable to gather more objective measures of career mentoring, LMX, or organizational commitment. Because our measures were obtained through a single survey, from a single respondent, this leaves open the possibility of common method and common source bias. Future research will want to examine the possibility of assessing not only the protégé's perspective, but also the mentor's understanding of the mentor-protégé relationship, as well. This may serve to validate the protégé's assessment of the degree and type of mentoring they receive.

6. CONCLUSION

In today's globally-driven marketplace, support for the IT workers that enable organizations' global reach is increasingly important. Yet, our understanding of the different support

mechanisms and their influence on organizational commitment for men and women, minority, and non-minority IT workers requires further development. The current study represents one step towards a better understanding of how organizations can provide leader support to enhance IT workers' commitment to their organization. We find that encouraging and facilitating leader-member relationships, especially for minority workers, and emphasizing the importance of career mentoring, especially for women, represent important avenues for retaining and supporting IT workers. By exploring these varied support mechanisms, it is our hope that this research will contribute to efforts made to gain insight into how best to support IT workers in the private sector.

7. REFERENCES

[1] Ahuja, M.K., 2002. Women in the information technology profession: A literature review, synthesis and research agenda. *European Journal of Information Systems*, 11(1): 20-34.

[2] Allen, D.G., Shore, L.M., and Griffeth, R.W., 2003. The role of perceived organizational support and supportive human resource practices in the turnover process. *Journal of Management*, 29(1):99-118.

[3] Allen, N.J. and Meyer, J.P., 1990. Organizational socialization tactics: A longitudinal analysis of links to newcomers' commitment and role orientation. *Academy of Management Journal*, 33(4): 847-858.

[4] Allen, T.D., Eby, L.T., Poteet, M.L., Lentz, E., and Lima, L., 2004. Career benefits associated with mentoring for protégé : A meta-analysis. *Journal of Applied Psychology*, 89(1):127-136.

[5] Aryee, S. and Chay, Y.W., 1994. An examination of the impact of career-oriented mentoring on work commitment attitudes and career satisfaction among professional and managerial employees. *British Journal of Management*, 5(4): 241-249.

[6] Askanasy, N.M. and Daus, C., 2002. Emotions in the workplace: The new challenge for managers. *Academy of Management Executive*, 16(1):17-86.

[7] Barnett, R.C. and Marshall, N.L., 1991. The relationship between women's work and family roles and their subjective well-being and psychological distress. In *Women, work, and health: Stress and opportunities,* M. Frankenhaeuser, U. Lundberg and M.A. Chesney Eds. Plenum Press, New York, NY, 111-136.

[8] Bartol, K.M. and Manhardt, P.J., 1979. Sex differences in job outcome preferences: Trends among newly hired college graduates. *Journal of Applied Psychology*, 64(5): 477-482.

[9] Baugh, S.G., Lankau, M.J., and Scandura, T.A., 1996. An investigation of the effects of protégé gender on responses to mentoring. *Journal of Vocational Behavior*, 49(3): 309-323.

[10] Brenner, O., Blazini, A.P., and Greenhaus, J.H., 1988. An examination of race and sex differences in managerial work values. *Journal of Vocational Behavior*, 32(3): 336-344.

[11] Buelens, M. and Van Den Broeck, H., 2007. An analysis of differences in work motivation between public and private

sector organizations. *Public Administration Review*, 67(1): 65-74.

[12] Burt, R.S., 1998. The gender of social capital. *Rationality and Society,* 10(1):5-46.

[13] Career Voyages, 2010. U. S. Department of Labor and U.S. Department of Education: Information technology. Retrieved March 27, 2013 from http://www.careervoyages.gov/infotech-main.cfm.

[14] Chen, Z.X. and Francesco, A.M., 2000. Employee demography, organizational commitment, and turnover intentions in China: Do cultural differences matter? *Human Relations*, 53(6): 869-887.

[15] Chevalier, M., 2008. TechRepublic and Global Knowledge: IT skills and salary report. Retrieved March 27, 2013 from http://www.ite.sfcollege.edu/TechRepublic_2008_salary_rep ort.pdf.

[16] Chin, W.W., 1998. Issues and opinion on structural equation modeling. *MIS Quarterly,* 22(1): 7-16.

[17] Chin, W.W., Marcolin, B.L., and Newsted, P.R., 2003. A partial least squares latent variable modeling approach for measuring interaction effects: Results from a monte carlo simulation study and an electronic-mail emotion/adoption study. *Information Systems Research*, 14(2): 189-217.

[18] Craig, C.A., Allen, M., Reid, M., Riemenschneider, C., and Armstrong, D., 2012. The impact of career mentoring and psychosocial mentoring on affective organizational commitment, job involvement, and turnover intention. *Administration and Society*, July 2012: 1-25.

[19] Cross, S.E. and Madson, L., 1997. Models of the self: Self-construals and gender. *Psychological Bulletin*, 122(1): 5-37.

[20] Dreher, G.F. and Ash, R.A., 1990. A comparative study of mentoring among men and women in managerial, professional, and technical positions. *Journal of Applied Psychology*, 75(5): 539-546.

[21] Dunegan, K.J., Uhl-Bien, M., and Duchon, D., 2002. LMX and subordinate performance: The moderating effects of task characteristics. *Journal of Business and Psychology,* 17(2): 275-285.

[22] Dunham, R.B., Grube, J.A., and Castaneda, M.B., 1994. Organizational commitment: The utility of an integrative definition. *Journal of Applied Psychology*, 79(3): 370-380.

[23] Fisher, C.D. and Ashkanasy, N.M., 2000. The emerging role of emotions in work life: An introduction. *Journal of Organizational Behavior*, 21(2): 123-129.

[24] Fornell, C. and Larcker, D.F., 1981. Evaluating structural equation models with unobservable variables and measurement error. *Journal of Marketing Research*, 18(1): 39-50.

[25] Gerstner, C.R. and Day, D.V., 1997. Meta-analytic review of leader-member exchange theory: Correlates and construct issues. *Journal of Applied Psychology,* 82(6): 827-844.

[26] Graen, G.B. and Uhl-Bien, M., 1995. Relationship-based approach to leadership: Development of leader-member exchange (LMX) theory of leadership over 25 years:

Applying a multi-level multi-domain perspective. *The Leadership Quarterly*, 6(2): 219-247.

[27] Greenhaus, J.H., Parasuraman, S., and Wormley, W.M., 1990. Effects of race on organizational experience, job performance evaluations, and career outcomes. *Academy of Management Journal*, 33(1): 64-86.

[28] Griffeth, R.W., Hom, P.W., and Gaertner, S., 2000. A meta-analysis of antecedents and correlates of employee turnover: Update, moderator tests, and research implications for the next millennium. *Journal of Management*, 26(3): 463-488.

[29] Guzman, I.R., Stam, K.R., and Stanton, J.M., 2008. The occupational culture of IS/IT personnel within organizations. *The DATA BASE for Advances in Information Systems*, 39(1): 33-50.

[30] Harris, K.J., Kacmar, K.M., and Witt, L.A., 2005. An examination of the curvilinear relationship between leader-member exchange and intent to turnover. *Journal of Organizational Behavior*, 26(4): 363-378.

[31] Hayes, F., 2003. Avoid burnout. *Computerworld*, 37(12): 58.

[32] Joiner, T.A., Bartram, T., and Garreffa, T., 2004. The effects of mentoring on perceived career success, commitment and turnover intentions. *Journal of American Academy of Business*, 5(1/2): 164-170.

[33] Joo, B.K.B., 2010. Organizational commitment for knowledge workers: The roles of perceived organizational learning culture, leader-member exchange quality, and turnover intention. *Human Resource Development Quarterly*, 21(1):69-85.

[34] Keil, M., Tan, B.C.Y., Wei, K.K., Saarinen, T., Tuunainen, V., and Wassenaar, A., 2000. A cross-cultural study on escalation of commitment behavior in software projects. *MIS Quarterly*, 24(2): 299-325.

[35] Kram, K.E. and Hall, D.T., 1989. Mentoring as an antidote to stress during corporate trauma. *Human Resource Management* 28(4): 493-510.

[36] Levinson, M., 2009. IT skills shortage spells opportunity for unemployed workers. Retrieved March 27, 2013, from http://www.cio.com/article/484303/IT_Skills_Shortage_Spel ls_Opportunity_for_Unemployed_Workers.

[37] Liden, R.C., Wayne, S.J., and Sparrowe, R.T., 2000. An examination of the mediating role of psychological empowerment on the relations between the job, interpersonal relationships, and work outcomes. *Journal of Applied Psychology*, 85(3): 407-416.

[38] Mathieu, J.E. and Zajac, D.M., 1990. A review and meta-analysis of the antecedents, correlates, and consequences of organizational commitment. *Psychological Bulletin*, 108(2):171-194.

[39] Murray, M., 1991. *Beyond the myths and magic of mentoring: What mentoring is—what it is not.* Jossey-Bass, San Francisco, CA.

[40] Nishii, L.H. and Mayer, D.M., 2009. Do inclusive leaders help to reduce turnover in diverse groups? The moderating role of leader–member exchange in the diversity to turnover

relationship. *Journal of Applied Psychology*, 94(6): 1412-1426.

[41] Noe, R.A., Greenberger, D.B., and Wang, S., 2002. Mentoring: What we know and where we might go. In *Research in personnel and human resources management*, G.R. Ferris and J.J. Martocchio Eds. JAI Press, New York, NY, 129-173.

[42] Nystrom, P.C., 1990. Vertical exchanges and organizational commitments of American business managers. *Group & Organization Management*, 15(3), 296-312.

[43] Payne, S.C. and Huffman, A., 2005. A longitudinal examination of the influence of mentoring on organizational commitment and turnover. *Academy of Management* Journal, 48(1): 158-168.

[44] Porter, L.W., Steers, R.M., Mowday, R.T., and Boulian, P.V., 1974. Organizational commitment, job satisfaction, and turnover among psychiatric technicians. *Journal of Applied Psychology*, 59(5): 603-609.

[45] Ragins, B.R., Cotton, J.L., and Miller, J.S., 2000. Marginal mentoring: The effects of type of mentor, quality of relationship, and program design on work and career attitudes. *Academy of Management Journal*, 43(6): 1177-1194.

[46] Reid, M., Allen, M., Riemenschneider, C., and Armstrong, D., 2008. The role of mentoring and supervisor support for state IT employee' affective commitment. *Review of Public Personnel Administration*, 28(1): 60-78.

[47] Riemenschneider, C., Allen, M., Reid, M., and Armstrong, D., 2006. The effects of mentoring to reduce stress in a state IT department during times of transformational change. *International Journal of Learning and Change*, 1(4): 429 - 445.

[48] Rutner, P., Hardgrave, B., and Mcknight, D., 2008. Emotional dissonance and the information technology professional. *MIS Quarterly Executive*, 32(3): 635-652.

[49] Sanchez-Franco, M.J., 2006. Exploring the influence of gender on the web usage via partial least squares. *Behaviour & Information Technology*, 25(1): 19-36.

[50] Scandura, T.A., 1997. Mentoring and organizational justice: An empirical investigation. *Journal of Vocational Behavior*, 51(1): 58-69.

[51] Scandura, T.A., Graen, G.B., and Novak, M.A., 1986. When managers decide not to decide autocratically: An investigation of leader–member exchange and decision influence. *Journal of Applied Psychology*, 71(4): 579-584.

[52] Seibert, S., 1999. The effectiveness of facilitated mentoring: A longitudinal quasi-experiment. *Journal of Vocational Behavior*, 54(3): 483-502.

[53] Tharenou, P., 1999. Gender differences in advancing to the top. *International Journal of Management Reviews*, 1(2): 111-132.

[54] Thatcher, J., Stepina, L., and Boyle, R., 2002. Turnover of information technology workers: Examining empirically the influence of attitudes, job characteristics, and external

markets. *Journal of Management Information Systems*, 19(3): 231-261.

[55] Thomas, C.H. and Lankau, M.J., 2009. Preventing burnout: The effects of LMX and mentoring on socialization, role stress, and burnout. *Human Resource* Management, 48(3), 417-432.

[56] Trauth, E.M., Quesenberry, J.L., and Huang, H., 2009. Retaining women in the US IT workforce: Theorizing the influence of organizational factors. *European Journal of Information Systems*, 18(5): 476-497.

[57] Vakola, M. and Nikolaou, I., 2005. Attitudes toward organizational change: What is the role of employees' stress and commitment? *Employee Relations*, 27(2): 160-174.

[58] Viator, R.E., 2001. The association of formal and informal public accounting mentoring with role stress and related job outcomes. *Accounting, Organizations and Society*, 26(1): 73-93.

[59] Viator, R.E. and Scandura, T.A., 1991. A study of mentor-protege relationships in large public accounting firms. *Accounting Horizons*, 5(1): 20-30.

[60] Wayne, S.J., Shore, L.M., and Liden, R.C., 1997. Perceived organizational support and leader-member exchange: A social exchange perspective. *Academy of Management Journal*. 40(1): 82-111.

[61] Weiss, H.M. and Cropanzano, R., 1996. Affective events theory: A theoretical discussion of the structure, causes, and consequences of affective experiences at work. *Research in Organizational Behavior*, 18(1): 1-74.

[62] Zeffane, R., 1994. Patterns of organizational commitment and perceived management style: A comparison of public and private sector employees. *Human Relations*, 47(8): 977-1011.

8. APPENDIX

Items retained in the final measurement model are marked with an asterisk (*).

PSYCHOSOCIAL MENTORING
1. Conveyed feelings of respect for you as an individual? (*)
2. Conveyed empathy for the concerns and feelings you have discussed with him/her? (*)
3. Encouraged you to talk openly about anxiety and fears that might detract from your work?
4. Shared personal experiences as an alternative perspective to your problems? (*)
5. Discussed your questions or concerns regarding feelings of competence, commitment to advancement, relationships with peers and supervisors or work/family conflicts? (*)
6. Shared history of his/her career with you? (*)
7. Provides suggestions concerning problems you have encountered at work? (*)
8. Encouraged you to try new ways of behaving on the job? (*)
9. Served as a role model?
10. Displayed attitudes and values similar to your own? (*)

Scale: 1=Not at all to 7=To a very large extent

CAREER MENTORING

1. Given or recommended you for challenging assignments that present opportunities to learn new skills? (*)
2. Given or recommended you for assignments that required personal contact with supervisors in different parts of the company? (*)
3. Given or recommended you for assignments that increased your contact with higher level managers? (*)
4. Given or recommended you for assignments that helped you meet new colleagues? (*)
5. Helped you finish assignments/tasks or meet deadlines that otherwise would have been difficult to complete?
6. Reduced unnecessary risks that could have threatened your opportunities for promotion?
7. Given or recommended you for assignments or tasks that have prepared you for higher positions? (*)
8. Kept you informed about what is going on at higher levels in the company or how external conditions are influencing the company?

Scale: 1=Not at all to 7=To a very large extent

LEADER-MEMBER EXCHANGE

1. I usually know where I stand with my manager. (*)
2. My manager has enough confidence in me that he/she would defend and justify my decisions if I was not present to do so. (*)
3. My working relationship with my manager is effective. (*)
4. My manager understands my problems and needs. (*)
5. I can count on my manager to "bail me out," even at his or her own expense, when I really need it. (*)
6. My manager recognizes my potential. (*)
7. Regardless of how much power my manager has built into his or her position, my manager would be personally inclined to use his/her power to help solve problems in my work. (*)

Scale: 1=Strongly disagree 7=Strongly agree

ORGANIZATIONAL COMMITMENT

1. I am willing to put in a great deal of effort beyond that normally expected in order to help this organization be successful.
2. I really care about the fate of this organization.
3. I am extremely glad that I chose this organization for which to work, over other organizations I was considering at the time I joined. (*)
4. I talk up employment in this organization to friends as a great place to work. (*)
5. I am proud to tell others that I work for this organization. (*)
6. I find that my values and this organization's values are very similar. (*)
7. For me this is the best of all possible organizations for which to work. (*)

Scale: 1=Strongly disagree 7=Strongly agree

Do Economic Recession and Gender Influence the Likelihood of Entry Job in IT for IT Graduates?

Chunmian Ge
National University of Singapore
chunmian@nus.edu.sg

Atreyi Kankanhalli
National University of Singapore
disatrey@nus.edu.sg

Ke-Wei Huang
National University of Singapore
huangkw@comp.nus.edu.sg

Xiqing Sha
National University of Singapore
xiqing@nus.edu.sg

ABSTRACT

Attracting and retaining women is a major concern in the IT profession. Existing literature has noted that female students are less likely to choose IT as an undergraduate major, while female IT professionals are more likely to leave the IT workforce. There is little study of an intermediate step i.e., if gender affects whether IT graduates take up their first job in IT. At the same time, the recession in developed economies has prompted research interest on its effects on IT jobs. This paper examines the intersection of these two phenomena i.e., it seeks to understand the influence of both gender and the recent recession on the likelihood of IT graduates taking up their first jobs in IT. It hypothesizes direct and interaction effects of gender and recession on the dependent variable. The hypotheses are tested through analyzing data from annual surveys of undergraduate students majoring in IT at a large public university over a 5-year period from 2007-2011 that includes the recent recession. As hypothesized, female IT graduates were found to be 7.5% less likely to enter IT jobs over this period than their male counterparts. We also found that the economic recession of 2009 has significant interaction with gender i.e., female IT students were 20.9% less likely to enter an IT job in 2009 than male IT students. We contribute to the literature by demonstrating that economic downturn and gender could significantly affect likelihood of entry job in IT, while most of the previous research considers the effects of individual characteristics. Our findings provide implications for IT students, IT employers, and government policy makers.

Categories and Subject Descriptors

H.0 General

Keywords

Entry Job in IT, Gender Difference, Economic Recession, IT Graduate

1. INTRODUCTION

"I am a new graduate and am looking for work in IT. What I would like to ask all of you, is if you could go back in time would you still choose IT?"

—— question asked on an online forum[1]

The above quote illustrates a salient question in the minds of fresh IT graduates, since the first job is important for their future career development [1, 2]. While an IT job may hold various advantages such as a casual or flexible work environment e.g., a jeans and T-shirt culture, some IT jobs are notorious for their stressful nature, long working hours, and need to continuously update skills due to rapidly-changing technologies [3]. Therefore, IT students may prefer non-IT careers, which negates the time and resources invested in educating them. Thus, it is vital to understand the factors that may affect fresh IT students' take up of IT and non-IT jobs.

On one hand, individual characteristics such as gender are likely to play an important role in determining one's first job. Gender difference in the IT discipline has been widely studied (e.g. [4]). These studies are typically motivated by the need to attract and retain females in the IT workforce. There are two main streams of research regarding gender and the IT profession. One stream focuses on examining gender differences in undergraduate students' decisions to pursue an IT major (e.g. [5]). The other stream aims to study gender effects on IT careers (e.g., differences in IT job turnover). However, there is limited understanding and study of the gender differences in IT graduates' likelihood of taking up an IT job as their first job. A related study by Kuhn and Joshi [6] examined gender similarities and differences in IT job attribute preferences among undergraduate IT students.

On the other hand, external factors could also have significant impacts on the entry into an IT job. A prominent exogenous factor is the condition of the economy. Particularly, the 2008 financial crisis has been recognized as the most significant economic downturn since the Great Depression of the 1930s [7]. It is likely that the IT labor demand of employers would be affected by this macro-economic shock. In other words, IT graduates' likelihood of entering an IT job could vary due to the contraction of business and reduced employment in a recession. However, there is a lack of studies examining the impacts of the economic recession on new IT graduates' entering an IT job, given that economic influence is suggested as an important construct as per the individual differences theory of gender and IT [8].

---

[1] http://serverfault.com/questions/100541/if-you-could-go-back-in-time-would-you-still-choose-it

The goal of this study, therefore, is to examine the effects of gender, economic recession, and their interaction on the likelihood of fresh IT graduates entering an IT job. This is accomplished by surveying the first employment of undergraduate students completing an IT major in a large public university from 2007 to 2011. As hypothesized, female IT students were found less likely to enter IT jobs than their male counterparts. As also expected, gender and the recession (assessed in 2009 as the year after the financial crises) had a significant interaction effect i.e., fresh female IT undergraduates were even less likely to take up an IT job in 2009 than in other years. This study contributes by improving our understanding of the effects of gender and economic recession on new IT graduates entering an IT job. It also provides implications for IT students, IT employers, and government policy makers. Further analyses being planned are discussed at the end of the paper.

2. LITERATURE REVIEW

2.1 Gender and IT Career

Prior research has shown that gender influences both individual's career IT decisions and opportunities in the IT workforce [9]. In fact, there exists substantial research investigating gender effects in the IT discipline. Among these, one stream of research has examined gender difference in students' decisions to pursue an IT major. Here, male college undergraduates were found to be more likely to choose an IT major than females, as males scored higher on computer self-efficacy, attitudes towards IT careers, and outcome expectations (e.g. [10]). These differences in beliefs may be explained from the social construction perspective. This view suggests that girls and boys are given different signals in a variety of ways in their formative years [11]. Specifically, females are often discouraged from taking up technology-related subjects and interests and their expertise in these areas may be under-valued [12]. These gender-based norms put pressure on men and women to conform to prescribed normative roles [8]. With the technology emphasis in IT subjects, as girls grow up, they may be less likely to choose an IT major to study [13].

Another stream of the research focuses on exploring gender differences in IT careers and IT job turnover. Generally speaking, males tend to congregate in technical and managerial jobs [14]. Thus, it could be expected that the IT workforce would tend to be dominated by males [15]. One reason why female IT professionals experience a greater desire to move out of IT jobs is due to less favorable chances of promotion (e.g. [16, 17]). Additionally, female IT professionals reported higher stress levels than males [18], and are more likely to leave the workforce due to both work stress [19] and family reasons [20, 21]. Accordingly, in a meta-analysis of 33 studies about the antecedents of IT turnover intention, gender is identified as a significant antecedent [9] i.e., female IT professionals are more likely to leave IT jobs. Other than individual attributes such as gender, external factors such as economic conditions could also have significant impacts on IT careers and the take up of IT jobs.

2.2 Gender and Economic Recession

The 2008 financial crisis began with the bursting of the housing bubble in 2007 and its impact continues in the labor market. There was more unemployment due to this recession than at any time since the Great Depression [7]. Three basic hypotheses have been put forward in the literature to predict the impact of

recession on women's employment in general i.e., the flexible reserve or 'buffer' hypothesis, the segmentation hypothesis, and the substitution hypotheses [22]. The *buffer hypothesis* states that women are a flexible reserve such that they are drawn into the labor market in good times and are removed in bad times. In other words, companies prefer to hire male employees whenever available. The *job segmentation hypothesis* is based on gender-typing of occupations. It posits that if an economic downturn hits male-dominated industries more than female dominated industries, then male unemployment rate would be higher. As per the *substitution hypothesis*, women are considered as cost-saving substitutes for men as the recession intensifies. In other words, during a recession, companies may hire more female employees to cut wage costs. We draw the implications of these hypotheses for female employment in the IT sector as shown in Table 1.

Table 1. Summary of hypotheses regarding the impact of economic recessions

Hypothesis	Buffer	Segregation	Substitution
Female Employment in IT	Decrease more than males	Not relevant	Increase more than males

Of the three hypotheses, the job segregation hypothesis does not predict how female employment rate could be affected during a recession for a male-dominated industry such as IT. Therefore, it is less relevant to our study. However, the buffer and substitution theories predict opposite effects on female employment in IT during a recession. Compared to the substitution hypothesis, the buffer hypothesis could be more relevant to our study. This is because women are typically not recognized as cost-saving substitutes for men in the IT industry according to an IT compensation study by Ang et al. [23], which found that gender was not a significant predictor of either base compensation or total compensation of IT professionals. In this manner, our study can add to the literature by validating which one of the buffer and substitution theories would apply better to explain female employment in IT jobs during the recession.

Other than direct effects, the external economic environment could interact with gender to affect fresh undergraduates' IT career entry. However, even with the extensive research on the impacts of gender difference on IT major and career decisions, there are few studies [24] examining the impact of an external economic shock on IT careers. Laumer and Eckhardt [24] observed that in the last economic recession, there was a significant decrease in IT personnel's perception of career opportunities in IT, while other factors such as their job satisfaction, organizational commitment, and turnover intention stayed similar in 2008 and 2009. Change in the perception of IT career opportunities during a recession may also affect students' IT career entry. Overall, there is a need for a more comprehensive understanding of the direct and interaction effects of gender and economic recession on the likelihood of IT undergraduates taking up their first job in IT.

3. HYPOTHESES DEVELOPMENT

Prior research has found that females are less likely to choose an IT major and more likely to leave IT jobs, as discussed in the previous section. According to the social constructionist perspective, individuals' perceptions are socially constructed, accepted, and internalized. Thus, men are socially perceived to be well-suited to perform stereotypically masculine roles whereas women are viewed to fit well in stereotypically feminine roles [8]. The IT profession is considered to be male-dominated and possessing a masculine culture, as technology is inherently masculine in character [25]. It is, thus, expected that females will be less likely to take up an IT career compared to males due to these social norms.

In addition, female students were found to have lower outcome expectations regarding an IT career [10], in terms of how satisfied a student thinks he/she would be in an IT career. The stereotype of the average computer worker as an introverted male [26] would likely affect outcome expectations and attitudes towards IT jobs [10], and in turn lead to fewer female IT graduates entering IT jobs.

At the same time, IT employers' attitudes towards female newcomers could also affect the likelihood of female graduates' entry into IT jobs. Prior research has found that male IT newcomers were expected to perform better, reported a higher quality of work relationships, and felt more empowered than female IT newcomers [27]. This suggests that IT employers may prefer male IT newcomers due to past experience or socially constructed biases. Based on the above arguments, we hypothesize that,

H1. *For their first job, female undergraduate students who major in IT are less likely to enter an IT job than their male counterparts.*

At the same time, an economic recession may influence IT graduates' first jobs due to business contraction and less employment. Bansak et al. [28] compared the three previously mentioned hypotheses by examining the impact of recession on gender-related segregation of nine occupations[2], which also include professionals and technicians. They found that the buffer hypothesis dominates the other two hypotheses. According to the buffer hypothesis, it is more difficult for women to obtain jobs in general during a recession since employers' would not draw on them as reserves but would rather discard them. Although not stated in the original buffer hypothesis, we believe that this effect would be stronger in male-dominated industries, such as the IT industry [29]. IT companies may prefer male applicants because they may perceive that the nature of IT jobs and culture fits male workers better and the attrition rate of male workers has been lower than females, as discussed in the literature review. During an economic downturn when job openings reduce and the number of rookie job applicants remains similar, IT employers can cherry-pick the job applicants they prefer and thus reduce the employment of female IT students.

Besides, high-achieving male IT graduates who normally target well-paying jobs, e.g., high-salary finance jobs, in good times may also seek IT jobs in bad times due to the downsizing of the financial industry and the fact that IT companies survived the economic recession relatively well [24]. An increasing number and quality of IT job applicants would lead to higher competition levels in the IT job market. The increasing competition may also reduce the likelihood of females' entering an IT job. As a result, we hypothesize that:

---

[2] The nine occupations are: Executive/Senior Level Officials and Managers, Professionals, Technicians, Sales Workers, Administrative Support Workers, Craft Workers, Operatives, Laborers and Helpers, and Service Workers.

H2. *For their first job, female undergraduate students who major in IT are less likely to enter an IT job during a recession than in other times.*

4. METHOD AND DATA

4.1 Data and Coding

We obtained our dataset from a graduate employment survey in a large public university in Singapore. The Singapore government has the vision of establishing an Asia innovation hub of technology industries and has implemented economic incentives to attract major software companies to the country, which greatly increases the demand for skilled IT labor and leads to a highly competitive IT labor market [30]. Therefore, it is crucial to study the determinants of entering an IT career in the context of Singapore.

The survey we drew from is conducted annually and anonymously by the university. The subjects are undergraduate students who have just graduated from the university 6 months before. Most of them graduated in May. Our dataset consisted of all students graduating with a bachelor's degree in computing. The survey includes the graduates' demographic information and first employment particulars. In addition, almost all of the graduates are working in Singapore. Our sample consists of annual surveys from 2007 to 2011, a time frame in which the 2008 financial crisis occurred. For post-1990 recessions, the full effects of a recession on employment were not realized until the recession passed [31]. This is also the year that the 2008 financial crisis affected Singapore. The unemployment rate was also highest in Singapore during year 2009[3]. The unemployment rate in year 2009 was 36.4% higher than that in year 2008. Hence, we chose the year 2009 as the relevant year to examine the exogenous effect of the 2008 financial crisis on the first job of IT graduates (see Figure 1).

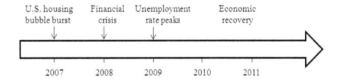

Figure 1. Timeline of the 2008 Financial Crisis

To decide whether the first job of an individual in our sample is IT or non-IT in nature, a PhD student in this area manually went through and classified all the records by considering the company name, industry sector, occupation and job description of students' first jobs. The judgment was made primarily based on the job function description and additionally based on the company's nature of business. The classification was validated by two IS professors. Examples of IT jobs included programmer, software developer, IT designer and analyst, while examples of non-IT jobs included sales and marketing personnel, accountant, and bank teller.

4.2 Logit Model

Logit model is used for predicting the outcome of a binary variable based on one or more explanatory variables. This type of

---

[3] http://www.mom.gov.sg/statistics-publications/national-labour-market-information/statistics/Pages/unemployment.aspx

model has been widely used in social science research [32]. We specify the following logit model to examine the impact of economic recessions.

$$f(X_i) = \beta_0 + \beta_1 Gender_i + \beta_2 Gender_i * Recession_i + ControlVars + \varepsilon, \quad (1)$$

$$Pr(ITJob_i = 1 \mid X_i) = \frac{e^{\beta x}}{1 + e^{\beta x}}. \quad (2)$$

where i denotes the individual IT graduate.

Table 2. Summary Statistics and Control Variables

Category		Pct (Mean)	Std. Dev	Variable
First Job	IT Job	76	0.41	Equals 1 if IT Job and 0 otherwise
	Non-IT Job	24		
Gender	Female	23	0.42	Equals 1 if female and 0 otherwise
	Male	77		
Race	Chinese	80	0.40	*Benchmark Chinese*
	Indian	8	0.27	Equals 1 if Indian
	Malay	2	0.14	Equals 1 if Malay
	Other Races	10	0.30	Equals 1 if Other
Major	CNM[4]	13	0.34	Equals 1 if major is Communications and Media
	CBio	2	0.13	Equals 1 for Computational Bio.
	CEng	25	0.43	Equals 1 for Computer Engg.
	CS	22	0.41	*Benchmark Computer Science*
	EC	15	0.36	Equals 1 for Elect. Commerce
	IS	23	0.42	Equals 1 for Information Syst.
Citizenship	Foreigners	31	0.46	Equals 1 for Foreigner
	Permanent Resident	8	0.28	Equals 1 for PR
	Citizen	61	0.49	*Benchmark Citizen*
Fin. Support	Fin Assistance	4	0.19	Equals 1 if financially assisted
	Scholarships	19	0.39	Equals 1 if schol. holder
	Loan	39	0.49	Equals 1 if on student loan
	Self-financed	38	0.49	*Benchmark self-financed*

The dependent variable, $ITJob_i$, is a binary variable that equals one if the first job of the individual graduate is an IT job and zero if it is a non-IT job. $Gender_i$ is a binary variable that equals one if the individual graduate is female, and zero if male. $Recession_i$ is another binary variable that equals one if the student graduated in the year 2009, and zero otherwise. $Gender_i * Recession_i$ represents the interaction effect of gender and recession. $ControlVars$ indicates a series of control variables as shown in Table 2. ε is the error term. The probability of individual i taking up an IT job is shown in Equation (2).

---

[4] CNM in this study is computer-oriented. It aims to train students for a career in interactive and digital media technologies. The program includes modules such as programming methodology, database systems and so on.

Table 2 lists the control variables in this model. Individual characteristics such as race and citizenship are included because these variables could be related to students' job choices or employers' recruiting preferences. Year dummies are also added in the model. The table also reports the summary statistics of our sample with 919 observations over 2007-2011.

5. PRELIMINARY FINDINGS

We estimated four models where model 1 consists of gender and the year dummies. Model 2 also considers the impact of economic recession, in addition to the variables in model 1.

Table 3. Logit Model Estimation Results

	(1) IT Job	(2) IT Job	(3) IT Job	(4) IT Job
Gender	-0.574***	-0.343*	-0.474**	-0.202
	(0.001)	(0.089)	(0.014)	(0.367)
Gender*Recession		-0.973**		-1.127**
		(0.017)		(0.011)
Indian			-0.754**	-0.766**
			(0.019)	(0.017)
Malay			0.467	0.452
			(0.479)	(0.489)
Other Races			-0.449	-0.512
			(0.176)	(0.125)
CNM			-1.254***	-1.252***
			(0.000)	(0.000)
CBio			-2.865***	-2.865***
			(0.000)	(0.000)
CEng			-0.753**	-0.747**
			(0.012)	(0.012)
EC			-2.083***	-2.085***
			(0.000)	(0.000)
IS			-1.075***	-1.061***
			(0.000)	(0.000)
Foreigners			0.479*	0.504*
			(0.063)	(0.052)
PR			-0.020	-0.073
			(0.953)	(0.831)
Fin Assistance			0.166	0.306
			(0.712)	(0.508)
Scholarships			-1.012***	-1.022***
			(0.000)	(0.000)
Loan			0.254	0.245
			(0.217)	(0.235)
Year 2007	0.184	-0.089	0.229	-0.070
	(0.484)	(0.760)	(0.417)	(0.823)
Year 2008	0.391	0.145	0.415	0.161
	(0.191)	(0.651)	(0.214)	(0.650)
Year 2010	0.154	-0.123	0.318	0.015
	(0.496)	(0.635)	(0.194)	(0.958)
Year 2011	-0.359*	-0.640**	-0.305	-0.625**
	(0.096)	(0.011)	(0.192)	(0.021)
Constant	1.282***	1.490***	2.348***	2.578***
	(0.000)	(0.000)	(0.000)	(0.000)
Observations	919	919	919	919
Log-likelihood	-496.8	-494.0	-448.6	-445.4
AIC	1005.6	1002.0	935.2	930.8
Pseudo R^2	0.022	0.028	0.117	0.123

p-values in parentheses * $p < 0.10$, ** $p < 0.05$, *** $p < 0.01$

Model 3 builds on model 1 by adding control variables including race, major, citizenship, and financial support type. Last, model 4 builds on model 2 by adding control variables. The results of model tests are shown in Table 3.

The main effect of gender is significant and negative in models 1-3, indicating that female students are less likely to be placed in IT jobs. In other words, the models suggest that when we do not separate recession from normal years, *H1 is supported*. Further, the interaction term of gender and recession is significant in both models 2 and 4 indicating that *H2 is supported*.

Table 4 reports the marginal effects of logit regression. Model 4 shows that during normal years, female IT graduates are 3.2% less likely to enter IT jobs than male IT graduates. In addition, female IT graduates are 20.9% less likely to enter IT jobs than male IT graduates during recession. In other words, female IT graduates are 17.7% less likely to enter IT jobs in 2009 than in other years. The results for control variables also show that race, major, citizenship and the type of financial support could be significant predictors of IT job entry of IT graduates.

Table 4. Marginal Effects of Logit Regression

	(1)	(2)	(3)	(4)
Gender	-0.103***	-0.061*	-0.075**	-0.032
Gender * Recession		-0.172**		-0.177***

p-values in parentheses * $p < 0.10$, ** $p < 0.05$, *** $p < 0.01$

6. IMPLICATIONS AND FUTURE RESEARCH

It has been observed that the more diverse and inclusive the IT workforce, the more likely IT solutions will address a broad range of issues [33]. However, the IT workforce continues to be a male-dominated such that attracting and retaining women remains a major concern in IT [4, 6]. Our study adds to the literature by showing that even if they graduate with an IT degree, female students are less likely than males to take up an IT job as their first job. This finding addresses a step between the two streams of existing literature that female students are less likely to choose IT as a major and female IT professionals are less likely to continue an IT career. With our finding, it seems that females may not enter (or may leave) the IT profession in all three stages i.e., before university, after university, and after taking up an IT job. Thus, it is important for IT educators and recruiters to work towards alleviating females' negative attitudes towards an IT career in all three stages.

Further, this study finds that during the 2009 financial meltdown, the gender segregation effect in IT was aggravated such that a significantly lower proportion of female IT students were placed in IT jobs. This finding suggests that for those IT companies that are able to hire during the economic recession, it may be a great opportunity for them to recruit more female IT graduates. Female IT graduates may also benefit from this knowledge for their job search. Last, government policy makers may need to be aware of this finding and urge IT companies to keep a stable female employment for a diversified IT workforce during an economic recession.

Continuing this work, we plan to examine the impacts of economic recessions in more details. One direction is to study how salary may affect IT graduates' career decisions. Job seekers typically make a tradeoff between the salary prospects and finding a job they enjoy. High-performing IT students may choose to work in non-IT jobs with higher salary even if they like the IT profession, whereas poor-performing IT students may still choose an IT career because the salary offered is the best among all the options available to them. Thus, we can investigate gender

differences and the substitution relationship between IT and non-IT jobs during normal and recession times. Another potential direction is to further classify IT jobs into finer categories to investigate the gender differences in taking up different IT job classes. Collecting information about job openings from job search websites could help us in modeling IT labor demand to shed more light on our research objectives.

7. REFERENCES

[1] J. B. Forbes, 1987, "Early Intraorganizational Mobility: Patterns and Influences," *Academy of Management Journal*, vol. 30, pp. 110-125.

[2] J. H. Greenhaus, G. A. Callanan, and V. M. Godshalk, 2009, *Career Management*: Sage Publications.

[3] WetFeet, 2009, *Careers in Information Technology*. Philadephia: PA.

[4] E. M. Trauth, J. L. Quesenberry, and H. Huang, 2009, "Retaining Women in the Us It Workforce: Theorizing the Influence of Organizational Factors," *European Journal of Information Systems*, vol. 18, pp. 476-497.

[5] A. Y. Akbulut and C. A. Looney, 2007, "Inspiring Students to Pursue Computing Degrees," *Communications of the ACM*, vol. 50, pp. 67-71.

[6] K. Kuhn and K. Joshi, 2009, "The Reported and Revealed Importance of Job Attributes to Aspiring Information Technology: A Policy-Capturing Study of Gender Differences," *The Data Base for Advances in Information Systems*, vol. 40, pp. 40-60.

[7] H. S. Farber, 2012, "Unemployment in the Great Recession: Did the Housing Market Crisis Prevent the Unemployed from Moving to Take Jobs?," *The American Economic Review*, vol. 102, pp. 520-525.

[8] E. M. Trauth, C. C. Cain, K. Joshi, L. Kvasny, and K. Booth, 2012, "Embracing Intersectionality in Gender and It Career Choice Research," in *Proceedings of the 50th annual conference on Computers and People Research*, Milwaukee, USA.

[9] D. Joseph, K. Y. Ng, C. Koh, and S. Ang, 2007, "Turnover of Information Technology Professionals: A Narrative Review, Meta-Analytic Structural Equation Modeling, and Model Development," *MIS Quarterly*, vol. 31, pp. 547-577.

[10] N. Heinze and Q. Hu, 2009, "Why College Undergraduates Choose It: A Multi-Theoretical Perspective," *European Journal of Information Systems*, vol. 18, pp. 462-475.

[11] G. Kolata, 1984, "Equal Time for Women," *Discover*, vol. 5, pp. 24-27.

[12] C. Cockburn and S. Ormrod, 1993, *Gender and Technology in the Making*. London: Sage.

[13] M. K. Ahuja, 2002, "Women in the Information Technology Profession: A Literature Review, Synthesis and Research Agenda," *European Journal of Information Systems*, vol. 11, pp. 20-34.

[14] D. Tomaskovic-Devey and S. Skaggs, 2002, "Sex Segregation, Labor Process Organization, and Gender Earnings Inequality," *American Journal of Sociology*, vol. 108, pp. 102-128.

[15] D. Joseph, W. F. Boh, S. Ang, and S. A. Slaughter, 2012, "The Career Paths Less (or More) Traveled: A Sequence Analysis of It Career Histories, Mobility Patterns, and Career Success," *MIS Quarterly,* vol. 36, pp. 427-452.

[16] J. J. Baroudi and M. Igbaria, 1994, "An Examination of Gender Effects on Career Success of Information Systems Employees," *Journal of Management Information Systems,* vol. 11, pp. 181-201.

[17] M. Igbaria and J. J. Baroudi, 1995, "The Impact of Job Performance Evaluations on Career Advancement Prospects: An Examination of Gender Differences in the Is Workplace," *MIS Quarterly,* vol. 19, pp. 107-123.

[18] V. Sethi, R. C. King, and J. C. Quick, 2004, "What Causes Stress in Information System Professionals?," *Communications of the ACM,* vol. 47, pp. 99-102.

[19] D. J. Armstrong, C. K. Riemenschneider, M. F. Reid, and J. E. Nelms, 2011, "Challenges and Barriers Facing Women in the Is Workforce: How Far Have We Come?," in *Proceedings of the 49th SIGMIS annual conference on Computer personnel research*, San Antonio, USA.

[20] Q. Huang and M. Sverke, 2007, "Women's Occupational Career Patterns over 27 Years: Relations to Family of Origin, Life Careers, and Wellness," *Journal of Vocational Behavior,* vol. 70, pp. 369-397.

[21] C. K. Riemenschneider, D. J. Armstrong, M. W. Allen, and M. F. Reid, 2006, "Barriers Facing Women in the It Work Force," *The Data Base for Advances in Information Systems,* vol. 37, pp. 58-78.

[22] J. Rubery, 1988, *Women and Recession*. New York: Routledge and Kegan Paul.

[23] S. Ang, S. Slaughter, and K. Y. Ng, 2002, "Human Capital and Institutional Determinants of Information Technology Compensation: Modeling Multilevel and Cross-Level Interactions," *Management Science,* vol. 48, pp. 1427-1445.

[24] S. Laumer and A. Eckhardt, 2010, "Analyzing It Personnel's Perception of Job-Related Factors in Good and Bad Times," in *Proceedings of the 48th annual conference on Computer personnel research*, Vancouver, Canada.

[25] M. Wilson, 2004, "A Conceptual Framework for Studying Gender in Information Systems Research," *Journal of Information Technology,* vol. 19, pp. 81-92.

[26] S. McConnell, 2003, *Professional Software Development: Shorter Schedules, Better Projects, Superior Products, Enhanced Careers*: Boston: Addison Wesley.

[27] G. Chen and R. J. Klimoski, 2003, "The Impact of Expectations on Newcomer Performance in Teams as Mediated by Work Characteristics, Social Exchanges, and Empowerment," *Academy of Management Journal,* vol. 46, pp. 591-607.

[28] C. Bansak, M. E. Graham, and A. A. Zebedee, 2012, "Business Cycles and Gender Diversification: An Analysis of Establishment-Level Gender Dissimilarity," *The American Economic Review,* vol. 102, pp. 561-565.

[29] E. L. Chao and P. L. Rones, 2006, "Women in the Labor Force: A Databook."

[30] S. A. Slaughter, S. Ang, and W. Fong Boh, 2007, "Firm-Specific Human Capital and Compensation Organizational Tenure Profiles: An Archival Analysis of Salary Data for It," *Human Resource Management,* vol. 46, pp. 373-394.

[31] K. M. Engemann and H. J. Wall, 2010, "The Effects of Recessions across Demographic Groups," *Federal Reserve Bank of St. Louis Review,* vol. 92, pp. 1-26.

[32] A. C. Cameron and P. K. Trivedi, 2005, *Microeconometrics: Methods and Applications*: Cambridge university press.

[33] R. Florida and G. Gates, 2004, "Technology and Tolerance: The Importance of Diversity to High-Technology Growth," *Research in Urban Policy,* vol. 9, pp. 199-219.

Going It All Alone In Web Entrepreneurship?
A Comparison of Single Founders vs. Co-Founders

Olav Spiegel
University of Cologne
Albertus-Magnus-Platz
50923 Cologne, Germany
+49 221 470-5319
spiegel@wim.uni-koeln.de

Puja Abbassi
University of Cologne
Albertus-Magnus-Platz
50923 Cologne, Germany
+49 221 470-5396
abbassi@wim.uni-koeln.de

Daniel Schlagwein
University of New South Wales
Australian School of Business
Sydney UNSW 2052, Australia
+61 2 9385 6487
schlagwein@unsw.edu.au

Kai Fischbach
University of Bamberg
An der Weberei 5
96047 Bamberg, Germany
+49 951 863-2890
kai.fischbach@uni-bamberg.de

ABSTRACT

There is a considerable amount of entrepreneurial activity in the information technology (IT) industry, especially in the Web. Many claim that the founders are the single most critical factor in startup success. The entrepreneurial self-efficacy theory and the jack-of-all-trades theory suggest that founders with diverse skills and broad experience will be able to successfully create a business alone. Alternatively, social capital theory suggests that founders who have high social capital and who engage in social networking will be able to go alone. Others, however, claim that team building is crucial for startup success as to bringing complementary skills together.

In this study, we investigate if having a diverse skill set, higher experience, or more social connections is indeed a determinant of single founders, while co-founders have more specialized (yet complementary) skills. Our results are derived from analysis of 91 Web startups and their 183 (co-) founders. Contradicting existing theory, we could not find determinants for starting a new business alone. However, we find that co-founders do indeed complement each other's skills.

Our results suggest that existing entrepreneurial theory needs to be expanded and revised to accommodate for the contradictions found and that future research is required in this area.

Categories and Subject Descriptors

K.1 [**Computing Milieux**]: The Computer Industry – *statistics, suppliers;* K.7.0 [**The Computing Profession**]: General; K.6.1 [**Management of Computing and Information Systems**]: Project and People Management – *staffing.*

General Terms

Management, Performance, Economics, Human Factors

Keywords

Web entrepreneurship, startups, founders, co-founders, founding teams, social networks, entrepreneurial self-efficacy theory, jack-of-all-trades theory, team diversity, human capital, social capital

1. INTRODUCTION

"IT is the magic ingredient that inspires and most often enables contemporary entrepreneurial endeavors" [21]. Despite the considerable amount of entrepreneurial activity in the IT industry, little is known about actual founders and founding teams in this context [48]. We would like to contribute to a better understanding of what we call *Web entrepreneurship* – startups that make intensive use of the Internet and web technologies.

Since Schumpeter's [55] days, entrepreneurship has been a fruitful research field, resulting in typologies of entrepreneurs (e.g., [65, 69]), as well as theories on factors leading to entrepreneurship, including the entrepreneurial self-efficacy theory [15] and the jack-of-all-trades theory [41]. However, to our knowledge, those theories have only been applied to single entrepreneurs so far and not to teams of entrepreneurs or co-founders. Theory suggests that diversity [35] and heterogeneity of skills within (founder) teams can be beneficial [12, 36, 45].

Our research is guided by the following question: What differentiates single founders from co-founders? In other words, why do some people found alone and others in teams? We aim to show that, as theory would imply, single founders have more relevant entrepreneurial skills, have more experience, and are better connected than co-founders. On the other hand, we aim to provide evidence that team formation is driven by the need to gain access to complementary resources, resources that can compensate for individual skill deficits. Finally, we want to investigate whether single or co-founders are more successful.

The paper is organized as follows. In the next section, we provide a literature review and develop a theoretical framework for our study. Then, we discuss our research method and data. Following that, we present our empirical findings. Finally, we discuss these findings against the existing entrepreneurial theory as well as implications for research and practice. We conclude with a summary and provide a research outlook.

2. LITERATURE REVIEW AND THEORETICAL BACKGROUND

In this section, we provide some theoretical background about our research context, and develop hypotheses based on a review of the existing literature.

2.1 Web Entrepreneurship

Entrepreneurship has been studied intensively since Schumpeter [55] laid the grounds for this research field in the early 20th century. Web entrepreneurship falls into this larger stream of research. Information Technology (IT) has become increasingly important in this field: *"Our steadfast belief is that IT is the magic ingredient that inspires and most often enables contemporary entrepreneurial endeavors"* [21]. Compared to IT startups in general, Web startups are new ventures that do not only use IT to support their business processes, moreover they are using the Internet and associated technologies – often coined as 'Web 2.0' [52] – to create and implement new business ideas. Different other terms have been used in the past, including *"e-entrepreneurship"* [40], *"pure dot.com firms"* [56], and *"Internet businesses"* [46]. Despite the considerable amount of entrepreneurial activity in the IT industry, especially in the Web, little is known about actual founders and founding teams in this context [48].

2.2 Entrepreneurs (Single Founders)

Looking at the person of the entrepreneur, several frameworks have been suggested to understand the factors (i.e. the characteristics of a person) leading to entrepreneurship. Especially the (entrepreneurial) self-efficacy theory and the jack-of-all-trades theory have been brought forward to explain disposition to entrepreneurship. In addition to those human capital factors, social networking and social capital have been used to explain entrepreneurial success.

2.2.1 Entrepreneurial Self-Efficacy

Self-efficacy refers to the ability of a person to independently solve problems, complete tasks, and reach his/her goals [7]. In the entrepreneurial context, self-efficacy refers to self-reported *"confidence in having the relevant skills for running one's own business"* [19]. Chen et al. [15] specified a measurement construct of entrepreneurial self-efficacy (ESE) as being comprised of self-efficacy in five managerial functions: innovation, marketing, management, risk-taking, and financial control. Besides those generic skills, entrepreneurs in the Web context need to have some domain-specific abilities. For instance, computer efficacy includes additional dimensions (such as technologies and design skills) that are relevant specifically in the IT context [16]. We have adapted computer efficacy to the specific context of Web entrepreneurs in this study.

We suggest that single entrepreneurs and co-founders can be differentiated based on their degree of entrepreneurial self-efficacy, i.e., the number of specific entrepreneurial skills. In the case of single founders, all or most of these traits need to be present in one person:

> HYPOTHESIS 1: Single entrepreneurs have a higher degree of entrepreneurial self-efficacy (more entrepreneurial skills) than co-founders

2.2.2 The Jack-of-All-Trades Theory

The 'jack-of-all-trades' view of entrepreneurship suggests a balance of skills, breadth of education, and number of roles served in prior job positions as predictors of entrepreneurial success [41, 42, 68].

For the case of single founders, we expect that they can be differentiated from co-founders based on a higher education and greater work experience:

> HYPOTHESIS 2: Single founders have a higher education and greater work experience than co-founders

2.2.3 Social Networking and Social Capital

The concept of social capital has become increasingly popular and has found broad acceptance and application beyond its origins in the social sciences [2], including the field of information systems research [71]. Social capital is *"the sum of the actual and potential resources embedded within, available through, and derived from the network of relationships possessed by an individual or social unit"* [49]. Networks are not only very relevant for individuals but are also an important resource for the firm [30].

Oliver Bussmann, Chief Information Officer of SAP, has recently stated that *"you're putting your executive career at risk if you're not social"* [28]. This "socialness" refers to the use of social networking to expand executives' viewpoints and knowledge. Access to knowledge is the most important resource for companies [32, 51], especially in the networked economy [57].

Entrepreneurship is inherently a network activity [23]. There have been many studies addressing the importance of personal and business networks in the success and/or survival of startups [11, 12, 61, 67]. This is especially true in earlier stages of startups [9, 24, 39]. There are three essential processes in the early stages of startups, where networks play a crucial role: *"discovery of opportunities, securing resources, and obtaining legitimacy"* [24]. Furthermore, access to diverse information and resources has been shown to have a positive effect on entrepreneurial success [11].

Online social networks support the maintenance of existing connections as well as the formation of new social ties [25]. In this sense, online social networks, such as LinkedIn, facilitate access to information and resources. Thus, social networking is crucial for the generation of social capital. Recent research showed a positive relationship between an entrepreneur's LinkedIn network size and entrepreneurial survival [60]. Founding teams are able to compensate for disadvantaged network constellations of co-founders, i.e. their lack of social capital, which single founders cannot. Thus, for single founders, social networking plays an even more pivotal role.

> HYPOTHESIS 3: Single entrepreneurs are more engaged in social networking and have more social capital than co-founders

2.3 Entrepreneurial Teams and Diversity

In recent years, research has paid increasing attention to entrepreneurial teams [17, 34], recognizing that many new startups are not founded by lone entrepreneurial heroes [54, 63]. Cooney [17] defines entrepreneurial teams as *"two or more individuals who have a significant financial interest and participate actively in the development of the enterprise"*. In our research context, most of the team members described their position as 'co-founder', which is very different from a regular employee who gets paid for the job only.

Different factors may lead to team entrepreneurship, including personal reasons [29] and diversity considerations [45]. Research on team diversity and team outcomes is very comprehensive, and a recent meta-analytic review confirmed the positive impact of task-related diversity on team performance [36]. However, diversity (and its synonyms like heterogeneity) is an ambiguous concept as there are three distinctive types: separation, variety, and disparity (see [35] for a detailed discussion). In this research context, we are referring to diversity as variety, which can be summarized as *"composition of differences in kind, source, or category of relevant knowledge or experience among unit members"* [35]. Research showed that diversity of skills among a team of entrepreneurs can decrease uncertainty risks in the innovation process [45]. Such heterogeneity in teams may relate to both knowledge and viewpoints. Diversity of skills may help the co-founder team to identify opportunities between otherwise unconnected fields and hence lead to something new as the essential for innovative startups [12]. The heterogeneity of the top management team of startups has been found positively related to capital accumulation during an initial public offering (IPO) [72] and growth [59]. However, to avoid enduring conflict and increase constructive conflict, inner cohesion in teams is essential [26].

Summarizing, we hypothesize that the creation of entrepreneurial teams is driven by diversity considerations in the sense that co-founders complement each other in a variety of skills. More specifically, we hypothesize that co-founders complement each other in the skills underlying entrepreneurial self-efficacy (see discussion on ESE above); these are the skills that are required to become an entrepreneur.

> *HYPOTHESIS 4: Co-founders in entrepreneurial teams are selected complementing each other's ESE skills to increase the overall diversity (variety).*

2.4 Startup Performance and Funding

"The most compelling research finding about new venture teams to date is that team founded ventures appear to achieve better performance than individually founded ventures" [14]. As noted before, heterogeneity of the top management team of startups is positively related to IPO proceeds [72] and growth [59]. Stam and Schutjens [62] have also shown that team startups tend to have significantly higher startup capital than solo startups.

Performance and success of startups is not generally defined, especially in their early phases. For instance, actual revenues (if any at all) do not fully represent a startup's value. Typical successes for tech companies, especially web startups, are exits in the form of Initial Public Offerings (IPOs) or being acquired by an established company. The IPO rate or acquisition rate of portfolios is often a measurement for the success of venture capitalists (VCs) [1]. VCs are the primary source of selection for startups that have not yet exited [8]. Hence, funding received through these *"confirms the quality of the company and decreases the uncertainty about its potential success. [...] The credibility associated with a funding event – emanating from the information available to the VC firm as well as its reputation – gives a strong signal about the quality of the startup"* [20]. This is in line with other studies that measure the potential success of a startup as a function of external funding [8, 12, 20].

In line with existing theory, we would expect that founder teams would be able to raise more external funding than single founders.

> *HYPOTHESIS 5: Founding teams (co-founders) are able to raise more external funding than single entrepreneurs*

3. DATA AND RESEARCH METHOD

We have used a quantitative empirical approach to test our hypotheses against a data set of Web startups, their founders, and the characteristics of the founders.

3.1 Data Sources

We used a data set of 91 Web startups, 183 (co-) founders and their personal characteristics. The data set was compiled specifically for this study by utilizing two main data sources: the web database CrunchBase [18] and the professional networking site LinkedIn [44].

CrunchBase is a free public database, which is part of TechCrunch, a network of technology-oriented blogs and other web properties recently bought by AOL [5]. As of March 30, 2013, the database listed 118,774 companies, 154,011 people, and 34,168 funding rounds [18]. CrunchBase has a focus on startups and entrepreneurial companies [31]. The CrunchBase data are collected using a crowdsourcing [37, 38] approach: everyone is invited to contribute knowledge. CrunchBase has a large user community supported by a professional team from TechCrunch. The information can be accessed directly by means of an open application programming interface. We used a Java-based parsing program to download a complete dump for further processing on a local database.

LinkedIn is the world's largest professional online network with more than 200 million members in over 200 countries [50]. We believe the personal information presented on LinkedIn to be reasonably correct for the purpose of our study. This is in line with recent studies that found information available through online social networks to be quite accurate [6, 33]. Since the LinkedIn User Agreement prohibits any use of automated methods like software and scripts to access their data [43], we manually visited all founder profiles and extracted the relevant information for our attributes.

3.2 Sampling Strategy and Data Set

Our sampling strategy has been as follows. First, we selected only startups that were US-based to reduce the impact of other factors outside of the interest of this study (such as national culture). Second, we selected only startups that received seed funding in the year 2011 to make the data set coherent in terms of time (avoiding impact from, for example, the financial crisis) as well as stage of development. Finally, we selected only Web startups (category 'Consumer Web' on CrunchBase) to ensure homogeneity and comparability in our sample. Applying this selection strategy resulted in a first set of 103 companies. After removing 12 entries, because either the respective company was not active any more (e.g., website was taken offline) or the funding information could not be confirmed by alternative sources (e.g., self-declared only), we resulted with a set of 91 startups. Next, we identified the respective founder(s) of each startup using information from CrunchBase, LinkedIn, AngelList [4], press releases, and 'About Us' pages. This resulted in 183 individuals. For each one of them, we manually searched for the corresponding LinkedIn profile, where we could match 171 founders (93%).

Table 1: Overview of data and attributes

Startups	Company attributes	Name Number of founders Amount seed funding received in 2011
Founders	*Demographic data*	Name Gender Ethnicity Location (i.e. U.S. state)
	Education and work experience	Highest degree earned Total years of education Total years of work experience Number of prior work positions Prior consulting experience (dichotomous) Prior founding experience (dichotomous) Prior employee experience (dichotomous) Prior experience as venture capitalist (dichotomous) Startup sole position at time of founding Founder still active in startup (as of June 2012)
	Entrepreneurial self-efficacy (ESE) attributes	Innovation skills (dichotomous) Marketing skills (dichotomous) Management skills (dichotomous) Risk-taking skills (dichotomous) Financial control skills (dichotomous)
	Computer efficacy attributes (adapted to Web context)	General IT skills (dichotomous) Design skills (dichotomous) Web technology skills (dichotomous)
	Social networking attributes	LinkedIn profile Number of LinkedIn connections

All findings on the individual level will be based on this set of 171 founders with LinkedIn profiles (only the analysis on the number of founders per startup is based on the 183 founders), if not stated otherwise.

The type of data gathered is summarized in Table 1 below. Most of the attributes could be derived directly from the LinkedIn profiles or the CrunchBase website. For the entrepreneurial self-efficacy and computer efficacy attributes we used research team triangulation (see [22]). Chen et al. [15] provide some suggestions to assess the different self-efficacies. For instance, risk-taking is described as *"take calculated risks, make decisions under uncertainty and risk, take responsibility for ideas and decisions, work under pressure and conflict"* [15]. We selected the corresponding attributes based on the descriptions of prior jobs and educational background, e.g., if there was prior founding experience we drew the conclusion that the person must be "risk-taking". While the original entrepreneurial self-efficacy construct was self-reported and self-evaluated by the survey participants [15], we believe that our objective approach based on natural data delivers at least equally good results. Entrepreneurial self-efficacy refers to one's perceived confidence in performing domain-specific tasks, thus, describing the ability to fulfill this task in a job description should be a sufficiently good proxy.

3.3 Statistical Methods

First, we conducted a descriptive statistical analysis of the data to identify the major characteristics of the data set. Second, we performed Pearson's Chi-2 tests to compare the entrepreneurial self-efficacy attributes of single entrepreneurs with co-founders. Third, we applied Chi-2 tests in combination with two-sample *t*-tests to differentiate founders on their education and work experience. Fourth, we used two-sample *t*-tests to compare the average number (mean) of LinkedIn connections. Fifth, we used

one-way ANOVA (analysis of variance) to differentiate between the number of founders in a startup and the coverage of skills on the company level. Sixth, we analyzed the relationship between number of founders and the amount of funding received. As the explanatory variable is nominal and the explained variable continuous, we calculated Spearman's rank correlation coefficient (rho) and Kendall's Tau-b to test for correlations. We used the software IBM SPSS 21 for all statistical analyses.

4. FINDINGS

In this section we summarize our findings. First, we present some descriptive statistics about the founders and startups in our data sample. Next, we present the findings in light of our hypotheses.

4.1 Descriptive Statistics

Most of the startups in our sample are founded by two co-founders (45.05%). Single entrepreneurs account for (28.57%), as shown in Table 2 below.

Table 2: Number of founders per startup

(Co-) Founders	Startups	Percentage
1	26	28.57%
2	41	45.05%
3	21	23.08%
4	3	3.30%
Total	**91**	**100.00%**

The majority of founders declared the United States as their place of residence (which is unsurprising as we looked only at US startups). Less than 10% live outside, primarily in Europe and

India. For the US residents, we found a similar geographic distribution in our sample compared to earlier examinations [53]. As shown in Figure 1 below, the dominant states for Web startups are California (39%) and New York State (22%).

Figure 1: Geographic distribution of US-based founders

Our sample had a majority of male, white founders, as shown in Table 3 below. Overall, the gender ratio is very unequal (except for the Asian sub group, where it is balanced). The distribution in terms of ethnicity is not representative of the US overall population [66].

Table 3: Founders by sex and ethnicity

	Sample			
Ethnicity	**Female**	**Male**	**Total**	**US overall**
White	7.60%	71.35%	78.95%	80.98% "White"
Arabic	0.00%	1.17%	1.17%	
Indian	1.75%	8.19%	9.94%	4.65% "Asian"
Other Asian	4.68%	4.68%	9.36%	
Black	0.00%	0.58%	0.58%	13.14%
Total	**14.04%**	**85.96%**	**100.00%**	**98.76%**

Almost half of the founders in our sample have a Bachelor's degree as their highest degree before they start their own business, as shown in Table 4 below.

Table 4: Highest degree earned

Highest degree	**Founders**	**Percentage**
No information	15	8.77%
Other education	18	10.53%
College	7	4.09%
Bachelor	84	49.12%
Master (incl. MBA)	42	24.56%
PhD	5	2.92%
Total	**171**	**100.00%**

The entry 'No information' represents the group of founders that did not have any information on education in their LinkedIn profiles. 'Other education' relates to founders that started with a first degree but did not finish yet, or they took some other classes that did not result in a degree.

4.2 Single Founders vs. Co-Founders

In this section we are comparing the single founders against the co-founders to find evidence for our above-mentioned hypotheses.

4.2.1 Entrepreneurial Self-Efficacy

We performed a series of Chi-2 tests to test the dependence between being a single vs. co-founder and the 8 dimensions included in our entrepreneurial self-efficacy construct. The results are given in Table 5 below. We did not find a significant differentiator between single founders and co-founders in any of the ESE dimensions. In addition, we tested for the total number of ESE dimensions covered by an individual and compared single founders and co-founders. The average of the number of ESE dimensions is almost identical between the two groups: 3.27 for single founders and 3.20 for co-founders. Again, the difference was not significant.

Table 5: Number of founders vs. ESE

ESE-Dimension	**Single founders**		**Co-founders**	**Pearson Chi-2 S.**
Marketing skills	31.82%	<	36.73%	0.654
Innovation skills	36.36%	>	32.65%	0.739
Mgmt. skills	63.64%	<	70.07%	0.542
Risk-taking skills	40.91%	<	50.34%	0.409
Financial skills	54.55%	>	44.22%	0.364
Design skills	9.09%	<	9.52%	0.948
General IT skills	50.00%	>	45.58%	0.698
Web tech. skills	40.91%	>	31.29%	0.369
Count ESEs (maximum 8)	Avg.3.27	>	Avg. 3.20	0.892
Individuals	**22[1]**		**147**	**-**
[1] Excl. two single founders due to incomplete LinkedIn profiles				

In addition, we tested for differences across the complete 2x8 matrix, as well as single founders against teams of two founders only. In both cases the results were either not significant or contradictory. This can also be seen in Table 5 when looking at the direction of the difference.

Overall, there is no clear indication that single founders have more ESE skills as hypothesized. These results are in contradiction to the above mentioned entrepreneurial self-efficacy theory (see discussion).

Hence, we can reject Hypothesis 1:

HYPOTHESIS 1: Rejected. No support that single entrepreneurs have a higher degree of entrepreneurial self-efficacy (more entrepreneurial skills) than co-founders

Characteristics	Single founders	Co-founders	Overall	Pearson Chi-2 significance
Consulting experience	18.18%	21.77%	21.3%	0.702
Founding experience	31.82%	42.18%	40.8%	0.357
Employee experience	90.91%	95.24%	94.7%	0.399
Venture capitalist exp.	13.64%	4.08%	5.3%	0.063
				Two-sample t-test significance
Prior job positions	Avg. 3.91	Avg. 4.42	Avg. 4.36	0.444
Years of higher education	Avg. 4.45	Avg. 3.82	Avg. 3.90	0.661
Years of work experience	Avg. 7.82	Avg. 9.21	Avg. 9.03	0.137
Years of education and work combined	Avg. 10.68	Avg. 11.74	Avg. 11.60	0.212
Individuals	**22**[1]	**147**	**169**	-

[1] Excl. two single founders due to incomplete LinkedIn profiles

Table 7: Number of LinkedIn connections

LinkedIn connections		This data sample			LinkedIn survey[2]	LinkedIn statistics[3]
		Single founders	Co-founders	Overall		
Low	0 - 49	4.2%	3.4%	3.5%	11.5%	
	50 - 99	4.2%	8.2%	7.6%	20.0%	
Medium	100 - 199	8.3%	10.9%	10.5%	20.3%	
	200 - 299	8.3%	11.6%	11.1%	17.0%	
	300 - 399	8.3%	16.3%	15.2%	13.4%	
	400 - 499	8.3%	10.2%	9.9%		
High	500 - 999				12.8%	
	1000 - 2999	58.3%	39.5%	42.1%	3.6%	
	3000 - 9999				1.3%	
Total		**100.0%**	**100.0%**	**100.0%**	**100.0%**	
Average		**852.2**[1]	**703.5**[1]	**724.4**[1]	**387.7**[2]	**94.9**[3]

[1] Assuming the same distribution of values in the "High" bin as for the participants in the user survey. Calculated based on the midpoints of the bins
[2] Survey among 306 LinkedIn users [10]. Average connections calculated based on the midpoints of the bins
[3] Average LinkedIn member's 2nd degree network has 9,000 people [58], equivalent to SQRT(9000) = 94.9 direct connections on average

4.2.2 Jack-of-All-Trades

We analyzed the groups of single founders and co-founders for differences in education and work experience, such as prior consulting experience. The results are summarized in Table 6. Again, we applied Chi-2 tests to test for statistical significance between any pair of variables. There was no significant differentiator between single founders and co-founders. We can only see an indication (p=0.063) that single founders rather had prior experience as a venture capitalist (VC) than co-founders.

There are no significant differences between single founders and co-founders. Thus, we can reject hypothesis 2:

HYPOTHESIS 2: Rejected. No support that single entrepreneurs have a higher education and greater work experience than co-founders

4.2.3 Social Networking

As we can see in Table 7, single founders have 852.2 LinkedIn connections on average, compared to 703.5 for co-founders. For both types of entrepreneurs, this is considerably higher than the 387.7 connections per user in a recent survey [10], and 94.9 connections on LinkedIn across all users [58]. Because the LinkedIn profiles do not reveal the exact number of connections > 500 we have estimated those values based on some reasonable assumptions (see comments below Table 7).

Table 8: Complementarity of ESE Skills in Founder Teams

(Co-) Founders	Startups	Average Binary Euclidean Distance Between Founders[1]	Average ESE Coverage on Founder Level	Average Increase of ESE Coverage	Average ESE Coverage on Company Level
1	22	-	3.3 out of 8	-	3.3 out of 8
2	36	3.0 out of 8 (37.2%)	3.7 out of 8	1.5	5.2 out of 8
3	19	3.1 out of 8 (38.2%)	2.8 out of 8	2.6	5.4 out of 8
4	3	2.9 out of 8 (36.8%)	2.8 out of 8	3.2	6.0 out of 8
Total	**80**[2]	-	-	-	-

[1] Defined as (B+C)/M, where
B = number of variables "present" in case i and "absent" from case j
C = number of variables "absent" from case i and "present" in case j
M = number of variables observed for both cases i and j
see [70] for details
[2] For this analysis we removed 11 startups, because we could only calculate changes in ESE and founder distance if the information on all founders was complete

In order to statistically validate the indicated difference in network size between single founders and co-founders we again applied a *t*-test. However, the difference in the average number of LinkedIn connections was not statistically significant ($p=0.504$). Thus, we cannot show that single entrepreneurs are more engaged in social networking and we need to reject our hypothesis.

> *HYPOTHESIS 3: Rejected. There is no significant difference in social networking between single founders and co-founders.*

4.3 Complementarity of ESE Skills in Founder Teams

In this section we are further investigating the team constellations in founding teams. More specifically we are interested in validating whether the founding team formation follows a pattern, i.e. seeking a co-founder with complementary skills. The results are summarized in Table 8 above.

In summary, the results support our hypothesis that founder team formation is driven by the search for complementary team members. The average Binary Euclidean Distance between any two founders in founder teams is about three, meaning that on average co-founders differ in three out of eight ESE dimensions. This is also reflected on the company level. For instance, in startups with two co-founders, on average the founders cover 3.7 ESE dimensions, while on the company level the coverage is at 5.2 dimensions. Thus, in this case co-founding results in an increase of ESE dimension coverage of 1.5 on average. To clarify, the average distance between founders and the average increase of ESE coverage on the company level are not the same, as the following example illustrates. Consider two founders, one with five ESE dimensions and the other with one more complementary skill. By definition, the distance between the two is six; however the increase of ESE coverage on company level is only one. Still, this one more unique skill might be very valuable for the startup.

In the case of two founders the complementarity becomes also obvious when looking at the different job titles that founders have. In most cases there are combinations of Chief Executive Officer (CEO) on the one side and Chief Technology Officer (CTO)/Chief Operating Officer (COO) on the other side.

In order to statistically validate these observations we applied one-way ANOVA (analysis of variance) with four groups based on the number of founders and ESE coverage on company level as dependent variable. Levene's test of homogeneity of variances between groups was not significant ($p=0.561$), thus we can assume equal variances. ANOVA determined that there is a statistically significant difference between groups ($p<0.001$). More specifically, Scheffé's post-hoc test revealed that the single founders are statistically different from all groups of co-founders, but the startups with two, three or four founders do not differ significantly ($\alpha=5\%$). In summary, the increase of ESE coverage going from one to two founders is statistically significant, but the effect from adding more founders is not.

Based on above results we showed that co-founders indeed complement each other's skills. Thus, we could confirm our hypothesis:

> *HYPOTHESIS 5: Confirmed. Co-founders complement each other's ESE skills*

4.4 Amount of Funding

On average, single founders received the highest funding of about $700,000. Startups with more founders received less funding on average. The standard deviation is quite high for all cases, indicating that the data is spread across a large range. This is also supported by the values for minimum funding ($10,000) and maximum funding ($4,000,000) in the sample. See Table 9 below for more details.

Table 9: Funding information

(Co-) Founders	Startups	Mean	Std. dev.
1	26	$699,744	$943,148
2	41	$603,220	$611,476
3	21	$410,643	$449,441
4	3	$466,667	$485,627
Total	**91**	**$581,855**	**$689,133**

At first glance, there seems to be a (negative) correlation between the number of founders and the average amount of funding.

However, when testing the correlation, Spearman's rank correlation coefficient (rho) and Kendall's Tau-b were both not statistically significant. Even after excluding some potential outliers the results did not change. Consequently, our hypothesis needs to be rejected:

> *HYPOTHESIS 5: Rejected. Founding teams (teams of co-founders) are not able to raise more external funding than single founders*

5. DISCUSSION

In this section we first summarize and discuss our research results. Next, we highlight our contributions and address some limitations. Finally, we describe some implications for theory and practice.

First of all, our study shows some interesting **demographics**. For example, we find that for ethnicity in our sample the portion of Asian founders is high (19%) compared to the general population [66]. We can also see that the portion of female founders is very low (14%). This is indicative of the much-criticized gender gap [64] in IT. However, the percentage of women in our sample is higher than in earlier studies [13]. Black founders are much underrepresented; there was only 1 out of 171 entrepreneurs.

The **geographic distribution** of founders across the US is not very surprising and in line with prior findings [53]. California with the San Francisco Bay Area and New York State with the Greater New York City Area are widely recognized to be the most vibrant hot spots for entrepreneurial activities [63].

From the **general attributes and characteristics** we can gain some interesting insights into the career paths of founders. First, we see that more than 40 percent of founders in our sample have prior founding experience, which could be interpreted as a signal for investors that investing in this startup is less risky. This can be true even when the prior founding experience was a failure [27, 47]. Second, we find that almost all founders have prior work experience, 9 years on average in more than four different positions. This indicates that entrepreneurs usually build upon a solid basis of general work experience, which brings with it additional factors, for example access to resources and social connections. Third, we were surprised to find that around half the founders in our sample do not state their position at this startup as their sole position, which leads to assumptions that there might be some diversification in place on the side of founders to decrease the high risk associated with startups.

Surprisingly, we could not find any significant **determinants for being a single founder**, the hypotheses based on entrepreneurial self-efficacy, the jack-of-all-trades theory, and social networking did not hold against our data. This indicates that there must be other factors that are relevant for the decision to co-found in a team or go it all alone that we could not account for. For instance, Forster and Jansen [29] report that every entrepreneur in their study had the desire to partner, but they could not find the right partner yet. Also, there might be personality traits such as being an individualist vs. team-player that can make the difference. Looking closely at our results we can see an indication that experience and access to resources could actually matter. In the group of the single founders there are relatively more individuals with prior experience as venture capitalist, but the difference is not very significant ($p=0.063$). Still, this might indicate that a venture capitalist might be more inclined to go it alone based on her personal experience and resources at hand. In addition, we could see that single founders have a higher average number of social ties than co-founders, but the difference was not significant.

However, it could indicate that single founders might compensate for their lack of co-founders with an extended network of outside resources. This could be one of the factors that influence a founder to go it all alone. If a single founder has enough of the right external resources in her network and the venture is suitable for working with freelancers and other external workers, she could be more inclined to try it without a formal co-founder.

However, we found that co-founders indeed have **complimentary skill sets** and with that could confirm our hypothesis. Thus, at least part of the decision to co-found and the choice for the specific co-founder(s) is based on complementing a founder's own skill set. This is also reflected in the job titles of co-founders. In addition, we can see in our analysis that in startups with three or four co-founders the average coverage of ESE dimensions by each founder is lower than in startups with only two co-founders. This indicates a higher level of specialization and clearer division of responsibilities made possible by the increase of manpower in the team. Notably, we identified some co-founders that were socially connected before starting the new business, i.e., former classmates, brothers, or even a married couple. Hence, existing social connections and ties could be an additional explanation for co-founding. Overall our findings are in line with prior research that suggests that entrepreneurial teams are either formed for interpersonal or resource-seeking reasons [29].

Lastly, contrary to some previous research we could not find any significant **difference in funding** based on the number of founders in a startup. This indicates that the number of founders or the fact of having co-founders is only one of many factors that play a role in evaluating the potential of a startup and the corresponding investment by a venture capitalist, especially in the early seed stage that our companies were selected on. One of the main differentiators here could be the selection of the underlying business model (see for instance [3, 73]).

Our research makes some **contributions** to research in three areas. First, we add to the IS discipline a better understanding of Web startups, especially their characteristics and founder demographics. Second, we add to the field of entrepreneurship research a new facet and new perspective on the entrepreneurial self-efficacy construct. We show that the underlying required domain-specific skills need not necessarily be present altogether in single founders, but can also be composed by complementary co-founders. Third, we provide support that entrepreneurial team formation is indeed based on resource-seeking behaviors, i.e. the selection of co-founders is driven by the search for complementary resources.

As an empirical study, this research is not without **limitations**. First, our study is based on a sample of 91 startups and 183 founders, only 24 of which are single founders. This sets a natural limitation on the ability to show statistical significance in analyses. The differences between single and co-founders regarding entrepreneurial self-efficacy, experience, and social networking are rather small. Thus, we suggest future work to aim for a bigger sample size especially when it comes to the inclusion of single founders. Second, our data is only a snapshot of the situation. As entrepreneurship is inherently very dynamic, future studies could try a longitudinal approach to show the dynamic development, e.g. founding team formation and evolution over time. Third, we gathered our data from publicly available sources. This constrains the set of available attributes compared to specifically designed surveys. Also, the data might potentially be biased, e.g., due to founders not reporting or exaggerating the importance of prior job positions. We strongly believe that our data is sufficiently correct for the purpose of our research. As outlined above, recent studies found information available through online social networks to be pretty accurate. Fourth, our conceptualization and measurement of the entrepreneurial self-efficacy construct is different from its original use. Still, we argue that objectively observed skills serve as a good proxy for the perceived self-confidence in a specific skill. Finally, some boundary conditions might apply. Our research focus was on US-based Web startups. We believe that the results will also apply to other industries that are characterized as being very knowledge-intensive as well as highly dynamic. Transferring the results to Web startups outside the US should be feasible, if cultural aspects do not play a stronger role in team formation.

Finally, our research has some **implications** for policy makers, theory and practice. First, the observed gender gap and the imbalance between ethnic groups indicates that policy makers should focus on specific initiatives and programs to foster entrepreneurial activities in those segments of the population as well. Also, universities should consider those imbalances when setting up or revising curricula in entrepreneurship. Second, even though we found support for our hypothesis on team formation we could not find antecedents for becoming a single entrepreneur or not. This could be approached in more detail in subsequent research. Third, for prospective future founders, our research implies that there is no simple rule to follow, when deciding to go it all alone or find one or more co-founders. The factors that play into this decision might be manifold and can only be answered by the founders themselves. This also leads to the implication for investors, not to discriminate startups based on the number of founders or complementarity of skills alone, but to look closer at the intangible connections found either inside the team or in the founders extended networks. Still, practitioners might want to consider our findings on complementarity of skills – and what kind of skills – when looking for co-founders.

6. CONCLUSION

Using a unique data set of 91 web startups and their 183 (co-) founders, we set out to analyze if there are determinants for going it all alone or co-founding. Surprisingly, and contradicting existing theory, we could not find any significant differences between single founders and co-founders based on entrepreneurial self-efficacy, experience, and social networking. However, we could show that entrepreneurial team formation is indeed driven by complementarity of co-founders' skills.

Our results motivate three further research options that need to be explored. First, due to limitations in the data available from the LinkedIn profiles, the hypotheses could be further tested using a traditional survey approach. Second, there could be other factors that determine the decision to go it all alone or co-found. As we mentioned above, private social connections or other life events that formed social bonds between co-founders might influence this decision. These connections could be explored in a further study. Also, we could show that the choice of a co-founder is at least partly based on complementarity in skills. Thus, future studies could take a more balanced approach to explaining the decision to co-found; looking into both private and professional factors. Third, as mentioned in the results, single founders could also be compensating for their lack of co-founders through an extended network of outside resources. We suggest shedding a light on the difference not only in size but also in diversity and usefulness of the social network of single founders compared to co-founders in future studies building on this research.

We see this study as a first step in understanding the research questions at hand. Building on this study, future work could employ bigger sample sizes and surveys to explore one or more of the promising indications we could find in our data.

7. REFERENCES

[1] Abell, P. and Nisar, T. M. 2007. Performance Effects of Venture Capital Firm Networks. *Management Decision* 45, 5, 923–936.

[2] Adler, P. S. and Kwon, S.-W. 2002. Social Capital: Prospects for a New Concept. *Academy of Management Review* 27, 1, 17–40.

[3] Al-Debei, M. M. and Avison, D. 2010. Developing a Unified Framework of the Business Model Concept. *European Journal of Information Systems* 19, 3, 359–376.

[4] AngelList. 2013. *AngelList - Home.* http://angel.co. Accessed 1 April 2013.

[5] Arrington, M. 2010. *Why We Sold TechCrunch To AOL, And Where We Go From Here.* http://techcrunch.com/2010/09/28/why-we-sold-techcrunch-to-aol-and-where-we-go-from-here/. Accessed 1 April 2013.

[6] Back, M. D., Stopfer, J. M., Vazire, S., Gaddis, S., Schmukle, S. C., Egloff, B., and Gosling, S. D. 2010. Facebook Profiles Reflect Actual Personality, Not Self-Idealization. *Psychological Science* 21, 3, 372–374.

[7] Bandura, A. 1982. Self-Efficacy Mechanism in Human Agency. *American Psychologist* 37, 2, 122–147.

[8] Baum, J. A. C. and Silverman, B. S. 2004. Picking Winners or Building them? Alliance, Intellectual, and Human Capital as Selection Criteria in Venture Financing and Performance of Biotechnology Startups. *Journal of Business Venturing* 19, 3, 411–436.

[9] Birley, S. 1985. *The Role of networks in the entrepreneurial process.* Cranfield School of Management, Cranfield.

[10] Breitbarth, W. 2012. *LinkedIn Infographic: What to know what others are doing?* http://www.powerformula.net/blog.html?p=2347. Accessed 1 April 2013.

[11] Brüderl, J. and Preisendörfer, P. 1998. Network Support and the Success of Newly Founded Business. *Small Business Economics* 10, 3, 213–225.

[12] Burton, M., Sørensen, J. B., and Beckman, C. M. 2002. 7. Coming from Good Stock: Career Histories and New Venture Formation. In *Research in the Sociology of Organizations.* Emerald (MCB UP), Bingley, 229–262.

[13] CB Insights. 2010. *Venture Capital Human Capital Report: January to June 2010.* http://www.docstoc.com/docs/49664597/Gender-and-Education-Demographics-Venture-Capital-Human-Capital. Accessed 1 April 2013.

[14] Chandler, G. N., Honig, B., and Wiklund, J. 2005. Antecedents, Moderators, and Performance Consequences of Membership Change in New Venture Teams. *Journal of Business Venturing* 20, 5, 705–725.

[15] Chen, C. C., Greene, P. G., and Crick, A. 1998. Does Entrepreneurial Self-Efficacy Distinguish Entrepreneurs from Managers? *Journal of Business Venturing* 13, 4, 295–316.

[16] Compeau, D. R. and Higgins, C. A. 1995. Computer Self-Efficacy. Development of a Measure and Initial Test. *MIS Quarterly* 19, 2, 189–211.

[17] Cooney, T. M. 2005. Editorial: What is an Entrepreneurial Team? *International Small Business Journal* 23, 3, 226–235.

[18] CrunchBase. 2013. *CrunchBase - Home.* http://www.crunchbase.com/. Accessed 1 April 2013.

[19] Davidsson, P. 2006. *Nascent Entrepreneurship. Empirical Studies and Developments.* now Publishers Inc., Hanover, MA, USA.

[20] Davila, A., Foster, G., and Gupta, M. 2003. Venture Capital Financing and the Growth of Startup Firms. *Journal of Business Venturing* 18, 6, 689–708.

[21] Del Giudice, M. and Straub, D. 2011. IT and Entrepreneurism: An On-Again, Off-Again Love Affair or a Marriage? *MIS Quarterly* 35, 4, III.

[22] Denzin, N. K. 1978. *The Research Act: A Theoretical Introduction to Sociological Methods.* McGraw-Hill, New York.

[23] Dubini, P. and Aldrich, H. 1991. Personal and Extended Networks Are Central to the Entrepreneurial Process. *Journal of Business Venturing* 6, 5, 305.

[24] Elfring, T. and Hulsink, W. 2003. Networks in Entrepreneurship: The Case of High-Technology Firms. *Small Business Economics* 21, 4, 409–422.

[25] Ellison, N. B., Steinfield, C., and Lampe, C. 2007. The Benefits of Facebook "Friends:" Social Capital and College Students' Use of Online Social Network Sites. *Journal of Computer-Mediated Communication* 12, 4, 1143–1168.

[26] Ensley, M. D., Pearson, A. W., and Amason, A. C. 2002. Understanding the dynamics of new venture top management teams: cohesion, conflict, and new venture performance. *Journal of Business Venturing* 17, 4, 365–386.

[27] FailCon. 2012. *About Us.* http://thefailcon.com/about.html.

[28] Fidelman, M. 2012. *SAP's CIO: You're Putting Your Executive Career at Risk if You're Not Social.* http://www.forbes.com/sites/markfidelman/2012/06/10/saps-cio-youre-putting-your-executive-career-at-risk-if-youre-not-social/. Accessed 1 April 2013.

[29] Forster, W. and Jansen, K. 2010. Co-Creating New Ventures: Attraction, Search, and Uncertainty in Founding Partnership Formation. *Frontiers of Entrepreneurship Research* 30, 10.

[30] Gnyawali, D. R. and Madhavan, R. 2001. Cooperative Networks and Competitive Dynamics: A Structural Embeddedness Perspective. *The Academy of Management Review* 26, 3, 431–445.

[31] Goldenson, M. 2011. *The Math of TechCrunch, Part 1: Is TechCrunch Still About Startups?* http://techcrunch.com/2011/06/12/math-of-techcrunch-startups/. Accessed 1 April 2013.

[32] Grant, R. M. 1996. Toward a Knowledge-Based Theory of the Firm. *Strategic Management Journal* 17, 109–122.

[33] Gross, R. and Acquisti, A. 2005. Information Revelation and Privacy in Online Social Networks. In *Proceedings of the 2005 ACM Workshop on Privacy in the Electronic Society.* WPES '05. ACM, New York, NY, USA, 71–80.

[34] Harper, D. A. 2008. Towards a Theory of Entrepreneurial Teams. *Journal of Business Venturing* 23, 6, 613–626.

[35] Harrison, D. A. and Klein, K. J. 2007. What's the Difference? Diversity Constructs as Separation, Variety, or Disparity in Organizations. *Academy of Management Review* 32, 4, 1199–1228.

[36] Horwitz, S. K. and Horwitz, I. B. 2007. The Effects of Team Diversity on Team Outcomes: A Meta-Analytic Review of Team Demography. *Journal of Management* 33, 6, 987–1015.

[37] Howe, J. 2006. The Rise of Crowdsourcing. *Wired Magazine,* 14.06.

[38] Howe, J. 2008. *Crowdsourcing: Why the Power of the Crowd is Driving the Future of Business.* Crown Publishing Group, New York, NY, USA.

[39] Johannisson, B. 1987. Beyond Process and Structure: Social Exchange Networks. *International Studies of Management & Organization* 17, 1, 3-23-23.

[40] Kollmann, T. 2006. What is e-Entrepreneurship? Fundamentals of Company Founding in the Net Economy. *International Journal of Technology Management* 33, 4, 322–340.

[41] Lazear, E. P. 2002. *Entrepreneurship.* Working Paper 9109. National Bureau of Economic Research.

[42] Lazear, E. P. 2004. Balanced Skills and Entrepreneurship. *American Economic Review* 94, 2, 208–211.

[43] LinkedIn. 2011. *LinkedIn - User Agreement.* http://www.linkedin.com/static?key=user_agreement. Accessed 1 April 2013.

[44] LinkedIn. 2013. *LinkedIn - Home.* http://www.linkedin.com/. Accessed 30 March 2013.

[45] Matlay, H. and Westhead, P. 2005. Virtual Teams and the Rise of e-Entrepreneurship in Europe. *International Small Business Journal* 23, 3, 279–302.

[46] McKnight, L. W., Vaaler, P. M., and Katz, R. L. 2002. *Creative destruction. Business survival strategies in the global Internet economy.* MIT Press, Cambridge, Mass.

[47] Mitchell, R. K., Mitchel, J. R., and Smith, J. B. 2004. Failing to Succeed: New Venture Failure as a Moderator of Startup Experience and Startup Expertise. *Frontiers of Entrepreneurship Research.*

[48] Mourmant, G., Gallivan, M. J., and Kalika, M. 2009. Another Road to IT Turnover: The Entrepreneurial Path. *European Journal of Information Systems* 18, 5, 498–521.

[49] Nahapiet, J. and Ghoshal, S. 1998. Social Capital, Intellectual Capital, and the Organizational Advantage. *Academy of Management Review* 23, 2, 242–266.

[50] Nishar, D. 2013. *200 Million Members!* http://blog.linkedin.com/2013/01/09/linkedin-200-million/. Accessed 1 April 2013.

[51] Nonaka, I. 1994. A Dynamic Theory of Organizational Knowledge Creation. *Organization Science* 5, 1, 14–37.

[52] O'Reilly, T. 2007. What is Web 2.0: Design Patterns and Business Models for the Next Generation of Software. *Communications & Strategies,* 65.

[53] Rao, L. 2011. *LinkedIn Takes A Deep Data Dive On Startup Founder Profiles.* http://techcrunch.com/2011/09/01/linkedin-takes-a-deep-

data-dive-on-startup-founder-profiles/. Accessed 1 April 2013.

[54] Reynolds, P. D. and Curtin, R. T. 2008. Business Creation in the United States: Panel Study of Entrepreneurial Dynamics II Initial Assessment. *Foundations and Trends in Entrepreneurship* 4, 3, 155–307.

[55] Schumpeter, J. 1911. *Theorie der wirtschaftlichen Entwicklung.*

[56] Serarois-Tarrés, C., Padilla-Meléndez, A., and del Aguila-Obra, A. R. 2006. The Influence of Entrepreneur Characteristics on the Success of Pure dot.com Firms. *International Journal of Technology Management* 33, 4, 373–388.

[57] Shapiro, C. and Varian, H. R. 2008. *Information Rules. A Strategic Guide to the Network Economy.* Harvard Business School Press, Boston, Mass.

[58] Sharma, M. 2012. *I to the We - What is the true reach of your LinkedIn Network?* http://blog.linkedin.com/2012/03/14/startup-of-you-data/. Accessed 1 April 2013.

[59] Siegel, R., Siegel, E., and Macmillan, I. C. 1993. Characteristics Distinguishing High-Growth Ventures. *Journal of Business Venturing* 8, 2, 169–180.

[60] Song, Y. and Vinig, T. 2012. Entrepreneur Online Social Networks - Structure, Diversity and Impact on Start-up Survival. *International Journal of Organisational Design and Engineering* 2, 2, 189–203.

[61] Spiegel, O., Abbassi, P., Fischbach, K., Putzke, J., and Schoder, D. 2011. Social Capital in the ICT Sector - A Network Perspective on Executive Turnover and Startup Performance (Research-in-Progress). In *Proceedings of the International Conference on Information Systems (ICIS).*

[62] Stam, E. and Schutjens, V. 2005. *The fragile success of team start-ups.* Discussion Papers on Entrepreneurship, Growth and Public Policy, MPI Jena 1705.

[63] Startup Genome. 2012. *Startup Ecosystem Report 2012.* http://blog.startupcompass.co/. Accessed 1 April 2013.

[64] Stephan, P. and El-Ganainy, A. 2007. The entrepreneurial puzzle: explaining the gender gap. *The Journal of Technology Transfer* 32, 5, 475–487.

[65] Stewart, W. H. and Roth, P. L. 2007. A Meta-Analysis of Achievement Motivation Differences between Entrepreneurs and Managers. *Journal of Small Business Management* 45, 4, 401–421.

[66] U.S. Census Bureau. 2010. *Resident Population by Sex, Race, and Hispanic Origin Status.* http://www.census.gov/compendia/statab/cats/population.html. Accessed 14 June 2012.

[67] Vissa, B. and Chacar, A. S. 2009. Leveraging Ties: The Contingent Value of Entrepreneurial Teams' External Advice Networks on Indian Software Venture Performance. *Strategic Management Journal* 30, 11, 1179–1191.

[68] Wagner, J. 2006. Are Nascent Entrepreneurs 'Jacks-of-all-Trades'? A Test of Lazear's Theory of Entrepreneurship with German Data. *Applied Economics* 38, 20, 2415–2419.

[69] Wagner, K. and Andreas, Z. 2008. *The Nascent Entrepreneur at the Crossroads. Entrepreneurial Motives as Determinants for Different Types of Entrepreneurs.* Discussion Papers on Entrepreneurship and Innovation. Swiss Institute for Entrepreneurship, Chur.

[70] Wishart, D. 1987. *Clustan User Manual.* Computing Laboratory, University of St. Andrews, Edinburgh.

[71] Yang, S., Lee, H., and Kurnia, S. 2009. Social Capital in Information and Communications Technology Research: Past, Present, and Future. *Communications of the Association for Information Systems* 25, 1, Article 23.

[72] Zimmerman, M. A. 2008. The Influence of Top Management Team Heterogeneity on the Capital Raised through an Initial Public Offering. *Entrepreneurship Theory and Practice* 32, 3, 391–414.

[73] Zott, C. and Amit, R. 2007. Business Model Design and the Performance of Entrepreneurial Firms. *Organization Science* 18, 2, 181–199.

Spaces of IT Intrapreneurial Freedom:
A Classic Grounded Theory

Gaetan Mourmant
IESEG
XLerateur Inc.
Vancouver, Canada
www.vba101.com
(604) 781-9698
gmourmant@gmail.com

Fred Niederman
St. Louis University
Operations and ITM
Cook School of Business
(314) 315-0941
niederfa@slu.edu

Michel Kalika
Paris Dauphine University
Scientific Advisor -
Business Science Institute
http://www.business-science-institute.com
Paris : +33 1 81 50 45 53 (9am-6pm)
Kalika.michel@gmail.com

ABSTRACT
This paper addresses the question of fostering and developing innovation in IT companies and IT departments. This paper uses a Classic Grounded Theory based on interviews with CEOs, CIOs, IT Managers and IT employees. Spaces of IT Intrapreneurial Freedom (SoIF) is the theoretical core category of our model. SoIF has several characteristics related to its establishment and maintenance (e.g. Protecting the SoIF, Leaving the space) and is composed of seven lower-level concepts (e.g. material SoIF, Organizational Freedom). In addition, through the development of SoIF, we suggest that CEO, IT entrepreneurs, CIO and IT managers can improve the retention and innovativeness of their best and most innovative IT intrapreneurial employees.

Categories and Subject Descriptors
K.7.1 [**The Computing Profession**]: Occupations

General Terms
Management, Human Factors.

Keywords
Innovation, Intrapreneurs, Spaces of Intrapreneurial Freedom, Entrepreneurial Turnover, Entrepreneurial Realization

1. INTRODUCTION
The recent departure of Marissa Mayer from Google to Yahoo! and her first actions to revitalize an innovation culture is another example of how maintaining IT innovation is crucial for IT companies and IT department employees. Indeed, this is the theme of this 2013 conference.

We address this issue by looking at IT intrapreneurship using a classic Grounded Theory approach with CEOs, Entrepreneurs, CIOs, IT Managers and IT intra/entrepreneurial employees. More precisely, we are looking for the main concern of practitioners when discussing an open question of the topic of innovation and intrapreneurship in their IT department/company. This quickly resulted into the following two main concerns. First, "how to

create and foster innovation in IT departments and IT companies ?", and second, "how to keep your most wanted intrapreneurial IT employees?". Because these questions are interrelated and draw upon similar conceptualizations we address them together in this paper.

The theory we introduce in this paper has a core category named *Spaces of IT Intrapreneurial Freedom* (SoIF). We discuss how these SoIF are created and fostered in companies seeking for innovation and looking at retaining their intrapreneurial IT employees. SoIF is composed of several lower-level concepts (e.g. *material SoIF*, *Organizational Freedom*) and several aspects related to its establishment (e.g. *Protecting the SoIF*, *Leaving the space*). We also discuss the emerging theory with existing theory related to IT Entrepreneurial Turnover, specifically how, by using SoIF, organizations can reduce or postpone IT Entrepreneurial Epiphanies [1].

The rest of the paper is organized in the following way. First we review the literature, then we briefly introduce the theory. We then discuss the methodology and the theory more in depth. Finally, we discuss some limitations and future research.

2. LITERATURE REVIEW
In this section we explore the factors which help to foster IT intrapreneurship. We begin by defining intrapreneurship. Then, we show factors which aid in promoting an intrapreneurial spirit. Finally, we discuss the importance of SoIF for IT Entrepreneurial Employee Turnover

2.1 What is Intrapreneurship
Intrapreneurship – or corporate venturing – can be described as "the practice of developing a new venture within an existing organization to exploit new opportunity and create economic value [3]." In fact, Menzel et al. [4] posit that "anyone who behaves with entrepreneurial spirit within an existing organization... at any level and in any function... can be an intrapreneur.". In this paper, we look at the IT industry and how intrapreneurship is developed in an IT department or in IT companies, hence the term of IT Intrapreneurship.

2.2 Fostering IT Intrapreneurship Inside an organization
Management can potentially play a crucial role in fostering a work environment conducive to successful IT intrapreneurship. Firstly, it should encourage creativity and risk-taking [5-7]. Moreover, management should ensure the job satisfaction of its employees [7, 8]. Managerial support should also come in the

form of adequate IT infrastructure and resources [6]. Many even argue the importance of a company operating "on the frontiers of technology [7]."

Some managerial implications recommended by [8] to improve intrapreneurship are particularly relevant in an IT context: "offer and develop new products, develop their own technology, introduce technological newness and innovations, increase the autonomy of their units, improve co-ordination between the units and create a flexible organizational structure to advance business innovation". This focus on removing organizational barriers to intrapreneurship is also mentioned by Menzel et al. [4].

2.3 IT Entrepreneurial Employee Turnover

In the case of IT Entrepreneurial Employee Turnover – IT Employees deciding to quit their job to start their business - two streams of literature are interesting to study. The first is related to the classic reasons for IT turnover (see Joseph et al. [9] for a literature review on this topic) while the second is related to the decision to start a business. The approach developed by Mourmant et al., [1, 10, 11] combined turnover and nascent entrepreneurship literature by introducing the core category of IT Entrepreneurial Epiphany. Such IT *Entrepreneurial Epiphany* occurs when the employee/future entrepreneurs experience an "illuminating realization" that some or all of the necessary conditions for her to quit her job and start her own business have been met. For example, entrepreneurs, when talking about their *Entrepreneurial Epiphanies*, often include sentences such *as "I realized...", "... So that was my realization", "From there, it became clear...", "the exact moment you were waiting suddenly comes"*, etc. We suggest considering a larger range of realization and not only the illuminating realization, hence we use the concept of IT Entrepreneurial Realization (ER). This concept has 5 lower-level dimensions summarized in the following table:

Table 1: Table 1: Lower-level Concepts of IT Ent. Realization

Lower-level concepts & codes
The business game
Understanding the business game
Do I agree? (with the rules of the business game)
Necessary skills (e.g. do I have the necessary skills to play the game?)
Risk reduction
Comparing risks
Social Network and risk
Reality check
Voluntary naivety (Are people voluntarily naïve or are they just ignorant of what it takes to start a business?)
External environmental Context
Perceived opportunity and favorable context
Timing
Time pressure
The right moment
Long-term desire
End of a cycle
Long term reasons
Self-realization
Financial success
Independence (no structure, no time pressure)
Pleasure/passion
Lifestyle

3. THEORETICAL OVERVIEW

"If we were to follow a "purist" rendition of interpretive research [...], the theory would normally appear after the data presentation" (Anonymous, in Suddaby 2006, p. 637). Yet, following Suddaby's suggestion [12] for advanced clarity in the presentation of our arguments, we "employ the more traditional presentational strategy of providing a theoretical overview first, to preview the major findings and resulting model" (2006, p.637).

In this research, we define the core category of *Spaces of Intrapreneurial Freedom* (SoIF) as spaces (material or immaterial) in the company, whether these spaces refer to the whole company or just a portion (e.g. a department, a team) thereof. In those spaces, IT employees can benefit from Intrapreneurial Freedoms (e.g. Freedom to take risks, freedom to make mistakes, freedom to propose new ideas and take actions upon them, freedom to be autonomous). Here are examples of code related to the emergence of the concept of SoIF:

> *"I had to create a mini-environment, [an area] around being entrepreneurial"*, a CIO

In relation to the establishment of the SoIF, we mention the need for a protector of the SoIF from the possible bureaucratic pressure. This role could also be extended to the role of populating and protecting the eco-system of the space, for example through a drastic selection process of people showing specific characteristics (e.g. strong entrepreneurial spirit). We also introduce the importance of the responsibilities related to being a member of those SoIF. Such responsibilities should also be rewarded through an adequate process of recognition. Finally, we also discuss the importance of considering 'leaving the space' as a strong component of establishing and maintaining the SoIF.

In terms of the characteristics and lower level concepts of SoIF, we mention the following: Material SoIF (e.g. Bring Your Own Device) and Organizational Freedom (e.g. from bureaucratic rules). We also introduce five concepts that are highly interrelated: the freedom to have a global vision of the company/industry, which will allow the intrapreneur to recognize opportunities that are related to the company's goal. Once the opportunity is recognized, the freedom to innovate and create will be boosted by the freedom to make mistake (and of course, learn and remedy to those mistakes) and take reasonable risk, while having a great lifestyle embedding passion and pleasure.

4. METHODOLOGY

We follow a qualitative classic Grounded Theory Methodology, [13-17]. In particular, we iteratively use the following tools: open, selective and theoretical coding, 'memoing', sorting the memos, constant comparison and theoretical sampling in order to reach theoretical saturation. More specifically, the core category "Spaces of Intrapreneurial Freedom" emerged from the analysis of the first set of interviews with CEOs, CIOs, and IT employees. Each interview started with the following open question: "Should we foster Intrapreneurship, and if so, how?" (14 interviews). The core category emerged first as a code and then reached the status of core category during the analysis. Once SoIF was established as the core category, we recoded and analyzed previous interviews while conducting and analyzing additional interviews (N=10), following the process of theoretical sampling. Furthermore, we also performed an analysis of the literature, following Glaser's guidance, [16]. The goal of this process was to enrich the core category and reach theoretical saturation. The interviews were conducted with CEOs, entrepreneurs, CIOs, IT managers and IT employees. The interviews were conducted in France, China (Shanghai), Canada and US.

Regarding theoretical gaps in the literature, it is important to remind the reader that Classic (Glaserian) Grounded Theory Methodology reverses the "normal" way of doing research. Instead of starting with a literature review and finding a gap in the literature, the researcher starts with the data (e.g. interviews), identifies the main concern of the practitioners and analyzes how they continuously solve this main concern, hence leading to the discovery of the core category. Then, using GTM, we build up the theory from the data – and not as an answer to a theoretical gap in the literature. Once the emerging theory is solid enough, we did an "integrative placement" [14, p. 138] to integrate and weave our finding into the literature. Such approach aims at discussing and explaining our contribution, either in the form of confirmation-replication of previous findings and ideas, or by providing different theoretical lenses. Establishing the Space of Intrapreneurial Freedom (SoIF)

5. SPACES OF INTRAPRENEURIAL FREEDOM

5.1 Defining Spaces of Intrapreneurial Freedom

The core category of Spaces of Intrapreneurial Freedom (SoIF) is defined as spaces (material or immaterial) in the company, whether these spaces refer to the whole company or just a portion (e.g. a department) thereof. In those spaces, IT employees can benefit from Intrapreneurial Freedoms (e.g. Freedom to take risks, freedom to make mistakes, freedom to propose new ideas and take actions upon them, freedom to be autonomous). Here is an example of code related to the emergence of the concept of SoIF:

"I often encourage the creation of mini-research lab", *an IT entrepreneur (France)*

We now discuss and define more in depth this core category by exploring its properties, dimensions and lower-level concepts.

As mentioned, *space* or *spaces* can refer to part of the organization or the full organization. Indeed, an intrapreneurial culture can be found in a whole organization, only in some departments, or even just within a team. This is important as it gives back power to managers who want to foster intrapreneurship and innovation in a specific department - such as the IT department or a specific task-force team established to implement a Social Media project requiring high entrepreneurial spirit - while keeping the whole organization oriented towards a more top-down managerial style due, for example, to general strategy, industry regulation or strong bureaucratic culture. In Table 3 we summarize the relations between the various elements of the SoIF and the IT Entrepreneurial Realizations.

Table 2 summarizes the Properties and Lower-level concepts of Spaces of Intrapreneurial Freedom.

Table 2: Properties and lower-level concept of SoIF

Establishing and maintaining SoIF
•Protecting the SoIF
•The Protector(s) of the SoIF
•Populating the Space and Protecting its Eco-System
•SoIF and responsibilities
•SoIF and Recognition
•Formal and Informal SoIF
•Porosity
•Intensity of Intrapreneurship in the SoIF
•Leaving the space
Characteristics and Lower-level concepts of SoIF
•Material SoIF
•Organizational Freedom
•Freedom to Innovate and Create
•Freedom and Lifestyle
•Freedom to make mistakes and Risk-Taking
•Freedom and Opportunity Seeking
•Freedom to have a Global Vision of the Company/Industry

5.2 Establishing and maintaining SoIF

5.2.1 Protecting the SoIF

5.2.1.1 The Protector(s)/Initiator of the SoIF

The concept of SoIF is also related to boundaries that need to be protected. Based on our data and the literature [18], we found that the CEO, CIO or IT manager plays the role of protector (and/or initiator) of this space. Such protection is essential. For example one of the CIO mentioned:

"If there are too many bureaucratic issues, they will *leave".*

Or as a CEO stated:

"I remove barriers for the intrapreneurs"

Although the code of protector of the SoIF emerged from our data, it was notable how it coincided with the observations of Pinchot [3] who states that intrapreneurship "involves a role for the in-house sponsor, one who will finesse the corporate politics while the intrapreneur attends single-mindedly to making the idea a reality". In addition, instead of assigning just one protector, a company could have a whole team of protectors, for example, the company board or the actual members of the SoIF. As reported by one of our interviewee, such a role may involve a "mental battle" with the rest of the organization.

In the case of companies that do not show an overall entrepreneurial orientation [19, 20], those boundaries also refers to spaces that are protected from the non-entrepreneurial company's culture and could be used to foster specific research projects, [21]. One of our interviewee (an IT entrepreneur) spoke of creating mini-research labs, but under the constraints of the *responsibilities.* Another interviewee (CIO) mentioned the existence of specific projects geographically separated from the company in order to give them more independence and freedom.

5.2.1.2 Populating and Protecting the SoIF and its Eco-system.

Selection process. Another important aspect that emerged from our data is the important role of employee selection. For such spaces to work, the 'right' people are needed. Defining the right people is a challenging task. Among the various codes used by our interviewees (CIO, IT employees describing their recruitment process, IT Entrepreneurs), we find: *right mind-set, forward thinking innovators, openness, curious, trustable, kind and nice, reasonably artistic type, emotionally stable, life-long learners,* balance of *soft and technical skills, passionate, autonomous, responsible, reasonable risk-taker, conscientious,* and as a consequence, *very hard-working but still having a lot of pleasure.* Interestingly enough, those codes do not contradict themselves. Of course, such individuals are rare and represent a sort of ideal. These results strongly parallel the description of the entrepreneur found in the literature relating to personality traits [22 , 23], successful intelligence [24], entrepreneurial intuition [25], the jack-of-all-trades model [26-28] or passion [29], with maybe one notable difference in relation to risk taking. Indeed, the idea of a reasonable risk-taker intrapreneur could be opposed to the overconfident entrepreneur - often, but not always - reported in the literature. Based on our data and the literature [30 , 31 , 32 , 33 , 34 , 35 , 36 , 37 , 38], this would make a lot of sense that reasonable risk-taking intrapreneurs would tend to stay in a large company, while overconfident, cognitively biased or less risk-averse entrepreneurs will start their own business. Such hypothesis could be worth pursuing and testing.

As an illustration of a company very strict in selecting the right people, one interviewee (an IT employee working at this company) reported a process involving nine interviews for employees and six interviews for consultants - this specific company is ranked as a top company for which to work. Additionally, "they don't hesitate to fire people" to protect the "eco-system" when a recruiting mistake has been made; however, for the employee, making mistakes is ok, as long as they are transformed into a learning experience. Such a system of populating the SoIF could be complemented with self-selection processes, whereby members of the group introduce and/or support potential candidates. Regarding current IT employees, by fostering those SoIF and gradually transforming the corporate culture into an intrapreneurial culture, the rest of the employees may either follow their example, gradually evolving towards intrapreneurial behavior or complete intrapreneurs, or leave the company.

5.2.2 SoIF and responsibilities

SoIF are also related to responsibilities. Indeed, our data suggests that freedom, autonomy and independence have to be balanced by a certain number of safeguards. Among them, we cite *strict follow up* on the project by the manager and *discipline of quality* when delivering the final product; *focus on the task, the deliverable,* not the time spent; *high value-added* to and *ROI* of the project; *customer-centric* projects, which include an alignment of the intrapreneur's goals with those of the company. These responsibilities and safeguards vary in importance depending on the company and context, one can view these safeguards as reflecting the sort of constraints and realities that entrepreneurs face when confronted by the realities of the market

5.2.3 SoIF and Recognition

Recognition emerged at several levels in our data as a critical element in intrapreneurship. It could be linked to social recognition (e.g. the IT employee will present herself the result of her project in front of the client or the board of presidents). It is also an opportunity for the IT employee to shine. Recognition

could also be expressed by encouraging the intrapreneur during the realization of the project, accepting new ideas that make sense or promoting her in the hierarchy. Recognition has been mentioned as more efficient if more immediate, and not necessarily big. Finally, the financial motivations are clearly very important, especially if the product is successful. Depending on the company, stock-options could be a good way to retain employees by creating "golden handcuffs". Such financial mechanisms can be relatively complex with cyclical releases of stock options that can be cashed only after a certain period of time; otherwise, those stock options are lost. Those systems reduce the likelihood of an IT Entrepreneurial Realization related to *Long Term Reasons - Financial Success.* In addition*,* it also pushes the balance toward employment when comparing the risk of entrepreneurship with the potential loss of money for leaving the employed position. In that sense, it reduces the chances of an Entrepreneurial Realization [1] related to *Comparing the Risks.* That said it may only work with the type of employee for which money is a strong motivator. Of course, again, the emergence of recognition is clearly present in the IT Turnover literature, for instance through pay or promotability for high achievers [9].

5.2.4 Formal and Informal SoIF

SoIF can be related to formal groups of intrapreneurs, either created for a specific project or for on-going innovation. However, the SoIF is not necessarily formal. Indeed, Informal SoIF have also been encountered. For example, intrapreneurial people from among various departments in the organization may informally gather and start projects together without considering bureaucratic rules, and then, once the project is advanced enough, they may push it into the bureaucratic circuit with a much better chance of success as the project is already mature and "endorsed" by many members across the organization.

5.2.5 Porosity of the SoIF

In the case the SoIF is not at the scale of the company (e.g. an IT department or a team), the relation between the SoIF and the rest of the organization has to be carefully studied to avoid perverse effects. We term this "porosity" to describe an interface that has some solidity but allows for the passing of people and ideas across its boundary.

- This is of course related to the necessity to promote a *Global Vision of the Company/Industry* among the members of the SoIF. This will help avoiding an ivory tower syndrome where the members of the SoIF may feel that they belong to a group and not to the organization, hence falling in a trap of 'us' versus 'them'. This could lead to some potential and dangerous "push-back from other people who can't play by their rules".

- Another venue to avoid such a problem is to make sure that intrapreneurs are working with the whole organization. This is already implicit through a lot of other aspects (e.g. SoIF and Responsibilities, SoIF and opportunities).

Those two aspects should results in the intrapreneur having a coherent intrapreneurial behavior, i.e. aligning his actions with the goals of the company, as well as developing a better ability to spot intrapreneurial opportunities

5.2.6 Intensity of Intrapreneurship in the Space

SoIF may vary along the dimension of the intensity of intrapreneurship. It could go from a non-intrapreneurial setting, for example a bureaucratic administration, to the other extreme where intrapreneurship is cultivated and part of the culture. To illustrate, one of our CIO mentioned the of quick-win team where intrapreneurial behavior is encouraged for a short and limited project or task, in order to solve an urgent matter.

5.2.7 Leaving the space

If the employee still decides to leave the SoIF (e.g. the company), supportive approach such as entrepreneurial spin-off, and support at various levels: network, methodology, advices, technology, finance, future contracts [2 , 39 , 40]) from the company can be beneficial on several levels. For instance, it could generate corporate refocusing, "prosperity and well-being of regions, industry clusters and nations" or "a decrease of the administrative burden" [2]. Although those SoIF are designed to retain and develop intrapreneurs, eventually the most entrepreneurial employees will leave following shocks [41], Shifts of Understandings [11] and Entrepreneurial Realizations [1]. So delaying their departure and making it a positive experience could also be seen as a positive outcome of those SoIF; indeed as one of the CIO mentioned:

If retained too long, they might lose their entrepreneurial spirit - A Chineese IT entrepreneur.

In addition, the negative impact of such leaving could be decreased by the following actions:

- Implement a succession plan

- Teaming the entrepreneurs, hence the knowledge is shared

There is a balance between maximizing the length of stay and recognizing that they may not stay for a long period of time. This raises the question: of what tactics are most effective for maximizing the value of the intrapreneur during her or his tenure as well as methods for aiding in the transition to another venue.

5.3 Characteristics and Lower-level concepts of SoIF

We develop here the various lower-level concepts of SoIF that emerged from our data. These lower-level concepts are related to various types of freedom. We also discuss how they are related to the Entrepreneurial Realizations discussed previously.

5.3.1 Material SoIF

This concept emerged from several codes:

- *Personalization of the workspace*: Google is a good example of how employees create SoIF starting from their office. Depending on the type of company, the office may also be different (e.g. from closed cubicle to open spaces).

- *Technological Freedom – Bring Your Own Device (BYOD):* Each employee can use his own technological devices; PC, Mac, open source, etc. Interestingly enough, this may improve the testing and exploration of future applications, even though at first, a lack of standardization could lead to decreased productivity (maintenance of all the systems).

- *Clothes:* this is classic, but still very important, the ability to forego formal business clothes for clothes of one's choice. Hence, it also illustrates a degree of freedom inside the company. However, an informal dress code may also reflect a certain level of constraint; manner of dress indicate a group's identity, and in a "geek" environment, if one does not wear a 'Star Wars' t-shirt, one might not fit in.

- *Physical location of the space.* Our data and previous research has shown that new idea should be protected in a separate department to avoid being dismissed by the rules and processes of the governing rest of the organization [21]. This may be especially valid for some specific projects, such as a critical project, a new initiative.

- *Creation of (mini) research labs.* Following the example of Google, the creation of labs for innovation can also be a great way to foster intrapreneurship. This could be reproduced by SoIF such as mini-research lab where rules are more flexible and focus is on research & development.

- *Using Floating Desks.* One of our CIO suggested that by rotating all IT employees in the company using floating desks, they can hear what the workers are thinking and the workers see that they too make a contribution to the company, even if it takes a step or two to get the idea into the right hands. This is strongly related to the need of the IT department to be closely related to the business.

- *Freedom from tracking and spying devices/processes.* With the blurring of the boundaries between home and work, as well as the use of one device for both, tracking/spying devices or processes may hinder innovation and intrapreneurship by implementing a new type of rules, and threatening any risk-taking initiative.

5.3.2 Organizational Freedom

This freedom is directly related to the organization itself. This is one of the most important concepts as it was cited by all our interviewees. The codes related to this concept are discussed below and corroborate with previous findings, [4, 8]:

- Decentralization, agility of the structure, organization in autonomous and flexible clusters ,

- Flatten the structure and improve direct access to the decision-maker to streamline the decision making process and reinforce the notion that the employee's work is important or that he has some control or investment in the outcome.

- Reduce or delete

    o bureaucracy

    o power and political games

    o rules or make them reasonably flexible

    o excess formal procedures

Overall, such approaches will help the entrepreneur to "focus on the important project, rather than fighting the organization" (quote from an interviewee).

Our interviewees also reported that too much control kills innovation, as people may be scared to explore new ideas during working hours. With *Organizational Freedom*, employees are encouraged to reasonably explore new ideas, either as a rule (for example, the 20% time if Google) or an "informal encouragement". More formal and disciplined processes may then take over to industrialize the production.

Of course, the *Organizational Freedom factors* are clearly related to the first type of Entrepreneurial Realization, *understanding* and *agreeing with the rules of the business game* at the corporate level. The recognition that this business game no longer holds appeal for them is a strong realization for a majority of IT Entrepreneurs.

5.3.3 Freedom to Innovate and Create

This freedom could be seen as more specific to IT people and is related to the attractiveness of the IT department, in relation to its use of new technologies (cloud computing, big data, social media, etc.), resulting in a more stimulating environment needed to retain and motivate innovative IT employees. This concept can be linked to the *Entrepreneurial Realization* of *long term reasons* such as *passion* or *creativity*. In addition, support for innovative ideas has been found to be positively related to innovative performance [5].

5.3.4 Freedom and Lifestyle

In relation to the freedom to innovate, the freedom to *have fun*, have *pleasure*, *work in an exciting environment,* and *personal growth* is perceived as very important for fostering an innovative environment and retaining intrapreneurs. This is of course related to the *Entrepreneurial Realization* of *long term reasons, such as self-realization or lifestyle [1].*

5.3.5 Freedom to Make Mistakes and Reasonable Risk-taking

Innovation and intrapreneurship can be fostered through a culture that forgives, or even encourages mistakes, on the condition that something can be learned from those mistakes. Indeed, allowing mistakes is a strong mean to encourage a reasonable and rational risk-taking approach that could potentially lead to major innovation for the company. Additional consequences related to freedom to make mistakes are an *increase of self-confidence, suggesting new solutions, trying new solutions,* etc. The capacity to evaluate and take risks, and the increase of self-confidence are directly related to the *Entrepreneurial Realization* related to risk-reduction. Previous research also found that Tolerance for risk-taking is positively related to innovative performance [5].

5.3.6 Freedom to Seek Opportunities

This concept deals with the possibility for the intrapreneurs to recognize new opportunities, to pursue new projects, and to be a champion for these projects. Such projects involve the responsibilities discussed previously, and they usually represent a challenge for the intrapreneurs. If the intrapreneur is not allowed to pursue some of these opportunities, he may very well start to look outside the company for opportunities, and ultimately leave the company. He would then experience an Entrepreneurial Realization about *context and opportunity*.

Table 3: Relations between types of Entrepreneurial Realizations and SoIF

Lower-level concepts of Entrepreneurial Realization	Low-level concepts / codes	Lower-level concepts of SoIF
The business game	Understanding the business game	Freedom to have a Global Vision of the Company/Industry
	Do I agree? (with the rules of the business game)	Organizational Freedom
	Necessary skills (e.g. do I have the necessary skills to play the game?)	Freedom to innovate
Risk reduction	Comparing risks	Freedom to make mistakes and risk-taking
	Social Network and risk	Teaming and SoIF
	Reality check	
	Voluntary naivety (Are people voluntarily naïve or are they just ignorant of what it takes to start a business?)	Freedom to make mistakes and risk-taking, Freedom to seek opportunities
External environmental Context	Perceived opportunity	Freedom and opportunity –seeking
Timing	Time pressure	
	The right moment	
	Long-term desire	
	End of a cycle	Opportunity Seeking Freedom
Long term reasons	self-realization	Freedom and lifestyle
	financial success	SoIF and Recognition
	Independence (no structure, no time pressure)	
	Pleasure/passion	Freedom to innovate and create
	Lifestyle	Freedom and lifestyle Freedom to innovate and create

5.3.7 Freedom to Have a Global Vision of the Company/Industry

This is a very important aspect for IT intrapreneurs, considering the radical technological changes that are happening and will happen, especially in the realm of the integration and aggregation of various company systems of cloud or outsourced solutions.

Additionally, the necessity to propose added-value services, as well as the necessary collaboration with other department e.g. the marketing department to work on Big Data, Social Media or BI projects is also a strong factor supporting intrapreneurship. This is also supported in the literature, for example Antoncic and Antoncic recommends "providing sufficient information to employees about the effectiveness of implementing work tasks", [8].

5.3.8 SoIF and Entrepreneurial Realization

As discussed above and summarized in Table 3, all the Entrepreneurial Realizations are linked to the specific type of SoIF that emerged from our data. Those results were not obvious at the beginning of the study and resulted from additional memoing and constant comparison between the two models (SoIF and IT Entrepreneurial Realization). Our results suggest that the lower level concepts and characteristics of SoIF are interesting to consider when looking at reducing IT Entrepreneurial Turnover (IT employees leaving employment for entrepreneurship), specifically among the IT Intrapreneurial population.

For instance, by promoting organizational freedom, this could reduce the possible disagreement with the rules of the business game, hence reducing the chances for IT Entrepreneurial turnover. At the opposite, by providing a global vision of the industry, it could improve the employee's understanding of the business game, eventually leading to entrepreneurial turnover. Interestingly enough, the lower-level concepts and characteristics of SoIF may either reduce or increase the likelihood of IT Entrepreneurial Turnover. Future research may explore those aspects more in depth, but for each row of the table, we could easily draw some propositions to test.

5.4 Integration of the Results

We now relate all the properties and concepts of SoIF. We suggest that cultivating Spaces of Intrapreneurial Freedom (SoIF) at a departmental or organizational level fosters IT Intrapreneurship and innovation, as well as reduces unwanted IT turnover, in particular entrepreneurial turnover. We articulate the practical implications around the core category of SoIF. The protection of the space can be attributed to a champion or a team of champions, the *Protectors of the Space* that will "finesse" [18] the corporate politics while the intrapreneur "attends single-mindedly to making the idea a reality". At the corporate level, such protection can also be accompanied by the implementation of core values for the culture of the company (value of innovation, value of Intrapreneurship). When it comes to *Populating and Protecting* the eco-system of the space, we mentioned *hiring and/or developing the 'right' person* through a very selective process focusing on entrepreneurial mind-set rather than skills (that can be acquired later with this right mind-set). The SoIF does not come without *Responsibilities*, related to various aspects: we can cite *strict follow up* on the project by the manager and *discipline of quality* when delivering the final product; *focus on the task, the deliverable*, not the time spent ;

high value-added of the project and *ROI* of the project ; *customer-centric* projects for the intrapreneur. Those responsibilities also come with *Recognition* that may take different forms, such as *social recognition* (e.g. the IT employee will present herself the result of her project in front of the client or the board of presidents), encouragement, listening to the idea, letting the person acting upon it, and of course *financial recognition*.

Various characteristics and lower-level concepts of SoIF have been identified. For example, *Material SoIF* refers to the personalization of the office, the technology and its use, clothes, etc. *Organizational Freedom* refers to codes such as *decentralization, agility of the structure, autonomous* or *flexible clusters, flattening the structure* and finally *reduce or delete the bureaucracy*, the *power* and *political games*, the *rules* that are not reasonable and the *formal procedures* in excess. We mentioned the relation between the following characteristics of SoIF: The *Freedom to Innovate and Create*, while related to a certain *Lifestyle* (*fun, pleasure, exciting environment*) and favored by the possibility or even the encouragement to *Make Mistake* (and learn from them), as well as *Taking Reasonable Risks*. Those four Freedoms allow the IT Intrapreneur to pursue *Opportunities* triggered by a *Global Vision of the Company/Industry*.

Considering the triad *Global Vision of the Company/Industry, Opportunity* and *Responsibilities*, the intrapreneur needs to responsibly align his goals with those of the company, hence fostering the recognition of the best opportunities for the company. This may represents a real managerial challenge because of the intrapreneur's strong desire for independence [42]. Through cross-functional activities – for example, floating desks – the intrapreneur can enhance both his vision of the company, as well as his ability to spot opportunities that will be profitable for the company as a whole.

If understood by companies, this should result in a reduction of IT Entrepreneurial Turnover. For example, for a potential entrepreneur, if the rules of the organization are more aligned with intrapreneurship and if the *Protector of the SoIF* allows the intrapreneur to avoid having play too much politics to implement his ideas, the likelihood of the employee realizing that he disagrees with the rules of the corporate world should be reduced. Second, if the intrapreneur has the possibility to pursue his own ideas inside the organization, it reduces the chances the employee spots an opportunity outside the organization. Third, the employee may increase his passion and pleasure at work through the implementation of the *Freedom to Innovate and Create*.

Leaving the Space. If the employee still decides to leave the space, (i.e. the company); a supportive approach from the company can be beneficial. Although those SoIF are designed to retain and develop IT intrapreneurs, eventually the most IT entrepreneurial employees will leave following shocks [41], Shifts of Understandings [11] and Entrepreneurial Realizations [1]. So delaying their departure and making it a positive experience could also be seen as a positive outcome of those SoIF.

At the corporate level, *protecting the space* can even be achieved through the implementation of core values that will be translated into the culture of the company (value of innovation, value of Intrapreneurship). Such implementation will naturally be done by the *protector(s)*.

6. PRACTICAL IMPLICATIONS FOR HANDLING AND CULTIVATING SoIF

At the organizational level, we suggest that handling, mastering and fostering the emergence of the IT Spaces of Intrapreneurial Freedom is a powerful way for companies to maintain high level of innovation, but also to reduce IT Turnover.

The concept of SoIF emerged from our data and embeds several dimensions summarized in the following table. For each dimension of SoIF, we indicate the influence of Spaces of Intrapreneurial Freedom at the level of the IT department (HR resources, Innovation), as well as the level of the company (strategy).

Properties of Spaces of Intrapreneurial Freedom	Functional Politics of the IT Department - Human resources - Innovation	At the level of the company, including strategic moves.
A protector of the SoIF	Reinforcing the role of CIO, IT director and IT managers as protectors of their SoIF, either for specific teams or at the scale of the IT Department.	By implementing SoIF, the company or its actors can transform the culture of the company (with values of innovation and intrapreneurship), or reach hybrid situations allowing the cohabitation of SoIF within more traditional non-entrepreneurial company.
Populating and Protecting the Space and its Eco-System	We listed several characteristics of the intrapreneurial type, with a strong focus on the IT entrepreneurial mind-set rather than the skills themselves; skills that will have to be learned on a constant basis due to the fast-pace of IT innovation. Diversity is also an important characteristic to foster innovation. We also strongly insist on the selection and hiring process (e.g. up to 9 interviews are necessary to be hired in one of the highly innovative firms we studied) and the very strong reactivity in case of misfit: "they don't hesitate to fire people to protect the eco-system".	By populating those SoIF, the company brings and empowers innovative intrapreneurs, hence changing the dynamics of the organization. Depending on the size of the SoIF (team, department and company), the influence of the SoIF will be either limited or possibly extended to the whole organization.
	The list of codes relevant to this 'right' intrapreneur are listed below: *right mind-set, forward thinking innovators, openness, trustable, kind and nice, reasonably artistic type, emotionally stable, life-long learners,* balance of *soft and technical skills, passionate, autonomous, responsible, reasonable risk-taker, conscientious,* and as a consequence, *very hard-working but still having a lot of pleasure.*	
SoIF and Responsibilities	Probably the most important criteria to implement by HR, but also at the level of the company. We suggest having strong processes of assessment of the responsibilities related to SoIF. Among them, we mention *strict follow up* on the project by the manager and *discipline of quality* when delivering the final product; *focus on the task, the deliverable*, not the time spent ; *high value-added* of the project and *ROI* of the project ; *customer-centric* projects for the intrapreneur. Those responsibilities serve as safeguards to ensure that the objectives of the IT department are aligned with the SoIF.	
SoIF and Recognition	Recognition can be seen at two levels. Non-financial recognition, related to good managerial practices. For example, the IT employee presents herself the result of her project in front of the client or the board of presidents; the encouragement, listening of the ideas and letting the person acting upon it are other forms of recognition that could be very powerful. Of course, the second level is *financial recognition*.	At a company and strategic level, the same managerial practices of recognition can be applied. For example, having a practice of always recognizing who is/are at the origin of such idea or realization of very successful project will strongly encourage innovation at the company level. Related to financial recognition, we mentioned how recurring emission of stock option could create 'golden handcuff' and retain a certain type of Intrapreneurs, while attracting other intrapreneurs in the company.
Leaving the Space	If the employee still decides to leave the space and/or the company ; a supportive approach from the company can be beneficial on several levels such as Corporate refocusing, "Prosperity and well-being of regions, industry clusters and nations", "Decreasing the administrative burden" [2], positive image of the company and increased attractiveness to other intrapreneurs, future collaboration with former intrapreneurs.	

Characteristics and Lower-level concepts of SoIF		
Material SoIF	At the level of the IT department, acting upon the material side of the SoIF is relatively easy: altering a too formal dress code, allowing employees to personalize their desks, implementing Technological Freedom (Mac and PC are allowed), Freedom from tracking and spying devices/processes also emerged as an interesting practice that may reduce Innovation.	At the level of the company, material SoIF could be implemented through the Creation of (mini) research labs or the Physical location of the space.

Organizational Freedom	This is one of the most important concepts as it was cited by all our interviewees. We mention the following codes:
	
	• Decentralization, agility of the structure, organization in autonomous and flexible clusters ,
	• Flattening the structure and improving direct access to the decision maker to increase the rapidity of the decision making process, but also the feeling that the employee's work is important or that she has some control or investment in the outcome.
	• Reduce or delete
	  • bureaucracy
	  • power and political games
	  • rules or make them reasonably flexible
	  • formal procedures in excess
	
	Overall, such approaches help the intrapreneur to "focus on the important project, rather than fighting the organization" (quote from an interviewee). We also suggest to maintain the level of control to a low level as it 'kills the innovation" ; intrapreneurs become scary to explore new ideas while working. With Organizational SoIF, the employees are encouraged to reasonably explore new ideas, either as a rule (for example, the 20% time if Google) or just as an "informal encouragement". Depending upon the situations, once the innovation has been developed and implemented, more formal and disciplined processes may then take over to industrialize and rationalize the production.	

Freedom to Innovate and Create	This freedom could be seen as more specific to IT people and is related to the attractiveness of the IT department, in relation to its use of new technologies (cloud computing, big data, social media, etc.), resulting in a non-boring environment proper to retain and motivate young IT employees.	
Freedom and Lifestyle	In relation to the freedom to innovate, the freedom to have fun, have pleasure, work in an exciting environment, personal growth is perceived as very important for fostering an innovative environment and retaining intrapreneurs.	
Freedom to make mistakes and reasonable Risk-Taking	According to our interview, innovation and intrapreneurship can be fostered through a culture that forgives, or even encourages mistakes, at the condition that something is learned from those mistakes. Authorizing, or even encouraging those mistakes into the Spaces of Intrapreneurial Freedom can lead to major innovation for the IT department, but also for the company. In addition, allowing mistakes is a strong mean to encourage a reasonable and rational risk-taking approach that could lead to major innovation for the company.	
Freedom and Opportunity Seeking	This concept is related to the possibility for the intrapreneurs to recognize new opportunities, to suggest new projects to pursue and to be champions for this project. Those projects are of course related to the responsibilities discussed previously and they usually represent a challenge for the intrapreneurs. If the intrapreneur is not allowed to pursue some of those opportunities, he may very well start to look outside the company and recognize external opportunity ; leading him to pursue it and leave the company. He would then experience an Entrepreneurial Realization related to the context and the opportunity.	
Freedom to have a Global Vision of the Company/Industry	This is a very important aspect for IT intrapreneurs, considering the radical technological changes that are and will happen, especially in the realm of the integration and aggregation of the various systems of the company with the cloud/outsourced solutions, as discussed in the introduction. Additionally, the necessity to propose added-value services, as well as the necessary collaboration with other department (e.g. collaboration with the marketing department to work on Big Data and BI projects) is also a strong factor supporting intrapreneurship.	Depending on the industry, the competitiveness and other factors, the company can encourage the circulation of information allowing the employees to have a global vision, hence having the possibility to suggest and propose innovative solution and act upon them.
SoIF and Entrepreneurial Realization	This is an important finding of our study. In fact, all the Entrepreneurial Realizations (leading to entrepreneurship turnover have been found related to Spaces of Intrapreneurial Freedom. Hence implementing SoIF should strongly reduce the risk of ER, hence, reducing the risk of Entrepreneurial turnover.	

Table 4: Practical implications of SoIF

7. Conclusion

To conclude, we would like to raise a few limitations and future research questions.

Specificities to IS research. This study was conducted specifically with IT department and/or IT companies. Although some concepts may be more specific to the IT industry (e.g. technological freedom, freedom from tracking and spying devices), others are more generalizable to other fields such as engineering or marketing. The generalization beyond IT departments/companies would need to be confirmed by further cross-department/cross-industry studies. Hence, future research could look at how specific SoIF are to IT department/IT industry, compared to other department or other industries (more or less innovative).

Do all companies need SoIF? In some cases, the development of intrapreneurial behavior may not be appropriate. For instance, the industry or the company is highly regulated and therefore, such intrapreneurial behavior may lead to major mistakes and misunderstanding from co-workers. In other cases, the company needs to stabilize its profit and therefore will alternate an expansion/entrepreneurial phase with a stabilization/less entrepreneurial phase. This, of course will vary from one company to the other. Finally, in other cases, the SoIF may not fit some employees who are looking for an organized and ruled environment.

Socio-materiality and SoIF. Although not enough grounded in the data for now, future research should explore the relationship between sociomateriality and SoIF. What are the inter-connections? How one can explain the other? How could an in-depth understanding of sociomateriality lead to the creation of SoIF?

Expanding the analysis of emerging core categories. Some concepts may require more in-depth analysis. Following Glaser [17], we suggest that some of the concepts that emerged as lower-level concepts may very well deserve to be explored as core categories. For instance, the concept of porosity of the SoIF may have additional nuance and complexities or suggest hybrid forms that can be useful in less than ideal conditions.

When should we try to retain IT intrapreneurs rather than gracefully assist them in moving to other venues? Another future set of questions should focus on the degree to which SoIF is even capable of aiding the retention of entrepreneurially minded IT employees and under what conditions it is really better to in fact retain them. Indeed, it is possible that a CIO may only be able to delay their departure; several CIOs reported that such departure may be welcomed under specific conditions, hence it could be a benefit for some companies and circumstances to let go of their entrepreneurial IT employees. Similarly, the organization guiding an entrepreneurial spin-off is another valuable related phenomenon that is not yet well understood.

Is Freedom too strong ? One could argue that the term Freedom implies that the organization functions as a jail and that employees are prisoners. Well, in fact, from the point of view of the intrapreneur, expressions such as "the golden handcuffs", "it kills me" or "in this organization, people were rejecting their personal values" clearly expresses the perceived brutality of some organizations by the entrepreneur. Additionally, books such as "*Escape from the cubicle nation: From Corporate Prisoner to Thriving Entrepreneur*" (Pamela Slim), the French documentary "*J'ai très mal au travail*" (from J.M. Carré, 2007) and the movie

"*Human Resources*" all use similar analogies. That said, it is important to keep in mind that not all employees are unhappy in non-entrepreneurial organizations. Indeed, many people thrive in environments with rules and processes that keep the organization in order. We also interviewed several former entrepreneurs who could not stand the chaos and uncertainty of owning a business, and decided to become salaried employees once again, sometimes in intrapreneurial settings, sometimes in less intrapreneurial settings.

At the end of the day, it is hoped that the concept of SoIF can serve to link management practices, particularly in IS, with stimulating greater levels of innovation both within and beyond particular corporate environments. We have suggested a number of components of SoIF that can be examined individually for their contribution to the overall level of SoIF, on the differences between SoIF as intended by the firm and as experienced by employees, and potentially provide levers for management to affect levels of SoIF in their firm.

8. REFERENCE

[1] Mourmant, G. and Voutsina, K. From IT Employee to IT Entrepreneur: the Concept of IT Entrepreneurial Epiphany. City, 2010.

[2] Parhankangas, A. and Arenius, P. From a corporate venture to an independent company: a base for a taxonomy for corporate spin-off firms. Research Policy, 32, 3 2003), 463-481.

[3] Pinchot, G. Intrapreneuring: why you don't have to leave the corporation to become an entrepreneur. Harper & Row, New York, 1985.

[4] Menzel, H. C., Aaltio, I. and Ulijn, J. M. On the way to creativity: Engineers as intrapreneurs in organizations. Technovation, 27, 12 2007), 732-743.

[5] Alpkan, L., Bulut, C., Gunday, G., Ulusoy, G. and Kilic, K. Organizational support for intrapreneurship and its interaction with human capital to enhance innovative performance. Management Decision, 48, 5 2010), 732-755.

[6] Benitez-Amado, J., Llorens-Montes, F. J. and Perez-Arostegui, M. N. Information technology-enabled intrapreneurship culture and firm performance. Industrial Management & Data Systems, 110, 4 2010).

[7] Kenney, M. G., Khanfar, N. M. and Kizer, L. E. Practitioner Perspectives Of Information Technology Industry Intrapreneurship: An Exploratory Study. International Journal Of Management & Information System, 14, 1 2010), 35-40.

[8] Antoncic, J. A. and Antoncic, B. Employee satisfaction, intrapreneurship and firm growth: a model. Industrial Management & Data Systems, 11, 4 2011), 589-607.

[9] Joseph, D., Ng, K.-Y., Koh, C. and Ang, S. Turnover of information technology professionals: a narrative review, meta-analytic structural equation modeling, and model development. MIS Quarterly, 31, 3 2007), 547-577.

[10] Mourmant, G., Gallivan, M. J. and Kalika, M. Another Road to IT Turnover: the Entrepreneurial Path. Special issue of the European Journal of Information Systems on "Meeting the Renewed Demand for IT Workers." 18, 5 2009).

[11] Mourmant, G. and Voutsina, K. What Should I Understand? The Concept of Shift of Understanding, a Quote-Based Analysis. ACM Press, City, 2012.

[12] Suddaby, R. From the editors: What grounded theory is not. Academy of Management Journal, 49, 4 2006), 633.

[13] Glaser, B. G. and Strauss, A. L. The discovery of grounded theory: strategies for qualitative research. Aldine Transaction, 1967.

[14] Glaser, B. G. Theoretical sensitivity: advances in the methodology of grounded theory. The Sociology Press, Mill Valley, CA, 1978.

[15] Glaser, B. G. Doing grounded theory: issues and discussions. Sociology Press, Mill Valley, CA, 1998.

[16] Glaser, B. G. Getting out of the data. Sociology Press, Mill Valley, CA, 2011.

[17] Glaser, B. G. Stop, write. Sociology Press, Mill Valley, CA, 2012.

[18] Pinchot, G. I. Intrapreneuring: Why You Don't Have to Leave the Corporation to Become an Entrepreneur. University of Illinois at Urbana-Champaign's Academy for Entrepreneurial Leadership Historical Research Reference in Entrepreneurship, 1985.

[19] Wang, C. L. Entrepreneurial Orientation, Learning Orientation, and Firm Performance. Entrepreneurship: Theory & Practice, 32, 4 2008), 635-657.

[20] Wiklund, J. and Shepherd, D. Entrepreneurial orientation and small business performance: a configurational approach. Journal of Business Venturing, 20, 1 2005), 71-91.

[21] Chandler, A. Strategy and Structure: Chapters in the History of Industrial Enterprise. MIT Press, Cambridge, Mass., 1967.

[22] Zhao, H. and Seibert, S. E. The big five personality dimensions and entrepreneurial status: a meta-analytical review. Journal of Applied Psychology, 91, 2 2006), 259-271.

[23] Brandstätter, H. Personality aspects of entrepreneurship: A look at five meta-analyses. Personality and Individual Differences, 51, 3 2011), 222-230.

[24] Sternberg, R. J. Successful intelligence as a basis for entrepreneurship. Journal of Business Venturing, 19, 2 2004), 189-201.

[25] Blume, B. D. and Covin, J. G. Attributions to intuition in the venture founding process: Do entrepreneurs actually use intuition or just say that they do? Journal of Business Venturing, 26, 1 2011), 137-151.

[26] Lazear, E. P. Entrepreneurship. National Bureau of Economic Research, City, 2002.

[27] Lazear, E. P. Balanced skills and entrepreneurship. American Economic Review, 94, 2 2004), 208-211.

[28] Wagner, J. Are nascent entrepreneurs 'Jacks-of-all-trades'? a test of Lazear's theory of entrepreneurship with German data. Applied Economics, 38, 20 2006), 2415-2419.

[29] Cardon, M. S., Wincent, J., Singh, J. and Drnovsek, M. The nature and experience of entrepreneurial passion. The Academy of Management Review 34, 3 2009), 511-532.

[30] Busenitz, L. W. and Barney, J. B. Differences between entrepreneurs and managers in large organizations: Biases and heuristics in strategic decision making. Journal of Business Venturing, 12, 1 1997), 9-30.

[31] Camerer, C. and Lovallo, D. Overconfidence and Excess Entry: An Experimental Approach. The American Economic Review, 89, 1 1999), 306-318.

[32] Keh, H. T., Foo, M. D. and Lim, B. C. Opportunity Evaluation under Risky Conditions: The Cognitive Processes of Entrepreneurs. Entrepreneurship: Theory & Practice, 27, 2 (2002///Winter 2002), 125.

[33] Simon, M., Houghton, S. M. and Aquino, K. Cognitive Biases, Risk Perception, and Venture Formation: How Individuals Decide to Start Companies. Journal of Business Venturing, 15, 2 (2000/03// 2000), 113.

[34] Forbes, D. P. Are some entrepreneurs more overconfident than others? Journal of Business Venturing, 20, 5 2005), 623-640.

[35] Simon, M., Houghton, S. M. and Savelli, S. Out of the frying pan...?: Why small business managers introduce high-risk products. Journal of Business Venturing, 18, 3 2003), 419-440.

[36] Koellinger, P., Minniti, M. and Schade, C. "I think I can, I think I can": Overconfidence and entrepreneurial behavior. Journal of Economic Psychology, 28, 4 2007), 502-527.

[37] Lowe, R. A. and Ziedonis, A. A. Overoptimism and the Performance of Entrepreneurial Firms. Management Science, 52, 2 (February 1, 2006 2006), 173-186.

[38] Townsend, D. M., Busenitz, L. W. and Arthurs, J. D. To start or not to start: Outcome and ability expectations in the decision to start a new venture. Journal of Business Venturing, 25, 2 2010), 192-202.

[39] Dahlstrand, Ã. s. L. Growth and inventiveness in technology-based spin-off firms. Research Policy, 26, 3 1997), 331-344.

[40] Clarysse, B., Wright, M. and Van de Velde, E. Entrepreneurial Origin, Technological Knowledge, and the Growth of Spin-Off Companies. Journal of Management Studies, 48, 6 2012), 1420-1442.

[41] Niederman, F., Sumner, M. and Maertz, C. Testing and extending the unfolding model of voluntary turnover to IT professionals. Human Resource Management Journal, 46, 3 2007), 331-347.

[42] Carter, N. M., Gartner, W. B., Shaver, K. G. and Gatewood, E. J. The career reasons of nascent entrepreneurs. Journal of Business Venturing, 18, 1 (2003/01// 2003), 13.

9. ACKNOWLEDGMENTS

Our thanks to the CIGREF for supporting this project.

A Structured Review of IS Research on Gender and IT

Mike Gallivan
Robinson College of Business
CIS Department
Georgia State University
Atlanta, Georgia, USA
001 (404) 413-7363
mgallivan@gsu.edu

ABSTRACT

Despite many contributions to research on gender and IT – both empirical and conceptual – the IS field lacks an overall review of this stream of research. We provide such a review of IS research on gender and IT spanning 20 years, following the guidelines for conducting a "descriptive review" (King and He 2006). Focusing on IS journals and conferences, we identify over 190 papers in which the authors specifically mentioned one or more of a set of terms in their title, appendix or keywords (e.g., gender, sex, men, women, etc.). We identify the recurring authors in this research stream and we classify these authors' research methods, types of respondents studied, authors' epistemological stance and their gender theory-in-use. We identify four topic areas and, for each, we provide descriptive summaries of corresponding papers: IT ethics; IT careers and education; IT adoption and use; attitudes to telework. Many papers we located neglect to specify a clear theory-in-use regarding gender (i.e., whether the authors believe that observed differences between men and women are socially constructed, due to biological factors, or the result of other influences). We found few studies that regard men, who account for a majority of IT employees, as gendered or consider gender a relevant issue when studying male employees, teleworkers, or computer users. Authors of most papers seem to assume that the presence of women is necessary to trigger gender as an issue.

Categories and Subject Descriptors

K.3.2 Computer and Information Science Education; K.6 Management of Computing and Information Systems

Keywords

Gender, Scientometrics, Structured review.

1. INTRODUCTION

SIG MIS has been a leading venue for research on gender issues in IS field. Reaching back 20 years, SIG CPR featured its first pair of papers about gender as an issue in the IT workforce in 1993 (McLean et al. 1993; Tan & Igbaria 1993) and many papers thereafter. During the past six years, SIG MIS has featured many panels on gender issues (Guzman et al. 2008; Trauth et al. 2010)

and theoretically-informed empirical papers (Trauth et al. 2012). Of course, there are key papers on gender and IS in venues other than SIG MIS recently, including editorials (von Hellens, Trauth & Fisher 2012) and conceptual papers (Howcroft & Trauth 2008) in IS journals. There are some conceptual papers in key IS conferences (Trauth & Quesenberry 2006) and in non-IS journals, such as sociology (Adam, Howcroft & Richardson 2004).

We recognize the value of conceptual papers for their role in suggesting new theories and methods for studying a given topic area (Webster & Watson 2002). Yet, in addition to conceptual review papers, a separate type of review is one that offers a structured descriptive review (King & He 2005) of studies published in a given research stream. We offer such a descriptive review of prior work on gender and IS. In distinguishing four types of reviews, King and He (2006, p. 667) define descriptive reviews as those in which researchers:

> … introduce some quantification, often a frequency analysis of a body of research. The purpose is to find out to what extent the existing literature … reveals an interpretable pattern. To assure the generalizability of the results, a descriptive review often involves a systematic search of as many as [possible] relevant papers in an investigated area, and codes each selected paper on certain research characteristics, such as publication [year], research methodology, main approach … and outcomes.

We begin by summarizing some recent conceptual papers (i.e., 2006 or later) published in SIG MIS and elsewhere, noting the problems that the authors identified as requiring new theory or methods. Next, we describe our research methods for conducting a structured review of gender and IS research. We then present our results in a structured fashion. Despite our efforts to classify over 185 journal and conference papers we found in 35 journals and 6 conferences, we found many that we could not classify in terms of authors' espoused theory of gender (i.e., their beliefs about the source of any differences between men and women).

2. CONCEPTUAL DEVELOPMENT

Empirical studies of women in the computer workforce date back to the early 1980s (e.g., Olerup et al 1984). In a recent editorial for a special issue on interventions to encourage more women to enter IT jobs, von Hellens, Trauth and Fisher (2012, p. 345) note that: "the first papers in the area of women and computing, as it was then called, were being published in the early 1980s." While there was early interest in this topic in the computer science community, the first papers in the IS literature emerged a decade later – first, in an information science journal (Kling 1990), then at the SIG CPR conference (McLean et al 1993; Tan & Igbaria 1993), and later still in IS journals (Baroudi & Igbaria 1994; Truman & Baroudi 1994). There have been some descriptive reviews of specific topics related to gender and IT – one of attitudes to computers in a social science journal, *Computers in Human Behavior* (Whitley 1997) and in education journals (Reinen & Plomp 1997; Volman & van Eck 2011).

Since we focus on papers in IS journals and conferences, we situate the beginning of this research stream in 1990. Since that time (especially during the past decade), research on gender in the IT workforce has become an ongoing theme at two conferences: SIG MIS and AMCIS. In the last decade, there have been special issues on gender in two journals: *Information Technology & People* (Adam, Howcroft & Richardson 2002) and *Information Systems Journal* (von Hellens et al. 2012), plus a special issue on critical research that included gender research (Kvasny & Richardson 2006).

Although the topic of sex differences in IT adoption and usage has been less centralized in special issues, there has been substantial research analyzing the uptake of IT by women and men (e.g., Venkatesh & Morris 2000) – or, depending on the age group – girls and boys. There are scores of studies examining differences between men and women in IT attitudes and IT use, but, a previous review criticized early empirical studies in this area as having "difficulty explaining the phenomena it apparently uncovers as it does not adequately theorise the construct of gender" (Adam, Howcroft & Richardson, 2004, p. 227).

Conceptual reviews have the potential to suggest new, future directions for research. At the same time, they also provide an opportunity to look back and take stock of what we have learned and what insights we should leverage in the future (Webster & Watson 2002). Over the past decade, key conceptual papers have appeared – for example, focusing on factors that attract women to the IT workforce and sustain, or conversely, discourage them (Ahuja 2002). A second conceptual paper that evaluated the studies on gender and IS published in the 1990s found that many studies lack theoretical clarity about what accounts for observed differences between men and women (Adam et al. 2004). We label this as the authors' espoused theory of gender, drawing on terminology from Argyris and Schön (1974). Trauth and Quesenberry (2006) explored this issue, identifying three types of undertheorizing: pre-theoretical research (i.e., studies that compare men and women without articulating any theory or beliefs about sex differences); implicit-theoretical research (i.e., studies where authors fail to articulate their beliefs about sex differences); and insufficient theoretical research (studies that mention a theory about gender but fail to account for existing within-sex variation among women or among men).

Despite these benefits of these important conceptual papers, one type of review work is lacking: a consolidated review of gender research published in IS journals and conferences. We provide a comprehensive, structured review of this body of work. Below, we describe our research methods and the set of IS outlets we searched to find the relevant body of work on gender and IT. We then provide structured summaries of this work – dividing the literature into four topics: IT ethics; IT careers and education; IT adoption and use; and attitudes to telework. For each topic, we summarize five aspects of corresponding papers: the total number of studies, the type of research methods used, the type of subjects involved, researchers' epistemological stance and their espoused theory of gender. In reviewing the papers that match each topic, we identify patterns that emerged from our review.

3. RESEARCH METHODS

To identify the set of papers on IS and gender, I searched the titles, abstracts, and/or keywords of papers published in academic journals for one or more of the relevant terms: sex, gender, men, women, boys, girls, female, or male. In order for us to retain a paper in our review, it had to contain one or more of these terms in its abstract or keyword. It also had to appear in one of the outlets listed in Appendix 1A (IS academic journals) and Appendix 1B (IS conferences). With help from a graduate student, I read each paper's abstract and research methods sections, skimmed other sections, and classified each paper according to these categories:

3.1 Classification Scheme

3.1.1 Subject Areas
    IT Ethics

    IT Careers & Education

    IT Adoption and Use

    Attitudes toward Telework

3.1.2 Epistemological Views
    Critical Research

    Interpretivism,

    Positivism

3.1.3 Authors' Espoused Theory of Gender
    Critical Feminism

    Essentialism

    Individual Differences Theory of Gender

    Social Constructionist

3.1.4 Research Methods
    Conceptual paper

    Empirical, quantitative survey methods

    Empirical, quantitative experimental methods

    Empirical, qualitative methods (interviews, case study, etc.)

    Empirical, mixed methods (qualitative and qualitative)

    Empirical analysis of archival/secondary data

For each empirical study, we identified the number of informants or subjects, the type of subjects (e.g., employees in organizations, undergraduate, graduate, or secondary school students), the number of men and women, and subjects' country of origin.

4. RESULTS

We first report the some basic descriptive data regarding the papers we found. Table 1 identifies the names and affiliations of authors who appeared on 4 or more papers – with Eileen Trauth (18 papers) and Jeria Quesenberry (9 papers) leading the list. Most of the frequent authors are women – with the exception of two men: Magid Igbaria (6 papers) and Mike Gallivan (4 papers). Table 2 lists the journals and conferences containing the most papers, with AMCIS (Americas Conference on Information Systems) having the most total papers or panels: 25.

papers	Author Name	Country	University Affiliation
18	Eileen Trauth	USA	Penn State University
9	Jeria Quesen-berry	USA	Penn State Univ. / Carnegie Mellon Univ.
7	Alison Adam	UK	Salford University
7	Sue Nielsen	Austra-lia	Griffith University
6	Deborah Armstrong	USA	University of Arkansas / Florida State University
6	Anita Greenhill	Austra-lia/UK	Griffith University / Univ. of Manchester
6	Liisa von Hellens	Austra-lia	Griffith University
6	Cindy Riemen-schneider	USA	Univ. of Arkansas / Baylor University
6	Magid Igbaria	USA	Drexel University
6	K.D. Joshi	USA	Washington State University
6	Melanie Wilson	UK	Manchester Business School
5	Lynette Kvasny	USA	Penn State University
4	Monica Adya	USA	Marquette University
4	Manju Ahuja	USA	Indiana University
4	France Belanger	USA	Virginia Technical Institute
4	Mike Gallivan	USA	Georgia State Univ.
4	Debra Howcroft	UK	Salford University
4	Margaret Reid	USA	Univ. of Arkansas
4	Helen Richardson	UK	Salford University

Table 1: Number of Papers by Author

Table 2: Papers by Publication Outlet

# papers	Name of Journal or Conference
25	Americas Conference on IS (conference)
21	Information Society
18	Information Technology & People
17	Communications of the ACM
13	ACM SIG MIS (conference)
12	European Journal of Information Systems
10	Database for Advances in IS
8	Communications of the AIS
7	IEEE Transactions on Professional Communication
6	European Conference on IS (conference)
6	Information Systems Journal
6	Journal of Information Technology
5	MIS Quarterly
4	IEEE Transactions on Engineering Management
4	Australasian Conference on IS (conference)

Next we identify the papers corresponding to each topic and, for each topic, we classify papers based on the research methods, type of respondents, authors' on authors' epistemological stance, and espoused theory of regarding gender. We did not include conference panels in this detailed coding for two reasons: first, panels often include a mix of different topics; second, many published abstracts of conference panels are very brief – lacking space to describe the issues that presenters will discuss. The number of papers for each topic was as follows:

Topic 1: 15 papers – IT Ethics

Topic 2: 60 papers – IT Adoption and use

Topic 3: 80 papers – IS careers and education

Topic 4: 18 papers – Attitudes toward telework

Topic 1: IT Ethics

The first research topic we summarize is IT ethics (see Table 3). There were 15 studies belonging to this topic that mentioned one or more appropriate terms in their title, abstract or keywords. Of these, two were purely conceptual (Adam 2001a; Westfall 2000), 12 were quantitative, empirical studies and one was a qualitative study (Adam & Amanfo 2000). Nine out of 13 empirical studies used student subjects; the four exceptions were ones that analyzed responses to ethical scenarios for among IT managers and employees (Kuo et al 2006), managers only (Adam & Amanfo 2000) or general Internet users (Gattiker & Kelley 1999; Young & Case 2009). Most of the empirical studies were comparative studies of men and women; as a result, nearly all studies had balanced sets of men and women respondents – with the average ratio of women 43% (ranging from 18% to 57%).

Of the two conceptual papers, one author adopted a critical research perspective (Adam 2001a), while another espoused an interpretive stance (Westfall 2000). Of the 13 empirical studies, all were positivist hypothesis-testing studies, with the exception of the one qualitative empirical study (Adam & Amanfo 2000). Although the other 12 empirical studies were quantitative, we classify three of them as descriptive, atheoretical studies because they lacked any a priori hypotheses or theory (Cronan et al. 2006; Khazanchi 1995; Young & Case 2009). All other studies were positivist, theory-testing studies featuring hypotheses focusing on expected differences between men and women with regard to unethical IT behavior, such as software piracy.

One limitation of this set of studies, despite the benefit of having balanced sets of respondents by gender, 70% of studies were conducted with U.S. subjects (often students). There are also several studies with students from other countries.

Table 3 – Studies about IT Ethics		
Authors	**Year**	**Publication Outlet**
Adam	2001	Information & Organization
Adam & Ofori Amanfo	2000	Ethics & IT
Cronan, Foltz & Jones	2006	Communications of ACM
Gattiker & Kelley	1999	Information Systems Res.
Khazanchi	1995	J. Business Ethics
Kreie & Cronin	1998	Communications of ACM
Kuo, Lin & Hsu	2006	Journal of Business Ethics
Lending & Slaughter	1999	SIG CPR conference
Loch & Conger	1996	Communications of ACM
Masrom & Ismail	2008	ACIS conference
McCarthy, Halavi & Aronson	2005	Issues in IS
McMahon & Cohen	2009	Ethics & IT
Moores & Chang	2006	MIS Quarterly
Young & Case	2009	Issues in IS
Westfall	2000	Ethics & IT

As was the case for the atheoretical, descriptive quantitative studies of IT ethics (Cronan et al. 2006; Khazanchi 1995; Young & Case 2009), we found atheoretical papers in all topic areas of our review. Atheoretical, descriptive papers were most common in *Communications of the ACM*, which moved to a short-format, practitioner-focused style in the mid-1990s. Possibly owing to this shorter article format, authors lack sufficient space to state – or theoretically justify – any hypotheses. Instead, authors briefly introduce a topic, explain their research methods and results without stating any hypotheses or theory (Cronan et al. 2006).

In terms of authors' espoused theory of gender, we could not classify most of these papers into the available categories (e.g., essentialist, social constructivist, individual differences theory of gender, or others). Among such "unclassified" papers are three studies we mentioned above (Cronan et al. 2006; Khazanchi 1995; Young & Case 2009), plus three that contain *some* theory or hypotheses – but not with regard to authors' beliefs about the source of differences in the ethical beliefs or self-reported ethical behaviors of men and women (Gattiker & Kelley 1999; Gopal & Sanders 1997; McCarthy, et al 2005). Half of all the studies on IT ethics have an *unclassified* espoused theory of gender.

We classified authors' espoused gender theory as social constructivist if they stated or implied that differences between men and women related to ethical behavior or attitudes resulted from socialization or other social forces. There were three such studies (Kuo, Lin & Hsu 2006; Moores & Chang 2006; Westfall 2000). Conversely, we classified papers as having an essentialist theory of gender if they stated or implied that ethical beliefs were innately linked to being biologically male or female (Lending & Slaughter 2001). We coded one study as critical feminist (Adam & Amanfo 2000) and another as subscribing to the individual differences theory of gender (Trauth 2002), although this study of IT ethical behavior pre-dated the initial publication of the individual differences theory of gender by four years (Kreie & Cronin 1998). In their study, Kreie and Cronan argue that observable ethical beliefs emerge within a set of women (or a set of men) due

to actual life experiences or influential figures who shaped their beliefs, consistent with the individual differences theory:

> A person has internalized experiences, values, and beliefs which might collectively be called 'personal values.' [These] characteristics, such as gender, age, and education ... also affect one's view of what is ethical. – Kreie and Cronan (1998, p. 72).

Topic 2: IT Adoption and Usage

We identified 60 studies that mentioned gender or sex in the context of IT adoption and use. Most studies in this category were comparative studies of beliefs and IT adoption behaviors of men and women – with the exception of two that focused only on women's IT usage (Ingram & Parker 2002; Parmar et al. 2009). Most studies had balanced numbers of men and women – with the average ratio of women being 46%.

The majority of studies on this topic are positivist, hypothesis testing studies. Just 8% of studies were non-positivist, with these equally divided among interpretive studies (Saunders et al. 2009; Wilson 2002) and critical theory (Wilson 2004; Richardson 2009). We classified the other 92% of these studies as positivist, even if the authors did not explicitly state their epistemological orientation, because they tested hypotheses related to gender.

In terms of the authors' espoused gender theory, we were unable to classify most papers (at least 70%) as either essentialist, social constructivist, critical theory, etc. While some authors appear to suggest an essentialist belief that any observed differences between men and women are innate, we left these studies "unclassified" unless the authors specifically state that men and women differ in their IT beliefs or values due to innate biological factors. In contrast to the dominance of such papers with an "unclassified" espoused theory of gender, we identified 15% of studies as having a social constructivist view of gender. In these cases, the authors either used this exact phrase or implied that socialization was responsible for observed differences between men and women (Adam 2002; Hu, Al-Gahtani, & Hu, 2005; Ingram & Parker 2002; Shen, Lee, et al 2010). We labeled as social constructivist any papers that were theoretically grounded in sociology (e.g., sociolinguistics, Hwang 2010).

Among the 60 studies of IT usage, we did not find any papers that used Trauth's (2002) individual differences theory of gender (although for "IT Careers & Education," described below, we found many such studies).

Topic 3: IT Careers & Education

We found 75 papers corresponding to this topic alone, and these papers clustered into different subtopics – with each paper matching one or more of the subtopics. The subtopics are: (a) studies of college students' beliefs about IT careers, experiences with IT-related courses and the decision regarding a college major; (b) similar studies of pre-university students in middle or secondary school; (c) studies of IS and computer science (CS) faculty experiences and measures of scholarly output; and (d) studies of IT employees with regard to their job experiences and outcomes. While we sought to assign each of the 75 papers to one of these subtopics (based on which themes were dominant), some studies matched two or more subtopics, given the diversity of respondents participating in the study (e.g., students of various ages) or breadth of topics.

Table 4 – Studies about IT Adoption and Usage		
Author Names	**Year**	**Publication Outlet**
Ahuja & Thatcher	2005	MIS Quarterly
Baker, Al-Gahtani & Hubora	2007	IT & People
Bandyberry, Li & Lin	2010	AMCIS conference
Burnett, Beckwith, et al	2011	Interacting with Computers
Chai, Bagchi, Morrell, Rao & Upadhyaya	2009	IEEE Transactions on Prof. Communications
Chan, Gong, Xu &Thong	2008	PACIS conference
Djamasbi & Loiacono	2008	Decision Support System
Dutt & Srite	2005	AMCIS conference
Fedorowicz, Vilvovsky & Golibersuch	2010	Communications of the AIS
Gefen & Straub	1997	MIS Quarterly
Goss & Gupta	2003	Communications of ACM
Guo, Tan, Turner & Xu	2008	IEEE Transactions on Prof. Communication
Hartzel	2003	Communications of ACM
He & Freeman	2009	AMCIS conference
Ho, Lui & Ma	2003	International J. IT & D-M
Hope & Li	2003	ACIS conference
Hu, Al-Gahtani &Hu	2010	PACIS conference
Hu, Zhang, Zhang & Dai	2009	AMCIS conference
Hwang	2010	AMCIS conference
Ilie, Slyke, Green & Lou	2005	IRMJ
Kefi, Mlaiki & Kalika	2010	AMCIS conference
Kim & Han	2009	Journal of IT
Laosethakul & Bartczak	2001	AMCIS conference
Lind	2000	AMCIS conference
Maldifassi & Canessa	2009	Technology in Society
Middleton & Chambers	2010	IT & People
Morris, Venkatesh & Ackerman	2005	IEEE Transactions on Engineering Management
Parmar, Keyson & Bont	2009	Communications of AIS
Phang, Kankanhalli & Raman	2010	European Journal of IS
Powell & Johnson	1995	Decision Support System
Ranganathan, Seo & Babad	2006	European Journal of IS
Richards, Busch, et al.	2010	ACIS conference
Richardson	2009	IT & People
Saunders, Brown, Sipior, Zhang, Zigurs, et al.	2009	ECIS conference
Shade	1998	Information Society
Shen, Lee, Cheung & Chen	2010	Journal of IT
Simon	2001	Database for Advances in IS
Slyke, Belaner, Johnson	2010	Communications of AIS
& Hightower		
Slyke, Communale & Belanger	2002	Communications of ACM
Stenstrom, Stenstrom, Saad & Cheikhrouhou	2008	IEEE Transactions on Prof. Communication
Taylor	2004	European Journal of IS
Tong & Klecun	2004	IEEE TPC
Venkatesh & Morris	2000	MIS Quarterly
Wilson	2004	Journal of IT
Wilson	2002	IT & People
Zhang, Cheung, Lee, Chen	2008	AMCIS conference
Zhang, Lee, Cheung & Chen	2009	Decision Support System

4.1.1 Studies of college students' beliefs about IT careers and related IT curricula

We counted 27 studies of university students' attitudes and experiences with IT-related courses and their choice of college majors and careers. Bibliographical details for these studies appear in Table 5A. All 27 studies were quantitative, comparative analyses of men and women. Some of the comparative studies were atheoretical – again, with some of them appearing in Communications of the ACM (Cohoon 2001; Goss & Gupta 2010; Othman & Latih 2006). Some of these studies justified their focus on analyzing differences between men and women based on prior results, without offering any theoretical rationale for differences between men and women.

4.1.2 Studies of pre-university students' beliefs about IT careers and related IT curricula

We found five studies that solely or mostly focused on secondary students' attitudes to IT careers, as shown in Table 5B. With the exception of two studies focusing on high school girls only (Clayton et al. 2012; Dlodlo 2009), these studies compared attitudes of secondary school students based on sex. Of these studies in Table 5B, two are quantitative (Clayton, et al. 2012; Creamer & Meszaros, 2009), two are qualitative (Lang, 2012; Dlodlo, 2009), and one employed a mix of both sets of methods (Von Hellens, Nielsen, Greenhill & Pringle, 1997).

4.1.3 Studies of IS and Computer Science (CS) faculty experiences and outcomes

We found 9 studies that examined gender issues as related to IS and/or CS faculty. Seven of these were empirical studies – with there studies analyzing secondary data about male and female IS scholars (e.g., Cohoon, Nigai & Kaye 2011; Gallivan & Benbunan-Fich 2007; Kimery et all 2003), and three others that collected qualitative data through interviews (Cohoon 2001; Dlodlo 2009; Robertson et al. 2001). One conceptual paper reviewed prior work examining outcomes for men and women in other business disciplines (Gallivan & Benbunan-Fich 2008). By contrast, these authors show that such studies are lacking in IS.

4.1.4 Studies of IT Employees' Job Experiences

We identified nearly 50 studies of IT employees and/or managers, shown in Table 5D. Some papers are conceptual (Ahuja 2002; Cukier et al 2003; Tapia & Kvasny 2003; Von Hellens & Nielsen 2001), but over 90% of studies on this topic are empirical. Of the empirical studies, 60% are comparative studies of men and women in IT jobs; the other 40% analyzed the job experiences of women only (noted by * in Table 5D).

Table 5A – Studies about IT Careers and Education with University Students as Respondents

Author Names	Year	Publication Outlet
Akbulut-Bailey	2009	Communications of AIS
Baumann, Hambrusch & Neville	2011	Communications of ACM
Beyer, DeKeuster, Rynes & DeHeer	2004	AMCIS conference
Cohoon	2001	Communications of ACM
Creamer & Meszaros	2009	AMCIS conference
Croasdell, McLeod & Simkin	2011	IT & People
Cukier & Chauncey	2004	AMCIS conference
Gillard, Mitev & Scott	2007	Information Society
Guzman & Stanton	2009	IT & People
Harris & Wilkinson	2004	IT & People
Heinze & Hu	2009	European Journal of IS
Hersh	2000	IEEE Transactions on Engineering Management
Iyer, Chow, Zhao & Tate	2011	ICIS conference
Joshi & Schmidt	2006	Database for Advances in IS
Kizito	2011	Journal of Emerging Trends
Kuhn & Joshi	2009	Database for Advances in IS
Kulturel & Trauth	2012	AMCIS conference
Lang, Meyer, Niner, McKay & Lewis	2009	Communications of AIS
McDowell, Werner, Bullock & Fernald	2006	Communications of ACM
Nielsen, Von Hellens, Greenhill & Pringle	1998	SIG CPR
Othman & Latih	2006	Communications of AIS
Roberts, McGill & Hyland	2011	ACIS conference
Saifuddin, Dyke & Rasouli	2011	AMCIS conference
Sims, Vidgen & Powell	2008	Communications of AIS
Trauth, Cain, Joshi, Kvasny & Booth	2012	SIGMIS-CPR
Trauth, Joshi, Chong, Kulturel & Mahar	2010	AMCIS conference
Warrer, Young et al.	2012	AMCIS conference

4.1.5 Studies of IT Employees' Job Experiences

We identified nearly 50 studies of IT employees and/or managers, shown in Table 5D. Some papers are conceptual (Ahuja 2002; Cukier et al 2003; Tapia & Kvasny 2003; Von Hellens & Nielsen 2001), but over 90% of studies on this topic are empirical. Of the empirical studies, 60% are comparative studies of men and women in IT jobs; the other 40% analyzed the job experiences of women only (noted by * in Table 5D).

Table 5B – Studies about IT Careers & Education with Secondary Students as Respondents

Author Names	Year	Publication Outlet
Clayton, Beekhuyzen & Nielsen*	2012	Information Systems Journal
Creamer & Meszaros	2009	AMCIS conference
Dlodlo*	2009	Technology in Society
Hellens, Nielsen, Greenhill & Pringle	1997	PACIS conference
Lang	2012	IT & People

Table 5C – Studies about IT Careers and Achievements focusing on University Faculty

Author Names	Year	Publication Outlet
Cohoon	2001	Communications of ACM
Cohoon, Nigai & Kaye	2011	Communications of ACM
Dlodlo*	2009	Technology in Society
Gallivan & Benbunan-Fich	2006	SIG MIS conference
Gallivan & Benbunan-Fich	2007	IT & People
Gallivan & Benbunan-Fich	2008	IT & People
Kimery, Rinehart & Mellon	2003	AMCIS conference
Lamp	2007	Communications of AIS
Robertson, Newell, Swan, Mathiassen, Bjerknes	2001	Information Systems Journal

Table 5D – Studies about IT Careers and Education with IT Employees as Respondents

Author Names	Year	Publication Outlet
Adam, Griffiths, Keogh, Moore, Richardson & Tattersall*	2006	European Journal of IS
Ahuja [conceptual]	2002	European Journal of IS
Armstrong, Reid, Riemenschneider et al.	2011	AMCIS conference
Armstrong, Riemenschneider, Allen & Reid*	2007	Information & Management
Caputo & Morris	2010	International Journal of MIS
Coder, Rosenbloom, Ash & Dupont	2009	Communications of ACM
Cukier, Shortt & Devine [conceptual]	2002	Journal of IS Education
Dattero & Galup	2004	Communications of AIS
Dlodlo*	2009	Technology in Society
Guthrie, Soe, Yakura*	2009	AMCIS conference

Hersh	2000	IEEE Transactions on Engineering Management
Igbaria & Baroudi	1995	MIS Quarterly
Igbaria & Chidambaram	1997	IT & People
Joshi & Kuhn	2007	IT & People
Karr, Carroll & Lipford	2001	AMCIS conference
Khreisat	2009	Technology in Society
Kowtha	2008	IEEE Transactions on Engineering Management
Kvasny*	2003	ACM SIG MIS/CPR
Kvasny*	2006	Data Base for Advances in IS
Mbarika, Payton, Kvasny, & Amadi	2007	Information Society
McKinney, Wilson, Brook, Kelly & Hardgrave	2008	Communications of AIS
Morgan, Quesenberry & Trauth*	2004	AMCIS conference
Nielsen, von Hellens & Beekhuyzen	2004	ECIS conference
Okpara	2004	IT & People
O'Neill &Walker	2001	ECIS conference
Panteli	2012	Information Systems Journal
Panteli, Atkinson & Ramsay	1999	European Journal of IS
Quesenberry & Trauth*	2012	Information Systems Journal
Reid, Allen, Armstrong & Riemenschneider	2010	European Journal of IS
Richards, Busch & Venkitachalam	2010	ACIS conference
Riemenschneider, Armstrong, Allen & Reid*	2006	Data Base for Advances in IS
Timms, Lankshear, Anderson & Courtney*	2008	IT & People
Tapia & Kvasny	2004	SIG MIS/CPR
Tokunaga & Graham	1996	IEEE Transactions on Engineering Management
Trauth*	2002	IT & People
Trauth & Howcroft*	2006	IT & People
Trauth & Quesenberry*	2006	ICIS conference
Trauth, Quesenberry & Benjamin*	2008	Data Base for Advances in IS
Trauth, Quesenberry & Huang*	2009	European Journal of IS
Trauth, Quesenberry & Morgan*	2004	SIG MIS/CPR
Truman & Baroudi	1994	MIS Quarterly
Von Hellens & Nielsen [conceptual]	2001	Communications of ACM
Von Hellens, Pringle, Nielsen, Greenhill*	2000	AMCIS conference
Woodfield	2002	IT & People

In terms of authors' epistemological stance, 50% of the papers are interpretive; 43% are positivist, and just 6% were

critical research. The two critical papers (Adam, Griffiths et al 2006; Howcroft & Trauth 2008) seek to change the status quo, in terms of offering IT managers, teachers, and parents thought-provoking suggestions for modifying IT job attributes. Studies of IT employees reflect a greater balance between positivist and interpretive papers, compared to the other topics we reviewed above – where positivist studies dominated. In this set of papers on IT employees' career experiences, we also found greater balance regarding authors' espoused theory of gender. Unlike the previous topics– where "unclassified" papers dominated (i.e., where there was insufficient data to identify the authors' perspective), here we found a high ratio of papers that espouse a social constructivist perspective on gender or that subscribe to Trauth's (2002) individual differences theory of gender (with eight papers coauthored by Eileen Trauth and her colleagues).

A few studies either combined multiple espoused views of gender – such as one reflecting a blend of social constructivism and the individual differences theory of gender (Adya & Kaiser 2005), and one introducing standpoint theory to IS researchers (Kvasny 2006). Despite the greater balance among different espoused theories of gender, we still labeled several papers as "unclassified" – either because they were purely atheoretical (e.g., Coder, et al 2009) or because the theory and hypotheses included were focused on another phenomenon (i.e., antecedents to job satisfaction or job turnover, rather than an explanation of the source of gender differences).

As with the other topics, we found that authors interpreted their empirical results in terms of their espoused theory of gender. Authors who regard men and women as innately different tend to interpret any observed differences in beliefs or behavior as unchangeable, whereas those who regard such differences as resulting from social conditioning or life experiences likewise emphasize the importance of these factors in explaining results.

Relative to other topics that we reviewed above, the papers corresponding to this topic exhibited huge geographic diversity. While there were many studies of U.S. employees, at least 24 studies featured IS employees or managers in other countries. We identified three studies that combined respondents from multiple countries – Australia, Ireland and U.S. (Trauth 2002), Denmark, Sweden and the UK (Robertson et al., 1997), or a diverse set of 26 countries in Europe, Asia, and the Americas (Hersh 2000).

Topic 4: Attitudes toward Telework

The last topic was employees' attitudes and experiences regarding telework or working in virtual teams. Of the 18 papers belonging to this topic, three are conceptual (Greenhill & Wilson 2006; Wilson & Greenhill 2004; Wilson & Greenhill 2005) but most (11 papers) were quantitative studies; two were qualitative, empirical studies (Ocker 2007; McDonough 1999), and one combined qualitative and quantitative methods (Belanger 1999).

Nearly all of the empirical studies used student subjects – with six exceptions where the authors studied employees in business (Belanger 1999; Iscan & Naktiyok 2005; McCloskey, et al. 1998; Mokhtarian & Bagley 2000; Schiller et al. 2011) or members of online communities (Gefen & Ridings 2005). The majority of empirical studies are comparative (comparing beliefs and experiences of men vs. women regarding telework or their experiences with virtual teams). None of the empirical studies focused exclusively on women; however, three conceptual papers were focused on the implications of what the authors label "at home telework" for women specifically (Greenhill & Wilson 2006; Wilson & Greenhill 2004; Wilson & Greenhill 2005).

Table 6 – Studies about Telework		
Author Names	**Year**	**Publication Outlet**
Armstrong-Stassen, Landstrom & Lumpkin	2005	Information Society
Belanger	1999	Information & Management
Belanger	1999	IEEE Transactions on Prof. Communication
DeWester, Hah, Gervais & Siau	2009	AMCIS conference
Gefen & Ridings	2005	SIGMIS Database
Greenhill & Wilson	2006	European Journal of IS
Guthrie & Pick	1998	Journal of End User Computing
Iscan & Naktiyok	2005	Journal of IT
Lind & White	1998	AMCIS conference
Lind	1999	IEEE Transactions on Prof. Communication
McCloskey, et al.	1998	Journal of End User Computing
McDonough	1999	Decision Support System
Mokhtarian & Bagley	2000	Journal of American Society for Info. Science
Ocker	2007	IEEE Transactions on Prof. Communication
Pillis & Furumo	2007	Communications of ACM
Schiller et al.	2011	ICIS conference
Wilson & Greenhill	2004	ECIS Conference
Wilson & Greenhill	2005	ECIS Conference

Of the 18 papers, half the authors did not state an espoused gender theory; however, of those who did, most authors espoused social constructivism (Lind 1999; Pillis & Furumo 2007; Schiller et al 2011; Wilson & Greenhill 2004). Two papers adopted a critical Marxist view that women are oppressed by "at home" telework (Greenhill & Wilson 2006; Wilson & Greenhill 2005).

5. DISCUSSION

In this section, we draw general conclusions about the various analyses that we described above. We first offer some observations about the topic categories that we identified. The four topic categories are ones that we identified a priori – before searching the existing literature, rather than ones that emerged bottom up (however, the subcategories within "IT Careers and Education" emerged in a grounded fashion). While it was straightforward to assign most papers to one of the four subject categories, occasionally some papers spanned more than one category. This was the case for one conceptual review paper that dealt with "IT Careers and Education" as well as "IT Adoption and Use" (Adam, Howcroft & Richardson, 2004). With the exception of this broad conceptual paper, we found it fairly easy to assign papers to the four topics.

It is not surprising that, in an effort to reduce to set of papers to specific topic categories, some papers failed to match these categories. Indeed, a few papers did not correspond to any of the four topic areas – although the authors of such studies were clearly focused on gender issues in the context of IT use or use of information (Table 7). Such papers represent less than 4% of all the studies we identified.

A second general finding was the dominance of the term "gender" and the dearth of the word "sex" (or sexes) for referring to men and women. The word "gender" dominated by a ratio of more than 20:1. While this may not be surprising to those who are accustomed to reading academic literature that espouses a social constructivist perspective (for which the term "gender" is indeed appropriate), the dominance of the term "gender" was a surprising result in papers whose authors espouse an essentialist view that men and women are inherently different – or in papers whose authors neglect to articulate their espoused theory of gender. We found just four papers where the authors showed a clear preference for using the word "sex" rather than "gender" to refer to women and men (Hersh, 2000; Jørgensen & Grimstad, 2012; McLean et al. 1993; Ocker, 2007). Even papers where the authors clearly hold essentialist (biologically-based) beliefs about sex differences still show a preference for the word "gender" over "sex." We consider this an unusual result – one reflecting an apparent contradiction in terms: the word "gender" denotes a social constructivist view of how men and women are socialized to think and behave, rather than a view of innate differences rooted in biology. The fact that essentialist authors prefer the word "gender" rather than "sex" bears further analysis, given the definition of gender offered by Laura Kramer, author of *The Sociology of Gender* (2005, p. 2):

> Gender is … the totality of meanings that are attached to the sexes within a particular social system. More broadly, the gender system is a system of meaning and differentiation, linked to the sexes through social arrangements…We use sexes to refer to the categories that most contemporary societies define as physically based [in biology] ….

A third finding is that the concept of "gender" was only associated with women in the majority of studies we reviewed. In fact, most authors assumed that men lacked gender – in short, that being male was the norm, and that gender issues should only arise when women are introduced into the equation. For example, a study focused on information and exercise behavior of young men neglected to mention gender (Hirvonen et al. 2012), whereas many studies focusing just on women featured gender as a key concept. With the exception of one study that analyzed general beliefs regarding various IT skills as gendered (e.g., Trauth, Joshi et al. 2010) and two papers that feature gender as a central construct in an empirical study of an online community for gay men (Light 2007; Light et al. 2008), there is a pervasive assumption that gender is a relevant topic only when women are included as respondents. As a result, studies of men alone – or studies of jobs where men dominate (like IT jobs) – are regarded as irrelevant to gender. This assumption should be challenged – especially as the ratio of women in the IT industry has declined in the past decade to pre-1990 levels (von Hellens et al. 2012).

A final issue is that nearly 10% of the papers we retrieved from our searches were ones in which gender or sex differences was tangential to the main topic. In other words, despite the fact that the paper specifically mentioned gender or other specific term (e.g., sex, men, women) in its abstract or keywords – gender or sex differences were not mentioned in such studies. We created a typology to identify four reasons why such papers appeared in our search results. While some scholars might consider such studies to represent "errors of inclusion" (Benbasat & Zmud 2003) – meaning studies that do not belong in the search results; on the contrary, we believe that useful insights can be gained through such a typology that identifies each cluster of papers that were unrelated to the topic of gender or sex differences.

Low importance "Type 1" studies: Some papers do mention one or more of the key terms that we searched in their paper's abstract or keywords; however, the topic of gender or sex differences was irrelevant or only tangential to their study. One such paper mentioned gender differences in its abstract, yet the authors focused on non-gender aspects of the digital divide but without any gender analysis (Sims, Vidgen & Powell 2008).

Low importance "Type 2" studies: This category refers to papers where the authors mention one of the key terms in their paper's abstract, but where they did not hypothesize any sex-based differences in their study. Despite this fact, the authors conducted some (presumably exploratory) analysis of sex-based differences, which they then report in their results section and also mention in their abstract. These papers likely correspond to the category of pre-theoretical research (Quesenberry & Trauth 2006). There were various reasons why authors might have conducted comparative analyses for men and women, despite lacking any a priori hypothesis about their expectation for such differences: (a) there are no hypotheses in the paper at all; instead the authors collect analyze data without including a priori theory of any sort (Jorgensen & Grimstad 2012; Ocker 2007); or (b) some hypotheses existed in the study – but not with regard to anticipating any differences between men and women. Despite the absence of hypotheses, the authors of "Type 2" studies found sex differences in their data, which they considered important to mention in thr abstract (Heinze & Hu 2005; Kim & Han 2009).

Low importance "Type 3" studies: This was the largest group of papers: ones where the authors do mention one or more key terms that we searched for in their paper's abstract, and they do propose one or more hypotheses that anticipate sex-based differences. The authors do not specify what direction such gender difference will take. For instance, while they state that men and women will differ in terms of one or more constructs, the authors fail to articulate whether they expect women, as a group, to score higher or lower on the construct than men (Gattiker & Kelley 1999; Middleton & Chambers 2010; Masrom & Ismail 2008; Moores & Chang 2006; Okpara 2004; Phang et al. 2010; Saunders, Brown et al 2009; Warren et al. 2012). Since the authors state only that they expect to find some difference between men and women – but not a particular direction of difference – such studies seem to be "fishing" for results.

Low importance "Type 4" studies: In these studies, the authors do hypothesize about gender differences, however, their only reason for positing such differences is by citing prior research – rather than a theory that might account for such differences (Chan, Gong, Xu & Thong 2008; Ranganathan, Seo & Babad 2006; Skerlavaj, Dimovski & Desouza 2010). These papers also correspond to the category of pre-theoretical research (Quesenberry & Trauth 2006).

6. CONCLUSION

We provide a structured, descriptive review of the literature on gender and IS, identifying and classifying over 190 papers on this topic. Of course, there are some limitations of our study – namely that we have not sought to identify every paper published in every possible venue on this topic. While there may be other outlets – such as conferences in the IS field or non-IS journals (such as sociology, psychology, or management journals), we limited our search to 35 IS journals and 6 leading conferences. We intentionally excluded some IS conferences that lack a central search function – such as IFIP 8.2. We plan to perform further analyses – such as identifying the journal or conference outlets that publish the most studies that lack a clear statement of the authors' espoused theory of gender. Perhaps by drawing attention to such a lack of theoretical clarity, it may be possible to change editorial practices so that authors will be required to articulate their view of gender – describing what factors and forces (biological, institutional, social, etc.) lead to observed differences in the beliefs and behaviors of men and women regarding IT. We hope to continue in this line of work and ultimately, to draw attention to the need for researchers to provide theoretical clarity regarding their espoused theory of gender – regardless of whether authors hold views of gender that are currently popular or out-of-favor in other fields of study.

7. ACKNOWLEDGMENTS

Enormous thanks are due to Tianyi Zhang, research assistant and masters student in professional accountancy (MPA) at Georgia State University for her help with collecting and analyzing data.

8. REFERENCES

[1] Adam, A. "Computer ethics in a different voice," Information and Organization, 2001, 235-261.

[2] Adam, A. "Exploring the gender question in critical IS," Journal of Information Technology, 17, 2002, 59-67.

[3] Adam, A. and Amanfo, J.O. "Does gender matter in computer ethics?" Ethics & Information Technology, 2000, 37-47.

[4] Adam, A., Griffiths, M., Keogh, C., Moore, K., Richardson, H. and Tattersall, A. "Being an 'it' in IT: gendered identities in IT work," European Journal of Information Systems, 15, 2006, 366-378.

[5] Adam, A., Howcroft, D., and Richardson, H. "Guest Editorial: Special issue on gender and information systems," Information Technology & People, 15, 2002, 94-97.

[6] Adam, A., Howcroft, D. and Richardson, H. "A decade of neglect: reflecting on gender and IS," New Technology Work and Employment, 19, 2004, 222-240.

[7] Adya, M. and Kaiser, K. "Early determinants of women in the IT workforce: a model of girls' career choices," Information Technology & People, 18, 2005, 230-259.

[8] Ahuja, M. "Women in the IT profession," European Journal of Information Systems, 2002, 20-34.

[9] Argyris, C. and Schön, C. *Theory in Practice: Increasing Professional Effectiveness*, Jossey-Bass, 1974.

[10] Baroudi, J. and Igbaria, M. "Examination of gender effects on career success of IS employees," Journal of Management Information Systems, 11, 1994, 181-201.

[11] Belanger, F. "Workers' Propensity to telecommute," Information & Management, 35, 1999, 139-153.

[12] Benbasat, I. and Zmud, R. "The identity crisis within the IS discipline," MIS Quarterly, 27, 2003.

[13] Chan, K.Y., Gong, M., Xu, Y., and Thong, J.Y. "Examining user acceptance of SMS: an empirical study in China and Hong Kong," Proceedings of PACIS conference, 2008.

[14] Clayton, Beekhuyzen, J. and Nielsen, S. "Now I know what ICT can do for me!," Information Systems Journal, 22, 2012, 375-390.

[15] Coder, L., Rosenbloom, J., Ash, R., et al. "Economic and business dimensions increasing gender diversity in the IT work force," Communications of the ACM, 52, 2009, 25-27.

[16] Cohoon, J.M. "Toward improving female retention in the computer science major," Communications of the ACM, 44, 2001, 108-114.

[17] Cohoon, J.M, Nigai, S. and Kaye, J. "Gender and computing conference papers: women increasingly publish in ACM conference proceedings," Communications of the ACM, 54, 2011, 72-80.

[18] Creamer, E. and Meszaros, P. "Gender differences in factors that promote an interest in IT among high school and early and late college students," Proceedings of AMCIS conference, 2009.

[19] Cronan, T.P. Foltz, C. and Jones, T.W. "Piracy, computer crime and IS misuse at the university," Communications of the ACM, 49, 2006 84-90.

[20] Crook, C., Crepeau, R.G. and McMurtrey, M. "Utilization of the career anchor/career orientation constructs for management of IS professionals," Computer Personnel, 1991, 12-23

[21] Cukier, W., Shortt, D. and Devine, I. "Gender and IT: implications of definitions," Journal of IS Education, 13(1), 2003, 7-15.

[22] Dlodlo, M. "Access to ICT education for girls and women in rural South Africa," Technology in Society, 31(2), 2009, 168-175.

[23] Gallivan, M. and Benbunan-Fich, R. "Analyzing IS research productivity: an inclusive approach to global IS scholarship," European Journal of Information Systems, 16, 2007, 36–53.

[24] Gallivan, M. and Benbunan-Fich, R. "Exploring the relationship between gender and career outcomes for social scientists," Information Technology & People, 21, 2008, 178-204.

[25] Gattiker, U. and Kelley, H. "Morality and computers: attitudes and differences in moral judgments," Information Systems Research, 10, 1999, 233-254.

[26] Gefen, D and Ridings, C.M. "If you spoke as she does, sir, instead of the way you do: a sociolinguistics perspective of gender differences in virtual communities," database for advances in information systems, 36, 2005, 78-92.

[27] Gillard, H., Mitev, N., and Scott, S. "ICT inclusion and gender: tensions in narratives of network engineer training," Information Society, 23, 2007, 19-37.

[28] Gopal, R.D. and Sanders, G.L. "Preventive and deterrent controls for software piracy," Journal of Management Information, 14, 1997, 29-47.

[29] Goss, E. and Gupta, U. "Women and the Internet: is there an economic payoff?," Communications of the ACM, 46(9), 2003, 160-166.

[30] Guzman, I., Gallivan, M., Cohoon, J., Stanton, J., Bell, A., Quesenberry, J., Creamer, E. Adya, M., et al., "What Are we doing to improve recruitment and retention in IT majors?," Proceedings of 2008 ACM SIG MIS, 40-42.

[31] Heinze, N. and Hu, Q. "Why college undergraduates choose it: a multi-theoretical perspective," European Journal of Information Systems, 18, 2009, 18, 462-475.

[32] Hersh, M. "The changing position of women in engineering worldwide," IEEE Transactions on Engineering Management, 47(3), 2000, 345-359.

[33] Hirvonen, N., Huotari, M., Niemelä, R., and Korpelainen, R., "Information behavior in stages of exercise behavior change," Journal of the American Society for Information Science & Technology; 63, 2012, 1804-1819.

[34] Howcroft, D. and Trauth, E.M. "The implications of a critical agenda in gender and IS research," Information Systems Journal, 18, 2008, 185-202.

[35] Hu, S., Al-Gahtani, S.S., and Hu, P.J. "Examining gender effects in technology acceptance by Arabian workers," Proceedings of PACIS Conference, 2010, paper 76.

[36] Hwang, Y. "An Empirical investigation of normative, affective and gender influence on e-commerce systems adoption," AMCIS Conference 2010, paper 37.

[37] Ingram, S. and Parker, A. "The influence of gender on collaborative projects in an engineering classroom," IEEE Transactions on Professional Communication, 45, 2002, 7-20.

[38] Iscan, O. and Naktiyok, A. "Attitudes towards telecommuting: the Turkish case," Journal of Information Technology, 20, 2005, 52–63.

[39] Jørgensen, M. and Grimstad, S., "Software development estimation biases: the role of interdependence," IEEE Transactions on Software Engineering, 38, 2012, 677-693.

[40] Khazanchi, D. "Unethical behavior in IS: the gender factor," Journal of Business Ethics, 14, 1995, 741-749.

[41] Kim, B. and Han, I. "What drives the adoption of mobile data services? an approach from a value perspective," Journal of Information Technology, 24, 2009, 35-45.

[42] King, W. and He, J. "Understanding the role and methods of meta-analysis in IS research," Communications of the Association for Information Systems, 16, 2005, 665-686.

[43] Kling, R. "More information, better jobs?: occupational stratification and labor-market segmentation in the U.S. information labor force," Information Society, 7, 1990, 77-107.

[44] Kolko, B. "Representing bodies in virtual space: the rhetoric of avatar design," Information Society, 1998, 177-186.

[45] Kramer, L. The Sociology of Gender: An Introduction (2nd ed.), New York: Roxbury Press, 2005.

[46] Kreie, J. and Cronan, T.P. "How men and women view ethics," Communications of the ACM, 1998, 70-76.

[47] Kuo, F., Lin, C. and Hsu, M. "Assessing gender differences in computer professionals' self-regulatory efficacy concerning information privacy practices," Journal of Business Ethics, 73, 2007, 145-160.

[48] Kvasny, L. and Richardson, H. "Critical research in information systems: looking forward, looking back," Information Technology & People, 19(3) (2006), 196-202.

[49] Kvasny, L. "Let the sisters speak: understanding information technology from the standpoint of the 'other'," Database for Advances in Information Systems, 37, 2006, 13-25.

[50] Lang, C. "Sequential attrition of secondary school student interest in IT courses and careers," Information Technology & People, 25, 2012, 281-299.

[51] Lending, D. and Slaughter, S. "The effects of ethical climate on attitudes and behaviors toward software piracy," Proceedings of 2001 SIG CPR Conference, 198-200.

[52] Light, B. "introducing masculinity studies to IS research: the case of Gaydar," European Journal of Information Systems, 16, 2007, 658-665.

[53] Light, B., Fletcher, G. and Adam, A. "Gay men, Gaydar and the commodification of difference," Information Technology & People, 21, 2008, 300-314.

[54] Lind, M.R. "The gender impact of temporary virtual work groups," IEEE Transactions on Professional Communication, 42, 1999, 276-285.

[55] Masrom, M. and Ismail, Z. "Computer ethics awareness among undergraduate students in Malaysian higher education institutions," Australasian Conference on Information Systems, 2008.

[56] Mbarika, V., Payton, F.C., Kvasny, L., and Amadi, A., "IT education and workforce participation: a new era for women in Kenya?," Information Society, 23, 2007, 1-18.

[57] McCarthy, R.V., Halavi, L., and Aronson, J. "Information technology ethics: a research framework," Issues in Information Systems, 6, 2005, 64-69.

[58] McCloskey, D. Igbaria, M. and Parasuraman, S. "The work experiences of professional men and women who telecommute," Journal of End User Computing, 10, 1998.

[59] McLean, E.R., Tanner, J.R. and Smits, S. "Self-perceptions and job preferences of entry-level IS professionals: implications for career development," Computer Personnel, 1991, 33-43.

[60] McLean, E.R., Bryan, N., Tanner, J.R. and Smits, S. "The structure of job attitudes among entry-level IS professionals," Proceedings of 1993 SIG CPR conference, Athens, GA., 27-36

[61] Middleton, K. and Chambers, V. "Approaching digital equity: is wi-fi the new leveler?," Information Technology & People, 23, 2010, 4-22.

[62] Mokhtarian, P.L. and Bagley, M. "The impact of gender, occupation and presence of children on telecommuting," Journal of American Society for Information Science, 49, 2000, 115-134.

[63] Moores, T.T. and Chang, J. "Ethical decision making in software piracy: initial development and test of a four-component model, MIS Quarterly, 30, 2006, 167-180.

[64] Ocker, R. "A Balancing Art: the interplay of status effects on dominance in virtual teams," IEEE Transactions on Professional Communication, 50, 2007, 204-218.

[65] Olerup, A., Schneider, L., and Monod, E.Z. Women, work & computerization: opportunities and disadvantages, Proceedings of 1st Working Conference on Women, Work and Computerization, North-Holland, 1984.

[66] Othman, M. and Latih, R. "Women in computer science: no shortage here!," Communications of the ACM, 49(3), 2006, 111-114.

[67] Parmar, V., Keyson, D. and Bont, C. "Persuasive technology to shape social beliefs: a case of health IS for rural women in India," Communications of the AIS, 24, 2009.

[68] Phang, C.W., Kankanhalli, A., Ramakrishnan, K. and Raman, K. "Customers' preference of online store visit strategies," European Journal of Information Systems, 19, 2010, 344-358.

[69] Pillis, E. and Furumo, L. "Counting the cost of virtual teams," Communications of the ACM, 50, 2007, 93-95.

[70] Ranganathan, C., Seo, D. and Babad, Y. "Switching behavior of mobile users: do users' relational investments and demographics matter?," European Journal of Information Systems, 2006, 269-276.

[71] Reinen, I.J. and Plomp, T. "Information technology and gender equality: a contradiction in terminis?," Computers & Education, 28, 1997, 65-78.

[72] Richardson, H. "Taking a feminist approach to IS research and using the 'thinking tools' provided by sociologist Pierre Bourdieu," Information Technology & People, 2009, 26-35.

[73] Ridley, G. and Young, J. "Theoretical approaches to gender and it: examining some Australian evidence," Information Systems Journal, 22, 2012, 355-373.

[74] Robertson, M., Newell, S., Swan, J., Mathiassen, L. and Bjerknes, G. "The Issue of gender in computing: reflections from the UK and Scandinavia," Information Systems Journal, 11, 2001, 111-126.

[75] Saunders, C., Brown, S., Sipior, J., Zhang, X., Zigurs, I. and Loebbecke, C. "Gender and website design across cultures," Proceedings of ECIS conference, 2009, 171.

[76] Schiller, S., Nah, F., Mennecke, B. and Siau, K. "Gender differences in virtual collaboration on a creative design task," Proceedings of ICIS Conference, 2011, paper 12.

[77] Shen, A.X., Lee, M.K., Cheung, C. and Chen, H. "Gender differences in intentional social action: we-intention to engage in social network-facilitated team collaboration," Journal of Information Technology, 25, 2010, 152-169.

[78] Sims, J., Vidgen, R. and Powell, P. "E-learning and the digital divide: perpetuating cultural and socio-economic elitism in higher education," Communications of AIS, 22, 2008.

[79] Škerlavaj, M., Dimovski , V. and Desouza, K.C. "Patterns and structures of intra-organizational learning networks within a knowledge-intensive organization," Journal of Information Technology, 25, 2010, 189-204.

[80] Tan, M. and Igbaria, M. "Exploring the status of turnover and salary of it professionals in Singapore," Proceedings of 1993 ACM SIG CPR Conference, Athens, GA., 336-348.

[81] Tapia, A. and Kvasny, L. "Recruitment is never enough: retention of women and minorities in the IT workplace," Proceedings of 2003 SIG MIS/CPR Conference, 84-91.

[82] Trauth, E.M. "Odd girl out: an individual differences perspective on women in the IT profession," Information Technology & People, 15, 2002, 98-118.

[83] Trauth, E.M., Adya, M., Armstrong, D., Joshi, K.D., Kvasny, L., Riemenschneider, C. and Quesenberry, J. "Taking stock of research on gender and the IT workforce," Proceedings of 2010 SIG MIS Conference, Vancouver, British Columbia, 2010, 171-178.

[84] Trauth, E.M., Cain, C., Joshi, K.D., Kvasny, L. and Booth, K. "Understanding underrepresentation in IT through intersectionality," Proceedings of the 2012 SIG MIS Conference, Milwaukee, 56-62.

[85] Trauth, E.M. and Howcroft, D. "Critical empirical research in is: an example of gender and the IT workforce," Information Technology & People, 19, 2006, 272-292.

[86] Trauth, E.M., Joshi, K., Kvasny, L., Chong, J., Kulturel, S. and Mahar, J. "Millennials and masculinity: shifting tide of gender typing of ICT," Proceedings of AMCIS, 2010.

[87] Trauth, E.M. and Quesenberry, J. "Are women an underserved community in the IT profession?," Proceedings of International Conference on Information Systems, 2006, 1757-1770.

[88] Truman, G. and Baroudi, J.J. "Gender differences in the IS managerial ranks: an assessment of potential discriminatory practices," MIS Quarterly, 18, 1984, 129-150.

[89] Venkatesh, V. and Morris, M. "why don't men ever stop to ask for directions? gender, social influence and their role in technology acceptance and usage," MIS Quarterly, 24, 2000, 115-139.

[90] Volman, M. and van Eck, E. "Gender equity and information technology in education: the second decade," Review of Educational Research, 7, 2001, 613-634.

[91] Von Hellens and Nielsen, S. "Australian women in IT," Communications of the ACM, 2001, 46-52.

[92] Von Hellens, L., Trauth, E. and Fisher, J. "Editorial," Information Systems Journal, 2012, 343-353.

[93] Warren, J., Young, D. and Williams, K. "Personality, gender and careers in IT," Proceedings of AMCIS, 2012.

[94] Webster, J. and Watson, R.T. "Analyzing the past to prepare for the future," MIS Quarterly, 26, 2002, viii-xxiii.

[95] Westfall, R. "What is cyber-woman? the second sex in cyberspace," Ethics & Information Technology, 2, 2000, 159-166.

[96] Whitley, B.E. "Gender differences in computer-related attitudes and behavior," Computers in Human Behavior, 13, 1997, 1-22.

[97] Wilson, M. "Making nursing visible? gender, technology and the care plan as script," Information Technology & People, 15, 2002, 139-158.

[98] Wilson, M. "A conceptual framework for studying gender in IS research," Journal of Information Technology, 19, 2004, 81-92.

[99] Young, K.S. and Case, C.J. "Computer ethics: gender effects and employee Internet misuse," Issues in Information Systems, 10, 2009 598-603.

Table 7 – Papers That Do Not Correspond to Available Topic Categories			
Authors	**Year**	**Publication Outlet**	**General Topic**
Adam	2002	Journal of IT	Feminist epistemology
Howcroft & Trauth	2008	Information Systems Journal	A critical agenda for gender and IS research
Ingram & Parker	2002	IEEE Transactions on Prof. Communication	Influence of gender on collaborative projects
Jorgensen & Grimstad	2012	IEEE Transactions Software Engineering	Estimation biases in planning software development tasks
Kolko	1998	Information Society	Gendered nature of avatar design
Lim, Teo & Chin	2008	Communications of ACM	Cyber incivility in the workplace
Ridley & Young	2012	Information Systems Journal	Analysis of IT job skills specified in Australian classified advertising
Shachaf, Oltmann & Horowitz	2008	Journal of American Society for Info. Science & Technology	Service equality for men and women when using virtual reference services
Skerlavaj, Dimovski & Desouza	2010	Journal of IT	Knowledge-sharing via social networks within organizations

APPPENDIX 1: Journals Included in Literature Search

Accounting Management & Information Technology
Behavior & Information Technology
Communications of the ACM
Communications of the Association for IS
Database for Advances in Information Systems
Decision Sciences
Decision Support Systems
Ethics and Information Technology
European Journal of Information Systems
IEEE Transactions on Engineering Management
IEEE Transactions on Professional Communication
IEEE Transactions on Software Engineering
Information & Management
Information & Software Technology
Information and Organization
Information Resources Management Journal
Information Society
Information Systems Journal
Information Systems Research
Information Technology & People
Interacting with Computers
International Journal of Information Management
International Journal of IT & Decision Making
International Journal of Management & Info. Systems
Issue in Information Systems
Journal of American Society for Information Science
Journal of the Association for Information Systems
Journal of Business Ethics
Journal of Emerging Trends in Computing & I.S.
Journal of Information Systems Education
Journal of Information Technology
Journal of Management Information Systems
Journal of Organization and End User Computing
Journal of Systems & Software
MIS Quarterly
Technology in Society

APPPENDIX 2: Conferences Included in Literature Search

ACM Special Interest Group on Computer Personnel Research (SIG CPR) (pre-2004)
ACM Special Interest Group on Management Information Systems (SIG MIS) (after 2004)
Americas Conference on Information Systems (AMCIS)
Australasian Conference on Information Systems (ACIS)
European Conference on Information Systems (ECIS)
International Conference on Information Systems (ICIS)
Pacific Asia Conference on Information Systems (PACIS)

Stereotype Threat:
The Case of Black Males in the IT Profession

Curtis C. Cain
The Pennsylvania State University
College of Information Sciences and Technology
307G IST Building
University Park, PA 16802 USA
+1 814.865.8952
caincc@psu.edu

Eileen M. Trauth
The Pennsylvania State University
College of Information Sciences and Technology
330C IST Building
University Park, PA 16803 USA
+1 814.865.6457
etrauth@ist.psu.edu

ABSTRACT

An interview-based investigation of Black males was conducted to identify how individual identity, individual influences and environmental influences affect the academic pipeline for Black male students. Semi-structured interviews, informed by the Individual Differences Theory of Gender and IT, were conducted with Black males at a Predominately White Institution (PWI) and Historically Black College and University (HBCU) regarding the presence of stereotypes and how they may have combated these barriers. The results revealed that stereotypes and stereotype threat are prevalent among Black males pursuing IT careers and influence self-efficacy, identity, the academic environment and career choice.

Categories and Subject Descriptors

K.3.2 **[Computers and Education]**: Computer and Information Science Education.

K.7.1 **[The Computer Profession]**: Occupations.

General Terms

Management, Human Factors, Theory

Keywords

Ethnicity, race, individual differences, IT education, IT workforce, race, stereotypes, stereotype threat.

1. INTRODUCTION

In the United States of America, diversity is greatly needed in all professions as society needs role models and mentors for its youth [1]. The concept of identity and seeing oneself in a role opens the door to the possibility of one assuming that role. There is no lack of data supporting these claims. However, what is lacking is sufficient research to analyze and understand the problem, and provide the basis for interventions that could lead to the reversal of the trend. Black males are disproportionately underrepresented in higher education. Despite the dismal outlook for many Black males, there are those who successfully navigate through the

higher education system to attain a baccalaureate degree. These are the men able to provide new insights about Black males who do participate in this higher education system and persist, and perhaps their experiences illustrate strategies that may assist those who do not.

The number of Black males who attend and graduate from the nation's colleges and universities is steadily in decline and now at a critical and disturbing point [2]. This trend has recently captured more focused attention from educational researchers, sociologists, economists, and administrators in higher education [2]. Research indicates that this dilemma has roots that go back to elementary school and consequences that will influence future generations. The focus of this paper is IT, which is a part of STEM. The goal is to investigate the existence and impact of stereotypes on the dearth of Black males in the IT profession.

2. LITERATURE REVIEW

Significant research has been done on the digital divide, stereotypes and stereotype threat, academic pipeline and Black male identity, but they do not go far enough to explain the dearth of Black males' participation in IT. These issues combined have an impact on Black male participation in IT. In the upcoming sections, these issues are discussed in further detail. According to Mossberger, Tolbert & Stansbury (2003), the term digital divide, coined in the mid-1990s, describes patterns of unequal access to Information Technology (IT). Unequal access to IT was based on varying socioeconomic factors, such as education, race, gender, age and income. Blacks have historically been much less likely to have access to personal computers and thus have felt the greatest impact of the digital divide [3, 6, 8].

Indeed, researchers have studied how the digital divide and digital inequality influence underrepresented minority groups. For example, Kvasny & Keil (2006) conducted a case study in two Georgia cities, Atlanta and LaGrange, in response to the cities' attempts to readdress the digital divide [4]. Atlanta's initiative was to implement community-testing centers while LaGrange provided Internet with a set-top box. Their findings indicated that inequality was reproduced due to the lack of a mechanism that extended beyond access to usage. Their findings were similar to those found in DiMaggio & Hargittai's 2001 study [5]. Other studies have concurred with these findings that inequality exists socially, which deepens the issues of the digital divide [7].

Jackson et al.'s (2008) study of 172 Black children found that there are differences in how people of different ethnicities use the Internet and to what extent. They found that Black males use the Internet less intensely than Whites, Latinos, and Black females. Intensity refers to the ways the Internet is used and for how long.

The study also found that IT use predicted children's academic performance and that length of time using IT and the Internet was a positive indicator of academic performance [7].

In contrast, Black females were the most intense users of cell phones and use the Internet in more diverse ways than other groups. These findings suggest that Black males may not view IT as a field that they associate with [4, 8]. Jackson et al also found that Black females embraced technology in diverse ways, leading all groups in text messaging, searching the Internet for information, as well as searching for health related information [7]. Conversely, Black males lag behind other groups in IT usage with one exception: video gaming. This study emphasized that research and interventions should bring together culturally relevant tools to increase representation of Black males in computing and increase their level of technical awareness.

There has been a significant amount of research done on the adjustment, academic achievement, persistence, and rates of enrollment and graduation in postsecondary institutions. A large amount of the literature on Black males within educational environments, however, features quantitative studies comparing them with other subgroups. The academic pipeline has been the topic of contentious debate in a variety of different contexts. The academic pipeline refers to how individual, environmental and institutional factors influence, hinder or divert one from reaching a goal [9]. There are numerous versions of the pipeline for various subsets of the population. Researchers have studied pipelines related to minorities and women for completion of secondary, post-secondary, graduate and professional education [10, 11, 12].

Literature referring to leaks within the academic pipeline references the limited number of women and minorities in STEM disciplines [13, 14]. A 2003 study by Jackson using national databases discovered that there are wide gaps between Black males' and White males' educational attainment beginning with high school [35]. Margolis et al. (2008) posit that America struggles with a stratified intellectual class system for which there are unintended consequences of well-intended policies at every level [9]. They position the argument of inequality as the access and denial of access to Information Technology (IT), satisfactory educators and resources. "Research has shown that people with an actual connection at home, the ability to go online on a computer at home, are more engaged in a lot of different things than people who rely on access from work, a friend's house, or a phone," [15, 16]. However, stereotypes and stereotype threat have been shown to have an impact on Blacks' interests.

A stereotype is a widely held but fixed and oversimplified image or idea of a particular type of person or thing. Blacks are generally stereotyped, in the media, as superstitious, lazy, happy go-lucky, aggressive, intellectually inferior, ostentatious, active in sports, entertainers and poor performers in academics [17, 18 36, 37]. Black college students tend to obtain lower grades than their White counterparts, even when they enter college with equivalent test scores. Past research suggests that negative stereotypes of Black students' intellectual abilities play a role in this underperformance. Awareness of these stereotypes can psychologically threaten African Americans, a phenomenon known as "stereotype threat" [19], which can in turn provoke responses that impair both academic performance and psychological engagement with academics. Research has shown that Blacks, who enter a predominately white organization, feel that there is a pressure to disprove preconceived stereotyping. Many Blacks feel like they have to say the right thing, not say too much, or agree just to fit in. In many cases, the Black attempts to disprove stereotypes until their technical value can be exemplified to the organization and/or when the organization recognizes their value.

Thus, Blacks are susceptible to stereotype threat [18, 19, 20, 21, 33, 34]. Stereotype threat is defined as being at risk of confirming, as self-characteristic, a negative stereotype about one's group. In essence, stereotype threat is an internal characteristic. The presence of an actual stereotype may not exist but the individual is responding in a way that it is. Steele & Aronson (1995) performed four studies on 114 Black and White undergraduate students at Stanford University. Steele and Aronson entered the study with an assumption that Blacks internalized the stereotype of intellectual inferiority to Whites [18]. Their first study investigated the effect of stereotype threat on the intellectual performance of Black college students. Overall, the results showed the White students performed at a higher level than Blacks in each group. Results indicate that Blacks viewed the test as more biased compared to Whites. Black participants' self-ratings regarding performance were less than the White cohort. Thus, stereotype threat causes Black students to behave more aggressively, for fear of being stereotyped.

Vulnerability to stereotype threat may exist regardless of whether or not an individual assigns validity to that stereotype. Steele posits that an automatic reaction could occur in which an individual is aware of the assumption and therefore responds accordingly. The degree to which stereotype threat was experienced varies from person to person and often heightens depending upon which stereotype and is congruent with the context [21]. Steele's [19, 20, 21] work has shown that stereotype threat is the greatest hindrance to Black student success. Working to disprove the stereotype may seem everlasting and overwhelming, and may be impossible if certain individuals do in fact manifest characteristics of the stereotype [21].

When capable Black college students fail to perform as well as their white counterparts, the explanation often has less to do with preparation or ability than with the threat of stereotypes about their capacity to succeed [19, 21, 22, 24, 33, 34]. These threats emerge from both stereotypical representation and lack of representation in a particular domain. There is evidence to support the conclusion that stereotype threat between racial and low-income groups is a prominent factor hindering beliefs in one's ability to carry out tasks and engage in activities [23, 24].

Multiple problems result from IT being a predominately White male field. First, since there are fewer Black men and women in IT, their perspectives may not be brought to the forefront in policy, instruction, learning style and administration. Second, Black men and women may have a more difficult time adjusting to the discipline due to a lack of identity affiliation [7, [19, 20, 21, 33, 34]. Given the current economy, careers, which can offer lucrative pay and opportunity, are more important than ever. Blacks only represent 1.6 percent of those working in IT-related occupations, which can offer lucrative job opportunities [25]. The culmination of these issues motivates a need for a better understanding of the ways in which stereotypes and stereotype threat influence Black male students pursuing degrees in IT. With this in mind, this paper focuses on the following two research questions: *1) What stereotypes of Black males in IT fields exist? And 2) How do they enable understanding of Black male participation in IT?*

3. METHODOLOGY

The nature of inquiry for this study was interpretative, which focused on understanding the phenomenon of underrepresentation within the IT field. Semi-structured interviews, which allow for the flexibility to add to the interview guide based on responses from participants to broaden and deepen understanding [25] which the Individual Differences Theory of Gender and IT informed.

3.1 Individual Differences Theory of Gender and IT

The Individual Differences Theory of Gender and IT was developed as a theoretical alternative to two opposing perspectives on the topic of underrepresentation of women in the technical workforce, essentialism and social construction. The essentialist perspective attributes women's underrepresentation in IT to biological factors [26, 27]. In Trauth et. al's critique of essentialism they argue that while some relevant differences in ability maybe biologically based they are not based on gender. Further, essentialism does not add contextual factors, which may affect an individual's perspective or interaction with technology. The other perspective used to understand gender and IT is social construction, which describes gender as "two separate groups of men and women who are affected by two different sets of sociological influences. Hence, men and women are viewed as having different or opposing socio-cultural characteristics, which subsequently affect their relationship to and adoption of technology." [28, p. 23]. Social construction identifies social forces, which may shape the male or female life, but minimizes individual agency or different experiences that affect responses to those factors [29, 27]. Given the two differing theoretical perspectives of essentialism and social construction, they can be interpreted as describing partial elements of group homogeneity experienced by women in the IT workforce.

The Individual Differences Theory of Gender and IT, consists of three major constructs to explain gender variation in participation in the IT field: individual identity, individual influences, and environmental influences [29, 30, 31, 32]. The individual identity construct consists of two sub-constructs: personal demographics (e.g. ethnicity, socio-economic class, family background) and career items (i.e., type of IT work). The second construct, individual influences, consists of two sub-constructs: personal characteristics (e.g., educational background, personality traits) and personal influences (e.g., mentors, role models, and significant others). Lastly, the environmental influences construct consists of four sub-constructs related to the geographic region; cultural influences, economic influences (e.g. cost of living, cost of education), policy influences, and infrastructure influences (e.g. institutional climate) [29]. This theory is being applied to a new research domain for this study: Black males.

This study was conducted at a Predominately White Institution (PWI) and Historically Black College and University (HBCU). One institution is located in the Mid-Atlantic and the other in the South. Ten students were interviewed using the an interview guide (Trauth, 2002) derived and adapted from an National Science Foundation Grant which sought to explore the effects of race, ethnicity and socio-economic class on gender stereotyping of STEM disciplines [NSF Award #0204246].

The individual identity construct was applied in the studies to analyze ethnicity and family. The second construct, individual influences, was used to study the presence, or lack of, mentors and role models for Black males. Lastly, the environmental influences construct was adapted to examine the organizational and societal climate for Black males pursuing IT degrees [29].

3.2 Data Collection and Analysis

Semi-structured interviews were voice recorded and the interviewees were given pseudonyms to preserve their anonymity. Interviews ranged in length from thirty to ninety minutes. An interview guide was developed based on the three constructs of the Individual Differences Theory of Gender and IT. Open coding was then used to identify new themes that emerged from the interviews.

To further understand the data, the first author added reflexivity. As a Black male conducting research about Black male students, he is often asked about his role in his research. Interpretative work is influenced by the researcher, which introduces bias; however reflexivity is used to add transparency about how the researcher's perspective influenced the research. This is where reflexivity plays a major role. Reflexivity requires that researchers be consciously aware of how their interactions in the different stages of the research process influence the research participants. Reflexivity therefore assisted in understanding the interview data from Black males.

4. FINDINGS AND DISCUSSION

The constructs of the theory were used to analyze interview data on the presence of stereotypes and coping mechanisms of Black males who are studying IT education. The individual influences construct relates to stereotypes about personal characteristics (i.e. personality). The individual identity construct highlighted stereotypes related to race (i.e. ethnicity). The environmental influences construct presented stereotypes coming from the societal climate. Table 2, below, shows the results from this study highlighting stereotypes, quotations from interview participants and their connection to theoretical constructs.

The results guided by the interview guide provided by Trauth [27], provide evidence that the answer to the first question is yes; they knew stereotyping was likely to happen or that they have already experienced it, as shown in Table 2. The results provide evidence that the answer to the second question is that stereotypes have a varying influence on Black male participation in IT. Results indicate that Black males both succumb to and combat the stereotypes.

The findings of the study suggest three insights about the stereotyping of Black males in the IT field. One insight is the prevalence of Black males who wish to overcome stereotypes rather than succumb. Tom, Sebastian, Reggie and Mike combatted their stereotypes by responding in a way that disproved the stereotype. DJ on the other hand succumbed to the stereotype by acknowledging Black male representation in the media correlated to reality. A second insight is the acknowledgement that Black males understand that they will be stereotyped in an environment that is White male dominated. A third insight is that regardless of whether the student attends a Predominantly White Institution (PWI) or Historically Black College or University (HBCU), they understand that outside of the institutional structure there are barriers and overcoming these barriers are key to a successful career in IT. These findings give evidence that more research has to be done to identify ways to combat marginalization of Black males in the IT. With the benefit of these findings we will be able to better create future interventions. The pilot study shows that these problems still exist with the current generation and that current research has not alleviated these concerns for Black males.

The stereotypes identified by the interviewees align closely with the first author's personal experiences attending an HBCU for undergraduate school and then transitioning to a PWI for graduate education. Often times there was a sense of needing to combat stereotypes whether they presented themselves or not (i.e. stereotype threat). There was a sense of needing to prove oneself so as not to succumb to popular pop culture stereotypes and media stereotypes that correlate Black males to being lazy and ignorant.

Student	Institution
Tom	PWI
Sebastian	PWI
Reggie	HBCU
DJ	HBCU
Mike	HBCU

Table 1. Students' Institution Demography

These stereotypes may help people understand what one interviewee described as Black males living in a "ghetto" culture. The first author recalls a time when a professor stereotyped him as lazy and "ghetto" by the type of clothes he wore. There were certainly times where ethnic differences played a role in the necessity to disassociate with stereotypes. Whites often felt they did not need to disprove anything as they were already the dominant culture and thus felt they belonged in the IT field. With a dearth of Black faculty members in IT, the first author felt the need to solidify belonging and prevent marginalization. The interviewees attending PWIs made similar remarks about being marginalized because of so few Black students and faculty. Conversely, the students attending HBCUs spoke about stereotypes being attached to outside environmental factors (i.e. workplace environment). The lack of people of similar ethnicity and upbringing makes it difficult to feel welcomed into the field, something that leads to feelings of empowerment.

While attending an HBCU, the first author believes he was sheltered from stereotypes because the majority of the faculty and students were Black. Stereotypes did not begin to present themselves to him until he began participating in internships and proceeded into graduate school. He recalls his first internship as a database administrator where his White colleagues assumed he did not have the educational background to successfully redesign an antiquated system. He felt the need to disprove his critics. It was at that time that he began to notice differences between the Black male students and majority students. It was not until graduate school that he felt the pressure to conform to what the majority students did and distance himself from his own identity as a method to combat stereotypes. In similar fashion, issues of stereotypes also presented themselves in the interviews. Students at both PWIs and HBCUs have felt marginalized. Despite these issues, the interviewed Black males are continuing their education in IT. These findings give evidence that more research has to be done to identify ways to combat marginalization of Black males in the IT. With the benefit of these findings we will be able to better create future interventions.

Stereotype	Example	Impact	Response	Theoretical Construct
Black men are lazy	A team member said, "You don't need to come to any of the meetings, we'll put your name on the assignment." -Tom	Desire to combat stereotype	Tom took a lead role on the team project which challenged the stereotype.	Individual Influences (personality, mentors, role models, significant others)
Black men are unintelligent	A team member said, "Don't worry about doing anything. Your contribution can be the references" -Sebastian	Desire to combat stereotype	Sebastian challenged the stereotype by stating the will to participate in a larger portion of the project.	Individual Influences (personality, mentors, role models, significant others)
Black men are inexperienced about the IT field	An employer said, "It's ok if you haven't had any experience with infrastructure design." -Reggie	Desire to combat stereotype	Reggie stated that his participation in student-led organizations and internships combated the stereotype.	Individual Identity (IT work experience)
Black men live in "ghetto" culture	A team member said, "That's what I've seen in the music video." -DJ	Succumb to stereotype	DJ laughed and stated he has seen the video too.	Environmental Influences (attitudes, society, culture)
Black men are aggressive	A guidance counselor said, "There's no need to raise your voice, we watch TV." -Mike	Desire to combat stereotype	Mike challenged the perception by stating that Black men are not the aggressive people seen on television.	Environmental Influences (culture, individual influences, significant others)

Table 2. Stereotype Examples linked to Individual Differences Theory of Gender and IT

5. CONCLUSION

The findings, to date, of this research have implications for interventions and future research, which would lead to a better understanding of the factors influencing marginalization and subsequent underrepresentation of Black males in IT. In this paper, we show how Black males in IT are victims of stereotypes and self-impose stereotype threat. But more research is needed to explain how Black males were handling these issues and if they influenced career choice. Through qualitative inquiry, we identified some of the issues facing Black males. The findings from this study will add to the growing body of knowledge of minority groups within the IT field and inform subsequent interventions.

The results presented in this paper only begin to help us understand Black male adoption of the IT field. Further research is being conducted to identify other issues influencing Black male participation in IT. The ultimate goal of this research is add to the body of knowledge about minority group's participation in IT. One approach, which is the one presented in this paper, looks at not only ethnicity, but gender as a method to understand participation. One limitation of this research is that there were ten participants in our initial study. Another limitation is that the interviewees came from two universities. Efforts are underway to interview to broaden the participant pool, which include additional universities and additional participants.

6. ACKNOWLEDGEMENTS

This research is supported by a grant from the National Science Foundation (Graduate Research Fellowship) and the Pennsylvania State University's Africana Research Center.

7. REFERENCES

[1] Blake, M.B., Gilbert, J.E. 2010. "Black Computer Scientists in Academe: an Endangered Species?", The Chronicle of Higher Education – Diversity in Academe September 19, 2010

[2] Jackson, J., F.L. (2003). Toward administrative diversity: An analysis of the African American male educational pipeline. Journal of Men's Studies, 12(1), 43.

[3] Mossberger, K., C. Tolbert, and M. Stansbury. (2003). Virtual inequality: Beyond the digital divide. Washington, D.C.: Georgetown University Press

[4] Kvasny, L. and Keil, M. 2006. The Challenges of Redressing the Digital Divide: A Tale of Two U.S. Cities, Information Systems Journal, Vol.16. No. 1, pp. 23-53.

[5] DiMaggio, P. and Hargittai, E. (2001). From the 'Digital Divide' to `Digital Inequality': Studying Internet Use As Penetration Increases. Working Paper #15, Summer 2001.

[6] Kvasny, L. 2002. "Problematizing the Digital Divide: Cultural and Social Reproduction in a Community Technology Initiative". Ph.D. dissertation, Georgia State University, 2002.

[7] Jackson, L.A., Zhao ,Y., Kolenic, A., Fitzgerald, H.E., Harold, R. & Von Eye, A. (2008). Race, Gender, and Information Technology Use: The New Digital Divide. Cyber-Psychology & Behavior, 11, 4, pp. 437-442

[8] Kvasny, L., Payton, F., Mbarika, V., Amadi, A. and Meso, P. (2008). "Gendered Perspectives on IT Education and Workforce Participation in Kenya", IEEE Transactions on Education, Vol. 51, No. 2, pp. 256-261.

[9] Margolis, J., Estrella, R., Goode, J., Holme, J.J., Nao, K. 2008. Stuck in the Shallow End: Education, Race, and Computing. The MIT Press.

[10] van Anders, S. M. 2004. Why the academic pipeline leaks: Fewer men than women perceive barriers to becoming professors. Sex Roles, 51(9/10), 511.

[11] Evans, Z. 2001. Maintaining an open pipeline to higher education: Strategies that work. 18(8), 136.

[12] Hopkins, R. 1997. Educating black males: Critical lessons in schooling, community, and power. Albany: State University of New York Press.

[13] National Science Foundation, Division of Science Resources Statistics, Women, Minorities, and Persons with Disabilities in Science and Engineering: 2007, NSF 07-315 (Arlington, VA; February 2007). Available from http://www.nsf.gov/statistics/wmpd.

[14] National Science Foundation, Division of Science Resources Statistics, Women, Minorities, and Persons with Disabilities in Science and Engineering: 2009, NSF 09-305, (Arlington, VA; January 2009). Available from http://www.nsf.gov/statistics/wmpd/

[15] Pew Internet, a project of the Pew Research Center. Mobile Access 2010. http://www.pewinternet.org/~/media//Files/Reports/2010/PIP _Mobile_Access_2010.pdf

[16] Pew Internet, a project of the Pew Research Center. Social media & Mobile Internet Use Among Teens and Young Adults. February 2010

[17] Fein, S and Spencer, S., 1997. Prejudice as self-image maintenance: Affirming the self through negative evaluations of others., Journal of Personality and Social Psychology.

[18] Steele, C. M. and Aronson, J. (1995). Attitudes and Social Cognition: Stereotype Threat and the Intellectual Test Performance of African Americans. Journal of Personality and Social Psychology, 69, 5, 797-811.

[19] Steele, C.M. (2010). Whistling Vivaldi And Other Clues to How Stereotypes Affect Us, New York: W. W. Norton & Company, Inc.

[20] Steele, C. M. (1997). A Threat in the Air: How Stereotypes Shape the Intellectual Identities and Performance of Women and African Americans. American Psychologist, 52, 613-629.

[21] Davis, C., Aronson, J., and Salinas, M. 2006. Shades of Threat: Racial Identity as a Moderator of Stereotype Threat. Journal of Black Psychology 2006 32: 399.

[22] Shapiro, J. S., Neuberg, S. L. (2007). From stereotype threat to stereotype threats: Implications of a multi-threat framework for causes, moderators, mediators, consequences, and interventions. Personality and Social Psychology Review, 11, 107-130.

[23] Hamilton, T. 2009. "Understanding the Black College Student Experience: The relationships between Racial Identity, Social Support, General Campus, Academic, and Racial Climate, and GPA". Ph.D. dissertation, Seton Hall University, 2009.

[24] U.S. Department of Labor, U.S. Bureau of Labor Statistics. Labor Force Characteristics by Race and Ethnicity, 2011. http://www.bls.gov/cps/cpsrace2011.pdf

[25] Hsiung, Ping-Chun (2008). Teaching Reflexivity in Qualitative Interviewing, Teaching Sociology, vol 46, July, pp. 211-226.

[26] Trauth, E.M., Quesenberry, J.L., and Huang, H. (2009). "Retaining Women in the US IT Workforce: Theorizing the Influence of Organizational Factor." European Journal of

Information Systems. Special Issue on Meeting the Renewed Demand for IT Workers(18), 476-497.

[27] Trauth, E.M. (2002). "Odd Girl Out: An Individual Differences Perspective on Women in the IT Profession." Information Technology and People. 15, 98-118.

[28] Trauth, E.M., Quesenberry, J.L. (2007). "Gender and Information Technology Workforce: Issues of Theory and Practice." in Managing IT Professionals in the Internet Age. P. Yoong and S. Huff (Eds.) Hersey, PA: Idea Group Publishing: 18-36.

[29] Trauth, E.M., Quesenberry, J.L., and Huang, H. (2009). "Retaining Women in the US IT Workforce: Theorizing the Influence of Organizational Factor." European Journal of Information Systems. Special Issue on Meeting the Renewed Demand for IT Workers(18), 476-497.

[30] Trauth, E.M., Cain, C.C., Joshi, K.D., Kvasny, L. and Booth, K. (2012) "Embracing Intersectionality in Gender and IT Career Choice Research," Proceedings of the 2012 ACM SIGMIS-CPR (Milwaukee, WI).

[31] Morgan, A. J. 2008. "An Analysis of the Influences of Human Individual Differences on Web Searching Behavior among Black and Whites: A Case of Health Information Searching". Ph.D. dissertation, The Pennsylvania State University, 2008.

[32] Quesenberry, J.L. 2007. "Career Values and Motivations: A Study of Women in the Information Technology Workforce". Ph.D. dissertation, The Pennsylvania State University, 2007.

[33] Cain, C.C., Trauth, E.M. (2012). "Black Males in IT Higher Education in The USA: The Digital Divide in the Academic Pipeline Re-visited," Proceedings of the 18th Americas Conference on Information Systems (Seattle, WA).

[34] Cain, C.C. (2012). "Underrepresented Groups in Gender and STEM: The Case of Black Males in CISE," Proceedings of the 2012 ACM SIGMIS-CPR (Milwaukee, WI).

[35] Jackson, J., F.L. (2003). Toward administrative diversity: An analysis of the African American male educational pipeline. Journal of Men's Studies, 12(1), 43.

[36] Aronson, J. , Fried, C. & Good, C. (2002). Reducing the Effects of Stereotype Threat on African American College Students by shaping theories of intelligence. Journal of Experimental Social Psychology. 38, 113-125.

[37] Aronson, J. & Inzlicht, M. (2004). The ups and downs of attributional ambiguity: Stereotype vulnerability and the academic self-knowledge of African-American students. Psychological Science, 15, 12, 829-836.

Using Social Software for Enhancing IS Talents' E-Learning Motivation

Thomas Wirtky
Otto Friedrich University Bamberg, Germany
thomas.wirtky@uni-bamberg.de

Sven Laumer
Otto Friedrich University Bamberg, Germany
sven.laumer@uni-bamberg.de

Andreas Eckhardt
Johann Wolfgang Goethe University Frankfurt, Germany
eckhardt@wiwi.uni-frankfurt.de

Tim Weitzel
Otto Friedrich University Bamberg, Germany
tim.weitzel@uni-bamberg.de

ABSTRACT

In the aftermath of the global economic recession, 34% of all companies struggle to fill open positions. IS talents are the top-5 employees in demand. The countries' education systems are not flexible enough to provide enough workers with the right skills at the right point in time. E-learning could be part of the solution, if it were realizing its potential. The facts indicate that success of e-learning in the academic context is considerable, but users are not enough motivated to participate in corporate e-learning inhibiting life-long learning. Given the advent of social software and its potential to increase user motivation, this paper specifically develops a model predicting the impact of social software features on user motivation to participate in corporate asynchronous e-learning activities. Providing guidance for future e-learning research and implementations, it bases its findings on broad literature reviews.

Categories and Subject Descriptors

H.1.2 [**Models and principles**]: User/Machine Systems; K.3.1 [**Computers and education**]: Computer Uses in Education

General Terms

Management, Design, Human Factors

Keywords

HRIS, e-learning, motivation, social software

1. INTRODUCTION

A globally conducted survey among 38,000 companies indicates that 34% struggle to fill open positions in the aftermath of the global economic recession, and that Information Systems (IS) talents are the top-5 employees in demand [68]. The scarcity of talents stems, among other reasons, from the inflexibility of the countries' education systems to adapt to changes in skill demand. Even education systems praised and referenced for their flexibility such as Germany's dual education system seem to have difficulties with accelerated skill obsolescence due to the increasing pace of changes especially in technology-driven areas such as Information Systems (IS) [13,15,18,46,105].

The creative use of information technology (IT) appears to be the next logical step increasing the flexibility of education. E-learning was thought to be one of the fastest growing sectors [69]. It struggled in the beginning [66,107], but later enjoyed considerable success in academia [103]. Moreover, the recent advent of e-learning 2.0 promises a new era in technology enabled learning potentially providing the means for life-long learning even in dynamic areas such as IS [16,56,106]. This new version of e-learning is basically a combination of the former e-learning with social software, a synonymous term for web 2.0 as defined by O'Reilly, which basically refers to web-based software allowing users to not only consume information, but also to generate information and to socially interact with each other [35,76].

The challenge targeted in this paper is the still limited success of e-learning in the corporate context [37]. This research argues that the reason for this lack of success in the corporate context stems from neither the technology, nor the content, nor pedagogical design principles because these factors hardly differ between the academic and the corporate contexts. DeRouin et al. even found in their literature review that corporate e-learning participants generally react favorably [31], which suggests that technology, content and design are appropriate. Instead, comparing the academic and corporate contexts, differences in the environmental conditions rather explain the limited success of corporate e-learning, where programs need to be shorter, directly applicable and more self-directed than instructor-led [17,31]. While grades measure an academic student's short-term success, which are sometimes even directly dependent on e-learning participation, there is no direct connection between short-term success of a corporate employees and e-learning participation. Thus, motivation of the learner is different and more critical for corporate employees to participate [33,93].

Social software features are expected to increase motivation [20,98,101]. Although they are part of nearly all contemporary e-learning solutions, they are hardly implemented in the corporate context yet [7]. Research explaining which and how individual social software features increase motivation and guiding practitioners during design and implementation is unavailable [31], which calls for the research questions:

Why and how do social software features impact the motivation for corporate e-learning participation?

The answer could lead to corporate e-learning becoming successful and to life-long learning becoming more than a popular phrase. This research uses a narrow definition of e-learning to only include asynchronous technologies, i.e., technologies that provide electronic, time and place-independent access to knowledge, which is preprocessed for educational purposes. By contrast, synchronous technologies such as online conferencing and collaboration tools, which facilitate real-time distance trainings, are not included. This is due to the fact that social human interaction is already part of the definition of synchronous e-learning limiting the potential impact of additional social features on motivation.

In the following, this paper develops a model, which answers the research question, and provides an outlook in five sections. The first and second section review both current training motivation and social software literature. The third section describes the research context and identifies appropriate social software features. Combining all findings to a research model, the forth section also includes hypotheses on the impact of social software features on motivation. Finally, preparing for a future research stages, the fifth section of this paper outlines the envisioned research context, which is the previously mentioned dual education system, where interviews are already scheduled with IS talents.

2. COMPARISON OF TRAINING MOTIVATION MODELS

Current training motivation research serves as a foundation for this paper's research model. Since motivation research has a long history and cuts "across all subareas within psychology" [78], it is not surprising to find a diversity of corporate training motivation models in reputable journals of the last 20 years (see Table 1 for examples). Despite the models' differences, they also share common findings and constructs, which can be associated with more abstract motivational facets [23]. Thus, this section briefly presents an overview of motivational facets, a comparison of training motivation models by these facets, and an identification of the most comprehensive model as a basis for this research (for an extended discussion of motivational facets and the training motivation review please refer to [48,104]).

Figure 1 illustrates an overview of motivational facets, which is based on the general motivation model of Heckhausen and Heckhausen [48]. Individually, facets 1 and 2 – personal and environmental factors – have a long history of motivation research. Combined, Lewin suggested with his Field Force Theory that it is the product of both explaining behavior [64]. Porter and Lawler III, who extended Vrooms's Valence-Instrumentality-Expectancy model to one of the most complex motivation model, inspired facets 3 to 6 [79,97]. Their concepts of 'perceived equitable rewards' and 'satisfaction' are substituted by the more comprehensive concept of 'inequity' based on the relation of outcome to effort (facet 7) [1] and by a 'feedback loop' suggested by the Social Cognitive Theory (facet 9) [11]. Finally, the overview also borrows the concept of locus of control over the outcome [81], which is another outcome expectancy that is sometimes confused with perceived control from the theory of planned behavior (TPB) [6].

Table 1 contains the results of the comparison of training motivation models by the nine abstract motivational facets that Figure 1 illustrates. Hurtz and Williams contribute the most

comprehensive research model on training motivation with only minor limitations [53].

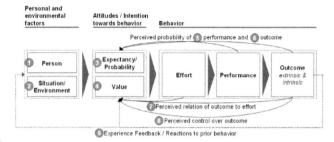

Figure 1: Overview of motivational facets [104]

Table 1: Comparison of training motivation models by nine motivational facets [104]

	(1) Person	(2) Environment	(3) Expectancy	(4) Valence	(5) Probability of performance	(6) Probability of outcome	(7) Inequity / Relation of outcome to effort	(8) Control over outcome	(9) Reactions to prior behavior
Birdi et al. [12]	●	●	●	-	●	●	-	-	-
Cheng [20]	●	-	●	●	●	●	-	-	-
Chiu et al. [21]	-	●	●	●	-	-	●	-	●
Clark et al. [22]	-	●	●	●	●	●	-	-	-
Garavan et al. [43]	-	●	●	●	●	-	-	-	-
Hurtz and Williams [53]	●	●	●	●	●	●	-	-	●
Maurer and Tarulli [71]	●	●	●	●	●	●	-	-	-
Noe and Wilk [75]	●	●	●	●	●	●	-	-	-
Tharenou [94]	●	●	●	-	●	●	-	-	-
Venkatesh [96]	●	-	●	-	●	●	-	-	-

3. SOCIAL SOFTWARE AND ITS IMPACT ON MOTIVATION TO USE TECHNOLOGY

After reviewing the training motivation literature in the previous section, this section will briefly review literature on the impact of social software on motivation to use technology. The term social software is synonymously used with web 2.0, which basically refers to web-based software allowing users not only to consume information, but also to generate information and to socially interact with each other (Ebersbach et al. 2011; O'Reilly 2005). The few available research contributions such as the three recent ones outlined in the following suggest a positive impact of social factors on motivation, but they do not provide suggestions how individual social software features impact motivation in a corporate e-learning environment, which inhibits especially practical use.

The first contribution is a research-in-progress publication whose authors opted against using an established, empirically supported research model in favor of a more general Person-Environment Fit based approach, which aims at explaining the impact of web 2.0 on system use [88]. Unfortunately, this ambitious attempt did not yield any findings yet, which could be relevant for the context of corporate e-learning. Empirical data of the second contribution supports the hypothesis that a website's socialness increases perceived usefulness, perceived ease of use, perceived enjoyment and the intention to visit a website [98]. The authors define socialness as the extent to which a website allows for human social interaction, and they test their hypothesis using video-based user interaction in an online shop. Although their finding is consistent with earlier findings regarding the usage of interactive videos in a synchronous e-learning environment, it is uncertain whether these findings are generalizable to an asynchronous, non-interactive e-learning context since non-interactive videos do generally not improve e-learning effectiveness [108]. The third contribution provides evidence for social factors to indirectly impact e-learning participation [20]. Unfortunately, the author defined social factors not as social software features, but as interpersonal and external influences.

Despite the mentioned concerns regarding the applicability of the findings to the asynchronous e-learning context, we generally conclude that social factors have a positive impact on motivation [20,101], in some cases even on more than one motivational facet [98], but the question which social software features to implement in order to maximize motivation in the corporate asynchronous e-learning context is still unanswered. This leaves practitioners without guidance for e-learning implementations and widens the already existing gap between them and academics in the area of e-learning [31].

4. DIFFERENTIATING SOCIAL SOFTWARE FEATURES

In order to examine the impact of social software in higher granularity than the existing literature, this section details the context and hypothesizes a list of social features applicable to this context.

4.1 Description of the context

Following the advice of DeRouin et al., we do not start with technology, but with the perspective of users [31], who could subdivide corporate e-learning participation into four steps. The first step entails the user's initial realization of a knowledge gap. This can either be self-induced due to curiosity or externally induced by someone else recommending or requesting the user to gain further knowledge. In a second step the user is searching for, evaluating and selecting an appropriate knowledge source. The actual transfer and absorption of knowledge potentially through e-learning participation comprises the third step, which as learning psychologists further differentiated into objectivist and constructivist learning [14]. Finally, in a forth step, the user needs to evaluate whether the initial knowledge gap is closed.

Social software could potentially play a pivotal role in each of the four steps. In the first two steps it could facilitate communication, whereas its role in the latter two steps extends to knowledge generation and exchange. It can be used in both objectivist and constructivist learning where technology requirements slightly differ [65].

This research exclusively focusses on the role of social software in step two, where the user decides on e-learning participation In theory, corporate knowledge management is responsible to support the user in identifying appropriate knowledge sources and to provide access to a diversity of sources. In reality, knowledge management and e-learning are organizationally and technically disjunct, although ideas of their combination are discussed on IS conferences for more than ten years [e.g., 30,57,75]. Thus, the user's actual decision to participate in corporate e-learning has to be preceded by the decision to enter a separate learning environment. Although we believe that this lack of integration is a major inhibitor of corporate e-learning success, we exclude knowledge management and focus our research on the e-learning environment commonly referred to as a virtual learning environment (VLE), which is defined as "computer-based environments that are relatively open systems, allowing interactions and encounters with other participants" [102]. Despite its definition, typical implementations of corporate VLEs do not allow users to interact with each other. They usually present the user a categorized sometimes even individualized list of available learning modules featuring short descriptions and a link to launch them i.e. a mean to access the content and to participate in e-learning.

4.2 Hypotheses regarding appropriate social software features

Social software features could enable user interactions in the corporate VLEs. Table 2 outlines hypotheses on which social software features are appropriate in the given context. For further details on each feature, please refer to the social technology literature [e.g., 35].

The appropriateness of social software features outlined in Table 2 is initially based on interviews with corporate users stating their preferences [104]. The results are not surprising because any additional support from others has a positive influence on system use [92]. Ratings and review comments of others are likely to impact e-learning usage in a VLE like they impact sales in an online shop, which researchers examined extensively including the importance of rating variance [90], the manipulation of online reviews [52], or the influence among reviewers [89]. Blogs, vlogs, asynchronous chats, status messages and wikis are not appropriate in supporting users' decision to participate because these features usually do not target individual e-learning modules and therefore do not provide the needed information on a timely basis.

This research extends the initial list in two ways. First, it argues that a functionality allowing to chat with other currently available users who might even have experiences with participating in a relevant e-learning module, could lead to targeted and timely information. Thus, the implementation of such a synchronous chat feature could have an impact on motivation to participate. Second, a RSS feature might also impact the motivation to participate [104], although it stretches beyond the context of a standalone VLE because it typically requires the integration with other corporate applications such as an employee portal [35].

Table 2: Appropriateness of social software features in asynchronous corporate e-learning environment (adapted from [104])

Social software feature	Appropriate in VLE?
Status notification (e.g., online, offline, or away) of others	
• peers	yes
• trainers/experts	yes
Synchronous communication such as chats	
• with online peers	yes
• with online trainers/experts	yes
Asynchronous communication such as messaging	
• with offline peers	no
• with offline trainers/experts	no
Comments on modules	
• from peers	yes
• from trainers/experts	yes
Comments on content	
• from peers	no
• from trainers/experts	no
Micro blogs such as short textual status updates	
• of peer users	no
• of trainers/experts	no
Blogs	
• of peers	no
• of trainers/experts	no
Vlogs	
• of peers	no
• of trainers/experts	no
Collaboration such as wikis	
• with peers	no
• with trainers/experts	no
Ratings on e-learning modules	
• from peers	yes
• from trainers/experts	yes
Tagging of content (folksonomy)	yes
Sharing of content with other online and offline users	no
Search for content/comments by contributor	yes
RSS feeds on new models, content updates, high scores, etc.	yes
Meta information on modules such as number of past participants, average result, and high scores	yes

5. RESEARCH MODEL

The model of Hurtz and Williams [53], which is strongly influenced by the theory of planned behavior [4], serves as a basis for this research. This section discusses modifications addressing both limitations of the basis such as conspicuous findings contrary to previously establish research and the incorporation of social software features. Figure 2 illustrates the final research model.

5.1 Personal factors

One limitation of the base model is the lack of personal factors. Despite a long history of well-known research on personal motivation, including personal motivation factors in the research model is challenging because researchers in the field appear to have worked independently and to have never agreed on an exhaustive set of distinctive personal motivation factors [e.g., 16,36,63,64]. Maslow, famous for his hierarchical grouping of motivational needs, even demanded to stop researching atomic personal motivational factors as they would never be complete, distinctive and helpful [70]. Despite his disapproval, research continued. Reiss for example published a list of 16 motives in 2004 [80], which subsequent research reduced to 11 only five years later [91].

Due to this ongoing discord, this research turns to intrinsic motivation as the innate source of all personal motivation factors [29], and incorporates the three intrinsic needs *autonomy*, *competence*, and *relatedness* of the Self-Determination Theory (SDT) [27,28,82]. SDT enjoys a growing research community [8,42,55], and, since Aristotle, academics and authors continuously stress the importance of intrinsic motivation [30,47,95]. All three human needs of SDT are particularly relevant to our context. *Autonomy* is defined as the level of perceived freedom in or control a behavior, which is particularly relevant to the training context as it does not only influence the decision to participate, but also training outcome [51]. *Competence* is an equivalent for self-efficacy [28], which is undisputedly a major factor in motivation, technology acceptance and learning [e.g., 10,23,24,25,100]. *Relatedness* is defined as the human need for belongingness and connectedness to other persons, groups, or cultures [83]. Neither the theory of planned behavior, nor the model of Hurtz and Williams include the notion of relatedness [4,53], which this research hypothesizes as crucial in explaining the impact of social software features on motivation.

SDT is not without criticism. For instance, Heckhausen and Heckhause criticize SDT's initially ambiguous definition of intrinsic, which later writings on SDT clarified [28,48]. Intrinsic motivation is not defined as a personal need or motive, but as enjoyment from the behavior itself [28,48]. Similar to Maslow [70], Heckhausen and Heckhausen further claim that a set of three personal needs might not be exhaustive, which is theoretically impossible to disprove. It remains interesting to note though that they do agree with McClelland's et al. distinction of implicit and explicit personal motives with the former being "affectively charged preferences for certain kinds of incentives (habitual propensities)" [62 in 43]. The major implicit motives are dominance, achievement and affiliation [75 in 43], which are nearly equivalents to SDT's autonomy, competence, and relatedness respectively.

In the research model, these three *Personal factors* of SDT are replacing the construct of *Perceived control* of the theory of planned behavior for two reasons. The first reason is a multitude of challenges surrounding the concept of *Perceived control*. Hurtz and Williams' findings regarding the concept differ from the established TPB literature in that the construct negatively correlates with *Actual behavior* [53], whereas it should positively correlate with the *Intention* to participate [3,4]. Other researchers also found "conceptual and methodological ambiguities surrounding the concept of perceived behavioral control", which Ajzen admits [6]. The second reason is a striking resemblance of *Perceived control* to *Personal factors*. The former consists of the two parts locus of control over behavior and self-efficacy [6], which SDT equivalently defined to autonomy and competence respectively. Interestingly, SDT even claims autonomy does not motivate a person if not paired with competence [40,84].

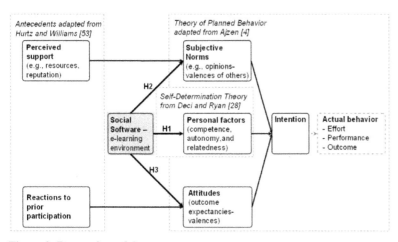

Figure 2: Research model

Table 3: Constructs and items of research model

Construct	Sample Item	Source(s)
Personal factors[1]		[27,28,82]
• Competence	"I do not feel very competent when I am participating in e-learning."	
• Autonomy	"I feel like I can make a lot of inputs to deciding on e-learning participation."	
• Relatedness	"I really like to interact with people in the e-learning environment"	
Environmental Support[1]		[53]
• Reputation	"Most people I know think that e-learning is beneficial."	
• Incentives	"Successful completion of e-learning is usually rewarded by our firm"	
• Resources	"Our company provides me enough "training time" for me to successfully complete e-learning activities"	
Subjective Norm		[4,39,53]
• Family opinion	"My family and friends pressure me to participate in e-learning activities"	
* valence	* "The opinion of my family and friends is important to me."	
• Supervisor opinion	see above	
* valence		
• Co-Worker opinion	see above	
* valence		
Reactions to prior experience		[26,53,59, 60,61,62]
• Ease of use experiences	"The e-learning system is rigid and inflexible to interact with."	
• Enjoyment experiences	"I have fun using the e-learning system."	
• Utility experiences	"Using e-learning increases my productivity"	
• Transfer experiences	"My behavior on the job has changed as a result of e-learning experiences."	
• Result experiences	"My department/unit has become more effective as a result of workers participating in e-learning."	
Attitudes		[2,5,53]
• Positive Expectancies * valences	"From successful completion of e-learning activities I expect acknowledgment from my supervisor(s)." * "Acknowledgement from my supervisor is important to me."	
• Negative Expectancies * valences	"From completion of e-learning activities I expect an increase in working hours." * "The reduction of working hours is important to me."	
Intention to participate	"In the near future, I intend to participate in e-learning activities"	[53,87]
Control variables:		
• Locus of control over outcome	"The outcome I expect of e-learning activities highly depends on my participation and my performance."	[63]
• Perceived inequity	"I feel injustice in our company because I unrightfully receive more/less recognition and reward from e-learning participation than my fellow colleagues"	[1]

1) Second-order hierarchical construct [9]

This research further argues that the new construct of *Personal factors* is also meaningful with regards to the Social Cognitive Theory. The often cited theory postulates that human motivation results from the triadic reciprocal interplay of environmental, personal, and behavioral factors [11], which relates well to the reciprocally influence of the three antecedents of *Intention*, which are *Subjective norm*, *Personal factors*, and *Attitudes*.

5.2 *Locus of control over outcome* and *Perceived inequity*

As illustrated in Table 1 Hurtz and Williams do not address motivational facets 7 and 8. The former is based on the theory of cognitive dissonance [38] and considered an expectancy of the effort-to-outcome relation relative to peers [1], and the latter is an expectancy of outcome [81]. Neither concept is included in the final research model illustrated in Figure 2 because their impact on motivation changes depending on a particular situation is therefore hardly generalizable in a model. Locus of control over the outcome on motivation is not always positive and depends on a person's preference to either avoid responsibility or take charge in a particular situation [81]. Similarly, the theory of perceived inequity, which claims that a person is motivated to act in order to establish justice, cannot consistently explain the impact on motivation without further antecedents and other actions than e-leaning participation. Ensuring that there is no impact on our model, we include there two concepts as control variables as outlined in Table 3.

5.3 *The impact of social software features on the motivation to participate*

Figure 2 illustrates the final research model including the factor *Social Software – e-learning environment*, which measures the extent to which social software features appropriate for this context (see Table 2) are implemented.

Summarizing the discussion of the previous sections, we expect *Social Software* features to impact *Personal factors* primarily because they provide the mean to satisfy the innate human need for relatedness. With regards to another personal factor competence, it would also be reasonable to believe that social software features provide the mean for others to raise it through persuasion, but prior research does not support this believe [10], which is why we believe relatedness to be the key in explaining the influence of social software.

H1: *'Social Software' positively impacts 'Personal factors'*.

According to Ajzen, Subjective Norms "are concerned with the likelihood that important referent individuals or groups approve or disapprove of performing a given behavior" [4]. As social software features in an LMS, allows a user to better know the opinion of potentially important referents, we further hypothesize an impact of 'Social Software' on 'Subjective Norms'

H2: *'Social Software' positively impacts 'Subjective Norms'*.

After completion of an e-learning module, participants can expect to have the opportunity to provide their own opinions, rakings and comments to others in the LMS using social software features. The theory of planned behavior captures these kind of raised outcome expectancies in the 'Attitudes' construct [4]. Since corporate employees are generally reluctant to contribute to rankings and discussions [57], we do expect a positive, but not a strong impact on 'Attitudes'.

H3: *'Social Software' positively impacts 'Attitudes'*

6. OUTLOOK AND RESEARCH CONTEXT OF IS TALENTS

We envision continuing this research in two steps. First, empirically supporting the previously developed research model using structured interviews in order to explain *why* social software impacts motivation, and second, using the research model as justificatory knowledge in a design science approach with the aim to explain *how* social software features impact motivation to participate in corporate e-learning. This section outlines both steps and the contextual choice in the following

6.1 Structured interviews

The interviews supporting the research model are structured because both social software and motivation theory have a long history and are well-defined. Social software features have been around for nearly ten years [35], and research on motivation theory date back to Aristotle [47].

The participants of choice are IS talents of Germany's dual education system for two reasons. The first reason is the rare implementation of social software features in today's corporate e-learning environments, which inhibits asking users for their actual opinions and requires asking them for their hypothetical opinions. The interview participants therefore need to be knowledgeable about social software, interested in the research topic, and experienced in corporate e-learning for the results to be meaningful. IS apprentices and students uniquely fulfill all three requirements. The dual education system requires corporations to fully employ apprentices and students. They spend half of their time in classes at a state-supported academic institution. Complementing and deepening the newly gained knowledge, they work the other half of their time in different departments of their individual employers. Usually, the employer's department of human resource development oversees their development, ensures that their practical experience matches the academic curriculum, and informs the academic institutions in case of necessary education changes. The young IS apprentices and students frequently use corporate e-learning on both a mandatory and a voluntary basis.

The second reason is that Germany's dual education system provides a successful, stable environment to provide lasting findings. Other more troubled economies by contrast, would constrain this research either through budget cuts on training and e-learning or through high unemployment rates leading to findings from extreme situations, which are less likely to be generalizable.

6.2 Design Science research

With a empirically proven model as a guidance and following the calls of other researchers [49,58], design science research appears to be an ideal approach in the area of e-learning. Behavioral science methods are less effective because researchable, successful implementations of corporate e-learning 2.0 implementations hardly exist, and because e-learning technology and trends are changing quickly which impedes the development of stable research models. By contrast, the design science process is ideal to extend boundaries to unknown research areas [32,45,50,99].

The artifact to be tested in this research would be a learning management system (LMS) with social software features implemented (as outlined in Table 2) in the corporate, asynchronous e-learning context. The experiments would follow an iterative trial-and-error approach [50], in order to identify an optimal implementation of social software features maximizing the users' motivation to participate measured in e-learning launches. One possible variation with regards to the implementation ratings could be to not only display and average score and some comments, but also to distinguish rating scores and comments by the source, which might add additional value to prospective users [36].

7. LIMITATIONS

The developed, cross-disciplinary research model currently lacks empirical support not only regarding the *Social Software* factor, but also regarding *Personal factors*. Furthermore, this paper does not discuss findings from related research on the users' willingness to collaborate in an e-learning environment and to contribute their opinions and their knowledge. They need to be discussed in the light of future empirical results, or future experiments. For example, the experiment needs to provide an environment of high social presence [57,77], of organizational encouragement [44], and of a structured and closed society such as the workforce of a corporation [54] in order to maximize user encouragement.

8. CONCLUSION

Human resource development, education, and learning are indisputably critical in today's recovering knowledge societies. Technology not only enforces this trend, but also provides the means to cope with it. Technology-enabled learning is the next logical step, but neither practitioners nor researchers mastered this step yet. The research model developed in this paper contributes to the closure of two gaps, the lack of understanding how individual social software features impact motivation in the corporate e-learning context and the general gap between researchers and practitioners in the e-learning area [31]. The contributed model combines contemporary training motivation theory with social software features, and it hypothesizes the impact of social software in an asynchronous corporate e-learning context. Practitioners may already use it as a starting point for their implementations, while researchers need to further substantiate it. The authors are committed to build on this model, to provide further insights on which technology features to use in order to ultimately help education to become more flexible and effective.

9. REFERENCES

[1] Adams, J.S. Towards an understanding of inequity. *Journal of Abnormal and Social Psychology 67*, 5 (1963), 422–436.

[2] Ajzen, I. and Fishbein, M. Attitudinal and normative variables as predictors of specific behaviors. *Journal of Personality and Social Psychology 27*, 1 (1973), 41–57.

[3] Ajzen, I. From intentions to actions: A theory of planned behavior. In J. Kuhl and J. Beckmann, eds., *Action control: From cognition to behavior*. Springer-Verlag, Heidelberg, Germany, 1985, 11–39.

[4] Ajzen, I. The theory of planned behavior. *Organizational Behavior and Human Decision Processes 50*, 2 (1991), 179–211.

[5] Ajzen, I. Nature and operation of attitudes. *Annual Review of Psychology 52*, (2001), 27–58.

[6] Ajzen, I. Perceived Behavioral Control, Self-Efficacy, Locus of Control, and the Theory of Planned Behavior. *Journal of Applied Social Psychology 32*, 4 (2002), 665–683.

[7] Andriole, S.J. Business impact of Web 2.0 Technologies. *Communications of the ACM 53*, 12 (2010), 67–79.

[8] Baard, P.P., Deci, E.L., and Ryan, R.M. Intrinsic Need Satisfaction: A Motivational Basis of Performance and Well-Being in Two Work Settings1. *Journal of Applied Social Psychology 34*, 10 (2004), 2045–2068.

[9] Bagozzi, R.P. and Edwards, J.R. A General Approach for Representing Constructs in Organizational Research. *Organizational Research Methods 1*, 1 (1998), 45–87.

[10] Bandura, A. Self-efficacy: toward a unifying theory of behavioral change. *Psychological Review 84*, 2 (1977), 191–215.

[11] Bandura, A. *Social Foundations of Thought and Action: A Social Cognitive Theory*. Prentice-Hall, Englewood Cliffs, N.J., 1986.

[12] Birdi, K., Allan, C., and Warr, P. Correlates and perceived outcomes of four types of employee development activity. *Journal of Applied Psychology 82*, 6 (1997), 845–857.

[13] Blechinger, D. and Pfeiffer, F. *Technological Change and Skill Obsolescence: The Case of German Apprenticeship Training*. Zentrum für Europäische Wirtschaftsforschung, Mannheim, Germany, 1996.

[14] Bodner, G.M. Constructivism: A theory of knowledge. *Journal of Chemical Education 63*, (1986), 873–878.

[15] Brauns, H. Vocational Education and France in Germany. *Journal of International Sociology 28*, 4 (1998), 57–98.

[16] Brown, J.S. and Adler, R.P. Minds on Fire: Open Education, the Long Tail, and Learning 2.0. *Educause Review*, January/February (2008), 16–32.

[17] Brown, K.G. and Ford, J.K. Using computer technology in training: Building an infrastructure for active learning. In K. Kraiger, ed., *Creating, implementing, and managing effective training and development*. Jossey-Bass, San Francisco, CA, 2002, 192–233.

[18] Buechtemann, C.F., Schupp, J., and Soloff, D. Roads to work: school-to-work transition patterns in Germany and the United States. *Industrial Relations Journal 24*, 2 (1993), 97–111.

[19] Cattell, R.B. *Personality and motivation structure and measurement*. World Book Co, 1957.

[20] Cheng, Y.-M. Antecedents and consequences of e-learning acceptance. *Information Systems Journal 21*, 3 (2011), 269–299.

[21] Chiu, C.-M., Chiu, C.-S., and Chang, H.-C. Examining the integrated influence of fairness and quality on learners' satisfaction and Web-based learning continuance intention. *Information Systems Journal 17*, 3 (2007), 271–287.

[22] Clark, C.S., Dobbins, G.H., and Ladd, R.T. Exploratory Field Study of Training Motivation: Infiluence of Involvement, Credibility, and Transfer Climate. *Group & Organization Management 18*, 3 (1993), 292–307.

[23] Colquitt, J.A., LePine, J.A., and Noe, R.A. Toward an integrative theory of training motivation: A meta-analytic path analysis of 20 years of research. *Journal of Applied Psychology 85*, 5 (2000), 678–707.

[24] Compeau, D.R. and Higgins, C. a. Computer Self-Efficacy: Development of a Measure and Initial Test. *MIS Quarterly 19*, 2 (1995), 189.

[25] Compeau, D.R. and Higgins, C. a. Application of Social Cognitive Theory to Training for Computer Skills. *Information Systems Research 6*, 2 (1995), 118–143.

[26] Davis, F.D. Perceived Usefulness, Perceived Ease of Use, and User Acceptance of Information Technology. *MIS Quarterly 13*, 3 (1989), 319.

[27] Deci, E.L. and Ryan, R.M. The "What" and "Why" of Goal Pursuits: Human Needs and the Self-Determination of Behavior. *Psychological Inquiry 11*, 4 (2000), 227–268.

[28] Deci, E.L. and Ryan, R.M. *Handbook of self-determination research*. University of Rochester Press, 2002.

[29] Deci, E.L. *Intrinsic motivation*. Plenum Press, 1975.

[30] Deming, W.E. *Out of the Crisis*. SPC Press, 1982.

[31] DeRouin, R.E., Fritzsche, B.A., and Sales, E. E-Learning in Organizations. *Journal of Management 31*, 6 (2005), 920–940.

[32] Dubin, R. *Theory Building*. Free Press, London, 1978.

[33] Dublin, L. If You Only Look Under the Street Lamps...or Nine e-Learning myths. *The e-Learning Developer's Journal*, June (2003), 1–7.

[34] Dunne, A. and Butler, T. Beyond Knowledge Management -- Introducing a Framework for Learning Management Systems. *European Conference on Information Systems (ECIS) Proceedings*, (2004).

[35] Ebersbach, A., Glaser, M., and Heigl, R. *Social Web*. UVK Verlagsgesellschaft mbH, Konstanz, 2011.

[36] Eckhardt, A., Laumer, S., and Weitzel, T. Who influences whom? Analyzing workplace referents' social influence on IT adoption and non-adoption. *Journal of Information Technology 24*, 1 (2009), 11–24.

[37] Fee, K. *Delivering E-Learning: A complete strategy for design, application and assessment*. Kogan Page Limited, 2009.

[38] Festinger, L. *A theory of cognitive dissonance*. Stanford University Press, 1957.

[39] Fishbein, M. and Ajzen, I. *Belief, attitude, intention, and behavior: An introduction to theory and research*. Addison-Wesley, Reading, MA, 1975.

[40] Fisher, C.D. The effects of personal control, competence, and extrinsic reward systems on intrinsic motivation. *Organizational Behavior and Human Performance 21*, (1978), 273–288.

[41] Freud, S. *Triebe und Triebschicksale*. Fischer, Frankfurt, Germany, 1952.

[42] Gagné, M. and Deci, E.L. Self-determination theory and work motivation. *Journal of Organizational Behavior 26*, 4 (2005), 331–362.

[43] Garavan, T.N., Carbery, R., Malley, G.O., and Donnell, D.O. Understanding participation in e-learning in organizations: a large- scale empirical study of employees. *International Journal of Training and Development 14*, 3 (2010), 155–168.

[44] Goodman, P.S. and Darr, E.D. Computer-Aided Systems and Communities: Mechanisms for Organizational Learning in Distributed Environments. *MIS Quarterly 22*, 4 (1998), 417.

[45] Gregor, S. and Jones, D. The Anatomy of a Design Theory. *Journal of the Association for Information Systems 8*, 5 (2007), 312–335.

[46] Hamilton, S.F. Germany and the United States in Comparative Perspective. *International Journal of Sociology 29*, 1 (1999), 3–20.

[47] Hardie, W.F.R. *Aristotle's ethical theory*. Clarendon Press, Oxford, 1980.

[48] Heckhausen, J. and Heckhausen, H. *Motivation and Action*. Cambridge University Press, Cambridge, UK, 2010.

[49] Herrington, J., Reeves, T.C., and Oliver, R. *A guide to authentic e-learning*. Routledge Chapman & Hall, 2010.

[50] Hevner, B.A.R., March, S.T., Park, J., and Ram, S. Design Science in information systems research. *MIS Quarterly 28*, 1 (2004), 75–105.

[51] Hicks, W.D. and Klimoski, R.J. Entry into training programs and its effects on training outcomes: A field experiment. *Academy of Management Journal 30*, 3 (1987), 542–552.

[52] Hu, N., Bose, I., Koh, N.S., and Liu, L. Manipulation of online reviews: An analysis of ratings, readability, and sentiments. *Decision Support Systems 52*, 3 (2012), 674–684.

[53] Hurtz, G.M. and Williams, K.J. Attitudinal and motivational antecedents of participation in voluntary employee development activities. *Journal of Applied Psychology 94*, 3 (2009), 635–53.

[54] Jarvenpaa, S. and Staples, D.S. The use of collaborative electronic media for information sharing: an exploratory study of determinants. *The Journal of Strategic Information Systems 9*, 2-3 (2000), 129–154.

[55] Johnston, M.M. and Finney, S.J. Measuring basic needs satisfaction: Evaluating previous research and conducting new psychometric evaluations of the Basic Needs Satisfaction in General Scale. *Contemporary Educational Psychology 35*, 4 (2010), 280–296.

[56] Joint-Research-Center. *Learning 2.0: The Impact of Web 2.0 Innovations on Education and Training in Europe*. Dictus Publishing, 2011.

[57] Kankanhalli, A., Tan, B.C.Y., and Wei, K.-K. Contributing Knowledge to Electronic Knowledge Repositories: An Empirical Investigation. *MIS Quarterly 29*, 1 (2005), 113–143.

[58] Kelly, A.E. Research as Design. *Educational Researcher 32*, 1 (2003), 3–4.

[59] Kirkpatrick, D.L. Techniques for evaluating training programs. *Journal of ASTD 13*, (1959), 3–9.

[60] Kirkpatrick, D.L. Techniques for evaluating training programs: Part 2—Learning. *Journal of ASTD 13*, (1959), 21–26.

[61] Kirkpatrick, D.L. Techniques for evaluating training programs: Part 4—Results. *Journal of ASTD 14*, (1960), 28–32.

[62] Kirkpatrick, D.L. Techniques for evaluating training programs: Part 3—Behavior. *Journal of ASTD 14*, (1960), 13–18.

[63] Lefcourt, H.M. Locus of control. In J.P. Robinson, P.R. Shaver and L.S. Wrightsman, eds., *Measures of personality and social psychological attitudes*. Academic Press, San Diego, CA, US, 1991, 413–499.

[64] Lewin, K. *The conceptual representation and measurement of psychological forces*. Duke University Press, 1938.

[65] London, M. and Hall, M. Unlocking the value of web 2.0 technologies for training and development: The shift from instructor-controlled, adaptive learning to learner-driven generative learning. *Human Resource Management 50*, 6 (2011), 757–775.

[66] Lytras, M. and Pouloudi, A. E-Learning☐: Just a Waste of Time. *Americas Conference on Information Systems (AMCIS) Proceedings*, (2001).

[67] Mandl, H. Implementation von E-Learning und Wissensmanagement - Ein mitarbeiterorientierter Ansatz. *Wirtschaftsinformatik (WI) Proceedings*, (2003).

[68] ManpowerGroup. Global talent shortage survey. 2012. http://www.manpowergroup.us/campaigns/talent-shortage-2012/pdf/2012_Talent_Shortage_Survey_Results_US_FIN ALFINAL.pdf.

[69] Martin, G., Massy, J., and Clarke, T. When absorptive capacity meets institutions and (e)learners: adopting, diffusing and exploiting e-learning in organizations. *International Journal of Training and Development 7*, 4 (2003), 228–244.

[70] Maslow, A.H. A Theory of Human Motivation. *Psychological Review 50*, 4 (1943), 370–396.

[71] Maurer, T.J. and Tarulli, B.A. Investigation of perceived environment, perceived outcome, and person variables in relationship to voluntary development activity by employees. *Journal of Applied Psychology 79*, 1 (1994), 3–14.

[72] McClelland, D.C., Koestner, R., and Weinberger, J. How do self-attributed and implicit motives differ? *Psychological Review 96*, (1989), 690–702.

[73] McDougall, W.U. *An introduction to social psychology*. John W Luce & Company, Boston, MA, US, 1918.

[74] Murray, H.A. *Explorations in personality*. Oxford University Press, New York, 1938.

[75] Noe, R.A. and Wilk, S.L. Investigation of the factors that influence employees' participation in development activities. *Journal of Applied Psychology 78*, 2 (1993), 291–302.

[76] O'Reilly, T. What Is Web 2.0. *Pattern Recognition 30*, 2005, 0–48. http://oreilly.com/web2/archive/what-is-web-20.html.

[77] Olivera, F., Goodman, P.S., and Tan, S.S. Contribution Behaviors in Distributed Environments. *MIS Quarterly 32*, 1 (2008), 23–42.

[78] Petri, H.L. and Govern, J.M. *Motivation - Theory, Research, and Applications*. Wadsworth Publishing, 2003.

[79] Porter, L. and Lawler III, E.E. *Managerial Attitudes and Performance*. Homewood, 1968.

[80] Reiss, S. Multifaceted Nature of Intrinsic Motivation: The Theory of 16 Basic Desires. *Review of General Psychology 8*, 3 (2004), 179–193.

[81] Rotter, J.B. Generalized expectancies for internal versus external control of reinforcement. *Psychological Monographs 80*, 1 (1966).

[82] Ryan, R.M. and Deci, E.L. Self-determination theory and the facilitation of intrinsic motivation, social development, and well-being. *The American psychologist 55*, 1 (2000), 68–78.

[83] Ryan, R.M. and Deci, E.L. Intrinsic and Extrinsic Motivations: Classic Definitions and New Directions. *Contemporary educational psychology 25*, 1 (2000), 54–67.

[84] Ryan, R.M. Control and information in the intrapersonal sphere: An extension of cognitive evaluation theory. *Journal of Personality and Social Psychology 43*, (1982), 450–461.

[85] Schultheiss, O.C. and Brunstein, J.C. Assessment of implicit motives with a research version of the TAT: Picture profiles, gender differences and relations to other personality measures. *Journal of Personality Assessment 77*, (2001), 71–86.

[86] Seufert, S. Work Based Learning and Knowledge Management☐: An Integrated Concept of Organizational Learning. *European Conference on Information Systems (ECIS) Proceedings*, (2000).

[87] Sheppard, B.H., Hartwick, J., and Warshaw, P.R. The Theory of Reasoned Action: A Meta-Analysis of Past Research with Recommendations for Modifications and Future Research. *The Journal of Consumer Research 15*, 3 (1988), 325–343.

[88] Soliman, M.A. and Beaudry, A. Undertanding individual adoption and use of social computing: A user-system fit model. *International Conference on Information Systems (ICIS) Proceedings*, (2010).

[89] Sridhar, S. and Srinivasan, R. Social Influence Effects in Online Product Ratings. *Journal of Marketing 76*, September (2012), 70–88.

[90] Sun, M. How Does Variance of Product Ratings Matter☐? *Management Science Furthcomin*, (2012).

[91] Sun, R. Motivational Representations within a Computational Cognitive Architecture. *Cognitive Computation 1*, 1 (2009), 91–103.

[92] Sykes, T.A., Venkatesh, V., and Gosain, S. Model of Acceptance with Peer Support: A Social Network Perspective to Understand Employees' System Use. *MIS Quarterly 33*, 2 (2009), 371–393.

[93] Tai, L. *Corporate E-Learning: An Inside View of IBM's Solutions*. Oxford University Press, New York, NY, USA, 2008.

[94] Tharenou, P. The relationship of training motivation to participation in training and development. *Journal of Occupational & Organizational Psychology 74*, 5 (2001), 599–621.

[95] Thomas, K.W. *Intrinsic Motivation at Work: What Really Drives Employee Engagement*. Berrett-Koehler Publishers, 2009.

[96] Venkatesh, V. Creation of Favorable User Perceptions: Exploring the Role of Intrinsic Motivation. *MIS Quarterly 23*, 2 (1999), 239.

[97] Vroom, V.H. *Work and Motivation*. New York, 1964.

[98] Wakefield, R.L., Wakefield, K.L., Baker, J., and Wang, L.C. How website socialness leads to website use. *European Journal of Information Systems 20*, 1 (2010), 118–132.

[99] Walls, J., Widemeyer, G., and El Sawy, O. Building an Information System Design theory for Vigilant EIS. *Information Systems Research 3*, 1 (1992), 36–59.

[100] Wan, Z., Compeau, D., and Haggerty, N. The Effects of Self-Regulated Learning Processes on E-Learning Outcomes in Organizational Settings. *Journal of Management Information Systems 29*, 1 (2012), 307–340.

[101] Wang, M., Vogel, D., and Ran, W. Creating a performance-oriented e-learning environment: A design science approach. *Information & Management 48*, 7 (2011), 260–269.

[102] Wilson, B.G. *Constructivist Learning Environments: Case Studies in Instructional Design*. Educational Technology Publications, Englewood Cliffs, NJ, 1996.

[103] Wirt, S., Choy, S., Rooney, P., Provasnik, S., Sen, A., and Tobin, R. *The condition of Education 2004 (NECS 2004-077)*. Washington, D.C., 2004.

[104] Wirtky, T., Laumer, S., Eckhardt, A., and Weitzel, T. Towards understanding social software and its impact on corporate e-learning motivation. *Wirtschaftsinformatik (WI) Proceedings (forthcoming)*, (2013).

[105] Witte, J.C. and Kalleberg, A.L. Matching Training and Jobs: The Fit Between Vocational Education and Emplyoment in the German Labour Market. *European Sociological Review 11*, 3 (1995), 293–317.

[106] Yang, H.H. and Yuen, S.C.-Y. *Collective intelligence and e-learning 2.0*. Information Science Reference, 2009.

[107] Zemsky, R. and Massey, W. Why the E-Learning Boom Went Bust. *The Chronicle of Higher Education 50*, July 9 (2004).

[108] Zhang, D., Zhou, L., Briggs, R.O., and Nunamaker, J.F. Instructional video in e-learning: Assessing the impact of interactive video on learning effectiveness. *Information & Management 43*, (2006), 15–27.

Motivating Students to Acquire Mainframe Skills

Brandon Phillips
University of North Texas
Information Technology
And Decision Sciences Dept.
1155 Union Circle
Denton, TX 76203-5017
+1-(940)-369-8513
brandon.phillips@unt.edu

Sherry Ryan
University of North Texas
Information Technology
And Decision Sciences Dept.
1155 Union Circle
Denton, TX 76203-5017
+1-(940)-565-3106
sherry.ryan@unt.edu

Gina Harden
University of North Texas
Information Technology
And Decision Sciences Dept.
1155 Union Circle
Denton, TX 76203-5017
+1-(940)-565-3174
gina.harden@unt.edu

C.S. Guynes
University of North Texas
Information Technology
And Decision Sciences Dept.
1155 Union Circle
Denton, TX 76203-5017
+1-(940)-565-3114
steve,guynes@unt.edu

John Windsor
University of North Texas
Information Technology
And Decision Sciences Dept.
1155 Union Circle
Denton, TX 76203-5017
+1-(940)-565-4147
john.windsor@unt.edu

ABSTRACT

There has been a perception in both industry and in academia that mainframe skills are obsolete. As a result, there has been a decline in curricula addressing these skills. However, recent evidence shows that many organizations are still actively supporting mainframe technologies and report a need for students graduating in information technology to be trained in those skills, especially as much of their current mainframe workforce moves toward retirement. This paper examines the question of what motivates students to acquire mainframe skills. To do so, this research is investigates IBM's Master the Mainframe contest, a competition that attempts to engender enthusiasm for acquiring mainframe skills and ensure an adequate supply of such skills to organizations relying on them.

Categories and Subject Descriptors

K.6.1 [**Management of Computing and Information Systems**]: Staffing, Training.

Keywords

Mainframes, legacy systems, motivation

1. INTRODUCTION

Three decades ago, technologists pronounced that "the mainframe is dead," but this has proved to be untrue. In fact, the demand has

returned for those skills and companies are finding a shortage of information technology (IT) graduates with those skills [20]. This misconception that mainframe skills are antiquated and not necessary in today's IT job market, leads to a perception gap concerning skill requirements between job seekers and job recruiters. When surveyed, job seekers reported that they placed mainframe skills at a lower priority level than both job recruiters and hiring managers [16].

Legacy mainframe systems require maintenance of vast amounts of code to be maintained and often integrated with web-based applications as e-commerce activities continue their growth in organizations [9]. Mainframe skills are vital to the modernization effort that companies engage in, in order to move out of a mainframe infrastructure [19]. There is also still a growing need for mainframe skills as current mainframe skilled workers are increasing in age and retiring, leaving a gap that needs to be filled [12].

Organizations moved away from mainframes in part because of their expensive hardware, software and licensing fees, in addition to the flexibility offered by new enterprise systems based on distributed architecture [11]. However, research shows these legacy systems are still in active use in many organizations [22]. Not only information systems (IS) managers, but also academic respondents report a need for IS curricula that includes COBOL and Customer Information Controls Systems (CICS) programming skills necessary to work on mainframes [3]. A study analyzing job advertisements to determine skill requirements of IT managers shows that those in the Fortune 500 work more on architecture and network related systems, including mainframes and security, than on hardware such as PCs [15].

Students may be concerned about the outsourcing of many mainframe skills or are drawn to newer programming languages. However, IT managers identify "familiarity with legacy systems" as one of the six key skills they feel IT graduates are lacking [22].

Indeed, research shows that even with the potential outsourcing of some mainframe skills, companies want to keep some of those skills in-house. Early in the decade outsourcing was prevalent, however, more recently, insourcing has become increasingly popular in order to enable businesses to grow their own IT capabilities in-house and reap the advantages of those capabilities [21]. While mainframe technologies were initially an easy target for outsourcing, companies relying on those legacy systems – combined with a desire to integrate them for internet applications – have a specific need for keeping those mainframe skills in-house [2]. In addition, because of the massive processing and storage management capabilities needed for business analytics and "big data", many analysts believe that mainframes provide a real solution for grappling with these issues [4]. It is therefore apparent that there is a need to address the educational and staffing requirements of those mainframe and legacy skills.

Mainframe education at the university level is nothing new; it has been around for decades. However, with the misconception that mainframes are not actively used in today's organizations, academia has decreased the resources spent on curriculum related to mainframe skills. In 2005 IBM started the Academic Initiative in order to advance mainframe studies and to both encourage schools to teach mainframe skills and to attract students to actively learn these skills. Between 2006 and 2009, IBM as part of their Academic Initiative program, surveyed its customer base to see which mainframe skills are needed the most.

Their results indicated that CICS, DB2, COBOL, and z/OS are still strongly required skills important to businesses and therefore hiring managers [26]. Out of the over 200 colleges and universities in Texas, only 8 currently participate in the IBM academic initiative to teach mainframe skills [25]. These courses are valuable to job seekers and to organizations that desperately need mainframe operators. More continues to need to be done in order to fill the need of mainframe skills in today's organizations.

As the baby-boom generation of workers continues its trek toward retirement, organizations will lose those retirees' valuable skills and experiences working with legacy systems. That includes the technologies those systems are based upon such as CICS, DB2, MVS, COBOL, etc. [10]. Thus, there are organizations with a heavy need for mainframe skills that face challenges in adequately replacing those skills [10]. Without adequate training in legacy technologies, where will the replacements of new IT professionals entering the work force come from?

IBM is involved in an initiative to spur enthusiasm for mainframe skills among educators and students alike entitled "Master the Mainframe Competition." In this present research we investigate this competition and seek to answer the research question, "What motivates students to acquire mainframe skills?" Using the macro-motivational Self-Determination Theory (SDT), we analyze the competition rules, articles, websites, Facebook postings, and blogs related to the competition and categorize student motivations. Because of the shortage of mainframe skills and the "graying" of mainframe programmers, this is a useful and important research question. The rest of the paper is as follows. First we discuss motivational theories, specifically highlighting SDT and its motivational categories. Next, we describe the Master the Mainframe Competition. Third, we analyze student motivations to participate in the competition. Because this paper is research-in-progress, we describe our future research and its potential significance.

2. LITERATURE REVIEW
2.1 Intrinsic vs. Extrinsic Motivation
Motivational theories have been an important part of many prior IS research studies. For example, one motivational theory, the Theory of Planned Behavior, has been used by numerous IS studies as a basis for understanding why a technology might or might not be adopted [5]. Motivation has also been recognized as one of the key factors that affect the success of learning. Student motivation has to do with students' desire to become involved in the learning process. It also relates to the underlying goals or purposes for engaging in learning. Learning motivation has been frequently been divided into two types: intrinsic and extrinsic. [17]. Intrinsic motivation refers to motivation that is driven by enjoyment or an interest in the task itself and exists internally within an individual instead of resulting from external pressure. Extrinsic motivation comes from outside of the individual so that an outcome will be attained [23]. Outcomes can be positive or negative. Common positive extrinsic motivators include money, good grades or trophies. Punishment is an example of a negative motivator. Both intrinsic and extrinsic motivation can work as driving forces that affect students overall performance [18].

2.2 Self Determination Theory (SDT)
While researchers often divide motivations into the two categories of intrinsic and extrinsic motivations, Self Determination Theory argues that motivations lie on a continuum, ranging from controlled to autonomous regulation. Deci and Ryan [6] proposed that when people are intrinsically motivated they feel a sense of autonomy. Conversely, when individuals are either rewarded or punished, they tend to feel pressured and controlled, and their basic need for autonomy is threatened. Other research has often considered extrinsic motivation as monolithic, but Ryan and Deci [6] argued it should be looked at as more granular and identified four categories of extrinsic motivation positioned on the controlled-autonomous continuum as shown in Figure 1. In addition to the framework shown in Figure 1 , we used Ke and Zhang's [13] application of SDT to open source developers' motivations to help provide a description of each SDT category in an IS context as discussed below.

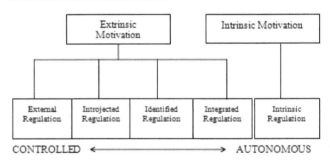

Figure 1. Self-Determination Theory (adapted from Deci and Ryan, [7])

With external regulation, an individual acts based upon the intention of obtaining a desired consequence or avoiding an undesired one. The impetus to participate in a behavior comes from outside sources, thus, the individual's behavior is significantly influenced or controlled by external forces. Examples in the IS literature of external regulation include enhancing the possibilities of job prospects and financial/salary rewards.

Next, introjected regulation is defined as an individual taking some sort of external demand but not fully accepting it as his or her own [6]. It represents partial internalization in which an individual feels somewhat controlled by tacit offers of others, or pride for actions that others assess as laudable, or guilt and shame for actions that others deem inappropriate or inadequate [6]. It often relates to ego involvement where individuals want to demonstrate their abilities or competence [6]. Examples of introjected regulation include: gaining recognition from peers, showing off work, and enhancing one's reputation within the community [13].

Identified regulation is related to individuals acknowledging the importance of the task or behavior in question and therefore accepting it as their own. They do so when they recognize and embrace the value of the activity. With identified regulation, individuals participate in the behavior with a greater feeling of autonomy and thus feel less controlled or obliged to perform the behavior [6]. Examples in the IS literature include identifying with a particular type of information systems development, seeing its value, and/or identifying with a development team [13].

Integrated regulation is when individuals incorporate or assimilate a new identification with their sense of who they are. According to Deci and Ryan [6]:

> Integrated regulation is similar to intrinsic motivation in that both are accompanied by a sense of volition and choice. Still, the two types of motivation differ in that intrinsic motivation is based on interest in the behavior itself, whereas integrated extrinsic motivation is based on the person having fully integrated the value of the behaviour. The latter is still a type of extrinsic motivation, for it remains instrumental to some other outcome, whereas with intrinsic motivation the activity itself is interesting and enjoyable.

2.3 IBM's Master the Mainframe Competition

With the need for mainframe skills still very much a reality in today's business world, IBM has for the last decade been instrumental in its partnership with the academic community. IBM sponsors a contest, Master the Mainframe, to motivate interest in high school and college level students and help them obtain valuable mainframe experience and skills. Through their partnership with over 643 schools and 56,000 students worldwide, IBM is sending a clear message that mainframe skills are in high demand. With the release of their new zEnterprise EC12 mainframe in August of 2012, IBM has demonstrated that the need for mainframe skills is still very much alive.

The Master the Mainframe competition allows students with little or no experience to be able to access mainframes and take courses to enhance their skills. The students compete in three parts. The first part is breaking the ice, which introduces the students to the world of mainframes and gets them comfortable navigating the user interface. The second part is the practical experience which entails more extensive programming, advanced commands, system setup, and advanced system navigation. This part also exposes students to various programing languages used in

application development on mainframes. The third and final part of the contest is the most challenging and also the most rewarding. It involves the students in a real world challenge and requires extensive work from the students over several weeks and perhaps even months. These scenarios are taken from real life situations encountered by experienced mainframe programmers. It is this final part that really ties everything together for the students and enables the students to see the real world applicability of what they have been learning. A look at IBM's Master the Mainframe Facebook page gives an indication of the popularity of the competition as well as the appreciation of the skills gained. The social media buzz indicates that the competition is a catalyst for a lot of students, who then go on to further develop their mainframe skills and ultimately land a job in the field.

3. ANALYSIS

In order to investigate the different types of motivation involved in students acquiring mainframe skills we conducted an online search focusing on sites that dealt with the Master the Mainframe competition including the IBM Master the Mainframe site, the Master the Mainframe Facebook site, various blogs devoted to Master the Mainframe, and news articles mentioning the competition. Many of the articles and online resources including blogs contained quotes from students and their feelings toward the Master the Mainframe competition. For this study, we analyzed the data using content analysis with an *a priori* coding scheme based upon the motivation types described earlier. Content analysis has been defined as a technique for compressing many words of text into fewer content categories based on explicit rules of coding [14]. With an *a priori* coding scheme, the categories are established prior to the analysis based upon theory [26]. Using this technique allowed us to match these quotes and narratives with their respective motivation type. We discuss these motivation types below.

3.1 External Regulation

People are motivated by external regulation due to an external acting influence. Students who are more motivated by prizes, rewards, as well as job and career opportunities choose to participate in the Master the Mainframe competition due to external regulation motivation. IBM entices students to participate in the competition with prizes including ASUS tablet computers, trips to the IBM mainframe lab, and other mainframe related clothing, bags, and more. Prizes are not the only draw; we see from participant quotes that acquiring mainframe skills to get a job is another source of external motivation for the contestants as well. IBM's Master the Mainframe page encourages participants to interact with their System z job board in order to match employers with mainframe students. This strengthens the argument that job placement as an external motivation factor is important. Some examples of external motivation are seen in the quotes from prior participants. This first quote is a clear example of job placement being an external motivating factor for this contestant.

> My participation and successful completion of Part One (I'm still working on Part Two) of the IBM Master the Mainframe Contest helped to get me a job at [an international bank] working as a Junior Systems Support Analyst. This position has never been offered to a student before and I never

would have been able to secure it without all that I have learned so far in the contest.

- Student, Georgian College

Another student involved in the competition stated a similar experience as noted below, and was able to use his mainframe skills to acquire an interview and subsequently an internship.

I participated in the Master the Mainframe competition last year and the mere mention of mainframe knowledge alone during an interview very likely earned me an internship over the summer scheduling jobs using TWS.

- Student, Missouri University of Science and Technology

3.2 Introjected Regulation

A second type of motivation is introjected regulation, which is motivation from an internalized, pressuring voice. This relates to students who participate in the Master the Mainframe competition to fulfill an ideal or goal they feel they must live up to. It often is associated with ego involvement and can be demonstrated by the desire to gain recognition from others. IBM has created a "Wall of Fame" which is an online list of participants who have completed the difficult Part Two of the competition. Students wishing to have "bragging rights", and have their name on the wall of fame, demonstrate introjected regulation.

For example, one student gleefully exclaims on his blog, "I find my name on the Mainframe Wall of Fame." This appears to be an important motivation for many students. When a student asked on the Master the Mainframe Facebook page whether the 2012 competition would continue the Wall of Fame, IBM assured them, "We'll keep updating the Wall of Fame as you keep knocking out those challenges." Through this public display of their accomplishments, introjected regulation is seen as a motivating factor.

3.3 Identified Regulation

Identified regulation is a form of motivation that we see in individuals who engage in activity as a means to their specific goal. This is an activity that they might not otherwise participate in. With regards to the Master the Mainframe competition, participants will compete in order to achieve a goal, such as skill development for their career, or education objectives. In this first quote, we see that this particular student is interested in the competition as a means to learn mainframe skills. *"Actually, I'm in it for the learning experience."*

-Student, Northeastern University

Another student clearly was interested in the competition for skill building:

Master the Mainframe has really given me an opportunity to broaden my horizons. I can now add another skill to my resume.

-Student, Georgian College.

These quotes give us insight into the participants' motivation and with learning experience and skill building as the goal of these two students, this clearly indicates Identified regulation.

3.4 Integrated Regulation

Integrated regulation is a form of motivation that arises when a person has fully integrated a motivation within himself or herself. The person's behavior is influenced by integrated regulation when they undergo self-examination and then internalize and assimilate the reasons behind an action. Students with this type of motivation can be identified with the phrase "I am a main framer." One example is from a student who stated:

The hands on experience with z/OS got me even more interested in the mainframe world.... I would recommend the contest to anyone who is interested in computer science and IT in general. Many people will never have a chance to interact directly with a mainframe, and this is a great opportunity.

- Student, Northern Illinois University

In the above quote, we see this participant has integrated the motivation to compete in the contest within him so much that he has become a proponent of the competition itself.

3.5 Intrinsic Regulation

Intrinsic regulation is inspired solely from the interest and enjoyment that a person finds in an activity. Many of the participants take part in the Master the Mainframe competition for the sole purpose and enjoyment as expressed by some quotes from past participants.

I am enjoying playing around with the mainframe! It is lots of fun! I appreciate this contest and am looking forward to spending many hours on your mainframe for part three :) Thank you so much for running such a cool contest.

- Student, Lake Sumter Community College

The contest has been fun and challenging so far. Thanks for hosting it.

- Student, University of Denver

I wanted to thank you all for the opportunity to participate and spend some time on a great platform and get to know it better. I just wanted to let you know how much fun it was and that I very much appreciate the time and resources you afforded to me.

- Student, University of St. Thomas

Thank you very much for doing this, the little bit I have done has been awesome so far. I can't wait to participate in another contest when I can really mainframe it up"

- Student, F.E. Madill Secondary School

In all of the above quotes, the motivation from these students is pretty clear, with words such as fun, cool, and awesome describing the competition. These types of feelings clearly indicate intrinsic motivation factors.

4. FUTURE RESEARCH

External motivation is a clearly a factor in the student's initial reason for joining the competition. With the competition's three phases, each stage being substantially more challenging for the contestants, it appears that as contestants progress from stage 1, to stage 2 and beyond, their motivation can become more internalized. Students may realize that they really enjoy the challenge of mainframe programming. Therefore, their reasons for continuing the competition may be different from those they initially started with.

This paper used SDT and identified all types of motivation at work in terms of students participating in the Master the Mainframe competition. SDT argues that the presence of external motivators decrease internal motivation [6]. This research found indications that this may not be true in this case. External motivation, in terms of prizes and potential future job opportunities, appear to be the initial motivators for students to become involved in acquiring mainframe skills. However, as they become more involved, they find that it is fun and intrinsically rewarding. To study this phenomenon further, stage 2 of the research will involve interviews with past participants. From these interviews, stage 3 will craft a survey to investigate how each of the various types of motivation is related to task effort and skill acquisition.

In addition to examining student's motivation for acquiring mainframe skills, during our research we found that IBM has a relationship with 8 colleges, in Texas in order to enhance mainframe skills curriculum. Further research could be done to examine the prevalence (or lack thereof)of curriculum in mainframe skills across the United States. In addition to exploring the lack of mainframe curriculum in higher education, the students of the schools that currently have mainframe courses or programs could give real insight into their motivation for participation in mainframe classes and their thoughts on the mainframe skills disparity.

5. CONCLUSION

Mainframe skills are in demand in the marketplace today. In order to supply the marketplace with IT professionals who have these requisite skills, students need to be trained in mainframe languages and procedures. This research investigated the case of IBM's Master the Mainframe competition to better understand how students can be motivated to acquire these skills. Using SDT as our theoretical framework, we found that IBM initially motivates students to participate in the competition through external regulation by offering prizes and touting the availability of mainframe related jobs. We found, however, evidence of all types of motivation ranging from controlled to autonomous motivation. Future research is needed in this area.

6. REFERENCES

[1] Ajzen, I. (1991). The Theory of Planned Behavior, *Organizational Behavior and Human Decision Processes*, 50(2), 179-211.

[2] Bullen, C. V., Abraham, T., Gallagher, K., Kaiser, K. M., and Simon, J. (2007). Changing IT skills: The impact of sourcing strategies on in-house capability requirements. *Journal of Electronic Commerce in Organizations*, 5(2), 24-37, 39-46.

[3] Carr, D., and Kizior, R. J. (2000). The case for continued COBOL education. *IEEE Software*, 17(2), 33-36.

[4] Database Trends and Applications. (2011). Big Data Workhorse. Retrieved from http://www.dbta.com/Articles/Editorial/Think-About-It/Big-Data-Workhorse---The-Mainframe-79352.aspx on March 15, 2013.

[5] Davis, F. D. (1989). Perceived usefulness, perceived ease of use, and user acceptance of Information Technology," *MIS Quarterly*, 13(3), 319-339.

[6] Deci, E. and Ryan, R. (2000). Self-determination theory and the facilitation of intrinsic motivation, social development, and well-being. *American Psychologist*, 55(1), 68-78.

[7] Deci, E. L., and Ryan, R. M. (2008). Facilitating optimal motivation and psychological well-being across life's domains. *Canadian Psychology*, 49, 14–23.

[8] Downey, J. P., McMurtrey, M. E., and Zeltmann, S. M. (2008). Mapping the MIS curriculum based on critical skills of new graduates: An empirical examination of IT professionals. *Journal of Information Systems Education*, 19(3), 351-363.

[9] Fleming, M., and Couturier, G. (2002). Managing the development of a mainframe-based inquiry system for the internet. *Industrial Management + Data Systems*, 102(3), 203-210.

[10] Gerth, A. B., and Rothman, S. (2007). The future IS organization in a flat world. *Information Systems Management*, 24(2), 103-111.

[11] Harbert, T. (2011). A new job for mainframes? *Computerworld*, 45(13), 20-25.

[12] Hewitt, Sue. "Defusing the demographic time-bomb." *Human Resource Management International Digest* 16.7 (2008): 3-5.

[13] Ke, W. and Zhang, P. (2010). The effects of extrinsic motivations and satisfaction in open source software development, *Journal of the Association for Information Systems*, 11(12), 784-808.

[14] Krippendorff, K. (1980). *Content Analysis: An Introduction to Its Methodology*. Newbury Park, CA: Sage.

[15] Lee, S. M., and Choong Kwon, L. (2006). IT Managers' requisite skills. *Communications of the ACM*, 49(4), 111-114.

[16] Lee, Sooun, and Xiang Fang. "Perception gaps about skills requirement for entry-level IS professionals between recruiters and students: an exploratory study." *Information Resources Management Journal (IRMJ)* 21.3 (2008): 39-63.

[17] Lepper, M. R. (1988). Motivational considerations in the study of instruction. *Cognition and Instruction, 5,* 289– 309.

[18] Lukmani, Y. M. (1972). Motivation to learn and language proficiency, *Language Learning,* 22(2), 261 - 273.

[19] McAllister, Andrew J. "The Case for Teaching Legacy Systems Modernization." *Information Technology: New Generations (ITNG), 2011 Eighth International Conference on.* IEEE, 2011.

[20] Nairn, G. (2008). The mainframe still needs to be mastered, *Financial Times,* (Nov 05), 5.

[21] Qu, Wen Guang, Wonseok Oh, and Alain Pinsonneault. "The strategic value of IT insourcing: An IT-enabled business process perspective." *The Journal of Strategic Information Systems* 19.2 (2010): 96-108.

[22] Pratt, M. K. (2012). Six key skills IT grads lack. *Computerworld,* 46(3), 18-20.

[23] Porter, L. W., and Lawler, E. E. (1968). Managerial attitudes and performance. Homewood. IL: Irwin-Dorsey.

[24] Ryan, R. (1995). Psychological needs and the facilitation of integrative processes. *Journal of Personality,* 63, 397–427.

[25] System Z Academic Initiative Program. (n.d.) Retrieved March 21, 2013, from http://www-03.ibm.com/systems/z/education/academic/schools_na.html#texas

[26] Weber, R. P. (1990). *Basic Content Analysis,* 2nd ed. Newbury Park, CA.

[27] Clabby Analytics (2011) Mainframe Skills Report – Sources of Mainframe Skill Training: Clabby Analytics

An Investigation of the Impact of Recertification Requirements on Recertification Decisions

Tanya McGill
Murdoch University
South St, Murdoch, 6150, WA, Australia
61 8 93602798
t.mcgill@murdoch.edu.au

Michael Dixon
Murdoch University
South St, Murdoch, 6150, WA, Australia
61 8 93606086
m.dixon@murdoch.edu.au

ABSTRACT

Certification has become a popular adjunct to traditional means of acquiring information and communication technology (ICT) knowledge and skills and many employers specify a preference for those holding certifications. Many ICT certifications include a requirement to recertify regularly, but little is known about the impacts of recertification requirements on the intention to maintain certification. This research explores the factors that influence the recertification decision. The perspectives of both ICT students and ICT professionals were sought. Both students and ICT professionals were very positive about the benefits of certification and highlighted that intrinsic desire for improved knowledge and skill, as well as job related benefits, motivated them to obtain certification and maintain it. The ICT professionals also emphasized the importance of certification to their employers. ICT professionals had strong knowledge of the recertification requirements for the certifications they held. This was not, however, the case for the ICT students; many students had little knowledge of what recertification might entail. A key factor contributing to intention to recertify was flexibility to seek higher paying jobs. The cost of recertification was not found to be a major issue. Support from employers in providing time for obtaining recertification was considered important. Given the huge range of different certifications available, and the varying value of these to the holder at different points in their career, ICT professionals appeared to take a strategic approach to the decision to recertify. Not surprisingly, they considered, and selectively chose, those which are worth recertifying given their current position and career aspirations.

Categories and Subject Descriptors
K.7.3 [**THE COMPUTING PROFESSION**]: Testing, Certification, and Licensing

Keywords: ICT Personnel, ICT Professionals, ICT Certification Recertification.

1. INTRODUCTION
Certification has become a popular adjunct to traditional means of acquiring information and communication technology (ICT) knowledge and skills and many employers specify a preference for those holding certifications. Certification intends to establish a standard of competency in defined areas. Unlike traditional academic degrees, certifications tend to be specific to narrow fields or even to individual products. They are designed to provide targeted skills that have immediate applicability in the workplace.

Previous research has considered the benefits and risks of ICT certification and its importance in obtaining employment, both from the student perspective [12,15,18] and from a workplace perspective [3-5,11]. Certification is perceived as an important factor in achieving employment. Students undertaking certification anticipate that it will lead to substantial financial benefits [15], ICT employees believe that it will benefit their careers [18] and managers making hiring decisions consider ICT certifications as important in validating skills and expertise [5].

Many ICT certifications include either a requirement to recertify regularly or a requirement to undertake a certain number of hours of professional development per year. The impact of the ongoing commitments associated with maintaining certifications has not previously been researched. The project described in this paper investigates the impacts of recertification requirements on the intention to maintain certification, and explores the factors that influence the decision to recertify. The perspectives of both ICT students who have yet to certify, and ICT professionals in the workplace who have previously obtained certifications, are considered.

2. BACKGROUND
Vendors such as Microsoft and Cisco Systems dominate the vendor specific certification market worldwide with qualifications such as Microsoft Certified Systems Engineer (MCSE) and Cisco Certified Network Associate (CCNA). Vendor neutral certifications such as those provided by the Institute for Certification of Computing Professionals (ICCP) and the Computer Technology Industry Association (CompTIA) also play an important role. Even relatively new fields have quickly introduced many certifications. For example in 2008 computer forensics had over 298 certifications [14]. ICT certifications have also become important for educational institutions in attracting students and placing graduates, with many universities aligning courses with certifications [10,13,19].

A number of studies have considered the benefits to employees of certification [e.g. 2,18]. These benefits appear to include: increased credibility, flexibility to change jobs, increased salary, and increased job security. These potential benefits are also a powerful incentive for university students to undertake certification as part of their studies [12,15]. These potential benefits therefore provide an incentive for those in the ICT industry, and those hoping to join it, to obtain certifications.

Employers have been shown to strongly value certification of employees and potential employees. Employers rely heavily on professional certifications when hiring ICT professionals to ensure a base level of required knowledge and skills and to improve skill levels through on-going professional development [5]. The credibility of the organization, via the credibility of its employees, has been found to be an important benefit for companies [2]. Certification of employees can also facilitate access to additional discounts, information, and support from vendors; the Cisco System Gold Certified Partnership program provides an example of this. This kind of benefit is rated very highly [2] and contributes to pressure being placed on employees to certify. Tim Herbert, the Vice President, Research, of CompTIA recently noted that the benefits of certification to organizations could be enhanced further via "Stronger links with education; easier methods of verification; greater understanding of what ICT certifications can and cannot do; and more organizational support for certifications as part of a professional development program." [5].

A number of authors have noted that the rapidly changing ICT knowledge base can mean that certification is not of lasting value [17,19,20]. In order to assure currency of knowledge, many certifications have regular recertification requirements. Despite the focus on benefits of ICT certification to the various stakeholders, little research has been done on employees and how the demands of recertification affect them as they progress through their career.

One of the key barriers to obtaining certification has been identified as the associated cost [22]. This is particularly the case when students are obtaining certification [12,15]. In their study, Hunsinger and Smith found that little more than half of the undergraduate student participants had the money to meet the costs of ICT certification. These costs can include textbooks, training sessions, travel, and examinations. Whilst financial benefits are a key benefit and incentive for initial certification [17] it is unclear that recertification provides additional financial benefits to balance the associated costs. However, as presumably those facing the requirement for recertification are more likely to be in employment, cost may be less of an issue for recertification. Many organizations will provide reimbursement of expenses incurred in obtaining the certification [7], and if this is not the case, employees should be better placed financially to meet the costs than those seeking their first ICT job are.

Finding the time to study and take examinations has also been identified as a issue for obtaining initial certifications [12], and is likely to be a continuing issue with recertification. Finding additional time to study for recertification may be even more of an issue than for initial certification as employees are enmeshed in their ongoing employment, and obtaining time release from employers seems likely to be an important factor in the decision to recertify.

In order to better understand recertification this study explores the factors that influence this decision. Factors considered include: the cost of recertification, employer support, the requirement for recertification to keep an existing job, and the possibility of recertification leading to a higher paid position. The perceptions of ICT students who are about to embark of their careers and who face a professional lifetime of commitment to maintaining their ICT knowledge are considered, as are those of ICT professionals in the work place who have previously obtained certification.

3. METHOD

The project involved two different types of data collection. Students undertaking courses that led to ICT certification completed an online survey, and ICT professionals were interviewed. Each of these phases of the study is described below.

3.1 ICT Student Data Collection

The student participants in the study were students enrolled in seven ICT courses at a Western Australian university. Students who successfully completed these particular courses could also pursue Cisco certification, as the courses made use of the Cisco curriculum. Potential participants (109 students) were contacted via email and invited to participate in the study by completing an online questionnaire. Completion of the questionnaire was voluntary and all responses were anonymous. The questionnaire took approximately 10 minutes to complete.

The questionnaire contained five main sections. The first group of questions obtained background information about the student participants. This included age, gender, and previous ICT experience. The second group of questions related to students' perceptions of the importance of industry certification for employment and gauged their intention to obtain certification. Those participants who were not currently working in the ICT industry were firstly asked to rate the importance of industry certification for obtaining their initial ICT employment. This item was measured on a 5 point scale ranging from (1) 'Not Important' to (5) 'Vital'. Those participants who were currently working in the ICT industry were instead asked to rate the importance of industry certification for getting ahead in their current employment. This question also used a 5 point scale ranging from (1) 'Not Important' to (5) 'Vital'. These questions were based on those used by McGill and Dixon [15].

In the third group of questions student participants were asked for their perceptions of the relative importance of various proposed benefits of certification. A list of eleven potential benefits of certification for ICT students [15] was presented. Each potential benefit was rated for importance on a 5 point scale ranging from (1) 'Not Important' to (5) 'Very Important' (see Table 3 for a list of the proposed benefits included).

The fourth section first explored students' knowledge of recertification requirements. These questions were developed specifically for the study. Participants were asked to rate their level of knowledge of recertification requirements for the certifications they could take based on their university studies on a 5 point scale ranging from (1) 'No knowledge' to (5) 'Detailed knowledge', and to describe the recertification requirements for CCNA, which was the initial and most commonly taken certification for these students. Participants were then asked how much influence they thought recertification would have on both their initial decision to obtain certification and on their decision to maintain certifications. These questions were answered on a 5 point scale ranging from (1) 'No influence' to (5) 'Large influence'.

The final section asked participants to indicate how important they considered a range of factors to be in their decision to maintain certification. These factors were derived from the literature on ICT certification [12,15,22], and were rated on a 5 point scale ranging from (1) 'Not Important' to (5) 'Very Important'.

3.2 ICT Professional Interviews

Australian ICT professionals who had obtained certifications at some point in their career were targeted for this research. They were contacted through snowball sampling. Potential participants were invited to participate via a telephone call or email. If they were interested they were sent an information letter and consent form. Interviews were at a time and location convenient to the participants and took approximately 30 minutes.

Interview questions were designed to be consistent with those in the student questionnaire where possible. Participants were first asked to provide some background information, focusing on their work in the ICT industry and the certifications they had obtained. They were also asked to provide their perceptions of the importance of certification to their employer. The next group of questions focused on the recertification requirements for the certifications they held. The final group of questions explored the participants' perceptions of the importance of a range of factors in influencing their decision to maintain certification. These factors mirrored those included in the student questionnaire. Participants were asked to both rate the importance of each factor on a 5 point scale ranging from (1) 'No influence' to (5) 'Large influence' and to discuss the influence of each. The qualitative responses to each question were classified into general themes. The themes were permitted to emerge from the data.

4. RESULTS

4.1 Student Perceptions

Forty four responses to the student survey were received. This corresponds to a response rate of 40.4%. The student participants had an average age of 25.9 years (with a range from 18 to 41) and were overwhelmingly male (93.2%). The gender proportions in this study are consistent with the low representation of females in ICT courses [6] and in particular with the very low proportion of females who are interested in networking courses [8]. The participants who had previously been employed in ICT related work had an average of 4.6 years experience. Table 1 summarizes some of the background information about the participants in this study.

Table 1. Background information about the student participants

	Number	Percentage
Gender		
Male	41	93.2
Female	3	6.8
ICT work experience (mean = 4.6 years)		
Yes	29	65.9
No	15	34.1
Intend to obtain certification?	38	86.4
Yes	3	6.8
No	3	6.8
Unsure		

The vast majority of the student participants (86.4%) intended to obtain some form of certification. Only three students indicated that they did not intend to pursue certification and three were unsure if they would. Whilst not all students enrolled in the targeted courses participated, given the centrality of certification to employment in networking, the responses appear likely to reflect those of non participants. This eagerness to undertake

certification reflects the widespread acceptance by students of its importance in obtaining employment [12,15,18]. CCNA was the most popular certification: 35 students (79.5%) intended to obtain it and six (13.6%) already held it. The second most popular certification was Cisco Certified Network Professional (CCNP) with 25 (56.9%) of the students intending to obtain it. Small numbers of participants also hoped to obtain a wide range of other certifications such as Cisco Certified Internetwork Expert (CCIE), Certified Information Systems Security Professional (CISSP) and Microsoft Certified Solutions Associate (MCSA).

ICT certification was perceived as very important for getting ahead if currently employed in the ICT industry, but not for getting an initial ICT job. The average importance rating given to ICT certification by those not currently employed in ICT was only 2.0 (out of 5), yet it was 4.1 for those currently employed in the ICT industry (see Table 2 below). The relatively high importance placed on obtaining certification by students who are already working in the ICT industry is consistent with previous research [15,18], and with research on the wider industry; for example, Alexander's [1] survey of 470 ICT contractors found that 83% of the contractors believed that ICT certifications were either 'very important' or 'somewhat important' to their prospects for career advancement.

Table 2. Perceived importance of certification for student participants

	N	Mean	SD	Min	Max
Importance of certification for initial job	29	2.0	1.2	1	5
Importance of certification for getting ahead in current job	28	4.1	0.9	2	5

The lower level of perceived importance for students who were not yet working in the ICT industry is unexpected. McGill and Dixon [15] found that students who had not yet obtained ICT employment rated certification even more highly than those currently in the industry. This difference may be due to the buoyant Western Australian economy resulting from a resources boom; students may anticipate that obtaining their initial job will be easy. Table 3 further explores the students' perceptions of the importance of initial certification by presenting the average perceived importance of each of the different benefits of certification. As can be seen, although in general students did not strongly believe that certification would be required to obtain initial employment, they were fully cognizant of its benefits. All the listed benefits were ranked relatively highly, with averages above the midpoint of the scale. The most highly ranked benefit in terms of importance was having a widely recognized qualification (rated 4.5 out of 5). ICT certifications are global and enable those who have them great flexibility in terms of obtaining employment around the world.

The next most highly ranked benefits related to the knowledge and skills that those obtaining certifications gain. Student participants perceived the knowledge and skills they obtain (4.4), and particularly the practical experience with real networking tasks (4.4) and experience with real equipment (4.4), as very important. This finding is consistent with the fact that the students were primarily undertaking Cisco certifications. Wilde [23] claimed that Cisco Systems has the most 'realistic' certification program, requiring those undertaking certification to perform real tasks, using real equipment. These relatively high rankings suggest that the intrinsic value of the knowledge and skill obtained during certification is perceived as important beyond the job related benefits that may eventuate.

Table 3. Benefits of certification as perceived by student participants

Rank	Benefits	N	Mean	SD	Min	Max
1	Widely recognized qualification	43	4.5	0.7	3	5
2	Greater knowledge/skill	44	4.4	0.6	3	5
2	Practical experience with real networking tasks	44	4.4	0.9	2	5
2	Experience with real equipment	44	4.4	0.9	1	5
5	Obtaining a formal marketable qualification	44	4.3	0.8	2	5
5	Able to apply for the increasing number of jobs that require certification	44	4.3	0.8	2	5
5	Increased credibility	43	4.3	0.8	3	5
8	Increased self-confidence	44	4.2	0.9	1	5
9	Higher salaries	44	4.0	0.8	2	5

Proposed benefits relating to the role of certification in improving opportunities to obtain jobs (4.3), and relating to credibility (4.3) and self-confidence (4.2) were fairly highly rated. These results are consistent with those of Hunsinger and Smith [12]. Improving employment opportunities is clearly important to those who undertake certification, but the slightly higher rankings of practical experience and improving knowledge and skill suggest that employment is not the sole motivation for undertaking certification. The perceived importance of practical experience obtained goes beyond just improving marketability.

Higher salaries was ranked last in terms of importance. Whilst potential salaries perhaps receive the most publicity in terms of benefits to holders of certifications, this ranking suggests that whilst important (4.0), salary is not the major driving factor for most students.

The perceptions of benefits were compared between those students who had some ICT related work experience and those who did not, using independent t-tests. The only benefit on which a significant difference was found, was higher salaries (4.28 versus 3.53, t(42)=3.12, p=0.03). Those with work experience valued the potential salary increases associated with certification more highly that those without work experience, perhaps because of knowledge about salaries gained in the workplace.

Ongoing access to some of the benefits of certification requires maintaining certification. Students were asked rate their knowledge of recertification requirements for the certifications they could take based on their university studies (see Table 4). There was a wide range of knowledge of recertification requirements for these certifications. The average level was 3.1 out of 5, but two students rated themselves as having no knowledge and only two considered themselves to have detailed knowledge. The students were also asked to describe the recertification requirements for CCNA, the most commonly

acquired certification. Only around half of the participants (21 students) answered this question. The key knowledge about recertification as a CCNA provided was that it entailed re-sitting exams and that it was required every three years. Nineteen students who had indicated they intended to obtain CCNA certification were unable to provide any information about what recertification might entail. Twelve students noted that the time period after which recertification was required was three years, and 12 were aware that recertification required an examination. Only six students noted that obtaining a higher qualification provides recertification for the lower qualification.

Table 4. Student knowledge of recertification requirements

	N	Mean	SD	Min	Max
Knowledge of recertification requirements	43	3.1	0.9	1	5
Amount of influence recertification requirements will have on **initial decision** to obtain certification?	42	3.2	1.3	1	5
Amount of influence recertification requirements will have on decision to **maintain** certifications?	42	3.4	1.2	1	5

Table 4 also summarizes the responses to the questions about the likely influence of recertification requirements on intention to obtain initial certifications and intention to maintain certifications by recertifying. Again there was a wide spread of responses. Five respondents (11.9%) felt that the requirements for recertification would not influence them at all in their decision to obtain initial certification, and four of these (9.5% of all respondents) did not anticipate the requirements influencing their recertification decision either. The majority of participants did, however, recognize that these requirements would play a role in their decisions to some degree, and responses to the two questions were strongly correlated (r=0.606, p<0.01), indicating that the factors that influence the initial decision to certify are likely to still be important in the decision to recertify.

Student participants were also asked to consider the factors that have been identified as relevant to the decision to certify and to rate their likely importance in the decision to recertify. Table 5 lists these factors in average importance order. All potential factors were generally perceived as fairly important, receiving mean ratings of above the mid point of the scale. Employer time release had the highest average rating (4.4), with employer financial support rated a little lower (3.9). It seems likely that from the perspective of a student, time will be in short supply once they start working full time, but money will be less of an issue. Consistent with this, certification costs was the second lowest ranked factor (3.8).

The second and third most highly ranked factors were flexibility to seek higher paying jobs (4.2) and recertification as a requirement for promotion (4.1); the student participants appeared to already be looking beyond their initial job to their future career progression. Recertification was seen as less important on average for keeping a current job (3.5).

The perceptions of the importance of factors that might influence the decision to recertify were compared between those students who had some ICT related work experience and those who did not, using independent t-tests. No significant differences were found. However, it is clear that there is a wide range of perspectives with each of the factors being considered extremely important by some participants, but with all factors except employer time release having some participants rating them relatively unimportant.

Table 5. Factors influencing recertification

Rank	Factors influencing recertification	N	Mean	SD	Min	Max
1	Employer time release	44	4.4	0.5	3	5
2	Enable flexibility to seek other higher paying jobs	44	4.2	1.0	1	5
3	Requirement for promotion	44	4.1	1.0	1	5
4	Employer financial support	44	3.9	1.0	1	5
5	Certification costs	44	3.8	1.0	2	5
6	Requirement for job already have	42	3.5	1.2	1	5

4.2 ICT Professional Perceptions

Twelve Australian ICT professionals who had obtained certifications at some time during their careers were interviewed. They ranged from 26 to 50 in age (with a median age of 37.5 years), and all but one were male. This low proportion of female participants is consistent with the Certification Magazine's 2009 Salary Survey, which found that 90% of those with certifications are male [16].

The ICT professionals had a wide range of experience in ICT (see Table 6). The number of years they had worked in ICT ranged from 5 years to 26 years (with a median of 11.8 years), and the number of jobs that the participants had held ranged from three to 10. There was also a very large range of time that they had held their current job: three months to 14 years. Four of them were considering changing jobs within the next year.

Table 6. Background information about the ICT professional participants

	Median	Min	Max
Time in the ICT industry	11.8 years	5 years	26 years
Number of ICT jobs held	6	3	10
Time with current organization	4 years	3 months	23 years
Time in current position	1.8 years	3 months	14 years

The ICT professionals had a wide variety of educational backgrounds: four had an ICT bachelor degree of some kind; six had undertaken postgraduate conversion qualifications, one had a sub-degree diploma in ICT and two had no tertiary ICT qualifications.

The importance of certification to the participants' employers was explored. Six of the ICT professionals considered it to be very important in their organization, and four of them believed that it was somewhat important. Only two interviewees felt that it was not important in their organization. Several different main reasons for the importance of certification to organizations were provided. The most common reason was to ensure that employees have the necessary skills to do their jobs (5 comments). This was seen to

be particularly important for new employees, though was also mentioned with respect to promotion. This is consistent with the existing literature on certification and hiring [5]. Having certified employees was also considered important as a means of establishing credentials for customers and potential customers (2 comments) as indicated by the following quotes:

Very important I think, since they use it as the primary means of proving the organizations qualifications, experience and ability to obtain new work.... We try to put a lot of emphasis on the fact that we have a lot of people who are very highly qualified and certified as well. Even to the point of actually getting recommendations from the vendors themselves.

Our customers they feel that if you are in this high tech area they need to see that our people are certified as well.

Where companies are resellers of hardware or software, partnership arrangements often require certain levels of certified staff, thus providing additional pressure for certification of employees [2]. Three participants mentioned this as a driver for their organization as reflected in the following quotes:

Certainly Microsoft certification as it gives us benefits as a partner.

We are dealing with Cisco technologies and other manufacturers who demand that the company must have people certified before they can even sell them those products. They don't want you to handle their products unless they know your people are certified.

All participants displayed good, accurate knowledge of the recertification requirements for the certifications they had obtained during their careers. All 12 ICT professionals still held some certifications; these included a wide range of Cisco, Microsoft, Novell, Prince, ITIL and Algosec certifications.

The different certifications held by the participants had a range of different requirements related to maintaining certification. Participants responded in a variety of ways to these requirements. Also, individual participants responded differently to different certifications they had held. Five main categories of responses were identified and are discussed below:

- *Recertify when it is required* (5 participants)
  When a particular certification had current relevance and importance to the participant, they undertook the actions required to recertify.

- *Maintain certification by obtaining a higher level certification* (3 participants)
  Obtaining recertification by gaining a new certification proved to be a strategic move for some participants. For example, one participant described renewing Cisco CCNA by obtaining Cisco CCNP:

  I've never had to take the same assessment twice. The reason for that is because I got my CCNA and then as that was about to expire you can update your CCNA for another 3 years by taking a CCNP level certification.

- *Let certification lapse* (3 participants)
  If a particular certification was no longer actively required, and the benefits not compelling, some participants would let it lapse:

  I haven't kept it up as it's not really relevant to my role.

- *Direct recertification not required* (6 participants)
  Some certifications did not have recertification requirements,

rather participants have to seek certification for each new relevant release, as one participants describes below:

> Like the Microsoft model where they release new versions of the certification and the old versions just become outdated. So that will be another thing that will have to be upgraded over time.

- *Recertification not yet required* (3 participants)

Participants did not appear to consider the onerousness of requirements from the certification body as a major factor driving their decision to recertify or not. It was notable, however, that the participants were strategic in their selection of what certifications to maintain. They appeared to have considered and selectively chosen those which are worth recertifying given their current position and career aspirations as indicated by the following quotations:

> ..since then I have decided to be more in coordination and management so I didn't see that there was a benefit for me to go down that track. As it wasnt going to benefit me personally so I didn't bother, I know it would have probably benefitted the company at the time.

> If I was to move jobs into another employer it would be extremely important, I would have to sit down and recertify myself.

Participants were also asked to consider the factors that have been identified as relevant to the decision to certify and to rate their likely importance in the decision to recertify. Table 7 lists the factors in average importance order. The flexibility to seeker higher paying jobs had the highest average rating (4.3) followed by employer support and time release (3.7). In general, recertification was seen as less important for holding a current job (3.6), or getting promoted within the organization (3.3). However it is clear that there is a wide range of perceptions with each of the factor being considered extremely important by some participants, and several as not at all important to at least one participant (certification costs, and employer support).

Table 7. Importance ratings for factors influencing recertification

Factor	Mean	Min	Max
Flexibility to seek higher paid jobs	4.3	2.5	5
Employer support (financial and time)	3.7	1	5
Requirement for current job	3.6	2	5
Required for promotion	3.3	1.5	5
Certification costs	3.1	1	5

As anticipated, overall the cost of recertification appeared to be the issue of least concern to the participants. Participant responses however encompassed a range of perspectives ranging from those who found recertification costs high and hard to justify – particularly the exams and the travel sometimes needed to take them – to those who found it expensive but considered it a worthwhile investment, and finally those for whom it was not an issue as costs were completely covered by their employer. The quotes below illustrate these perspectives:

> Certification can be a financial drain that is sometimes difficult to justify.

> I think the exams / books is a low cost but the exams can be more expensive costing thousands of dollars.

Microsoft and Cisco the initial thing is pretty cheap around the $200 range but once you get up to the CCIE level it starts becoming cost prohibitive for someone here in Western Australia and that is why I never took it any further.

> You have to have it, and yes cost is a factor, but you have to. Cost wouldn't stop me. It makes me more employable.

> [Costs] are important to me, but in my current position it is usually my employer who would pay for most of my certification and training costs.

> My employers have paid in the past so the cost is less real in those cases. So all of it is free.

Certification Magazine suggests that around 50% of those who seek certification have their cost covered by their employers [9]. So, whilst some employers provide support many do not, making employer support a more important issue than recertification costs. Several participants noted that employers who provide financial and/or time release support for certification and recertification are seen as more attractive than those that do not. As the following quote indicates, they also noted that by providing support to employees, employers signal the importance of ongoing certification to the organization:

> I think it is important as it shows that it has some importance to them. If they were unwilling to pay then I would think that it had little or no importance to them.

The flexibility to obtain higher paying jobs outside the current organization appeared to be more of a driver for recertification than either meeting the requirements of a current position or progressing within the same organization. Whilst several participants noted that they needed to demonstrate up to date knowledge to either keep their job or to gain promotion, a more common sentiment was that it was not so important once an initial position had been obtained within their firm:

> Staying here it has no importance

However, participants were mindful that certifications are a particularly important source of information to people who do not already know you, as indicated by the following quotes:

> If I wanted to go somewhere else I would definitely consider it worthwhile recertifying.

> ...because you have to be able to demonstrate more easily your level of skill to people who don't actually know you.

The ICT professional participants also identified a number of other factors that either have, or will, influence their decision to recertify. These are described below:

- *A desire to update knowledge* (6 participants)

Consistent with the students' strong desire to improve their knowledge and skills by gaining initial certifications, half of the ICT professionals mentioned they were motivated to recertify by a desire to update their knowledge; for example:

> So just expanding your knowledge, that is another factor – staying up to date, because the IT industry changes so fast if you don't recertify or sit any of these sort of courses you will be left behind.

- *Recertification is a requirement of stakeholders such as vendors or professional bodies* (2 participants)

For these participants the pressure to recertify extended beyond their immediate personal goals as illustrated by the following quotes:

We are dealing with Cisco technologies and other manufacturers who demand that the company must have people certified before they can even sell them those products.

It is critical for professional bodies to know that you are continuing to study. For example the ACS. I am a member of the ACS and they insist that you must meet a certain number of PDUs in a year, so for every certification that you are working on it counts as a number of PDUs that you can have. At the end of the year you have to fill in a form to show that you have been studying. So certification counts for that.

- *Availability of testing centers* (1 participant)
  Higher level certification often entails travel. This can influence decisions relating to whether recertification is a practical option and goes beyond straightforward cost and time issues:

  Availability of testing centres is actually a big thing. One of the problems with testing centre or certification at the moment is the whole planning of the activity. Obviously you want to be sitting your exam after you've had a reasonable amount of time to study for it, but you don't want too big a gap between when you have studies and when you sit your exam and that can be a problem. So not having access to a testing centre has been a problem in the past.

- *Recertification is associated with enhanced credibility or status* (3 participants)
  In addition to external factors, several participants noted that recertification was important from a personal perspective. It gave them a sense of achievement and pride; this is consistent with the findings of Anderson, Barrett and Schwager [2] and Sosbe, Hollis, Summerfield and McLean [21] and is illustrated by the following quotes:

  Well, status to be honest.

  So I think it is just important from a sort of pride perspective as well.

- *Time required* (2 participants)
  Regardless of whether employers provide time release for exams and training sessions, undertaking recertification requires a large investment of study time, and participants were very conscious of it. One participant highlighted that this affects not only those seeking recertification but also their families:

  But to justify the amount of money that I spend on it and the amount of time I spend studying is difficult. It is very very hard and can become painful and your spouse does not understand why you are doing this because you already have a job. And all that time is going, time you are supposed to spend with your family.

5. CONCLUSIONS

Recertification is integral to the professional life of many of those working in the ICT industry as indicated by the following participant:

So you become a perpetual student. But you are in a field that demands a kind of faith. You have to be always studying. Once you get tired of studying in this industry then you have to walk away from it and find something else to do.

In order to better understand the recertification choices that ICT employees make, this study explored the factors that influence these decisions. The perceptions of ICT students who were about to embark of their careers and who face a professional lifetime of commitment to maintaining their ICT professional status were considered, as well as those of ICT professionals in the work place who have previously obtained certification. The issues that were considered included: the cost of recertification, employer support, and the requirement for it to keep an existing job. Whilst all participants were from Australia, the issues highlighted are likely to be universal: future research in other countries is needed to confirm this.

Both students and ICT professionals were very positive about the benefits of certification and the vast majority of students who were taking courses that could lead to Cisco certification intended to obtain it. Both students and ICT professionals highlighted that intrinsic desire for improved knowledge and skill, as well as job related benefits, motivated them. The ICT professionals also emphasized the importance of certification to their employers.

With certification often comes the need for ongoing recertification. The ICT professionals interviewed for the study all had strong knowledge of the recertification requirements for the certifications they held. This was not, however, the case for the students who were surveyed; many students had little knowledge of what recertification might entail. Recertification might be seen as too far in the future to be of concern, but given that recertification is so central to ongoing employment in the ICT industry, those teaching courses that can lead to certifications should ensure that their students have an understanding of the long term implications of certification.

A key factor in motivating participants to recertify was flexibility to seek higher paying jobs. This was rated highest by the ICT professionals and second highest by the student participants. It appears that although they are either about to start their ICT career, or in its early stages, they are already very mindful of maximizing their career opportunities. The cost of recertification was not found to be a major issue for either group of participants so although the cost of initial certification can be prohibitive for students [12,15], students recognize that once they are employed this will be less of an issue, either because employer support is provided or because of their income. Support from employers in providing time for obtaining recertification was considered important by both groups.

Given the huge range of different certifications available, and the varying value of these to the holder at different points in their career, the ICT professionals that were interviewed appeared to take a strategic approach to the decision to recertify. This response is not surprising. They appeared to have considered, and selectively chosen, those which are worth recertifying given their current position and career aspirations. As Tate, Lichtenstein and Warren [22] noted, ICT professionals take risks when choosing certifications because it is difficult to know in advance whether a certain certification has longevity, and this is particularly the case in new areas. ICT professionals make judgment calls when the time comes to recertify. They consider both the intrinsic value of the certification and the obstacles to obtaining it. Organizations that rely on, and gain from, the certifications of their employees need to be mindful of this decision process and provide appropriate support.

6. REFERENCES

[1] Alexander, S., 1999. Sorting out certifications. *Computerworld*, Dec 13.

[2] Anderson, J.E., Barratt, K.S., and Schwager, P.H., 2005. Informing the HR hiring decision of IT personnel: The HR professional's view of IT certification, education and experience. *Informing Science Journal* 8, 281-302.

[3] Cegielski, C.G., 2004. Who values technology certification? *Communications of the ACM* 47, 10, 103-105.

[4] Cegielski, C.G., Rebman, C.M., and Reithel, B.J., 2003. The value of certification: An empirical assessment of the perceptions of end-users of local area networks. *Information Systems Journal* 13, 1, 97-107.

[5] CompTIA, 2011. CompTIA Industry Research: Executive Summaries of Key Topics 2010-2011. http://www.comptia.org/news/11-02-07/IT_Certifications_Grow_in_Importance_in_Hiring_Process_but_Employers_Challenged_by_Evaluation_Validation_Issues_CompTIA_Study_Finds.aspx.

[6] Computing Research Association, 2011. *Taulbee Survey Report 2009-2010*. Computing Research Association. http://www.cra.org/uploads/documents/resources/taulbee/CRA_Taulbee_2009-2010_Results.pdf.

[7] Ejiaku, S.A., Badamas, M.A., and Little, J.C., 2010. An examination of information technology certification: A measure of professional qualification. In *Business Research Yearbook*, R.A. Oglesby, H.P. Leblanc and M.G. Adams Eds. International Academy of Busness Disciplines, Beltsville, M.D., 119-125.

[8] Gras-Velazquez, A., Joyce, A., and Debry, M., 2009. *Women and ICT: Why are girls still not attracted to ICT studies and careers?* European Schoolnet (EUN Partnership AISBL). http://blog.eun.org/insightblog/upload/Women_and_ICT_FINAL.pdf.

[9] Green, E., 2009. Certification Magazine's 2009 Salary Survey. *Certification Magazine*, December.

[10] Hitchcock, L., 2007. Industry certification and academic degrees: complementary, or poles apart? . In *Proceedings of the 2007 ACM SIGMIS Computer Personnel Research Conference: The Global Information Technology Workforce* ACM, St. Louis, Missouri, USA, 95-100.

[11] Hunsinger, D., Smith, M., and Winter, S., 2011. A framework of the use of certifications by hiring personnel in IT hiring decisions. *Database for Advances in Information Systems* 42, 1, 9-28.

[12] Hunsinger, D.S. and Smith, M.A., 2008. Factors that influence information systems undergraduates to pursue IT certification. *Journal of Information Technology Education* 7, 247-265.

[13] Koziniec, T. and Dixon, M., 2002. ICT industry certification: Integration issues for post-secondary educational institutions in Australia. In *Proceedings of the Informing Science 2002 Conference*, Cork Ireland, 831-838.

[14] Lim, N., 2008. Escaping the computer-forensics certification maze: A survey of professional certifications. *Communications of the Association for Information Systems* 23, 547-574.

[15] McGill, T. and Dixon, M., 2005. Information technology certification: A student perspective. *International Journal of Information and Communications Technology Education* 1, 1, 19-30.

[16] Prokopeak, M., 2009. Certification Magazine's 2009 Salary Survey. *Certification Magazine*, December.

[17] Quan, J.J., Dattero, R., and Galup, S.D., 2007. Information technology wages and the value of certifications: A human capital perspective. *Communications of the Association for Information Systems* 19, Article 6.

[18] Rajendran, D., 2011. Does embedding an ICT certification help align tertiary programs with industry?: A study of CCNA workplace perceptions. *Journal of Applied Computing and Information Technology* 15, 1.

[19] Randall, M.H. and Zirkle, C.J., 2005. Information technology student-based certification in formal education settings: Who benefits and what is needed. *Journal of Information Technology Education* 4, 288-306.

[20] Ray, C.M. and McCoy, R., 2000. Why certification in information systems? *Information Technology, Learning, and Performance Journal* 18, 1, 1-4.

[21] Sosbe, T., Hollis, E., Summerfield, B., and McLean, C., 2005. CertMag's 2005 salary survey: Monitoring your net worth. *Certification Magazine*.

[22] Tate, N.J.A., Lichtenstein, S., and Warren, M.J., 2008. IT security certifications: Stakeholder evaluation and selection. In *Proceedings of the19th Australasian Conference on Information Systems*, Christchurch, 991-1001.

[23] Wilde, C., 2000. Demand for IT pros drives vendor certification growth -- but multiple-choice tests aren't always a true measure of skills and experience. *Information Week*, Sept 25, 214.

Identifying Skills for Entry-Level IT Consultants

Diane Lending
James Madison University
Computer Information Systems
Harrisonburg, VA 22807
1-540-568-3480

lendindc@jmu.edu

Thomas W. Dillon
James Madison University
Computer Information Systems
Harrisonburg, VA 22807
1-540-568-3015

dillontw@jmu.edu

ABSTRACT

In this paper, we present preliminary research into the skills that entry-level IT Consultants need. Our data sources are senior-level IT consultants from six different companies and senior IS students who had just completed an IT consulting class where they were mentored by 12 different consulting firms. We used focus groups and open-ended surveys to get rich detailed data and then analyzed the results. Based upon this, we expand the identified skills for an entry-level IT Consultant to include being able to cope with changes, taking a holistic view of a problem, knowing when to ask for help, being a self-starter and having good time management skills. We found that both written and oral communication skills were important and that senior consultants looked for entry level personnel who were well-rounded.

Categories and Subject Descriptors

K.3.2 [**Computers and Education**]: Computer and Information Science Education – *Curriculum, Information systems education*
K.6.1 [**Management of Computing and Information Systems**]: People and Project Management – *Staffing* K.7.1 [**The Computing Profession**]: Occupations

General Terms

Management

Keywords

Job skills, Consultant skills, IS Curriculum, Survey Development.

1. INTRODUCTION

Over the last twenty years the Information Technology (IT) field has migrated from the use of internal employees to the extensive use of external consultants. With this migration, the attributes (i.e. the technical and behavioral skill sets) for a successful Information Systems (IS) graduate have changed. The IT consultant needs to have strong communication and functional skills on top of their technical skills [6].

At our university which is located in the Mid-Atlantic part of the United States, our graduating IS students tend to be hired by consulting companies rather than for in house IT jobs. In particular, almost all of our best graduates are hired by consulting companies. With this in mind, we wondered whether our rather technically-focused IS curriculum is truly serving our constituents: hiring companies, students, and alumni. With that question in mind, we started a multipart study to determine what skills consultants need and how we can build a curriculum that covers those skills.

Our complete study will follow the following process:

1) **Qualitative Research**: The focus of the qualitative research will be on identifying IT consultant attributes such as technical skills, behavioral skills, entering the work force skills and established professional skills. This will be based upon focus groups and open-ended surveys of IT consultants who are at many different levels of their careers.

2) **Survey Design**: Based upon the focus groups and interviews, we will design a survey instrument to measure the importance of each of these skills in the IT consulting profession. Based upon Straub [13], we will validate the instrument.

3) **Quantitative Study**: The fully validated survey will be sent to IT consultants and to workers in other types of companies. We plan to analyze the two populations and check for differences between the skills wanted for a recent graduate. Based upon the quantitative and qualitative analysis, we will recommend an IS curriculum that provides IT consulting skills.

We are currently in the qualitative part of this study. This paper reports on early results from our qualitative analysis.

2. PRIOR RESEARCH

There is not much research into IT consulting skills specifically. Joshi, et al. [6] examined what it meant to be an excellent IT consultant, which they associated with being a top performer in an IT role in an IT consulting company. In one IT consulting company, they conducted focus groups into what this means, surveyed various stakeholders about top performers, and looked for incongruities among stakeholders. They found that all stakeholders found it of high importance that an entry-level top-performer have the ability to deliver, be committed, be cooperative, and be analytical. Some of their raters also found it to be high importance that this entry-level person be a quick learner and be able to manage relationships. In another study with this same data, Joshi and Kuhn [7] look at the gender typing of these critical attributes.

Most academic research into IT skills includes IT consulting as one of many jobs and does not investigate whether there are differences in needs for the IT consulting job. In this literature, the most relevant for our study is the work that focuses on the importance of technical and "soft" behavioral skills in career success. For example, Huang et al. [5] conducted a meta-analysis of the skills identified in academic research, practitioner publications, and job advertisements. They grouped IT skills into three categories: technical, business (e.g., business function knowledge and problem-solving skills), and humanistic skills (e.g., teamwork, leadership and communications skills). They found that the academic research tended to focus on all three areas, but humanistic skills were the least frequently cited. In addition, they found that practitioner publications focus on a rich set of technical skills but do not emphasize business and humanistic skills. Job skills in recent job advertisements did focus on all three sets of skills [5]. This was not necessarily true in earlier IS job advertisements, for example Gallivan, et al. [4] found that job advertisements between 1988 and 2003 focused on technical skills, and Todd, et al. [14] found similar results between 1970 and 1990.

The importance of the softer skills is occasionally shortchanged in academic research, for example, they are lumped into a single measure called "project management and other relevant business skills" in Lee & Mirchandani [11]. Other researchers recognize the importance of the softer skills and focus on them, e.g., [12]. Lee et al. [9] identified knowledge of human relations as a critical skill to be covered in the IS curriculum.

Much of the research in this area addressed the relative importance of various skills and how they are incorporated into the hiring or performance process. Other research identifies the relative importance in career advancement (e.g., Bassellier, et al., [1] which identifies the skills needed by IS managers or Lee [10] which looks at skill transferability as one advances in an IT career.)

Typically, the hard technology skills are the topics of the IS curriculum with courses designed to produce them. Soft skills such as problem solving, critical and creative thinking, oral and written communications, and team skills should be taught in all IS courses [2]. Students in a consulting class suggested that negotiating skills, communications skills, and teamwork were critical [8]. From a practitioner's perspective, customer communication, relationship management, and issue resolution skills were stressed [3].

3. QUALITATIVE RESEARCH METHODOLOGY

As noted above, we are currently in the qualitative step of our project. In this step, we are trying to build a list of IT consultant attributes and skills as identified by IT consultants at every level of employment about every level of employment at or below their level. We defined our levels of IT consultants as:

- Senior-level: Vice President or Partner
- Mid-level: 3 to 10 years of experience as an IT consultant
- Entry-level: 1 to 2 years of experience as an IT consultant
- New Hires: those who are in the process of being hired as an IT consultant

3.1 Focus Groups
We started with two focus groups, each with three senior-level consultants from three different companies, for a total of six senior-level consultants, all with vice president or partner in their title. Future focus groups will include mid-level and entry-level IT consultants.

In each senior-level group, we asked a series of six questions:

1) What skills are necessary for an entry-level IT consultant?

2) What attributes are necessary for an entry-level IT consultant?

3) What skills are necessary for a mid-level IT consultant?

4) What attributes are necessary for a mid-level IT consultant?

5) What skills are necessary for a senior-level IT consultant?

6) What attributes are necessary for a senior-level IT consultant?

The focus group meetings were taped and transcribed.

3.2 New-Hire Open-ended Surveys
We conducted a survey of students in a senior-level IT consulting class and asked them to identify the attributes necessary to be an entry-level IT consultant. Our consulting class is a closed-enrollment class, open only to those who apply and are accepted. Students who are accepted into the class are recommended by our faculty members. In this class, thirty students worked with consultants from 10 consulting firms from the Washington DC area. The course is team taught by an instructor and twelve consulting firms. As a course project, teams of three students, each team mentored by two consultants from a consulting firm, produce a proposal in response to an RFP. At the end of the semester, we asked our students, working in teams, to identify attributes that they think are necessary for entry-level IT Consultants. Most of the students had been interns at a consulting company the previous summer and most had already accepted permanent IT consulting jobs. This survey was conducted in the fall semester 2011 and will be repeated in fall 2012. All 30 students in the class responded.

3.3 Analysis
Each transcript and survey will be independently coded by two raters. At this moment, the entry-level consultant questions from the senior-level focus groups and the New-Hires survey have been analyzed. The process we used to code the data followed the process described by Joshi, et al. [6]. We started with an a priori coding scheme based upon Joshi's list of IT consultant attributes. As we found other attributes, we extended our coding scheme. Discrepancies between coders were discussed and reconciled.

4. RESULTS
Our classification scheme began with Joshi, et al.'s table [6] identifying critical attributes for entry-level IT personnel which is shown in Table 1.

Table 1: Attributes for Entry-level IT Personnel

A Priori Coding Scheme from Joshi, Kuhn, and Niederman [6]

Ability to Deliver	Interpersonally skilled
Able to build and manage credible relationships	Performs extra-role behaviors
Ambitious	Quick learner
Analytical and problem solver	Self-confidence
Assertive	Stands up under pressure
Business knowledge	Technical skills
Committed	Verbally skilled
Cooperative	

4.1 Focus-group new attributes for entry-level IT consultants

From our first two focus groups with senior-level IT consultants, we expanded the list of attributes for entry-level IT consultant to include seven new attributes. In the following section, we include the new attribute as well as sample text from the focus group transcripts where we felt it added to the discussion.

4.1.1 Balance of technology and business: understanding that technology solves business problems

"...That … as technology is … I want to understand, can they grasp a certain technology, get into roll up their sleeves, get their hands dirty, understand what's below the screen in making it work."

"I would add then to balance that out with the understanding of the business at some level and that you are not just knowing technology for technology's sake but you are learning it to solve a business problem and make a difference and make an improvement so the blend of understanding that's there and having just good analytical skills to understand what the core problem is and look at options and alternatives but being just good analysts breaking down a problem. That sort of thing."

"...the actual outcome is not to build a box, but what is that box going to solve in terms of business problem and the like."

4.1.2 Detailed-oriented

4.1.3 Enthusiastic/full of energy

4.1.4 Ethical

"...I think the things we look for in general around here some of your values, ethics, integrity, if you can glean some of that, that's what successful entry level people. That gets back to raising issues. I have worked with people who something's gone [wrong]. why didn't you raise the issue? Why didn't you talk about it? I don't know if that's more that falls into the integrity or ethics and

all that as much but it is one of those things that makes you question they got to know the timing and the right way to do that stuff. I would say in general, we look for some integrity, ethics, are key ones."

"Compassion. Let's be honest."

4.1.5 Know when to ask for help

"One other thing I was thinking you triggered when you said something about being the sponge and the learner, I think the bounds to that though is on the humility line of not being afraid to ask for help. Because especially with a new person, you want them to dig in enough , but you don't want them to spend 2 weeks trying to figure out if they had stopped and asked somebody a question they could have been on their way a lot sooner. So it is that balance of taking the initiative to figure it out, but know when to say I'm lost and I need some help."

"...it's not that you are going against your boss or somebody but knowing you can speak up in the right way to basically to raise an important issue or matter that's going to help the project, solve an issue or progress faster.

"Yea, even in an entry level person, you wouldn't them to say, "I don't think this is going to work, but I'm going to keep doing it." You'd want them to say, "Hey, are we really thinking about this right?"

4.1.6 Self-starter

4.1.7 Well-rounded

"I think part of it is they have a life outside of work as well. They have personal interests. They have a personality. It's not just all work. You know? There are things, whether it's participating on firm soccer teams or, you know, they want to be a part of the firm and not just the delivery of work."

"I've still got my scar from when I ruptured my Achilles playing softball for my corporate team. I don't do that anymore."

4.2 Survey of New-Hire Consultants attributes for entry-level IT Consultants

From analysis of our results of an open-ended survey of new-hire IT consultants, we expanded the list to include four new attributes and found support for four of the attributes identified by the senior IT consultants. We also found a few attributes mentioned just once which we will look for in other transcripts or surveys. In the following section, we include the new attribute with, where it adds value, sample text from open-ended surveys.

4.2.1 Flexible

"Consultants should [be] flexible. All consultants should be able to handle change."

"… accommodate hiccups that occur; adapt to change."

4.2.2 Holistic

4.2.3 Professional

"Consultants should be professional (speaking, dress, writing)"

"Consultants should maintain professionalism. Good oral/written communication, dress appropriately, show up on time."

4.2.4 Time Management Skills

"Consultants should have time management skills."

" A consultant has a lot on their plate. Needs to determine importance of work."

"… be well organized."

"… be able to manage time efficiently. Structure goals and tasks based on importance."

"… to prioritize/practice good time management."

4.3 Contrasts between a priori attributes and our findings

4.3.1 Change "Verbal Skills" to "Oral/Presentation Skills" and "Writing Skills"

In addition to the new attributes, we also noted that both our senior-level consultants and new-hire consultants clearly distinguished oral skills from writing skills. The verbal skills attribute used by Joshi et al. [6] focused more on oral presentation but our consultants identified both oral and written as important.

"One thing that we haven't brought up that we tend to talk about is communications, both written communications and oral communications. You just expect them to be able to write a complete sentence and write—you know, because they're—they could be writing documentation or proposal work or something and you've got to be able to write a convincing sentence or a paragraph on paper and all that."

"Yeah, and I think the big start to that is just when they talk. When you talk to people. I mean, I always think of replacing the wrong pronouns, you know, in a sentence. I mean, all of us—we're all—I mean, I don't profess to be an English expert, but I do know the finer points in—and when people speak, like, it should be, whatever. I did this versus we did it and sometimes people will combine it in a way that it makes it sound like we did when it was I did. .."

4.3.2 Committed versus Well-rounded

In addition, while the consultants interviewed by Joshi, et al. [6], identified being committed to the project to the point of being willing to sacrifice their personal life, our consultants pointed to the importance of being well-rounded. None of our consultants mentioned sacrificing personal life as an important attribute.

4.3.3 Move Networking from "Self-confidence" to "Able to build and manage credible relationships"

Our a priori classification scheme [6] included networking skills in the self-confidence attribute. However, our consultants and students seemed to place it more in the ability to build and manage credible relationships, e.g., "have good networking skills and be good at maintaining relationships."

4.4 Results to date

Our current classification scheme identifying critical attributes for entry-level IT personnel is shown in Table 2. The source is for each attribute is noted.

Table 2: Attributes for Entry-level IT Consultants
(Bold are new in this study)

Ability to Deliver (1,2,3)
Able to build and manage credible relationships. (1,2,3) **Now expanded to include networking (2, 3)**
Ambitious (1,2,3)
Analytical and Problem solver (1,2,3)
Assertive (1,2,3)
Balance of technical and business skills (2,3)
Business knowledge (1,2,3)
Committed (1 only)
Cooperative/team player (1,2,3)
Detail Oriented (1,2)
Ethical (2)
Enthusiastic/Full of Energy (2)
Flexible (3)
Holistic View (3)
Interpersonally skilled (1,2,3)
Knows when to ask for help (2,3)
Oral/Presentation Skills (1,2,3) **Split from Verbal skills in this study (2,3)**
Performs extra role behaviors (1,2)
Professional (3)
Quick learner (1,2)
Self-confidence (1,2)
Self-starter (2,3)
Stands up under pressure (1,2)
Technical skills (1,2,3)
Writing skills (1,2,3) **Split from Verbal skills in this study (2,3)**
Well-rounded (life beyond work) (2,3)

Sources:

1– A Priori Coding Scheme from Joshi, Kuhn, and Niederman [6]

2– Based upon focus groups with Senior-level IT Consultants

3– Based upon open-ended surveys of New-Hire IT Consultants

5. IMPLICATIONS

Ultimately, the goal of this study is to adapt our curriculum to the skills our constituents want to see in our graduates. Our early results suggest that a curriculum that aims at producing entry-level IT consultants, should include,

- Problem solving
- Dealing with changing requirements
- Balancing technical with business
- Which tool/technique is best for this problem?
- Networking and relationship building

- Presentation/know the audience
- Written and oral communications
- Know what's important
- Know what's convincing
- Time management skills
- Technical skills

6. CONCLUSION

This work reports on results from an early stage of a many-part study. We plan to hold at least six more consultant focus groups with senior, mid-level and entry-level consultants. We will repeat the survey of new-hire consultants in our consulting class. We will also look at consultant skills at multiple levels. We also plan a survey based upon our attributes. However even though based upon early and incomplete results, we have made some additions to the literature on what skills an entry-level IT consultant should have. In particular, our consultants feel that entry-level IT consultants should have a balance of technical and business skills, be ethical, be enthusiastic, be flexible, take a holistic view of a problem, know when to continue working and when to ask for help, have good oral skills, be professional, be a self-starter, have good written skills, and be well-rounded with a life beyond work.

7. REFERENCES

[1] Bassellier, G., Reich, B. H. and Benbasat, I. (2001) "Information Technology Competence of Business Managers: A Definition and Research Model," *Journal of Management Information Systems*, 17(4), pp. 159–182.

[2] Downey, J.P., McMurtrey, M.E., and Zeltmann, S.M. (2008) "Mapping the MIS Curriculum Based on Critical Skills of New Graduates: An Empirical Examination of IT Professionals," *Journal of Information Systems Education*, 19(3), pp. 351-363.

[3] Djavanshir G.R. and Agresti, W.W. (2007), "IT Consulting: Communication Skills are Key," *IT Professional Magazine,* 9(1), pp. 46-50.

[4] Gallivan, M. J., Truex, D. P. and Kvasny, L. (2004) "Changing Patterns in IT Skill Sets 1988–2003: A Content Analysis of Classified Advertising," *Databases for Advances in Information Systems*, 35(3), pp. 64–87.

[5] Huang, H., Kvasny, L., Joshi, K. D., Trauth, E., and Mahar, J. (2009) "Synthesizing IT Job Skills Identified in Academic Studies, Practitioner Publications and Job Ads," *Proceedings of SIGMIS CPR 09, May 28-30, 2009, Limerick, Ireland*, pp. 121-127.

[6] Joshi, K. D., Kuhn, K.M. and Niederman, F. (2010) "Excellence in IT Consulting: Integrating Multiple Stakeholders' Perceptions of Top Performers," *IEEE Transactions on Engineering Management*, 57(4), pp. 589-606.

[7] Joshi, K.D. and Kuhn, K.M. (2007) "What it takes to succeed in information technology consulting: Exploring the gender typing of critical attributes," *Information Technology & People*, 20(4), pp. 400-424.

[8] Komarjaya, J., Huifang, L, and Bock, G.-W. (2004). "Consulting from students' perspective," *Consulting to Management,* 15(2), pp. 29-33.

[9] Lee, D., Trauth, E. and Farwell, D. (1995) "Critical skills and knowledge requirements of IS Professionals: A joint academic and industry investigation", *MIS Quarterly*, 19(3), pp. 313–338.

[10] Lee C. K. (2005). "Transferability of skills over the IT Career Path," *Proceedings of SIGMIS CPR 05, April 14-16, 2004, Atlanta, Georgia*, pp. 85-93.

[11] Lee, K. and Mirchandani, D. (2009). "Analyzing the dynamics of skill sets for the U.S. information systems work force using latent growth curve modeling," *Proceedings of SIGMIS CPR 09, May 28-30, 2009, Limerick Ireland*, pp. 113-120.

[12] Purao, S. and Suen H. (2010) "Designing a Multi-Faceted Metric to Evaluate Soft Skills," *Proceedings of SIGMIS CPR 10, May 20-22, 2010, Vancouver, BC, Canada*, pp. 88-90.

[13] Straub, D.W. (1989) "Validating Instruments in MIS Research," *MIS Quarterly,* 13(2), pp. 147-169

[14] Todd, P.A., McKeen, J.D. and Gallupe, R.B. (1995) "The evolution of IS job skills: a content analysis of IS job advertisements from 1970 to 1990," *MIS Quarterly*, 19(1), pp. 1-26.

Information Systems in the Community: A Summer Immersion Program for Students from Historically Black Colleges and Universities (HBCUs)

Jeria Quesenberry
Carnegie Mellon University
224E PH, 5000 Forbes Avenue
Pittsburgh, PA USA 15213
+01 (412) 268-4573

jquesenberry@cmu.edu

Randy Weinberg
Carnegie Mellon University
224C PH, 5000 Forbes Avenue
Pittsburgh, PA USA 15213
+01 (412) 268-3228

rweinberg@cmu.edu

Larry Heimann
Carnegie Mellon University
224A PH, 5000 Forbes Avenue
Pittsburgh, PA USA 15213
+01 (412) 268-3211

profh@cmu.edu

ABSTRACT

Interest in information technology (IT) careers, in general, remains flat among college students and interest among women and non-majority students has even declined in recent years. Further, many researchers have expressed concern that students are ill-equipped to address many of the human, social, and ethical issues that typically arise in a technical context. At the same time, there is a growing body of work that suggests service-learning initiatives benefit all students, particularly women and minority students, in terms of stronger skill preparation and sense of collective belonging. The objective of this paper is to describe a six-week summer service-learning program aimed at addressing the under representation of African American students in the IT field. We found that the students experienced two significant outcomes: exposure to the skills necessary to enter the IT profession (e.g., project management, technical, and teamwork abilities); and participation in professional development opportunities that fostered a sense of belonging in the field.

Categories and Subject Descriptors

K.3.2 Computers and Information Science Education
K.6.1 Project and People Management

General Terms: Management, Human Factors, Theory

Keywords: IS Education, Service-Learning, African Americans, Race

1. INTRODUCTION

Many authors have written about the value of a diverse workforce in the era of information-driven globalization, networking, and fast paced social, technological, and economic change (e.g., Canton, 2007; Florida, 2005; Gravely, 2011). Canton explains that a smart, "diversity savvy workforce will be required to understand and align with the diversity in the global marketplace." Further, recruiting a diverse, high-tech, globally ready workforce will be an on-going challenge for organizations of all sizes (Canton, 2007). Yet, despite the substantial opportunities for well-prepared graduates entering the information technology (IT) workforce, increasing diversity in the field continues to challenge employers and university educators.

Attracting well-qualified women and non-majority employees, and students into the field, especially, has proven difficult in the US. Interest in IT careers, in general, remains flat among college students, and interest among women and non-majority students has even declined in recent years. For instance, data supplied by the 2010 Taulbee Report on overall enrollment in CS/CE/Information Systems programs at the undergraduate level shows numbers continue to be low for women and non-majority students.[1] Specifically, in AY 2010-2011 women accounted for 12.7% of awarded IT-related bachelor's degrees and Black/African Americans accounted for 4.6% of awarded IT-related bachelor's degrees. Recognizing the importance of increased diversity and inclusion, IT educators have brought this problem into focus through their professional associations and conferences. Likewise, active efforts of educators to foster an inclusive pipeline have been instrumental in address the 'leaky pipeline.'

At the same time, service-learning initiatives have gained attention in the IT field over the last several years. Researchers explain that the IT field has traditionally been characterized as a profession with deficiencies in communication and responsiveness to client need (e.g., Guthrie and Navarrete, 2004; Olsen, 2008; Tan and Phillips, 2005; Werner and MacLean, 2006). They argue that this may be a result of the typical IT college classroom experience that is usually based on solving fictitious, tightly bound technical problems as opposed to focusing on the political, teamwork or communication problems that arise when working on development projects in the professional world. Consequently, students have little practical classroom experience to equip them to address the complex human, social, and ethical issues that typically arise in a technical context.

This paper is structured as follows. First, we summarize existing research about the benefits of service-learning and its application in the IT discipline. We then describe an eight-year initiative to increase the pipeline of prospective IT professionals through an intensive summer program for students drawn from Historically Black Colleges and Universities (HBCUs). Next, we present findings from the interpretive research elements of the program.

---

[1] The Taulbee Survey is conducted annually by the Computing Research Association (CRA) to document trends in student enrollment, degree production, employment of graduates, and faculty salaries in academic units in the United States and Canada that grant the Ph.D. in computer science (CS), computer engineering (CE) or information (I).

Finally, we discuss service-learning projects and how they may be useful in increasing the representation of African Americans in the IT profession.

2. BACKGROUND

Service-learning is a pedagogical approach to learning where students apply course knowledge to solve a particular problem faced by a partner client in their local or global community. These partner clients are typically non-profit organizations who would not otherwise have means to address these problems without outside expertise and support. Jacoby (1996) states, "service-learning is a form of experiential education in which students engage in activities that address human and community needs together with structured opportunities intentionally designed to promote student learning and development" (p. 5). Service learning bridges the gap between classroom experience and application in the community.

Service-learning initiatives in the IT field are not new – in fact a variety of descriptive examples of these projects can be found in existing research. For example, Guthrie and Navarrete (2004) developed a service-learning project where college students in a web-development course worked with a partner elementary school to teach young children how to build a website for their class. Their research found that students' attitudes changed regarding the perception of clients and enjoyment of the project. Tan and Phillips (2005) conducted several service-learning projects where college juniors and seniors are partnered with local organizations to design and deliver a variety of systems including an eCommerce system for Heirloom Crochet Crafts, a human resources employee intranet for a regional bank, and a student accountability system for the university provost. Werner and MacLean (2006) have also conducted several service-learning projects where college students built a database system to track delivery of services to homeless people for a local shelter, an online application for Christmas gift sponsorship for a local charity, and a registration system for the local Urban League.

Service-learning in IT benefits both students and community partner organizations. Students build and improve their technical skills and capabilities, and build a greater understanding of the systems development lifecycle (e.g., Godfrey, 1999; Guthrie and Navarrete, 2004). Lazar and Lidtke (2002) found that service-learning initiatives give students an opportunity to experience user issues in a real-world environment, hence improving their ability to address political, communication, and ethical issues. Homkes (2008) argues that since service-learning is experiential learning and thus, allows for a more holistic and lasting learning by the students. Likewise, Tan and Phillips (2005) explain that students improve perceptions of career development, expression of values, understanding of self and world, and self-enhancement. These outcomes are significant given that companies are more likely to hire new employees with technical skills, team experience, ethical understanding, and social skills.

Recent research suggests that service-learning initiatives benefit all students, particularly women and minority students. For instance, Evans et al. (2009) highlight the benefits of service-learning as an instrument of individual and community involvement, and empowerment for students. Burge and Suarez (2005) also suggest that altering the traditional approach for teaching computer sciences can draw more African American students into the field and keep them there. They recommend

increasing the number of partnerships between educational institutions and local communities (e.g., non-profits, churches, etc.) in order to focus on computing career prospects and relevant gender/race specific issues. Likewise, Ferguson et al. (2006) found that partnerships with non-profit organizations tended to strengthen women's commitment to using computers to help others. The authors also found that students (including women and minorities) are more motivated to do a good job when they can see how their efforts are helping others.

Research also suggests that service-learning initiatives can encourage the recruitment and retention of female and minority students. For example, Tapia and Kvasny (2004) explain that for several reasons women and minorities have perceived the IT professions as not having the qualities they want in a job. They may view the work as difficult, isolating and lacking social interaction. Thus, they recommend the development of "educational efforts to change cultural perceptions of IT as male domain" (p. 89). Katz suggests that a main challenge for the retention of female and minority students in computer science lies in sustaining their interest. Given the many recruitment and retention challenges, it could be argued that employing a service-learning approach may help to address some of these issues about the profession.

In summary, the digital divide, coupled with the review of the research on service-learning, points to a need to apply a finer grain analysis to these areas of study. In an effort to better understand the lack of African Americans in the IT field and how service-learning initiatives can be used to support them in the workplace while address the enrollment gap, we explored the following research question: *How can service-learning projects help to address the under representation of African Americans in the IT profession?*

3. SUPPORTING DIVERSITY IN A SERVICE-LEARNING PROJECT COURSE

The Information Systems in the Community Summer Institute at Carnegie Mellon University was an intensive, 6-week, summer service-learning project in information systems for students from partner HBCUs. The program ran for eight years, starting in 2004. The program was designed to accomplish the following goals: 1) to create opportunities for promising students nominated from HBCUs to experience a 'leading edge' undergraduate IS curriculum; 2) to expose participating students to career opportunities and options for graduate study in IS; 3) to advance the University's commitment to diversity; and 4) to create links and joint opportunities with key faculty members at partner HBCUs.

The program was a highly compressed learning experience for participating students based on the regular undergraduate Information Systems curriculum. In six weeks, students learned the fundamentals of software development methods, teamwork, web development, and database programming. They practiced basic project management techniques and learned the importance of professional communications and personal accountability. As a service-learning experience, students applied their knowledge to a project for a real client in the public, charitable, or nonprofit sector in the Pittsburgh area.

Over the eight summers, 56 students from 11 partner HBCUs participated in the program. Students came from the following institutions: Clark Atlanta University, Elizabeth City State

University, Florida International University, Grambling State University, Hampton University, Kentucky State University, Lincoln University, Morehouse College, Oakwood College, Prairie View A&M University, and Spelman College. Students applied to the program upon recommendation of instructors at their home institutions. The participants ranged in age from 18 to 24 years old and represented a variety of ethnic backgrounds including: African American, Asian American, Afro-Caribbean, and African. Students in the program had declared majors in information systems, computer science, business administration, accounting, chemistry, and political science.

4. ANALYSIS OF STUDENT LEARNING

A major challenge associated with service-learning initiatives is the lack of assessment tools to determine the achievement of learning outcomes and instructional effectiveness. For instance, Ferguson et al. (2006) argues that we do not precisely know the intellectual impact of service-learning initiatives on student learning. The authors stress that concrete data is still needed to support these claims.

Given these challenges, we employed a variety of interpretive research techniques to assess student learning, curriculum effectiveness, and contributions to research goals during the program. These techniques were executed in the following manner. At the beginning of the program, a *pre-assessment questionnaire* was used to gather information about the students' background and to establish baseline knowledge of the learning objectives. At the conclusion of the program, face-to-face *individual qualitative interviews* were held with the students in order to inquire about their motivation for pursuing an information technology related degree and to understand their experiences in the summer program. A *post-assessment questionnaire* was also used to assess the students' knowledge of the learning objectives and their impressions of service-learning at the conclusion of the program. The questionnaires and interviews were used for the last four years of the eight year program and included feedback from 31 of the 56 students. Throughout the eight years of the program, participant observations and feedback (via face to face conversations not formal questionnaire results) were gathered from the students and community partner organizations.

We found the students experienced two significant outcomes: increased perception in their IT-related skills abilities (e.g., project management, technical and teamwork abilities); and participation in professional development opportunities that fostered a sense of belonging in the field.

4.1 Skills and Abilities for Preparedness in the IT Profession

A core learning objective of the program was to help students gain or build the skills and abilities necessary to enter the IT workforce. The program focused on a breadth and depth of skills across the field of IT including project management, the software development process, and application development. These skills helped strengthen the students' resumes and potentially gain the attention of IT workforce recruiters.

4.1.1 Project Management
During the first week of the program, the students visited their community partners' offices and held initial discussion sessions to gain a sense of the project. The following week, students further interviewed their project clients and conducted several follow-up meetings to determine the scope and nature of their projects. From these early interactions, an initial set of functional and non-functional requirements were created. This documentation was reviewed with the client and approved in a formal proposal presentation. With their project in hand, the students carefully managed the implementation, project scope, and communicated any project risks to their clients. At the completion of the six weeks, students delivered a fully-functional and deployed application to their client per agreed upon terms.

Students were consistently encouraged to consider the client's needs as the primary driver for all aspects of the project. At both the beginning and at the end of the program, students were asked to evaluate their experiences working with a "real client" to satisfy an information systems need on a scale of 1 to 5 (with 1 representing 'no experience' and 5 representing 'extremely high levels of experience'). At the start of the program, students reported an average of 2.22, or moderately low level of experiences. At the conclusion of the program this number increased significantly to 4.29, or extremely high levels of experiences (t=12.40, df=30, p<0.0001). This learning outcome was summarized by one of the students:

"I had never worked in a service-learning project before so this was my first time. I didn't think it would be so real-world. It was neat to make a change for a real client. I also learned a lot about how to work with a client and communicate with them."

Olsen (2008) speculates that students may not actually gain practice in the steps in the software engineering process. Hence, the program took a top-down, iterative development approach. Students learned that each decision they made about project design and deployment must be consistent with the needs of the client. Students also practiced techniques that address the planning, management, and tracking of projects. Managing scope, quality, and stakeholder expectations were emphasized throughout the project. To track project progress, students developed a detailed project plan. The project plan included a timeline, a list of required tasks and assignments, a task status worksheet, and an analysis of project risks. Students monitored project progress and risks and revisited the plan weekly. To manage their projects in a short time frame, students followed an agile methodology of the systems development lifecycle. As one student explained:

"We really focused on the importance of 'underpromisng and overdelivering' to the client. The last thing we want to do is create a project plan that is so aggressive we can't deliver. That would only let our client down in the end."

Students developed working iterations of their projects through stages of refinement and increasing functionality. With useable functionality provided to clients, early and regularly, students were able to get necessary feedback, expose problems and project risks along the way.

4.1.2 Technical Abilities
At both the beginning and at the end of the program, students were asked to evaluate their knowledge of various technologies (e.g., front-end and back-end web development languages, and database management systems) on a scale of 1 to 5 (1 representing 'no knowledge' and 5 representing 'extremely high

levels of knowledge'). At the start of the program, students reported an average of 2.34, or moderately low levels of knowledge. At the conclusion of the program this number increased significantly to 4.08, or very high levels of knowledge (t=10.64, df=30, p<0.0001). This learning outcome was summarized by one of the students:

"I wanted to get exposure to the technology during the program, which I was able to successfully do. It was great to gain both the theoretical and hand-on foundation."

Students learned and practiced technical skills necessary to implement their assigned projects. A range of web-based technologies were employed (e.g., HTML/CSS/JavaScript, PHP, Ruby on Rails, and MySQL). Intensive, group and individual hands-on instruction, lab sessions, and practice assignments helped students develop conceptual understanding and basic skills as quickly as possible. Improvement of skill was evaluated based upon the completion of lab sessions and practice assignments. Once the students had a familiarity of the technology, we applied it to meet clients' needs. As a cornerstone of agile methodologies, pair programming requires two individuals to work together on each module of code to be produced (Andres and Beck, 2004). Hence, to maximize learning, technically stronger students were paired with students whose strengths lied in analysis and design.

"I learned a lot especially about pair programming, information assurance and security."

4.1.3 Teamwork Abilities

Effective teamwork is essential for creating successful complex software systems, and especially so for the tight time schedule of this program. Entering the program, most students were generally competent programmers and academically accomplished. We verified this by reviewing applicant college transcripts (course work and grades) and experiences included on their resumes (internships, employment and listed skills). With few exceptions, however, incoming students did not have experience working on a software development team. At both the beginning and at the end of the program, students were asked to evaluate their experiences with working on teams to solve ill-defined information systems programs in a team-based environment on a scale of 1 to 5 (1 representing 'no experience' and 5 representing 'extremely high level of experience'). At the start of the program, students reported an average of 2.50, or moderately low levels of experience. At the conclusion of the program this number increased significantly to 4.34, or very high levels of knowledge (t=13.30, df=30, p<0.0001). This learning outcome was summarized by one of the students:

"The program helped to prepare me for life after college. For example, the group dynamics blew me away. Before coming here my knowledge about working in a team was mainly drawn from my instincts. Now I have real skills that I can go back and share with others at my school. I can share my knowledge of group dynamics and technical things."

Effective distributed leadership is important to the success of student team projects (e.g., Tomal, 2001). While individuals naturally gravitate toward tasks, and team roles that play to their strengths, the program offered students a safe environment in which to extend their skills in ways that contributed to the team's efforts. Almost all of the students (30 of the 31 questioned) felt this was the most important element they learned:

"The most important skill I learned this summer was time management and working with a team. Understanding that we all think that we are excellent natural team players, but it really takes a conscious effort to be an effective member of a team."

Another student felt:

"I've learned a lot from technical skills to teamwork. Even though we are all Black, we are a diverse group. So, we've learned a lot from each other."

Each person on the team took a leadership role in some way. One student was designated as Project Manager, another as Quality Assurance Manager and a third as Client Advocate. Students designated individuals to serve in other roles such as designer, lead programmer, or documentation editor as appropriate.

Students also learned to be alert for potential problems, and the instructors paid careful attention to student interactions and team dynamics. As interpersonal or team problems arouse, the faculty worked closely with the students to deal with them. For instance, two students shared that:

"Prior to coming to the summer program, most of my experiences with team projects were bad. The program exceeded my expectations and I leave with an understanding of teamwork and team dynamics that can be applied to almost anything in life."

"I have learned to be more cooperative in deciding and not just head-strong in your opinions. I can be hardheaded about how I want things to look. I have learned to be more open minded about other peoples' opinions."

Through interactions with their clients, the faculty, and each other, students realized the value and importance of effective teamwork. Throughout the program, the instructors coached students in teamwork, problem resolution, team leadership, and group motivation. We found that successful project teamwork required that the members demonstrated positive communication skills, initiative, cooperative spirit, and willingness to agree on a shared vision.

4.2 Professional Development and a Sense of Belonging in the IT Profession

Another core learning objective of the program was to expose students to professional development opportunities and foster their sense of belonging in the IT profession. At both the beginning and at the end of the program, students were asked to evaluate their knowledge of career opportunities, graduate school opportunities, and ethical/social issues of information systems on a scale of 1 to 5 (1 representing 'no knowledge' and 5 representing 'extremely high levels of knowledge'). At the start of the program, students reported an average of 2.94 or moderately low levels of knowledge. At the conclusion of the program this number increased significantly to 4.06 or moderately high levels of knowledge (t=7.67, df=30, p<0.0001). This learning outcome was summarized by one of the students:

"Prior coming to the summer program I felt like a big fish in a small pond. I leave this summer feeling like a bigger fish in a bigger pond."

When asked to describe their projects, the students often first talk about the challenges of learning new programming languages, databases, and server technologies. Most naturally focus, initially, on the technical aspects of their work, but as they progress on their projects, the importance of professional development, a sense of belonging, and commitment to the field became more evident. During the exit interviews, most of the students (26 of the 31 questioned) agreed that the program helped them to develop professionally and increased their commitment to the field. These students shared that the program helped them to be self-directed, and proactive, be sensitive to organizational politics, deal with ambiguity, and build communication abilities (written and oral). For instance, two students remarked:

"I learned new stuff I didn't know. I also learned what I didn't know."

"The program helped me see that this is a good major for me. I like it because I always keep learning. Most people see that as a negative, but for me it is a bonus to keep learning new things. I think the program helped me to see that I want to stay in the field after college."

During the six-weeks, students were exposed to a variety of career, and graduate opportunities while offering mentoring, and service-learning interventions. As a benefit of participation, students have had the opportunity to apply for graduate school at the University with the expectation of substantial scholarship support if admitted. Of the 56 students participating in the program, over 17 subsequently pursued master's degree programs in Information Systems Management at the University. Several others chose to pursue graduate education at other institutions before entering the workforce. The majority of the students (29 or the 31 question) intended to pursue future IT employment or graduate school, and felt the program helped to solidify their intentions. Overall, the students reported that the program was a positive growth experience, with potential long-term benefits for their professional development. For instance, a student shared:

"Initially, my post-graduation plans were to enter the workforce immediately. Through emersion into the Carnegie Mellon community, the summer program has definitely encouraged me to pursue a graduate degree."

Webster and Mirielli (2007) suggest that many service-learning projects may not provide students with significant opportunities for reflective processing or considerations of how their experiences are personally meaningful. Homkes (2008) encourages instructors to focus on student learning rather than product delivery or hours of effort. Consistent with this thinking, the program encouraged students to continuously reflect on their experiences. For instance, two students shared in their exit interviews:

"The best thing about the program is that it opened a lot of doors for me. It helped me to know what the real-world is like and what I want to do. There are not a lot of opportunities for young Black students like this. And it has been so valuable."

"This is a once in a lifetime experience. I learned more here in the first two weeks than I do back home. This program has opened my eyes to what I can actually do. The mindset you get from being at Carnegie Mellon helps to show that African-Americans can grow and foster in an environment of excellence. You realize how far you can go."

Students were also required to make a final public presentation of their project to the clients, faculty, and other invited guests. This was a formal affair – students were expected to practice their presentation and prepare content for accuracy, completeness, and brevity. This final presentation also gave students the opportunity to reflect on their work in a public way. The final presentation served as a substantial closure point for the project and is the last significant event in the term.

The contributions of the students also made a significant difference for the community partner organizations. Typically, small- to medium- size nonprofit organizations need, but lack, effective information-based management and operations tools such as streamlined databases, websites for client service, and effective communications capabilities. Summer projects are intended to address real community partner needs or opportunities, and are scaled to match students' capabilities, and limited timeframe. This factor helped to improve the students' commitment to service and coincidently their sense of belonging in the field. About half of the students (15 of the 31 questioned) participated in the program because they wanted to find ways to help the community with technology. For the most part, this was a benefit that students realized once the project came to a close. For instance, a student explained:

"What I enjoyed most about working with a service-learning project this summer was the 'life and social lessons' I gained that I wouldn't get at a traditional internship. The program was beyond my expectations."

Other students shared similar sentiments:

"What I liked most about the program was being able to help our client. It feels good to help a group who is so nice and helps others."

"I never worked in a community service project like this before. It gives me a sense of selfish self-worth."

"It touched my heart getting to help in the community."

5. LESSONS LEARNED AND IMPLICATIONS FOR FUTURE RESEARCH AND TEACHING

In this paper, we presented an analysis of a summer internship program in information systems that employed a service-learning approach. The program aimed at exposing talented post-secondary students from HBCUs to complex team collaboration, advanced technologies, software engineering methodologies, and professional norms.

In this article, we investigated how *service-learning projects could help to address the under representation of African Americans in the IT profession.* Our findings suggest a few conclusions in terms of both recruitment and retention. First, we found that the hands-on / real-world approach of a service-learning project helps build students' perceptions of their skills and their exposure to a variety of IT skills (e.g., project management, technical, and teamwork abilities). Thus, students are even more competitive as they enter the IT job market (in terms of position and salary expectations) and/or graduate school applications (in terms of diverse pedagogy experiences and internship experiences). We also found that the program helped to foster a sense of belonging in the IT field and encouraged or solidified the students' interest in remaining in the discipline. Finally, the collaborative nature of the program helped to build personal and professional networks among the students, instructors, and community partners.

After eight years of the program, several valuable lessons have informed our research and teaching. First, we found that it is possible to accept students with varying levels of preparation, from different schools, with different majors, and with different learning styles into an intensive program, and expect high quality results. In this study, we investigated students' *perception* of their IT skills; in future studies, we would like to evaluate their *assessed* skill abilities, and any improvements. We have also learned that the regular information systems core curriculum can be successfully streamlined, compressed, and packaged for delivery in a non-traditional, fast-paced, intensive setting. It is challenging, yet important, to establish a baseline of knowledge when students come with such a diversity of backgrounds. Along those lines, in future studies we would like to analyze the student data by university, student classification (year of study), by major, age, gender, and background. We believe it is critical for educational programs, and/or employers focus recruitment efforts on student aptitude or potential, not just prior skills or programming proficiency.

We have also learned that the most critical success factor in the project outcome, and the students learning was centered on the teams' ability work together. We had great success in mentoring the students in project management, and technical abilities. However, the teamwork component was much more challenging. We found that it required constant coaching, mentoring, and monitoring to do it well. We believe IT-related pedagogical strategies used in the classroom or in service-learning projects should have a foundation in the fundamentals of teamwork. Offering these learning opportunities to our students will help to prepare them for a highly interactive and collaborative workplace upon graduation.

Finally, we have learned that there is difficulty in offering this type of program particularly as it relates to forming the service-learning project. Instructors must be prepared to spend significant time building relationships with community partners. The right client, the right project, and the right match with a student team is difficult to establish, and should not be attempted lightly. In addition, much effort will be required of the instructor to mentor, and coach the students throughout the project. Further, identifying, and establishing appropriate assessment activities is critical in the evaluation of program success, and student learning.

In the future, we hope to find innovative ways to reshape, expand, and disseminate our findings and to magnify its impact beyond the immediate students and community partners. We are also focusing on ways to maintain significant partnerships with HBCUs, and others stakeholders interested in ways to increase the talent pool interested in careers in the IT profession.

6. ACKNOWLEDGMENTS

This research is funded by the Andrew W. Mellon Foundation (Grant #30900675).

7. REFERENCES

[1] Andres, C. and Beck, K. (2004). *Extreme Programming Explained: Embrace Change (2nd Edition) (The XP Series)*. Addison-Wesley Professional, New York.

[2] Canton, J. (2007). *The Extreme Future: The Top Trends That Will Reshape the World in the Next 20 Years*. New York: Penguin Group.

[3] Evans, S.Y., Taylor, C.M., Dunlap, M.R., Miller, D.S. (Eds.). (2009). *African Americans and Community Engagement in Higher Education: Community Service, Service-Learning, and Community-Based Research*. Albany, New York: State University of New York.

[4] Ferguson, R., Liu, C., Last, M. and Mertz, J. (2006). "Service-Learning Projects: Opportunities and Challenges." *Proceedings of the ACM SIGCSE Conference*, 127-128.

[5] Florida, R. (2005). *The Flight of the Creative Class: The New Global Competition for Talent*. New York: HarperCollins Publishers.

[6] Godfrey, P.C. (1999). "Service-Learning and Management Education A Call to Action." *Journal of Management Inquiry*, 8(4), 363-377.

[7] Gravely, M. J. (2011). *What Is the Color of Opportunity? New Realities at the Crossroads of Business and Race*. Cincinnati, Ohio: Impact Group Publishers.

[8] Guthrie, R.A., and Navarrete, C.J. (2004). "Service-Learning Impact on IS Students in a Web Development Course." *Information Systems Education Journal*, 2(12), 1-12.

[9] Homkes, R. (2008). "Assessing IT Service-Learning." *Proceedings of the ACM SIGITE Conference*, 17-21.

[10] Jacoby, B. (1996). "Service-learning in Today's Higher Education." In Jacoby, B. (Ed.), *Service-learning in Higher Education: Concepts and Practices*. San Francisco, California: Jossey-Bass, 3-25.

[11] Katz, S., Allbritton, D., Aronis, J., Wilson, C. and Soffa, M.L. (2004). "Increasing Diversity in the Information Technology Workforce: Implications from a Study of Factors that Predict Achievement in CS." *Proceedings of the 6th International Conference on Learning Sciences*, 612-612.

[12] Lazar, J. and Lidtke, D. (2002). "Service-Learning Partnerships in the Information Systems Curriculum." In Lazar J. (Ed.), *Managing IT/Community Partnerships in the 21st Century*, 1-16.

[13] Olsen, A.L. (2008). "A Service Learning Project for a Software Engineering Course." *Journal of Computing Sciences and Colleges (JCSC)*, 24(2) 130-136.

[14] Tapia, A. and Kvasny, L. (2004). "Recruitment is Never Enough: Retention of Women and Minorities in the IT Workplace." *Proceedings of the ACM SIGMIS CPR Conference*, 84-91.

[15] Tan, J. and Phillips, J. (2005). "Incorporating Service Learning into Computer Science Courses." *Journal of Computing Sciences in Colleges (JCSC)*, 20(4), 57-62.

[16] Tomal, J.A. (2001). "A Factors Approach for Studying Success on Student Software Development Teams." Doctoral Dissertation, University of Pittsburgh, Pittsburgh, Pennsylvania.

[17] Webster, L.D., and Mirielli, E.J. (2007). "Student Reflections on an Academic Service Learning Experience in a Computer Science Classroom." *Proceedings of the SIGITE Conference*, 207-211.

[18] Werner, M. and MacLean, L.M. (2006). "Building Community Service Projects Effectively." *Consortium for Computing Sciences and Colleges (CCSC) Conference*, 76-87.

Research in Progress / Teaching Systems Analysis and Design: What Do Students Really Need to Know?

Anne Powell
Southern Illinois University Edwardsville
Department of Computer Management
and Information Systems, School of Business
Edwardsville, IL 62026-1106
1-618-650-2590
apowell@siue.edu

Susan E. Yager
Southern Illinois University Edwardsville
Department of Computer Management
and Information Systems, School of Business
Edwardsville, IL 62026-1106
1-618-650-2917
syager@siue.edu

ABSTRACT

This research in progress describes a survey instrument and includes preliminary analysis results of responses from IS/IT professionals regarding Systems Analysis and Design (SA&D) course content and coverage. Questions focus on the skills, tools, development practices, and development methodologies considered most important for a new employee to know and have in their tool kit. We consider our findings in light of the IS 2010 Curriculum Guidelines, with an eye toward how our information can assist in course and curriculum design. We present preliminary results with next steps.

Categories and Subject Descriptors

K.3.2 [**Computers and Education**]: Computer and Information Science Education – *Information systems education.*
K.6.1 [**Computers and Education**]: Project and People Management – *Systems analysis and design.*

General Terms

Design, Theory

Keywords

Systems analysis and design, SA&D education, SA&D skills, SA&D tools, SA&D development, SA&D methodologies

1. INTRODUCTION

While much of the existing research collects data from faculty teaching Systems Analysis and Design (SA&D), we focus on what potential employers believe is important for our students to know. The following sections include literature review, details about the study, preliminary results, and next steps.

2. LITERATURE REVIEW

Three primary areas of research in systems analysis and design pedagogy have been examined in the research stream. One area of research focuses on course activities and cases to use in teaching the SA&D course. Course activities are designed to show ways to teach individual topics in the SA&D curriculum, including software inspection exercises [21], user participation in

requirements definition [7, 18], and writing and interpersonal skills [17]. Instructors of SA&D may also choose from published teaching cases for use in their own classes. These cases typically involve assignments covering the analysis, design, and development of a solution [e.g., 5, 10] and may involve specific roles for the student to play in a group project [e.g., 16]. Other cases are designed for use with object-oriented analysis and design methodologies [13].

More recently, a second popular area of research centers on the merging of the traditional/structured waterfall methodology and object-oriented methodologies. Several articles discuss ways to merge the two types of methodologies and the feasibility of teaching both in a single SA&D class [2, 6, 11, 19]. Object-oriented SA&D processes in the traditional SDLC model are defined [12], and the most common object-oriented diagrams used by practitioners are identified [8]. In addition, the agile methodology is often discussed as another viable methodology that could and should be included in an SA&D course [3].

A third primary area of research attempts to identify topics that should be included in a one-semester SA&D course. Academics who teach the SA&D course have provided much of the input on what topics to include. Avison, Cole, and Fitzgerald [1] present seven (7) reflections on teaching SA&D based on their thirty-plus years of experience with the course content (e.g., "Information systems development is core to the discipline of IS" and "Using case studies can give meaning and real-world context to the material"). Other researchers examine which topics academics believe should be included. In two research papers published eight years apart, topics found to be definitely important include: data flow diagrams, balancing of data flow diagrams, entity relationship diagrams, use of team projects, projects that use both data and process modeling skills, data modeling concepts in general, and skills in data collection [9, 20]. In addition, the 2003 study found decomposition diagramming, use of a CASE tool, and interviewing techniques to be important [20], while the 2011 study found project management skills as an additional topic of primary importance and use of a CASE tool had declined and become unimportant [9]. Both studies found the importance of teaching object-oriented SA&D to be controversial [9].

Less often, other research focuses on practitioners and their view of which topics are essential in an SA&D course. Alumni, one year out from graduation, provided insight into whether they believed the project completed in their SA&D course was beneficial. The vast majority believed working with a real client on a project was useful preparation and a realistic simulation of actual systems work [22]. In addition, 90% or more of the alumni working as systems developers believed that deliverables including entity-relationship diagram, testing plan, and implementation plan were relevant to their post-course experiences [22]. By examining job ads, skill sets found most essential for systems analysts [15] included development skills (i.e., analysis, implementation, general development, design), software skills (i.e., database, packages, operating systems/platforms), business skills (i.e., general business and function-specific), and social skills (i.e., communication and interpersonal). Finally, methods and approaches used by practitioners in industry – but not necessarily what they thought should be taught – were identified [14].

3. THE STUDY

Like many undergraduate MIS programs, we are in the midst of curriculum revision prompted by the recently published IS 2010 Curriculum Guidelines for Undergraduate Degree Programs in Information Systems. In conjunction with a broader evaluation of the extent to which we should adopt the model curriculum recommendations, we recognize the need to reassess the content of our SA&D course; and in doing so, we want to include the perspective of employers of our graduates. This leads to our research questions:

> **Research Question 1:** Which SA&D skills, tools, practices, and methodologies do our employers deem most important for new hires to know and be able to apply?

> **Research Question 2:** How can we integrate the input received from our employers with the IS 2010 Curriculum Guidelines recommendations for SA&D?

Acceptance and implementation of IS 2010 Curriculum Guidelines by AACSB-accredited undergraduate information systems programs across the U.S. is only now being evaluated [4]. Input from potential employers can provide guidance when considering possible curriculum modifications, especially while contemplating IS 2010 Curriculum Guidelines adoption.

The goal of our data collection is to determine what practitioners believe should be included in an introductory SA&D course. We created a questionnaire adapted from several previous surveys. To identify the methods and approaches that employees want new hires to understand, we drew from the survey used by Lang and Fitzgerald [14]. We pulled specific topics covered in an SA&D course from the surveys used by both Tastle and Russell [20] and Guidry et al. [9]. Specific features of systems projects were drawn from van Vlielt and Pietron [22]. We also added items based on our own experience in teaching the SA&D course.

We sent e-mail to approximately 120 alumni we are connected with through LinkedIn, requesting their assistance in getting our online survey to the right people within their organization. While not all of these alums work in an area that utilizes their education about SA&D, many replied directly that they would forward our request to the appropriate contacts within their organization.

The survey asked about the importance of skills and tools, the frequency of use of development practices and methodologies, and the size and industry of their organization. Appendix 1 includes the complete survey items, the source of the items, and the scale used to measure each item.

4. PRELIMINARY RESULTS

4.1 Respondents

One hundred (100) people responded to the survey. Demographic questions asked about 1) size of the organization, annual revenues, total number of employees, and total number of IS/IT employees, and 2) industry in which the organization operates. Fifty-seven (57) respondents provided annual revenues (ranging from \$3M to \$110B), 24 provided annual IS/IT budgets (\$100,000 to \$500M), 75 provided total number of employees (30 to 265,000), and 61 provided total number of IS/IT employees (2 to 200,000). Twelve respondents placed their organization in manufacturing and 62 chose service. An additional six selected both manufacturing and service.

4.2 What Students Need to Know

Allowable responses about the importance of skills and tools ranged from 1 = Definitely Unimportant to 5 = Definitely Important. To analyze the responses, we examined means. See Appendix 2 for results for all skills and Appendix 3 for results for all tools, both presented in descending order by "% of Somewhat Important and Definitely Important responses" within "Response Mean." A mean response of 4.5-5.0 was interpreted as a topic of critical importance, 3.5-4.49 of considerable importance, 2.5-3.49 of possible importance, 1.5-2.49 of little importance, and 0.00-1.49 of no importance.

Two skills were considered of critical importance (see Appendix 2): working in teams and working with end-users (means of 4.83 and 4.57, respectively). The rest of the skills fell into the considerable importance category except one – criteria for selecting projects rated only possible importance. Of particular interest were three skills of considerable importance that were all rated as either Somewhat Important or Definitely Important by at least 90% of the respondents: identifying problems in current systems (93%), identifying and assessing risks (90%), and requirements gathering techniques (93%). The only other skill that garnered at least 80% on this measure was identifying feasibility issues (82%).

We asked about 19 types of tools (see Appendix 3), four of which pertain to documentation. Three of the four documentation tools, and 12 of the other 15 tools, were judged to be of considerable importance. Only the ability to create user and technical documentation was rated as either Somewhat Important or Definitely Important by 90% of the respondents. Most important of the other tools was estimation of critical path of tasks (81% of respondents). The only other tool that garnered at least 80% on this measure was project scope statement (80%).

Allowable responses about how often development practices and methodologies were used included never, 1-25% of time, 26-50% of time, 51-75% of time, and 76-100% of time. In addition to examining means, we considered response frequencies to determine the percentage of respondents indicating usage over 50% of the time (responses of 51-75% and 76-100%). See Appendix 4 for results for all development practices and Appendix 5 for results for all development methodologies.

Under development practices, we asked if their company or department used CASE tools to model diagrams. Similar to the Guidry et al. [9] study, the ability to use and understand CASE tools was not found to be a widely needed skill of new hires, with only eight (8) respondents indicating that their company used CASE tools. We asked about four (4) development practices (see Appendix 4). In-house development was the most common development source (43 of 89 respondents indicated that they use in-house development over 50% of the time), followed by purchasing a package (18 of 87), outsourcing (12 of 88), and utilizing an application service provider (11 of 87). The most common response for in-house development was 51-75% of the time (24 responses). The most common response for purchasing, outsourcing, and application service provider were all 1-25% of the time (39, 42, and 50 responses, respectively).

Hybrid, customized, or proprietary in-house methodologies was reported as the most common approach/methodology for development (42 of 86 respondents indicated that they used this approach over 50% of the time). Structured/traditional, object-oriented, and Rapid/Agile methodologies were each used over 50% of the time by about a third of our respondents. Only 10% of respondents indicated that they used no methodologies over 50% of the time (see Appendix 5).

4.3 Industry and Size Differences

One-way ANOVA tests were conducted by breaking the responses into different groups. The 62 service industry responses were compared to the 12 manufacturing industry responses. Only two significant differences in importance were found between the two industries. The first, 'Estimation of Task Duration,' was rated significantly more important to service industries than to manufacturing industries (F=6.005, p=.017). Response means for service industries was 4.24 while the manufacturing mean was 3.58. The second item, 'Report Design Issues,' was rated significantly more important to manufacturing respondents (F=2.972, p=.089). No significant differences between manufacturing and service industries were found for any of the other survey items.

When running ANOVA tests based on size of company, responses were divided into large companies (75,000+ employees, n=20), mid-sized companies (5,000-55,000 employees, n=24), and small companies (30-3,800 employees, n=31). Two items were found to have significant response differences based on number of employees. The ability to create/use data flow diagrams was significantly less important for small companies (F=5.351, p=.007). Response means were 4.30 and 4.25 for large and mid-sized companies respectively and 3.55 for small companies. Likewise, small companies were significantly less likely to use structured/traditional methodologies for new development than large or mid-sized companies. While 58% of respondents from large companies and 50% of respondents from mid-sized companies reported using structured/traditional methodologies over 50% of the time, only 18% of small companies reported using structured/traditional methodologies over 50% of the time.

5. NEXT STEPS

With the data collected, one of the next steps includes analysis of "Other" responses regarding skills, tools, development practices, development methodologies, and organization industry classifications. We need additional analysis of results, possibly incorporating entropy and deviation [20], to allow us to utilize this valuable data from potential employers of our graduates. Reflection upon results in the context of both SA&D course content and coverage, plus a broader curriculum review in conjunction with IS 2010 Curriculum Guidelines, are next steps.

6. REFERENCES

[1] Avison, D., Cole, M., and Fitzgerald, G. 2006. Invited Paper: Reflections on Teaching Information Systems Analysis and Design: From Then to Now! *Journal of Information Systems Education* 17, 3 (Fall 2006), 253-6.

[2] Bataveljic, P., Eastwood, M., and Seefried, H. 2006. An Approach to Teaching Object-Oriented Analysis and Design. *Journal of Information Systems Education* 17, 3 (Fall 2006), 267-72.

[3] Batra, D., and Satzinger, J.W. 2006. Contemporary Approaches and Techniques for the Systems Analyst. *Journal of Information Systems Education* 17, 3 (Fall 2006), 257-65.

[4] Bell, C.C., Mills, R.J., and Fadel, K.J. 2013. An Analysis of Undergraduate Information Systems Curricula: Adoption of the IS 2010 Curriculum Guidelines. *Communications of the Association for Information Systems* 32 (Jan 2013). DOI= http://aisel.aisnet.org/cais/vol32/iss1/2.

[5] Cappel, J.J., and Gillman, Jr., J.R. 2011. Teaching Case: Jay's Collectibles. *Journal of Information Systems Education* 22, 2 (Summer 2011), 111-5.

[6] Carte, T.A., Jasperson, J. (Sean), and Cornelius, M.E. 2006. Integrating ERD and UML Concepts When Teaching Data Modeling. *Journal of Information Systems Education* 17, 1 (Spring 2006), 55-63.

[7] Costain, G., and McKenna, B. 2011. Experiencing the Elicitation of User Requirements and Recording them in Use Case Diagrams through Role-Play. *Journal of Information Systems Education* 22, 4 (Winter 2011), 367-80.

[8] Dobing, B., and Parsons, J. 2006. How UML is Used. *Communications of the ACM* 49, 5 (May, 2006), 109-13.

[9] Guidry, B.N., Stevens, D.P., and Totaro, M.W. 2011. The Systems Analysis and Design Course: An Educators' Assessment of the Importance and Coverage of Topics. *Journal of Information Systems Education* 22, 4 (Winter 2011), 331-45.

[10] Guidry, B.N. and Totaro, M.W. 2011. Teaching Case: Convention Center Management: A Systems Analysis & Design Course Project. *Journal of Information Systems Education* 22, 1 (Spring 2011), 15-7.

[11] Harris, A.L., Lang, M., Oates, B., and Siau, K. 2006. Systems Analysis & Design: An Essential Part of IS Education. *Journal of Information Systems Education* 17, 3 (Fall 2006), 241-8.

[12] Khoo, B. 2011. A Process-Based Analysis of Object-Oriented System Analysis and Design. *International Journal of Management & Information Systems* 15, 1 (First Qtr 2011), 123-30.

[13] Khoo, B. 2009. Evaluating the Effectiveness of the Constructionist Approach to Object-Oriented Systems Analysis and Design Pedagogy. *Review of Information Systems* 13, 4 (Fourth Qtr 2009), 59-66.

[14] Lang, M., and Fitzgerald, B. 2006. New Branches, Old Roots: A Study of Methods and Techniques in

Web/Hypermedia Systems Design. *Information Systems Management* 23, 3 (Summer 2006), 62-74.

[15] Lee, C.K. 2005. Analysis of Skill Requirements for Systems Analysts in Fortune 500 Organizations. *The Journal of Computer Information Systems* 45, 5 (Summer 2005), 84-92.

[16] Mitri, M., and Cole, C. 2007. Teaching Case: A Systems Analysis Role Play Case: We Sell Stuff, Inc. *Journal of Information Systems Education* 18, 2 (Summer 2007), 163-8.

[17] Pomykalski, J.J. 2006. Teaching Tip: Interleaving Modeling and Writing Activities in Systems Analysis and Design. *Journal of Information Systems Education* 17, 3 (Fall 2006), 249-52.

[18] Ramiller, N.C., and Wagner, E.L. 2011. Communication Challenges in Requirements Definition: A Classroom Simulation. *Journal of Information Systems Education* 22, 4 (Winter 2011), 307-17.

[19] Rob, M.A. 2006. Dilemma between the Structured and Object-Oriented Approaches to Systems Analysis and Design. *The Journal of Computer Information Systems* 46, 3 (Spring 2006), 32-42.

[20] Tastle, W.J., and Russell, J. 2003. Analysis and design: Assessing actual and desired course content. *Journal of Information Systems Education* 14, 1 (Spring 2003), 77-90.

[21] Tyran, C.K. 2006. A Software Inspection Exercise for the Systems Analysis and Design Course. *Journal of Information Systems Education* 17, 3 (Fall 2006), 341-51.

[22] van Vliet, P.J.A., and Pietron, L.R. 2006. Information Systems Development Education in the Real World - A Project Methodology and Assessment. *Journal of Information Systems Education* 17, 3 (Fall 2006), 285-93.

Appendix 1: Survey Questions

Question 1: On a scale of 1 (definitely unimportant) to 5 (definitely important), new hires for my organization/department should have an understanding/knowledge of:
Working in teams[1,3]
Working with end users
Criteria for selecting projects
Identifying feasibility issues[4]
Identifying and assessing risks
Identifying problems in current systems
Estimation of task duration
Requirements Gathering techniques
Managing change requests
Purpose of RFP/RFI/RFQ/ITB
User interface design issues[1,3,4]
Report design issues
Internal control design issues
Information security design issues
General design issues (layout, text, navigation, color)
Other (please specify)
Question 2: On a scale of 1 (definitely unimportant) to 5 (definitely important), new hires for my organization/department should be able to create:
User and technical documentation[4]
Cost-benefit and payback analysis[1,3]
Business case for proposed system
Project scope statement[1,4]
Other (please specify)
Question 3: On a scale of 1 (definitely unimportant) to 5 (definitely important), new hires should be able to create/use these tools:
Gantt chart/network diagram
Activity dependency diagram[1,3]
Critical path of tasks
Process models[1,3]
Data flow diagram (DFD)[1,3,4]
Use case diagram[1,3]
Functional decomposition diagram[1,3]
Entity-Relationship diagram[1,3,4]
Class diagram[1,3]
Structure chart[4]
Sequence diagram[1,3]
Activity diagram
State-transition diagram[1,3]
Data dictionary
Decision table/tree
Other (please specify)
Question 4: Does your company/department use CASE tools to model diagrams? If no, please proceed to the next question. If yes, please list below:
Question 5: For new systems development in your area, how often are new systems developed through (scale= Never, 1-25% of time, 26-50% of time, 51-75% of time, 76-100% of time):
In-house development?
Outsourcing?
Purchasing a package?
Application Service Provider?
Other (please specify)
Question 6: For new systems development in your area, what percentage of time is spent using these approaches/methodologies for development (scale= Never, 1-25% of time, 26-50% of time, 51-75% of time, 76-100% of time)?
Hybrid, customized, or proprietary in-house methodologies[2]
Structured/Traditional methodologies[2] (e.g., SDLC, Waterfall, Yourdon, SSADM)
Iterative or incremental methodologies[2] (e.g., Spiral, RUP, Iterative Design)
Rapid/Agile methodologies[2] (e.g., RAD, XP, SCREM, DSDM)
Application Service Provider
Object-Oriented development methodologies/approaches[1,2,3] (e.g., OOAD, UML, J2EE)
ERP system configuration
No methodologies used/ad hoc development[2]
Other (please specify)

[1]Guidry, Stevens, and Totaro (2011); [2]Lang and Fitzgerald (2006); [3]Tastle and Russell (2003); [4]van Vliet and Pietron (2006)

Appendix 2: SA&D Skills

Skills	Response Mean	Category	% of Somewhat Important and Definitely Important responses
Working in teams	*4.83*	*Critical Importance*	*100%*
Working with end users	*4.57*	*Critical Importance*	*95%*
Identifying problems in current system	4.49	Considerable importance	93%
Identifying and assessing risks	4.38	Considerable importance	90%
Requirements gathering techniques	4.37	Considerable importance	93%
Identifying feasibility issues	4.17	Considerable importance	82%
Estimation of task duration	4.09	Considerable importance	78%
Information security design issues	4.06	Considerable importance	78%
User interface design issues	4.03	Considerable importance	79%
Managing change requests	3.91	Considerable importance	74%
General design issues	3.84	Considerable importance	78%
Report design issues	3.81	Considerable importance	72%
Internal control design issues	3.70	Considerable importance	63%
Purpose of RFP/RFI/RFQ/ITB	3.52	Considerable importance	58%
Criteria for selecting projects	3.44	Possible importance	55%

Appendix 3: SA&D Tools

Tools	Response Mean	Category	% of Somewhat Important and Definitely Important responses
User and technical documentation	4.37	Considerable importance	*90%*
Project scope statement	4.05	Considerable importance	*80%*
Critical path of tasks	4.00	Considerable importance	*81%*
Use case diagram	3.92	Considerable importance	75%
Data flow diagram	3.92	Considerable importance	74%
Decision table/tree	3.89	Considerable importance	74%
Business case for proposed system	3.88	Considerable importance	74%
Process models	3.88	Considerable importance	74%
Entity-relationship diagram	3.85	Considerable importance	69%
Data dictionary	3.75	Considerable importance	66%
Sequence diagram	3.72	Considerable importance	64%
Gantt chart/network diagram	3.71	Considerable importance	68%
Activity diagram	3.57	Considerable importance	57%
Class diagram	3.55	Considerable importance	55%
Activity dependency diagram	3.50	Considerable importance	57%
Functional decomposition diagram	3.39	Possible importance	48%
Structure chart	3.35	Possible importance	47%
Cost-benefit and payback analyses	3.32	Possible importance	51%
State-transition diagram	3.24	Possible importance	39%

Appendix 4: SA&D Development Practices

Development Practices	Response Mean	Responses > 50% / Total responses	% of > 50% responses
In-house development	3.35	43 / 89	48%
Purchasing a package	2.63	18 / 87	21%
Outsourcing	2.32	12 / 88	14%
sApplication Service Provider	2.22	11 / 87	13%

Appendix 5: SA&D Development Methodologies

Approaches/Methodologies for Development	Response Mean	Responses > 50% / Total responses	% of > 50% responses
Hybrid, customized, or proprietary in-house methodologies	3.15	42 / 86	49%
Structured/traditional methodologies	2.88	30 / 86	35%
Object-oriented development methodologies/approaches	2.73	30 / 86	35%
Rapid/Agile methodologies	2.63	29 / 87	33%
ERP system configuration	2.33	18 / 86	21%
Iterative or incremental methodologies	2.10	13 / 86	15%
Application Service Provider	1.95	8 / 85	9%
No methodologies used/ad hoc development	1.79	8 / 81	10%

Behavior and Expectations of Mobile Job Seekers: An Industry Study Focusing on Job Boards

Stephan Böhm
RheinMain University of Applied Sciences
Department of Design Computer Science Media
Wiesbaden, Germany
stephan.boehm@hs-rm.de

ABSTRACT

The market share of mobile devices like smartphones and tablets is growing rapidly. These devices are increasingly used to access the services offered on the Internet. Time spent online has started to shift considerably from desktop and laptop computers to mobile connected post-pc devices. In certain areas, mobile usage has already exceeded the access and traffic generated by desktop computers. This development also affects the usage behavior and expectations of job seekers when accessing job ads and other job-related information online. In this context the paper at hand presents a study analyzing the behavior and user expectations of job seekers using mobile devices in Germany. The study shows that the majority of smartphone and tablet users have already accessed job ads and used job search applications ("apps") through these devices. Moreover, many of those respondents who have already accessed job ads with a post-pc device also expect to be able to apply for a job via smartphone and tablet.

Categories and Subject Descriptors

A.1. [**General Literature**]: Introductory and Survey. H.4.0. [**Information System Applications**]: General; H.4.3. [**Information System Applications**]: Communication Applications – *Internet.*

General Terms

Management, Measurement, Documentation, Human Factors

Keywords

Mobile Media, Mobile Recruiting, E-Recruiting, Mobile Job Ads, Mobile Job Apps, Mobile Job Boards, User Expectations, Status Quo Analysis

1. INTRODUCTION

Internet access and user installation of application software have been supported by mobile devices for many years [3]. However, device limitations, bandwidth restrictions, insufficient usability and prohibitive pricing for mobile data prevented the mass market from adopting these new technologies. The majority of mobile subscribers continued to use their devices for voice telephony and messaging services. It was the introduction of the Apple iPhone in the year 2007 that gave new impetus to the industry. But many HR managers remained skeptical about the potential of these technologies for their discipline. At that time, the majority of them used a simple feature phone or a blackberry. When confronted with the term "mobile recruiting" they often imagined candidates typing an application letter or writing a resume on these devices. This is still a strange scenario considering the former and current limitations of mobile devices. The tremendous success of the iPhone and the following smartphone generations produced by other hardware manufacturers changed their opinion: Some innovation leaders started to launch mobile-optimized career websites, used QR codes on their job advertisements, or developed application software ("apps") for mobile recruiting [4].

In Germany some studies and empirical findings on the HR manager's perspective on mobile recruiting have been available since 2009. These studies have identified a growing relevance of mobile recruiting as well as its deployment between 2009 and 2011 [6]. A more recent study on general recruiting trends from 2012 reports that 5.7 percent of the top 1,000 companies in Germany offer mobile applications for job seekers on mobile devices (such as smartphones, tablets, etc.). About 10 percent offer mobile-optimized job ads. Overall, almost half of the respondents believe that the increasing use of mobile devices will have a major impact on recruiting. More than one-third (36.7 percent) consider addressing candidates via mobile devices to be useful for recruitment. About a third believes that candidates will apply for jobs via mobile devices. However, when questioned on current external trends and internal challenges in the area of recruitment, "always on" and mobile recruiting were of relatively low importance for the participants and ranked among the last places in the list of rated trends and challenges [19].

These results are consistent with the observation in practice that HR managers are now aware of "mobile recruiting" but that there is still a lack of budgets and resources specifically assigned for mobile recruiting activities in most companies. Hence it has to be questioned whether HR management departments have implemented the required tools and instruments to track and analyze the share of requests and responses within their online recruiting channels that are generated through mobile devices like smartphones and tablets. However, growing mobile Internet usage and resulting user expectations may force companies to take action by generating a pull for mobile-optimized content and services. *Emma Frazer*, senior industry head for recruitment at *Google UK* has recently stated that one of five recruitment related search queries come from a mobile device [11]. At the same time this would mean that companies could lose up to 20 percent of their potential candidates if they do not mobile-optimize their e-recruiting activities on the Internet. Against this background this paper analyzes the usage behavior and user expectations of mobile job seekers with a focus on job boards. The paper is structured as follows: section 2 gives some background on mobile Internet usage in Germany and the concept of mobile recruiting. The approach of the study and the results are presented in sections 3 and 4. Implications for employers and providers of job boards and recruitment are discussed in section 5.

2. BACKGROUND

2.1 Mobile Recruiting

There is still a lack of research on mobile recruiting. Only a few scientific publications [e.g. 6, 10, 12, 13, 14, 15] and industry studies or guidelines [e.g. 16, 18, 20] have been published up to today. However, mobile recruiting can be defined as "… any organizational information provided for or delivered to a mobile device in order to attract and hire potential applicants and employees."[6] In this context mobile recruiting can be interpreted as a field of e-recruiting, dealing with the particularities as well as the challenges and opportunities of addressing potential candidates through mobile devices. In a narrower sense mobile recruiting focuses on activities related to candidate contact and the application process. In practice mobile recruiting is often used in a more comprehensive way and subsumes the deployment of mobile media technologies throughout all the activities within the recruiting funnel as shown in figure 1.

Mobile Recruiting in a Broader Sense

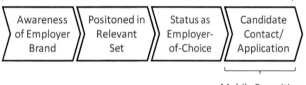

Figure 1. Mobile Recruiting in the "Recruiting Funnel" [9]

A wide range of mobile media technologies can be used for mobile recruiting and are already being deployed in practice. Mobile social media, mobile web, SMS and mobile apps are the most frequently used mobile media technologies in Germany according to a 2011 survey among HR Managers [6]. The growing popularity and the innovative character of mobile media technologies can be used at the beginning of the recruiting funnel, e.g. to increase awareness of an employer brand. But mobile media technologies can also be deployed to generate a direct impact on the relationship between employer and job candidate or the application process by improving efficiency or providing added value compared to conventional desktop-based processes:

- *Ubiquity:* Candidates can be addressed regardless of time and place, i.e. anytime and anywhere. This can be used to improve availability or response times. Information needs can be satisfied in the situation and at the time they occur and do not have to be postponed to the availability of a desktop computer with Internet access.

- *Context-sensitivity:* Up-to-date smartphones are equipped with a variety of sensors to present the requested information in relation to the current usage context. This can be used to reduce complexity of search requests or to improve relevance through context-sensing, i.e. by automatically detecting the location in order to filter job ads.

- *Usability and convenience:* User interfaces of modern mobile devices support gesture control and are equipped with touch screens. They are often easier to use than the interfaces of traditional desktop systems. Furthermore they can adapt very flexibly to different usage situations and provide a wide range of media formats. This allows flexible adaptation of the media

richness to the type of task or communication. Another driver for convenience is the fact that mobile devices are immediately ready for use without a time consuming boot-up sequence.

- *Personalization:* Smartphones are very personal devices assigned to a specific personal profile/identity and configured to personal needs. Furthermore, many mobile operating systems support social media integration. The user can very easily interact with social networks and use the functionality of the mobile device to upload personal information.

- *Real World Connection:* In most cases user interaction on desktop computers is initiated by user input via keyboard or mouse. The user interacts while the usage context is predominantly static. This is different in mobile environments in which this context varies widely. Here user interaction can be triggered by events or linked to real-life objects (e.g. mobile tagging[13]). Furthermore, the view on the real world can be augmented by computer generated virtual information (e.g. augmented reality).

Mobile recruiting is about considering and deploying these value drivers in a company's e-recruiting activities. It is important to understand, that providing mobile-optimized access to existing e-recruiting services and applications is only the first step to implementing a mobile recruiting strategy. These activities may be driven by a usage shift from desktop to mobile and the threat of losing potential candidates if this trend is missed by an employer. In a second phase employers will need to focus more on value drivers of mobile media technologies to differentiate from competitors.

2.2 Mobile Internet Usage

The use of mobile devices to access the Internet has increased dramatically in Germany over the last five years. According to *Accenture's Mobile Web Watch* study [1], only 13 percent of Internet users accessed the Internet via their mobile phones in 2008. The percentage of mobile Internet users increased to 28 percent in 2011 and more than doubled to 58 percent today as stated in the newest *Mobile Web Watch 2012* study. Smartphones are the most preferred devices for mobile Internet access (used by 50 percent of the respondents) followed by netbooks (28 percent) and tablets (17 percent). Eighty-five percent of mobile Internet users access the Internet once a day or more with their mobile devices. However, age is still a differentiating factor with regards to mobile internet usage: in Germany 27 percent of the respondents to the *Accenture* study over 50 years use mobile Internet but 82 percent in the age group 14 to 29 years [2].

Mobile apps are an important driver of mobile usage and can be used for device personalization by selecting and installing a set of applications aligned to user needs. Sixty-seven percent of the respondents of the *Accenture* study in Germany have downloaded a mobile app on their mobile device in 2012. The most popular types of apps are information apps. Mobile apps of this type have been downloaded by 81 percent of German mobile app users followed by entertainment apps (58 percent). According to the *Google Mobile Planet* study German smartphone users have an average of 24 apps installed on their devices – 9 of these applications are used regularly. Smartphones have established themselves as an indispensable companion in everyday life for many people. Sixty-four percent of the participants of the *Google Mobile Planet* study would not leave the home without their device. Forty percent of the smartphone users search on their devices every day. Smartphones are used on the go (88 percent) but also at home (97 percent) or at work (72 percent) [8].

However, this market data should be interpreted cautiously. The percentage of mobile Internet users is often determined by asking the participants for a single usage experience thus disregarding the intensity or frequency of usage. Therefore it must be considered that the increase of mobile Internet users is not reflected by e.g. the distribution of page views on websites accessed by mobile and desktop devices. According to *StatCounter*, a web analytics service, the percentage of page views generated from mobile devices has grown from 2.01 percent to 5.45 percent in Germany between October 2011 and October 2012. The distribution differs according to region. In the US the share of mobile page views has grown from 7.05 percent to 11.42 percent during this time. This data shows that the majority of web usage is still generated by desktop computers but user and usage growth rates show strong signals that this might change in the near future [17].

It is obvious that these market trends will affect the Internet usage behavior of job seekers when looking for job descriptions or other career related information. Therefore, employers as well as providers of job boards, career management, and other recruitment services have to review and revise their e-recruiting strategies. They need to monitor mobile media trends and usage to define and implement appropriate strategies on how to support mobility and seamless cross device integration for the services they offer.

3. METHODOLOGY

The objective of the study at hand was to analyze behavior and expectations of mobile job seekers by focusing on the services offered on job boards. The study was conducted online in cooperation with a German job board provider between June and July 2012. The online questionnaire and the study were announced on the job board website and in an email newsletter from the provider. The questionnaire consisted of five parts and a total of thirty questions in German. All the results presented in the next section provide an approximate English translation. Overall 1,343 respondents participated in the study. The number of respondents here and in the following varies because the participants were not forced to answer all questions or due to filter questions. Table 1 shows the demographics of the survey respondents.

Table 1. Demographics of the Survey Respondents

Age	14 - 19	1	0.1%
	20 - 29	123	9.2%
	30 - 39	360	26.8%
	40 - 49	502	37.4%
	50 +	322	24.0%
	n/a	35	2.6%
Gender	Female	477	35.5%
	Male	820	61.1%
	n/a	46	3.4%
Position	Apprentice/Student	7	0.5%
	Graduate	99	7.4%
	Professional	635	47.3%
	Executive	484	36.0%
	n/a	118	8.8%
Smartphone or Tablet Owner	Yes	934	69.5%
	No	409	30.5%
Total	N	1,343	100.0%

The majority of the respondents are older than 30 and male. The reason for this is that the cooperating job board addresses job seekers in the target groups of professionals and executives. The job board does not provide career information for apprentices and students which explains the very low participation rates in these segments. Against this background it has to be considered that the following study results mainly represent the usage behavior and user expectations in the segments of job seeking professionals and executives. More than two thirds of the respondents own a smartphone or tablet (69.5 percent). A quarter (25.1 percent) of the respondents stated to use more than one device. The distribution of the answers on the type of phone was as follows: smartphones with touch screen (50.7 percent), smartphone without touch screen (9.6 percent), tablets (18.2 percent), other mobile devices (21.5 percent). Android (42.3 percent) was the most popular smartphone platform followed by iOS (33.7 percent). Conversely, due to the popularity of the iPad, Apple's iOS (67.3 percent) is preferred over Android (29.2 percent).

4. RESULTS

The following section presents findings of the study on the usage behavior and user expectations of the participants in the areas of (1) job ads, (2) mobile apps and (3) an application for jobs via mobile devices. As mentioned earlier, it has to be taken into consideration that these findings mainly represent job seekers in the segments of professionals and executives searching for career information on job boards.

4.1 Mobile Job Ads

Job boards aggregate job ads, also referred to as job descriptions or job listings, from different employers and provide search engine capabilities to find job offers according to the job seeker's profile, qualifications, and career objectives. Sixty-two percent of the respondents that own a smartphone or tablet have already used such a mobile device to read a job ad. Job boards are the most popular source of this information and used by 77.8 percent of the mobile job seekers as shown in fig. 2.

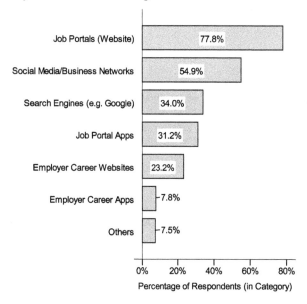

Figure 2. Sources of Job Ads Used on Mobile Devices (N=577)

Many of the respondents have read job ads on their smartphone or tablet at home (70.7 percent), when travelling (64.5 percent) or in other situations on the go (61.9 percent). One-third (33.3 percent) of the respondents have used their mobile devices to search for job ads while at work. These results show that the usage of mobile devices is not only driven by ubiquity but also by convenience when using these devices at home, and by privacy issues when using it at work instead of a corporate desktop computer. In general, the majority of mobile job seekers expect the job ads to be optimized for their mobile devices: An adaption to the smaller screen size is demanded by 89.8 percent and 57.9 percent want the content itself to be reduced to its essence. Different media formats are not expected – only 2.6 percent would prefer a video instead of a job description when using a mobile device. When asked how job boards can be optimized for mobile devices, most of the respondents voted for functions to save the job ads they have read or to forward search results (e.g. using email) as shown in figure 3. These results also emphasize the need to design the functions of a job board in close alignment to the target group. Professionals and executives are generally quite flexible regarding their place of employment – thus not interested in using a job portal function to search for jobs in the close vicinity.

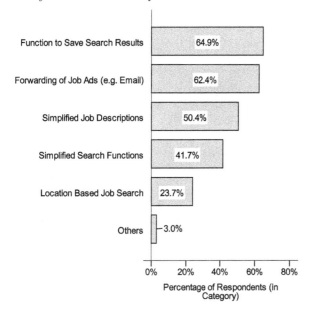

Figure 3. Expectations regarding Mobile Optimization of Job Boards (N=569)

As mentioned above, there are still smartphone and tablet owners who have not read job ads on their mobile devices yet. However, 76.1 percent of these job seekers can imagine doing so in the future. Compared to the usage behavior of existing mobile job seekers, there are higher shares of potential users who are expecting to use mobile apps for job searches. Another interesting finding is that fewer potential mobile job seekers can imagine searching for job ads on mobile devices at home (60.1 percent) or at work (18.7 percent). This again could be an indicator that ubiquity is given too much importance and that real usage is – especially for tablets – driven by other factors like usability or convenience.

4.2 Mobile Apps

Mobile apps are another way to provide mobile optimized access to job ads and other contents and services of job board providers. Many (46.2 percent) of the smartphones and tablet owners who have already read a job ad on their mobile devices have already used such a mobile job board app. Most of the responding mobile job board app users see the greatest advantages of these applications in (push) notifications about new job ads (72.0 percent) as shown in figure 4. Improved performance (51.7 percent) and clari-

ty (43.7 percent) are other important reasons for using an app instead of the web-based job board with a mobile device.

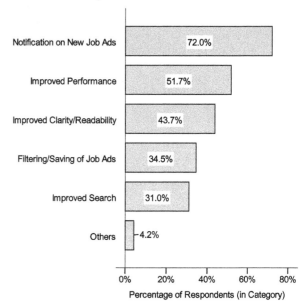

Figure 4. Perceived Advantages of Mobile Job Board Apps (N=261)

However, 53.8 percent and thus the majority of the smartphone and tablet users who have already read job ads on their devices are not using mobile job board apps. Most of these non-users refrain from the use of this kind of mobile apps due to privacy concerns (73.7 percent). Mobile apps can obtain rights to access data on the mobile device such as contacts and addresses. The pure existence of this functionality and its potential abuse may worry some of the users, especially in situations like job related searches where professionals and executives with an existing employment relationship necessarily want to remain anonymous. Another important reason for not installing a job board app is that many of the respondents (39.3 percent) do not see a value add compared to the search on the website or it is not opportune to do so (37.2 percent) – e.g. because they are using a corporate device.

These findings are consistent with the technical characteristics of mobile apps. In general, native apps are able to interface (more) directly with the device's native features, data and hardware. Compared to websites and web apps they also perform faster and do not rely on an online connection [5, 7]. However, many of these advantages are not relevant for job boards. The data on the job boards is stored and processed by servers. Mobile devices are primarily used as front-ends or clients to define search queries and present the resulting job listings to the user. For this reason apps also require an online connection. With regard to standard features of job boards native apps hardly offer advantages vs. mobile-optimized websites or web apps.

4.3 Applying for Jobs via Mobile Devices

A successful job search can culminate in the job seeker's intention to apply for the company. If the job search is conducted on a smartphone or tablet the limitations of these devices may force the job seeker to switch to a desktop computer to proceed. To prepare an application the applicant may need to have access to information that is stored on the hard drive of his computer or the desktop is chosen because it is more convenient to work with longer texts on these devices. The required change of media may result in a delay or abortion of the application process. However, in many cases it can be sufficient to provide a short text and a link to a personal profile (e.g. in a social media/business network) to allow the candidate to be screened by the employer. Another approach could be to store some prepared documents in the user profile of a job board user account. In this case the mobile device is just used to trigger the sending of these application documents if an appropriate job ad is found.

The participants of the study were asked if they could imagine using these different alternatives to apply for a job by using mobile devices. The results are shown in table 2.

Table 2. Mobile Application via Smartphone or Tablet

Share of respondents[1] that can imagine using their smartphone or tablet to ...

... create a letter of motivation	Yes	226	27.0%
	No	612	73.0%
... keep an a resume up-to-date	Yes	324	38.7%
	No	514	61.3%
... fill out a simple application form	Yes	662	79.0%
	No	176	21.0%
... apply with short text and link to profile	Yes	578	69.0%
	No	260	31.0%
1) Smartphone or tablet owners who have read or can imagine reading job ads on their mobile devices.	N	838	100.0%

The most popular option is to fill out a simple application form (79.0 percent) followed by an application by a short text and a link to a profile (69.0 percent). A smaller share of the respondents would accept even more effort for a mobile application by creating a letter of motivation (27.0 percent) or updating a resume (38,7 percent) from a smartphone or tablet. These questions on job application via mobile devices may sound very visionary. However, 6.4 percent of the respondents stated that they have already used their smartphone or tablet to apply for a job. In addition, 30.2 percent of the respondents expect an attractive employer to provide an option for comfortable mobile application.

5. IMPLICATIONS

Mobile recruiting has been identified in prior studies as being a trend that is discussed within HR departments. However, the dramatic growth of mobile Internet usage as well as the shift of Internet usage from desktops to mobile devices may force companies to step-up their mobile recruiting activities very soon. Otherwise employer and job boards are in danger of forgoing the growing number of job seekers that access job ads from mobile devices. A first step must be to establish appropriate analytic tools to track the share of mobile access and traffic within the e-recruiting channels. As a second step a mobile recruiting strategy is required to define how to cope with the usage shift towards mobile devices and how to improve efficiency, provide a value-add, and differentiate from competitors when deploying mobile media technologies for recruiting.

The findings of this study show that job seekers in Germany are already using their smartphones and tablets for job searches on a wide scale. They expect mobile-optimized service offers that allow for an efficient and convenient job search with mobile devices. More sophisticated mobile offerings like mobile video or location based search are not the focus (of the professional and executive job seekers) yet. Against this background, employers and providers of job boards should focus their activities on the provision of mobile-optimized websites or web apps before getting en-

gaged in the development of (native) mobile apps. Many users expect the option to apply for a job via mobile device but only a very small proportion of job seekers have used this up to now. Employers should utilize this phase to test and evaluate different alternatives when providing such an option (e.g. impact on quality and quantity of applications) and to adapt the internal recruitment processes (e.g. to establish a two step approach by screening mobile applications before requesting a more comprehensive application from appropriate candidates).

6. REFERENCES

[1] Accenture 2008: Mobile Web Watch 2008: Das Web setzt zum Sprung auf das Handy an. http://www.accenture.com/SiteCollectionDocuments/Local_ Germany/PDF/MobileWebWatch2008.pdf. Accessed 06.11.2012.

[2] Accenture 2012. Mobile Web Watch 2012: Special Edition: Germany, Austria, Switzerland. http://www.accenture.com/SiteCollectionDocuments/PDF/A ccenture-Study-Mobile-Web-Watch-Germany-Austria-Switzerland-EN.pdf. Accessed 06.11.2012.

[3] Andersson, C., Freeman, D., James, I. Johnston, A., and Ljung, S. 2006. Mobile Media and Applications. Chichester, Wiley.

[4] Böhm, S., and Jäger, W. 2009. Mobile Recruiting 2009: Ergebnisse einer empirischen Studie zur Bewerberansprache über mobile Endgeräte. Hochschule RheinMain.

[5] Böhm, S., Jäger, W., and Niklas, S. J. 2011. Mobile Applikationen im Recruiting und Personalmarketing. *Wirtschaftsinformatik und Management*, 3/ 4, 14–22.

[6] Böhm, S., and Niklas, S. J. 2012. Mobile Recruiting: Insights from a survey among German HR Managers, Proceedings of the 2012 ACM Special Interest Group MIS Computers and People Research Conference (SIGMIS CPR 2012), Milwaukee, Wisconsin, 117-122.

[7] Fling, B. 2009. Mobile Design and Development. Sebastopol, O'Reilly.

[8] Google 2012: Our Mobile Planet: Understanding the Mobile Consumer. May 2012. http://www.thinkwithgoogle.com/insights/uploads/607368.pd f/download/. Accessed 06.11.2012.

[9] Jäger, W., and Böhm, S. 2012. Mobiles Personalmarketing und Recruiting. In: Beck, C. (Hrsg.), Personalmarketing 2.0, 2. Aufl. Köln, Wolters Kluwer.

[10] Laumer, S., Eckhardt, A., and Weitzel, T. 2010. Electronic Human Resources Management in an E-Business Environment. *Journal of Electronic Commerce Research*, 11/4, 240-250.

[11] Mobile Recruitment Conference 2012: 1 in 5 Recruitment Searches are Now Mobile. http://mobilerecruitmentconference.com/2012/10/08/1-in-5-recruitment-searches-are-now-mobile/. Accessed 08.11.2012.

[12] Niklas, S.J. Strohmeier, S., and Böhm, S. 2012. Mobile Job Board Applications – Which are the Key Success Factors? A Literature Review and Conceptual Framework, Proceedings of the 4th European Academic Workshop on Electronic Human Resource Management 2012, Nottingham, UK.

[13] Niklas, S.J., and Böhm, S. 2011. Increasing Usage Intention of Mobile Information Services via Mobile Tagging, Pro-

ceedings of the 5th International Conference on Mobile Ubiquitous Computing (UBICOMM 2011), Lissabon, Portugal, 98-104.

[14] Niklas, S.J., and Böhm, S. 2011: Applying Mobile Technologies for Personnel Recruiting – An Analysis of User-Sided Acceptance Factors, *International Journal of eBusiness and eGovernment Studies,* 3/1, 169-178.

[15] Niklas, Susanne J. 2011. Mobile IS Success in Personnel Marketing: a Consumer-based Analysis of Quality and Perceived Value, Proceedings of the 2011 ACM Special Interest Group MIS Computer Personnel Research Conference (SIGMIS CPR 2011), San Antonio, Texas, 91-95.

[16] Potentialpark 2011. Mobile Recruitment: A Thriving Trend Amongst Job Seekers. http://www.potentialpark.com/wp-content/uploads/2011/12/Potentialpark-Results-Release-2011-Mobile-Recruitment.pdf. Accessed 07.11.2012.

[17] StatCounter 2012: StatCounter Global Stats. http://gs.statcounter.com. Accessed 07.11.2012.

[18] Web-Based Recruitment 2012. How to Get Ready for Mobile Recruitment. http://web-based-recruitment.com/free-guides/. Accessed 08.11.2012.

[19] Weitzel, T., Eckhardt, A., von Stetten, A., Laumer, S., Maier, C., and Cuhl, E. 2012. *Recruiting Trends 2012.* Otto Friedrich Universität Bamberg, Goethe Universität Frankfurt am Main, ISS Chris Universität Bamberg, monster.de, Bamberg & Frankfurt.

[20] Wheeler, K., Alder, M., and Martin, D. 2012. Mobile Recruiting Guide 2012. http://s3.amazonaws.com/pocketrecruit/assets/MobileRecruitingGuide2012FINAL2.pdf. Accessed 08.11.2012.

Research-in-Progress: Economic Elements of Collective Memory in IT Occupational Culture

Tim Jacks
Southern Illinois University Edwardsville
Rte 157, Edwardsville, IL, USA
618-650-2424
tjacks@siue.edu

Prashant Palvia
University of North Carolina at Greensboro
1400 Spring Garden Street, Greensboro, NC, USA
336-334-4818
pcpalvia@uncg.edu

ABSTRACT

With a backdrop of economic turmoil in recent history composed of a severe recession and slow recovery, there is timely motivation to explain the important role that collective memory plays in occupational culture. Based on the lens of cultural sociology and Halbwach's theory of collective memory, the findings uncover the heroes and origin stories that form the collective memory of the IT occupation in order to answer the research question "What are the important elements of collective memory in IT occupational culture?" The findings include elements of economic downturns, layoffs, outsourcing, job-hopping, 9/11, Silicon Valley, and increased regulation, as well as common heroes and origins. A hermeneutic interpretation is offered to further explain the importance of the results for both theory and practice.

Categories and Subject Descriptors

K.7.1 [The Computing Profession]: Occupations

Keywords

IT occupational culture, IT professionals, collective memory, economic factors

1. INTRODUCTION

Information Systems (IS) research on culture has typically focused on two levels of analysis: national and organizational (Leidner & Kayworth, 2006). However, research at the level of occupational culture is still nascent. This study focuses on the occupational culture of Information Technology (IT) professionals. Despite some ambiguity in who is and who is not considered to be in the IT workforce (Kaarst-Brown & Guzman, 2005), IT professionals are defined here as *people who work within a formal IT department or fulfill the role of IT for an organization*. For example, IT professionals include those who specialize in Systems Analysis & Design, Programming, Applications, Database Administration, Telecommunications, Infrastructure Support, IT Project Management, and IT Operations.

The IT profession is developing its own occupational culture that is distinct from organizational culture (Guzman, 2006;

Ramachandran & Rao, 2006; Nord et al, 2007; Gregory, 1983). Organizational culture is the dominant pattern of basic assumptions, perceptions, thoughts, feelings, and attitudes held by members of an organization (Schein, 1985). Occupational culture, in contrast, is not bounded by a single organization, but rather bases its culture on specific expertise, similar tasks, and a sense of itself as a distinct occupational group (Trice, 1993). Occupational culture, thus, spans across all organizations. Leidner & Kayworth (2006) point out that "what has received the least amount of attention in the literature on IT and culture is the very notion of an IT culture" (p.371). This study examines IT occupational culture as cultural attitudes that members of the IT occupation share (Nord et al., 2007; Guzman, 2006).

The study of IT occupational culture (ITOC) is important for two reasons. First, "culture affects action" (Swidler, 1986, p. 281). Culture has a causal effect on IS behavior at different levels, including national, organizational, and occupational (Karahanna, Evaristo, and Srite, 2005). IT occupational culture, in particular, defines shared meanings and expected behaviors for IT professionals (Nord et al., 2007). Second, cultural conflict can arise when two or more groups interact that do not share the same core set of values (Leidner & Kayworth, 2006; Nord et al., 2007). Thus, when the IT occupational group interacts with a different occupation, such as business managers, the result can be cultural conflict (Guzman, 2006; Nord et al., 2007).

Prior studies on ITOC have focused on the structural components that comprise an occupational culture and how those components pertain to ITOC. The historical element of culture, however, is missing from such frameworks. With a backdrop of economic turmoil in recent history composed of a severe recession and slow recovery, there is timely motivation to explain the important role that collective memory plays in occupational culture. This study examines the research question "What are the important elements of collective memory in IT occupational culture?" An interpretive approach based on the lens of cultural sociology, in general, and Halbwach's theory of collective memory, in particular, will address the research question. While the data collection has been completed as well as the qualitative coding, detailed results will be provided at the conference. The interview data set is part of a larger research project on ITOC, but the lens of collective memory is a new offshoot that moves the project forward in a new direction.

2. LITERATURE REVIEW

Culture is commonly understood as 'the way things are done around here', but this is an oversimplification (Schein, 1999). Culture can consist of the categories and plans for action shared by a group as well as the shared understandings people use to coordinate their activities (Harper & Lawson, 2003). Hofstede defines culture as "the collective programming of the mind that distinguishes the members of one group or category of people from others" (Hofstede & Hofstede, 2005, p. 4), and this is one of the most popular definitions in IS literature (Leidner & Kayworth, 2006). Despite the obvious appeal for an IS audience, Hofstede emphasizes that people are not "programmed" in the same way that computers are.

Hofstede's definition succinctly highlights the collective aspect of culture at a group level; however it may underemphasize the deeper meanings of culture. To contrast with Hofstede, Clifford Geertz, the noted anthropologist, says "The concept of culture I espouse. . . is essentially a semiotic one. Believing, with Max Weber, that man is an animal suspended in webs of significance he himself has spun, I take culture to be those webs, and the analysis of it to be therefore not an experimental science in search of law but an interpretative one in search of meaning" (Geertz, 1973, pp. 4-5). This definition highlights the perspective that culture is more important than simply differentiating one group from another. Culture is paramount because it provides meaning in our day-to-day lives and cultural sociologists tend to use Geertz' definition of culture (Griswold, 2004). "Geertz, and Weber before him, took culture to involve meaning… how people in social contexts create meaning" (Griswold, 2002, pp.12-13). Culture is "an historically transmitted pattern of meanings embodied in symbols, a system of inherited conceptions expressed in symbolic forms by means of which men communicate, perpetuate, and develop their knowledge about and attitudes toward life" (Geertz, 1973, p.89).

Trice (1993) explores the defining characteristics of occupational cultures in detail with his Theory of Occupational Culture. In this framework, occupational cultures exist apart from organizational culture and become a source of conflict due to occupational cultural differences. Seven characteristics that separate out an occupational culture are identified as 1) Esoteric knowledge and expertise, 2) Extreme or unusual demands, 3) Consciousness of kind, 4) Pervasiveness, 5) Favorable self-image and social value in tasks, 6) Primary reference group, and 7) Abundance of cultural forms (Trice, 1993). This framework has been used in more recent IS literature to verify that there is, indeed, the existence of such a thing as 'IT occupational culture' because it conforms to these seven characteristics (Guzman et al., 2004; Guzman & Stanton, 2004; Guzman et al. 2006; Ramachandran and Rao, 2006). For example, esoteric knowledge and technical jargon are prime examples of what separates IT people from other people in an organization.

It is important not to overstate the homogeneity of IT occupational culture. Certainly there are differences between members and even sub-groups (hardware people vs. software people, for example). The three-way perspective of culture is an important tool to include in any cultural analysis. The three-way perspective indicates that culture may be analyzed as 1) integrated, 2) differentiated, or 3) fragmented (Martin, 2002). Integration sees consensus and consistency in shared perceptions and this is the primary perspective for this research. Differentiation, on the other hand, examines inconsistent interpretations and differing subcultures within a group. Finally, fragmentation emphasizes the role of paradox, ambiguity and tension with a culture for which there may be no easy explanations. All three may be used simultaneously for a richer interpretation of culture and this three-way view of culture has

also been advocated for IS research in particular (Kappos & Rivard, 2008).

One of the many gaps in our knowledge of ITOC is in identifying the critical elements of collective memory that are shared by members of the occupation. If organizations can be viewed as interpretive systems with their own collective memory (Stein & Zwass, 1995), this study proposes that occupations can be viewed as interpretive systems in a similar way. In other words, what specific elements of collective memory have helped to shape IT occupational culture over time? The theory of collective memory is typically used in cultural sociology research to help explain interpretive systems (Daynes, 2010; Fine, 1992).

Maurice Halbwachs, a student of both Emile Durkheim and Max Weber, emphasized the role that collective memory has in shaping culture (Halbwachs, 1992). Collective memory is not literal history, but the shared *interpretation* of history that was experienced and lived by a social group (Halbwachs, 1992). He used the Durkheimian view of collective representations and wanted to identify how people mythologize their own pasts (Coser, 1992). Collective memory is a cohesive force for a social group because it identifies the group's heroes and group origins (Coser, 1992). For Halbwachs (1992), the estrangement experienced between different social groups is due to their not sharing enough collective memories. If two groups do not share common experiences, they will not interpret the meaning of the past or the present in the same way (Coser, 1992). Furthermore, this disparity in meaning will be passed on to each generation as they continually reshape their collective memories (Smith & Riley, 2009).

Occupational groups have their own memories that their members have constructed over a long period of time (Coser, 1992). The collective memory of a group is an important aspect of the culture of a social group (Connerton, 1989). While it is individuals who are doing the remembering, not groups or institutions, those individuals are part of a specific group context and use that context to both remember and re-interpret their past (Coser, 1992). Collective memory has been used in management research (Walsh & Ungson, 1991) and IS research (Stein & Zwass, 1995) for organizations. But it has not yet been studied at the occupational level in the context of the IT profession.

If culture is "an historically transmitted pattern of meanings embodied in symbols" (Geertz, 1973, p.89) and "the sum total of all the shared, taken-for-granted assumptions that a group has learned throughout its history" (Schein, 1999, p. 29), then any analysis of occupational culture should address the influence of collective memory, i.e., the shared history and interpretation of that history by the group's members (Brief & Nord, 1990). For example, Fine (1996) situates his study of restaurant workers in the history of restaurants. Interpretations of the meaning of any work activity are driven by our interpretations of the past (Brief & Nord, 1990; Allan, 2001; Halbwachs, 1992). Relevant past events in shared history can include economic events and institutions (Brief & Nord, 1990; Daynes, 2010). There are historical events that have impacted the IT occupation in significant ways. Some events include Y2K, 9/11, the dot-com boom and bust, outsourcing and offshoring trends, the rise of the Internet, and the rise of compliance regulations. A closer examination of the elements of collective memory in ITOC will serve to expand our knowledge.

3. METHODOLOGY

In order to answer the research question, an interpretive approach is appropriate for focusing on shared interpretations of meaning for theory-building. Qualitative semi-structured interviews with 25 IT professionals were conducted, asking open-ended questions about various aspects of ITOC.

As Guzman (2006) examined perceptions of IT occupational culture by *students* who were preparing to enter the field of IT, this study extends that work to address the context of those who have been in the profession for at least 7 years (enough time to be fully socialized into the occupational culture). The three selection criteria for interview candidates were:

1) IT professionals who had worked in the field at least 7 years.

2) They had worked in multiple organizations in IT departments, not just one company for their entire career.

3) They were not members of IT management.

IT managers tend to share more in common with business management culture and overall organizational culture than with IT occupational culture (Guzman et al., 2004; Iivari & Huisman, 2007), therefore IT managers were excluded. A large IT services recruiting firm was extremely helpful in providing contacts that met the selection criteria.

Each interview lasted from one hour to two hours. All interviews were conducted face-to-face, tape recorded and then immediately transcribed. All the transcriptions were then provided to the interviewees for validation that the right information was captured and they were allowed to make corrections or amendments. These steps serve to increase the reliability of data gathered in an interview process (Yin, 2003).

Analysis in qualitative research means sorting out the structures of significance or codes and interpreting their meaning for a wider audience (Geertz, 2002). Therefore, the analysis of the interview data involved several stages including 1) coding, 2) content analysis, and 3) hermeneutic interpretation. While the unit of data collection is the individual, the unit of analysis is the occupational group level because the results are being generalized to this group level. The unit of analysis is the unit about which descriptive and explanatory statements are to be made (Babbie, 1992).

Coding is the process of transforming raw data into a more quantitative form (Babbie, 1992) although qualitative data is not the same as quantitative data (Richards, 2005). The aim of codifying is "to arrange things in a systematic order" (Saldana, 2009, p. 8). While the coded data is not quantitative, many techniques of content analysis are based on coded data, including word-frequency counts, key-word-in-context listings, classifications of words into content categories, content category counts, and retrievals based on content categories and co-occurrences (Weber 1990). All of these techniques were used in the coding process.

Two forms of content analysis in the qualitative analysis software Dedoose were used. The first was a simple code frequency count across all the imported transcripts. When conducting qualitative analysis, the frequency of a symbol, idea, or subject matter can be interpreted as measuring its importance, attention, or emphasis (Krippendorff, 2004). The second form of content analysis is in code co-occurrence. Co-occurrence coding is the process of simultaneously coding a passage or overlapping passages with multiple codes because human speech does not always lend itself to a single idea for each paragraph or even each sentence

(Saldana, 2009). Co-occurrence charts were helpful in quickly finding examples of relationships, for example, how economic layoffs have led to extreme or unusual demands in the workplace.

4. PRELIMINARY RESULTS

The variety of backgrounds of the interviewees is shown in the demographics in Table 1.

Table 1. Interviewee demographics

ID	Age	Years in IT	Sex	IT Function	IT group size	Org size	Current industry	Education
1	33	11	M	Programmer	50	21000	Education	Masters IS
2	32	14	M	Mainframe	200000	400000	Technology	Masters IS
3	35	12	M	Developer	500	96000	Technology	Masters IS
4	55	20	M	Mainframe	18	24000	Manufacturing	Bachelors IS
5	33	11	M	Support	1000	200000	Retail	Associates IS
6	42	21	M	Support	1000	200000	Retail	Bachelors CS
7	36	14	F	Project mgr	600	26000	Manufacturing	Bachelors IS
8	43	25	F	Business Analyst	15	3000	Education	Bachelors
9	34	15	M	Programmer	4	2500	Education	Bachelors
10	46	25	M	Consultant	1	1	Manufacturing	Bachelors IS
11	37	11	M	DBA	32	1500	Healthcare	Masters IS
12	26	8	M	DBA	30	300	Financial	Bachelors IS
13	34	12	M	Consultant	5	5	Manufacturing	Associates BUS
14	48	25	M	Network Admin	600	26000	Manufacturing	Bachelors CS
15	39	15	M	Consultant	6	11	Manufacturing	Bachelors BUS
16	42	19	M	DBA	300	10000	Financial	Bachelors CS
17	42	16	F	SysAdmin	25	1300	Legal	Bachelors
18	31	14	M	Security	25	3000	Nonprofit	Bachelors BUS
19	44	11	M	App Architect	2000	40000	Financial	Bachelors CS
20	42	18	F	DBA	50	500	Healthcare	Bachelors IS
21	35	14	M	SysAdmin	24	2000	Healthcare	Associates IS
22	33	11	M	SysAdmin	25000	200	Financial	Associates IS
23	36	17	F	Consultant	7000	7000	Technology	Bachelors
24	38	12	M	SysAdmin	7	300	Publishing	Associates IS
25	35	13	M	SysAdmin	500	24000	Retail	Associates IS

In general, the data reveal strong support for the idea of a collective memory in IT occupational culture. There are many examples of historical events that are interpreted similarly by members of the IT occupation. The strongest themes had to do with economic factors. Table 2 shows a frequency count of the relevant collective memory codes. Space does not permit a complete list of all codes used in the analysis.

Table 2. Frequency count of codes

Economic downturns including layoffs (47)	82
Heroes	45
Job security	30
Parent	27
Origin ("fell into")	21
Technological history	20
Job hopping	18
9/11	15
Increased compliance/regulation	12
Silicon Valley	9
Outsourcing	9
Political	8
Y2K	4

The theme of economic growth and decline with resulting layoffs for IT workers was the most frequent narrative among the interviewees. The dot-com boom and bust directly impacted those who were working during this time of rapid technological expansion in the late 1990s followed by an abrupt economic halt in the early 2000s. There were many examples of job loss or job-switching during this time period due to the economy. Stories of being laid off and losing an IT job due to economic conditions were both common and painful to recount. Interviewees made it clear that losing a job is a devastating life change, and not simply an economic change in status. Of the 82 references to the economy, 47 were directly related to layoffs within the IT occupation. Of the 47, 15 were tightly intertwined with 9/11 and/or outsourcing based on code co-occurrence.

Eventually after 9/11 they scaled back their IT department from 8 people in Charlotte to one and I wasn't the one guy. I had to look for work elsewhere. (#5)

That was around the 9/11 time, because I remember actually sitting at home, I had just gotten married. I actually got laid off 4 days before I got married. I had the wedding invitation on the refrigerator at work. (#25)

I remember telling my Dad "I'm not going anywhere." ... I ended up getting laid off a month after 9/11. (#16)

I was there the day the layoffs happened at [a large bank]! First time [they] had ever laid anyone off in, what, 150 years of being in existence? That was a tough day for them. That was a really tough day for them. I really felt bad for the guys (lowered tone of voice)...because you know IT people think they're invincible (raises voice) and indispensable... and they're not! They're just not! (#8)

I wasn't fired, I was outsourced, but it's the only job I've ever lost in my adult life and it was tricky because I know it's not personal, but it felt very personal to me at that time. I almost lost my house. I couldn't find another job. It felt very <u>personal</u> to me. ...I just never in a million years thought...because I had always done great at my jobs, I always had good reviews, I never even made a lateral move, you know? So here I was with no job and...you learn. You learn that you're not indispensable! (#17)

It was at the height of the dot com, I mean this was in 2000. When I got hired there, stock prices were about $147 a share, and a year later when I was laid off it was less than $2. It was just basically a situation where you got laid off because the company imploded. (#19)

Through a reduction of 50%, probably even more...yeah, it's more. When I was there the first time, we had about 20 people in the department, and now we're down to seven. (#24)

When the interviewees were asked "Who are your IT heroes?" the answers were extremely varied but generally fell into three categories. Teachers in school were identified 7 times, a past colleague or mentor 13 times, and industry people 12 times (see Table 3).

Of the "past colleagues" category, in every instance, the context of the quote was that the admired person had *taught* them something important. So there is strong evidence that teachers, whether in that role formally or informally, are considered heroes for IT employees. It is worth noting that Bill Gates and Steve Jobs were mentioned by four different people as *not* being examples of IT heroes because they were considered business people. Parents were mentioned three times, and not having any IT heroes at all was the response from five people.

Identifying heroes is an important element of collective memory and so is identifying origin stories (Coser, 1992). Origin stories overlapped between career origins and industry origins out of

Table 3. Examples of industry heroes

Person	Known for
Richard Stallman	Free Software Foundation
John Carmack	Gaming developer
Al Stevens	Dr. Dobbs
Ben Forta	Cold Fusion
Linus Torvalds (twice)	Linux
37 Signals	Development
David Hanson	Ruby on Rails
Nintendo	Gaming
John Strand	Security
Scott Lowe	VMWare
Roddie Perlman	Spanning Tree protocol

Silicon Valley. The origin story had many common themes including a parent bringing home a computer at an early age and then a lack of formal preparation for the IT field later in life.

I purely fell into it, and I lucked out. (#17)

I'm in IT because I fell into it. (#9)

It was by accident. I thought that I wanted to be a teacher. (#7)

I started out, I wanted to be a journalist. So I got into IT sideways. (#1)

I didn't really know what I wanted for a career. (#5)

I stumbled into IT and programming. (#4)

I never intended...I just had to pick something..."you have to!" "I'm like uhhh, I don't want to!" Until of course then I graduated, it's like to only really marketable skill I have is computer stuff. (#8)

In terms of the origins of the industry, these stories mainly related to the culture of what life was like in Silicon Valley in the 90s, i.e., the glory days of the profession. There is evidence here that IT people tend to mythologize the past as most group cultures do.

It was a crazy culture. When you went into the office, everybody was casual, people came in shorts, the business people came in in suits, we had a game room that had arcade games and a PlayStation 2, foosball, pinball, there was a pool table, Ping-Pong table, a snack bar in there that they kept stocked constantly. ... We had anything you wanted, you just asked the receptionist and she'd get it stocked in the snack room. I mean it was just a crazy time, there were parties going on, startups happening left and right. It was a wild ride. I'm sorry it didn't last longer. (#6)

We were in this special place [Silicon Valley in the late 90s] where maybe my experience is not reflective of other people's experiences in less innovative environments. It was pretty loose out there in terms of the different business ideas people were trying out at the time, with all the startup stuff. We had a bunch of people who had never really managed anything, people fresh out of business school, had a great business idea and got some venture capital for it. So that really colors, I think, the way that I'm going to tell you that history, to me, kind of comes out of that and into this more structure, more bureaucratic, less fun [environment] (#1)

At that time in the economy in the world, I could pretty much pick anywhere I wanted to go in the United States and find a job. And we literally did that. We took a paper from South Carolina and cruised some want ads and contacted some head hunters and they paid my way down, my moving expenses and everything else. Ah, the good old days! (#4)

As the economy grew worse, there came increasing compliance legislation such as Sarbanes-Oxley, health care privacy, and changing credit card security standards that led to an evolving culture of regulation. The new compliance culture meant that companies were exerting more control over IT functions and this increased scrutiny has been felt strongly and sometimes bitterly by IT personnel. If the origin stories harken back to the halcyon days of growth, freedom, and fun at work, then the current view of the occupation is bleak by comparison. In addition to layoffs and outsourcing, the current environment faces more regulation, less innovation, and less job security. Changing economic conditions clearly made IT workers much more risk-averse and less entrepreneurial. Interviewees that were willing to "go out on their own" into consulting during the height of the dot.com boom are now settling for more stable jobs with regular hours. While an aging work force may contribute to this preference for stability, it was clear that this was a choice driven by perceptions of an unstable economy.

Everyone's fearful of a job right now. (#4)

I mean, we've lost...I've told you about the IT staff, and we've lost about 50% of the people in the company over the last 3 or 4 years. And it's probably going to get worse. (#24)

Right now everybody's afraid to leave a good thing, once the economy turns around that will probably resume. (#2)

The main ones obviously with what I've been through is all the smaller shops that are more exciting and fun to work at are few and far between. With all the people I know, except for a handful of people that work at big companies. You don't see the start-ups like you did in the late nineties. You don't see the new business... not like it was back in the late nineties, early 2000s.(#19)

Especially in the economic environment we're in right now, most IT departments have been trimmed and the demands are higher than they were before, because there are fewer people! They work very hard. They work a lot of hours, sometimes for even less pay than they made before sometimes. (#15)

Yeah, the employer, they know they have you. There's not a lot of jobs out there. Employers gain. Employers gain. They lay off people and they rehire. They think that one person should be able to do 3 people's jobs and do it as effectively. I think that's the big negative with what I'm seeing. People are just overworked. (#20)

Over the past 3 or 4 years, I've kind of taken on a different perspective as far as IT as a whole, and I see things sort of differently now. Maybe it's because the economy and how things have to be justified now, ...and this is one of the things that I try to tell the younger guys there, you know, everything that we do, there has to be either a cost savings associated with it, or revenue generated associated with it. (#24)

---

5. DISCUSSION AND INTERPRETATION

While everyone's individual work experiences differ, there are remarkable commonalities that were observed in the data. By applying the "principle of the hermeneutic cycle" (Klein & Myers, 1999) and moving from the individuals' experiences (the parts) to the larger context of the occupation (the whole) and back again, a pattern of shared meaning emerges. If stories of group heroes and group origins are important for collective memory, then what kind of overall portrait is painted by these narratives?

In general, there is a tragic motif to the overarching narrative. The common origin story includes an early adolescent experience with

computers full of the joy of discovery and learning. But this is quickly followed by a lack of formal preparation for a career in IT. The narrative goes like this: "I will never forget the day that (Mom/Dad/other family member) brought home our first computer. It was a (Commodore/Atari/Apple/IBM) and I fell in love with it!" The narrative typically continues with "I never planned to work with computers, I just fell into IT." Despite differing contexts, the interviews share a collective memory of what it was that brought them into a career in IT.

After falling into IT, there is a strong collective memory of the "good old days" of the dot.com boom when companies had money, were willing to reward IT talent with stock options in the company, and allowed a loose, almost adolescent, work environment focused on play. During this golden age, there is a shared perception that "job-hopping", moving from one company to another in quick succession for better pay, was an occupational phenomenon *particular* to the IT profession. (Whether this is actually true or not, this is the shared perception in collective memory.) It was during this period that "heroes" emerged. The commonality of the industry heroes in Table 3 above is that most were developers and all were creators of something new, profound, and meaningful (new applications, new languages, new operating systems, new methods). But the real heroes were those who taught what they had discovered.

Then as the dot-com bubble burst, shortly after 9/11, layoffs devastated the IT workforce as companies downsized. However the traumatic impact of these layoffs was even greater for the IT occupation than other occupations due to their previous history of quick advancement and feelings of being indispensable or invincible. IT workers emerged from this period of layoffs in the 2000s older, wiser, and more focused on keeping a decent job than on exciting new entrepreneurial ventures. There is a new shared understanding that everyone is dispensable now and something about the good old days of fun, creativity, and innovation has been lost.

On a more practical level, this hermeneutic portrait does help clarify an important area of IS research. If cynicism, defined as mental distancing from one's work (Ply et al., 2012), work exhaustion (Moore, 2000), and job (dis)satisfaction (Joseph et al., 2007) are common in the IT occupation, then these are not merely individual psychological attributes but may, in fact, owe their pervasiveness to deeply ingrained historical influences based on the collective memory of the occupation.

Based on the results, this research proposes that Halbwach's theory of collective memory can be successfully applied to the occupational level of analysis with fruitful results. An occupational system may be viewed as an interpretive system of collective memory and this is an important contribution to research. The contribution to practice includes important advice for today's business leaders: if you want to be a hero for your IT employees, be a teacher for them!

6. REFERENCES

[1] Albrechtsen, E. "A Qualitative Study of Users' View on Information Security." *Computers & Security* (26:4) 2007, pp. 276-289.

[2] Allan, G. *The Patterns of the Present.* State University of New York Press: Albany, 2001.

[3] Babbie, E. *The Practice of Social Research.* Sixth edition. Wadsworth Publishing: Belmont, CA, 1992.

[4] Brewerton, P. and Millward, L. *Organizational Research Methods: A Guide for Students and Researchers.* Sage Publications: Thousand Oaks, CA, 2001.

[5] Brief, A., and Nord, W. (Eds.) *Meanings of Occupational Work.* Lexington Books: Lexington, MA, 1990.

[6] Coser, L. "Introduction" in Halbwachs, M. *On Collective Memory.* The University of Chicago Press: Chicago, 1992.

[7] Creswell, J. *Qualitative Inquiry & Research Design.* Sage Publications, LosAngeles, 2007.

[8] Geertz, C. *The Interpretation of Culture.* Basic Books: New York, 1973.

[9] Geertz, C. "Thick Description: Toward an Interpretive Theory of Culture" in *Cultural Sociology.* Spillman, L. (Ed.) Blackwell Publishers: Oxford, 2002.

[10] Gregory, K. "Native-View Paradigms: Multiple Cultures and Culture Conflicts in Organizations." *Administrative Science Quarterly* (28) 1983, pp. 359-376.

[11] Griswold, W. *Cultures and Societies in a Changing World.* 2nd ed. Sage Publications: Thousand Oaks, CA, 2004.

[12] Guzman, I. "'As You Like I.T.': Occupational Culture and Commitment of New Information Technologists." Unpublished dissertation. 2006.

[13] Guzman, I., and Stanton, J. "Culture Clash! The Adverse Effects of IT Occupational Subculture on Formative Work Experiences of IT Students." *Americas Conference on Information Systems, 2004.*

[14] Guzman, I., Stanton, J. Stam, K., Vijayasri, V., Yamodo, I., Zakaria, N., and Caldera, C. "A Qualitative Study of the Occupational Subculture of Information Systems Employees in Organizations." *SIGMIS 2004, Tucson, Arizona.*

[15] Halbwachs, M. *On Collective Memory.* The University of Chicago Press: Chicago, 1992.

[16] Harper, D. and Lawson, H. (Eds.) *The Cultural Study of Work.* Rowman & Littlefield Publishers: New York, 2003.

[17] Hofstede, G. and Hofstede, J. *Cultures and Organizations: Software of the Mind.* New York: McGraw-Hill. 2005.

[18] Iivari, J. and Huisman, M. "The Relationship Between Organizational Culture and the Deployment of Systems Development Methodologies." *MIS Quarterly* (31:1) March 2007, pp. 35-58.

[19] Joseph, D., Ng, K., Koh, C., and Ang, S. "Turnover of IT Professionals: A Narrative Review, Meta-Analytic Structural Equation Modeling, and Model Development". *MIS Quarterly* (31:3) 2007, pp. 547-577.

[20] Kaarst-Brown, M. and Guzman, I. "Who is 'the IT workforce'?: Challenges Facing Policy Makers, Educators, Management, and Research. *SIGMIS-CPR 2005.*

[21] Kappos, A. and Rivard, S. "A Three-Perspective Model of Culture, Information Systems, and their Development and Use". *MIS Quarterly* (32:3) September 2008, pp. 601-634.

[22] Karahanna, E., Evaristo, J., and Srite, M. "Levels of Culture and Individual Behavior: An Integrative Perspective." *Journal of Global Information Management* (13:2) 2005, pp. 1-20.

[23] Klein, H. and Myers, M. "A Set of Principles for Conducting and Evaluating Interpretive Field Studies in Information System." *MIS Quarterly* (23:1) 1999, pp. 67-94.

[24] Krippendorff, K. *Content Analysis: An Introduction to its Methodology.* Sage Publications: Thousand Oaks, CA, 2004.

[25] Leidner, D., and Kayworth, T. "A Review of Culture in Information Systems Research: Toward a Theory of Information Technology Culture Conflict." *MIS Quarterly* (30:2), June 2006, pp. 357-399.

[26] Martin, J. *Organizational Culture: Mapping the Terrain.* Sage Publications, Thousand Oaks, CA, 2002.

[27] Moore, J. "One Road to Turnover: An Examination of Work Exhaustion in Technology Professionals." *MIS Quarterly* (24:1) 2000, pp. 141-168.

[28] Nord, J., Nord, G., Cormack, S., and Cater-Steel, A. "IT Culture: Its Impact on Communication and Work Relationships in Business." *International Journal of Intercultural Information Management* (1:1) 2007, pp. 85-107.

[29] Ply, J., Moore, J., Williams, C., and Thatcher, J. "IS Employee Attitudes and Perceptions at Varying Levels of Software Process Maturity" *MIS Quarterly* (36:2) 2012, pp. 601-624.

[30] Ramachandran, S. and Rao, S. "An Effort Towards Identifying Occupational Culture among Information Systems Professionals." *ACM SIGMIS-CPR 2006.*

[31] Richards, L. *Handling Qualitative Data: A Practical Guide.* Sage Publications: Thousand Oaks, CA, 2005.

[32] Rubin, H. and Rubin, I. *Qualitative Interviewing: The Art of Hearing Data.* Sage Publications: Thousand Oaks, CA, 1995.

[33] Saldana, J. *The Coding Manual for Qualitative Researchers.* Sage Publications: Thousand Oaks, CA, 2009.

[34] Schein, E. *Organizational Culture and Leadership.* Jossey-Bass Publishers: San Francisco, 1985.

[35] Schein, E. *The Corporate Culture Survival Guide.* Jossey-Bass Publishers: San Francisco, 1999.

[36] Smith, P., and Riley, A. *Cultural Theory: An Introduction.* 2nd Edition. Blackwell Publishing: Oxford, 2009.

[37] Stein, E. and Zwass, V. "Actualizing Organizational Memory with Information Systems." *Information Systems Research* (6:2) 1995, pp. 85-117.

[38] Swidler, A. "Culture in Action: Symbols and Strategies." *American Sociological Review* (51:2) 1986, pp. 273-286.

[39] Trice, H. *Occupational Subcultures in the Workplace.* ILR Press: Ithaca, New York, 1993.

[40] Walsh, I., Kefi, H., and Baskerville, R. "Managing Culture Creep: Toward a Strategic Model of User IT Culture." *Journal of Strategic Information Systems* (19:4) 2010, pp. 257-280.

[41] Walsh, J. and Ungson, G. "Organizational Memory." *Academy of Management Review* (16:1) 1991, pp. 57-91.

[42] Weber, R. *Basic Content Analysis.* 2nd ed. Sage Publications: Thousand Oaks, CA, 1990.

[43] Yin, R. *Case Study Research: Designs and Methods.* Sage Publications: Thousand Oaks, CA, 2003

Inter-Sourcing: Alternative IT Sourcing Solutions Using Student Interns

Mari W. Buche
Michigan Technological University
1400 Townsend Drive
Houghton, MI 49931
1+ 906-487-3440
mwbuche@mtu.edu

ABSTRACT

Information Technology (IT) sourcing decisions are motivated by cost savings, skills acquisition, and staffing flexibility. The research in progress introduces a new alternative in sourcing, inter-sourcing. This practice incorporates the benefits of offshoring and outsourcing, while eliminating many of the challenges. University interns perform IT projects for corporations as employees of satellite offices. This paper presents the emergent themes from exploratory interviews with directors of three satellite offices, university staff members, and the director of the associated business incubator. Implications for theory and practice are discussed, along with future directions for this research.

Categories and Subject Descriptors

K.6.1 [**Project and People Management**]:

General Terms

Management.

Keywords

Inter-Sourcing; IT Sourcing; IT Internships; IT Education.

1. INTRODUCTION

There is a high level of interest in sourcing decisions within industry, including projects involving information technology (IT) [13]. The generally accepted fundamental drivers of outsourcing IT work include cost reduction, skills access, and flexibility in staffing [14]. Heikkilä and Cordon summarize the primary drivers as: "Scarcity of capital; lack of know-how; flexibility and the need for quick response or small production; speed or time to market; asset utilization or spare capacity; and, economies of scale" [6]. Outsourcing is defined as a contractual arrangement whereby a company hires an outside vendor to perform specific business activities for a fee. "IS sourcing refers to the entire set of processes ranging from *initiating* and *preparing* the decision to provide an organization's IS function(s) in-house or externally by a legally independent service provider (or some combination of the two options); *making* the *decision*; *implementing* the decision; and *evaluating* and potentially *changing* or *confirming* (i.e. renewing) the decision," [7]. This can involve either full transfer of IT responsibilities or partial (selective) work [11].

Offshoring is a specific type of outsourcing that involves sending work to firms that operate outside of the national borders of the corporate parent office [4]. As reported in previous studies, there are numerous challenges that companies face when they engage in outsourcing arrangements: "Transfer of know-how that encourages new competitors; changes in the balance of power in the industry; dependency, confidentiality and security issues; and, fear of opportunism" [6]. Decision makers are encouraged to maintain direct control and monitoring capabilities over any business processes that impact corporate advantage [15]. The common assumption is that it is acceptable to outsource any processes that are not tied to the firm's core competencies. There is a variety of sourcing approaches to choose from, including selective IT sourcing, as compared to the "all or nothing" approach [11]. Given the current economic climate, companies are eager to experiment with business models that include cost reduction measures, particularly decreasing labor costs.

Strategic use of human resources is not a new concept, but finding a mutually beneficial solution to optimize limited resources, specifically human resources, is an ongoing managerial concern [8]. For example, Kosnik, Wong-MingJi and Hoover [9] describe five models of human resource supply chains. The two in-sourcing models they discuss are local contracting and HR centralizing. The three outsourcing models include purchasing HR, non-staffing HR, and staffing HR. Although these models apply to human resources, rather than IT, the fundamental decision making process can be applied to both disciplines. For instance, the motivation behind the decision is constant across fields.

Sourcing options tend to include the fundamental aspect of forging external relationships [11]. Corporate executives would prefer to have arrangements with vendors that share their goals in a stable partnership. Many outsourcing agreements have failed in the past due to a misalignment of goals between participating entities. A solution that encompasses the advantages of both insourcing and outsourcing is a new alternative we have designated "inter-sourcing". Inter-sourcing is defined as the mutually beneficial contractual arrangement between a company, a university, and student interns for the completion of specified project outcomes. The entities involved in the alliance share common goals, to provide quality solutions for individual IT development projects. The "client" is often a manager within the parent company who presents the team with a problem or opportunity, and mentors the team through analysis, design, development, and implementation.

To our knowledge, this is the first study to investigate the unique relationship defined by the term inter-sourcing. Given the practicality of these alliances, there is unlimited potential for growth and research in this area. The purpose of this preliminary investigation is to discover best practices companies can adopt to create value from inter-sourcing alliances. Specific research questions guiding this investigation are:

RQ1: What are the key factors that influence the success of inter-sourcing relationships?

RQ2: What are the drivers for creating inter-sourcing alliances?

RQ3: What are the expected benefits of inter-sourcing?

The remainder of this paper begins with a brief discussion of the stakeholders of inter-sourcing followed by a literature review on business strategy and sourcing decisions. Then, the methodology for the preliminary study is outlined, along with the results from the interviews. The paper presents a discussion of the key themes that emerged from content analysis of the data collection. The final section contains contributions to theory and implications for practitioners.

2. INTER-SOURCING STAKEHOLDERS

Inter-sourcing is a hybrid approach to IT sourcing that contains the best elements of outsourcing and insourcing, while mitigating the negative effects of both approaches. To employ a somewhat trite saying, it's a "win-win" (or, more accurately, a "win-win-win") solution [3]. As stated, the three stakeholders share common goals, namely:

a. Companies are eager to acquire cutting-edge skills without paying a premium for expensive technology experts. They would like to avoid paying for training costs to keep the skills of their employees current. And, they would ideally choose collaborations that are easy to implement, with minimal supervisory requirements. In some sectors, there is continuing talk of an IT skills shortage. Companies participate in university-sponsored career fairs in order to attract high-quality student interns and, if the intern is a good fit, offer permanent positions to graduates who possess the appropriate skills.

b. Most universities are constantly searching for opportunities to enrich their educational curriculum with real world experiences. Enhancing the curriculum with internships and co-ops provides experiences beyond the traditional classroom and textbook environment. Maintaining close ties with industry also ensures that the curriculum remains current, instilling valuable and useful academic content.

c. Students desire challenging, hands-on experiential learning with tangible personal benefits. They, ultimately, wish to obtain rewarding, full-time employment post-graduation. In that regard, developing identifiable skills that are valued by employers, and expanding their professional networks, would be important outcomes [2]. A significant benefit for students is that they can concurrently attend classes while participating in a valuable internship experience. Many students have said that they would like to take advantage of internships and co-ops, but they cannot justify lengthening their time to graduation, with the added living expenses and fees.

The primary difference between the proposed inter-sourcing and the common internship program is the role of a satellite office, acting as a mediator within the arrangement. Inter-sourcing encourages a project-oriented relationship that allows interns to develop knowledge while exercising problem-solving skills in a hybrid academic/industry environment. Although not required, another important stakeholder is a business incubator (or business accelerator). This agency might provide a geographical location (office space), technical support, Internet connectivity, legal (e.g. patent) advice, financial services, and business professional guidance, as needed [1]. The existence of a business incubator facility can be very attractive, especially for large companies, since the fundamental components and services have already been resolved.

3. BUSINESS STRATEGY AND SOURCING DECISIONS

In the 1990s companies were eager to focus on core competencies, and outsourcing was a realistic approach for handing off tangential tasks to another firm positioned to perform those functions more efficiently [10][12]. This substantial change in business strategy has created opportunities for outsourcing non-core processes, such as IT. Another factor influencing a rise in outsourcing of IT is the fact that many executives doubt the essential value of IT, making it appealing as a candidate for outsourcing [11]. The "age of the megacontracts", common in the 1990's, has come to an end. Companies are reluctant to enter into binding, long-term contracts. There were many risks associated with that practice; vendors failed to keep up with the ever-changing technology, the vendors stopped focusing on the alignment of IT with the company's business processes, and changes in key personnel led to dissolution of shared understandings. Basically, companies continue to evolve, but the outsourcing contracts are often too stringent to adapt.

Lacity, Willcocks and Feeny [11] present four distinct strategies based on purchasing style (transaction or relationship) and purchasing focus (resource or result). Inter-sourcing most appropriately fits the "preferred supplier" strategy since the satellite office maintains a relationship with the parent company and provides IT solutions, but doesn't actually take over ownership of the system. The responsibility for the outcomes remains with the project managers. The work performed by the interns is often of high importance, and this enables the IT departments at the parent companies to take on other projects that would be delayed or ignored.

The attractiveness of selective outsourcing is its flexibility and modular response [11], to benefit from specific aspects of IT and business alignment. Inter-sourcing, likewise, provides the flexibility witnessed using selective outsourcing. The parent company can determine which processes to assign to the satellite office, without fear of disclosure to competitors. This is a significant benefit over traditional outsourcing; the vendor might simultaneously be working for the company's rival, raising the suspicion of shared information across corporate boundaries.

In none of the cases included in this study did the satellite office completely take over the IT function. The student teams completed assignments that were allocated by managers from the parent headquarters. Many of the interns worked for both the director of the satellite office and the project manager from the parent office. This dual reporting arrangement gave students more exposure to corporate mentors and familiarity with supervisors in positions of authority. Some of the projects had the added benefit of exposing the interns to greater visibility throughout the company. For example, a student project team was tasked with providing the networking communications capabilities for the weekly teleconferences between the company headquarters and the satellite office. If the network failed, the student team would have been held accountable for that outcome.

4. METHODOLOGY

A qualitative methodology is most appropriate for this exploratory study, with the intention of extracting relevant information from case studies in the pursuit of greater understanding and theory development [5]. The researchers interviewed representatives from two of the three stakeholder groups (company representatives and university academic staff). A stratified, convenience sampling technique was used to identify interviewees. Each interview lasted more than 45 minutes, and were recorded and transcribed with the consent of the participants. The researcher followed an interview protocol (Appendix) and probed for detail. A rigorous content analysis revealed several key themes. This research project is in an early stage of development, therefore the findings from this investigation will be used to create a research model. The theoretical model will be evaluated with data gathered from additional stakeholders, including student interns. Participating companies were selected based on their convenient location and inter-sourcing ties to the local university. The researcher has worked with the director of the Smart Zone on past projects involving new technology ventures.

The multiple case study approach [16][17] will be used to develop the framework of best practices and to test the theoretical model. The preliminary sample includes both successful and discontinued arrangements. This provides additional insight into the necessity of relationship building as part of an inter-sourcing partnership. The comparative extremes introduced in this study were continuation versus abandonment of the satellite office, and the variation in specific purposes of the partnership arrangement (i.e. work product/outcomes versus feeder employees for the corporation). Not all of the projects were IT-related; some were engineering projects. However, the technical nature of the work involved presented useful interactions that inform the IT sourcing phenomenon.

5. RESULTS
5.1 Case Study Participants

In order to develop a broad understanding of the advantages and disadvantages of inter-sourcing relationships, we interviewed participants with a variety of perspectives. The satellite offices were all affiliated with the SmartZone business accelerator (business incubator), so the director was included in the study. This individual helped to explain the purported benefits of including larger corporations under the organizational umbrella. With the primary goal of creating jobs in the local community, this arrangement clearly contributes to that objective. The three participating firms employed, on average, 20 student interns and one or two permanent hire directors/supervisors for each of the satellite offices. And, they all intend to increase that number over the coming years except the one firm that has closed the satellite office. The industries represented are automobile manufacturing, aviation, and electronic services. The descriptive statistics of interviewees (Table 1) are: mainly males (83%), all had at least a bachelor's degree (100%), and most were 50 years of age or older (67%). Each of the office directors possessed background expertise relevant to the work produced by the interns. None of the directors received formal training in organizational development; they relied on their personal work experiences to develop the satellite offices and the basic structure of the working relationships. Two of the three had worked for the parent company before transitioning to the role of director, so

professional networks had already been established in those instances. All three directors were responsible for hiring student interns. Working out the logistical details with the human resources departments could have gone more smoothly for the third director; the other two parent companies simply followed their traditional procedures for processing student interns. Involvement by corporate executives varied greatly between the three sites. In one case, a team of corporate executives travelled to the location to participate in the "grand opening" kick-off event. The other two were treated as isolated sites, physically distant and distinct from the parent companies. Not surprisingly, one of those was the inter-sourcing relationship that was discontinued.

Table 1. Descriptive statistics of interview sample.

Characteristic	Description (Percentage)
Role	Student Intern (0)
	Director, Satellite Office (50%)
	University Liaison (33%)
	Other (17%)
Age Range	18-24 (0)
	25-34 (17%)
	35-50 (17%)
	51-61 (50%)
	62+ (17%)
Gender	Male (83%)
	Female (17%)
Education Level Completed	High School Diploma (0)
	Some Undergraduate Work (0)
	BA/BS Degree (50%)
	Some Graduate Work (17%)
	Master's Degree (33%)
	Doctoral Degree (0)
Area of Concentration	Mechanical Engineering
	Business
	High Education
	Mathematics
	Computer Science

5.2 Key Concepts and Best Practices

Based on a preliminary literature review and observations of three inter-sourcing satellite operations, a list of key concepts was created. The initial interviews (Appendix) provided insights and quotations to shape the framework for this study. The concepts are not presented in any particular order, and they are not intended to be an exhaustive list. These results will continue to expand as interviews are completed and analyzed. Although the specific details varied by case, the following are generalizations from the data collected.

5.2.1 Start-Up Challenges

According to directors of the satellite offices, some of the initial concerns include physical space requirements, computer equipment, network and communication infrastructure, security (e.g. VPN channel), and corporate system access for student interns. From a contractual perspective, it was essential for the directors to explicitly state their responsibilities and expectations.

The director of the business incubator was keenly interested in the projected growth (i.e. number of jobs created) and services the satellite office would require. Fees and rent were negotiated, and press releases were communicated to the local media. The collaboration between the incubator and the satellite offices created an opportunity for positive publicity. The inclusion of

Fortune 500 companies was a direction for the incubator, a different model for the use of the facilities and services. For instance, the pricing model for rent was revised to recognize their greater financial capacity, compared to startup companies.

It was essential to develop a sense of buy-in from the project managers and corporate executives. Challenging, but achievable, projects were solicited. The director was responsible for persuading the decision makers that the benefits produced by the satellite office would clearly exceed the costs involved. Enthusiasm, clear vision, and a positive attitude were essential for getting the satellite offices off the ground. Although there is risk involved in this type of venture, the potential value to the stakeholders is evident.

Corporate human relations must work out the legal details of payroll and compensation for the interns. However, most of the companies that would engage in inter-sourcing have experience with hiring college interns. This procedure doesn't have to be any different from that standpoint.

5.2.2 Data Security
The interns potentially have access to sensitive corporate data. In addition to signing non-disclosure agreements, they are trained to understand the huge ethical responsibility of their positions. One answer for protecting electronic communication is to encrypt the data and establish Virtual Private Networks (VPNs). The interns were able to access the corporate network as if they were at the parent business location. Physical security was also a concern, and locks were used to control access to work spaces. The level of security varied with the probability and potential loss associated with the data involved. For example, some of the satellite offices use motion detectors and other intrusion detection devices to monitor the physical work space.

5.2.3 Ongoing Challenges
To maintain momentum and establish a solid reputation, there needs to be a corporate champion who is passionate about making the project successful. Open and continuous communication is vital. And, dedicated students must be willing to juggle the demands of schoolwork and an internship. They are held accountable for the outcomes, and poor performance reflects badly on the satellite office. It could even jeopardize the continuation of the inter-sourcing arrangement. Not everyone in the parent company will support the implementation, so exceeding expectations is the objective.

5.2.4 Vulnerabilities
It's always possible that the parent company could pull the plug on the inter-sourcing satellite office without explanation or prior warning. That raises the question: Should there be long-term contracts? If the satellite office is closed, student interns will be harmed the most. They were counting on that employment and potential career trajectory. What obligation does the company have to the interns, if any? This did occur at one of the case study sites during the research project. Without prior warning or explanation, the satellite office was closed at the end of the calendar year, and the director was called back to the parent company. The university representatives were shocked by the closure, and several people tried to get the executives to reverse their decision. It is still unclear why the inter-sourcing arrangement was discontinued, but directors must be aware of the possibility.

5.2.5 Measurements of Success
An important part of sustaining the agreement will rely on a proven track record of success. Directors and the project managers should create practical metrics to objectively document achievement. Although not a guarantee, being able to produce testimonials from satisfied project managers could help to protect the future of the office. Another consideration is the timeline for projects. With predictably high turnover of student interns, will projects be held to the same work schedule? In particular, some directors expect interns to work longer hours in the summer months. Is that a reasonable expectation? Is there a target ROI that must be reached, and is it identical to the divisions at the parent company? These details need to be worked out as the inter-sourcing contract is developed.

5.2.6 Progression and Outcomes
Companies are facing difficulties in hiring employees with the desired technical skills and expertise. One of the case study participants has established the satellite office as a means of recruiting students upon graduation. Regarding the long-term relationship with student workers, will the interns be "fast-tracked" to permanent positions with the parent company? They have already been socialized into the corporate culture and learned many of the standard operating procedures. One might assume that this intensive training would often translate into a job offer. The directors interviewed agreed that the internship gave these students specific projects to discuss at the interview, and these applicants were able to "talk the talk", using the company shared language and jargon.

5.2.7 Miscellaneous Issues
Other questions the research will address are: What industries, projects, and tasks are ideal for this type of sourcing arrangement? What personality traits and leadership styles are optimal for directors of this type of office? How often should the office staff/director communicate results to the corporate office? Other topics will emerge from the data during analysis, so this list is only a framework based on the present understanding of the subject.

6. CONCLUSION
This paper introduced the concept of inter-sourcing IT projects, an innovative sourcing strategy that mitigates some of the commonly identified disadvantages of traditional offshoring. Inter-sourcing creates synergistic alliances between companies, universities, and college students in an internship format based upon contractual agreements. The director of a satellite office acts as the liaison, attracting challenging projects and allocating tasks to student interns based on demonstrated skills and abilities. Project managers from the parent companies remain actively involved in the assignments, providing ongoing feedback on project requirements, procedures followed, and quality of implementations. The continuity of the relationship is maintained, even though turnover of student interns is cyclical. Peer learning is a fundamental aspect of IT project development since students must continuously share their knowledge in order to keep projects on target. Ownership of projects is a natural result of the time and effort expended, and the interns develop deep knowledge of their processes.

Additional outcomes of the experience were discussed by the directors. For instance, interns developed many business professional skills that went beyond the IT projects they were involved in. These interns performed better in formal interviews when the time came, exhibiting confidence and communication skills that exceeded typical interactions of their peer group. They also developed a strong grasp of the jargon and understood the culture of the company, enabling them to converse on relevant topics with corporate representatives. The internship experience forced them out of their comfort zones; they practiced public speaking, writing summaries for a variety of audiences, and asking for assistance when they had questions. The direct benefit to the parent company is the continuous flow of "cutting edge" technical skills provided by interns.

This paper described the key issues and challenges to be considered in developing this type of arrangement. To date, the research team has completed six interviews of directors of satellite offices, the incubator CEO, and university contacts in who oversee the internship program. The next step is to interview student interns who are, or have been, affiliated with these case study offices and project managers who participated in sending work assignments to these offices. The interviews will be content analyzed for emerging themes and comparisons across case studies. These representatives contribute unique perspectives on how to improve on the relationships and define best practices. A minimum of 30 interviews are planned for the data collection phase of the project. Roughly equal representation from the various satellite offices will be targeted, with a balance of roles included. The anecdotes and quotations will add richness to the findings presented in the final report.

Although a discontinued site was included in the case study, it is not possible to determine the specific reasons for the closure. These factors were not communicated to any of the study participants, leaving many questions unanswered. Some of the interviews include speculation and personal theories developed by the individuals impacted by the decision. However, the implication is that directors need to secure strong support at the parent company, and maintain relationships with those key decision makers. Communicating the accomplishments of the satellite office is one way to attempt to ensure continuation of the inter-sourcing partnership. Corporate politics can have a profound impact on the creation and continuation of sourcing arrangements, despite the measurable value created. One aspect that makes inter-sourcing appealing is the low switching costs required to implement the relationship. However, as was apparent in this case study, that feature also makes it very easy for management to reverse course.

This study contributes to the theoretical research of IT sourcing decisions. Inter-sourcing is a new alternative, establishing a hybrid solution that incorporates substantial cost savings (i.e. reduced labor expense) and corporate recruiting (i.e. skills development and acquisition). The next step is to create a theoretical model based on the emergent themes discussed in this paper. Testing the model will lead to increased understanding of this alternative approach. By including all of the stakeholders involved in these inter-sourcing contracts, the implications will encompass multiple relevant perspectives. Practitioners will benefit from the best practices, adding another sourcing option to the management decision space.

A future research study might include community representatives, such as from the local Chamber of Commerce or the City Manager, to add a broader view of the benefits to the community – that is, keeping money in the local economy, retaining industry

that would not have occurred otherwise, and creating stronger bonds between the university and businesspeople. Tracking student interns following graduation would also provide a view of the longitudinal benefits of these experiences. Additionally, interns could be instructed to maintain personal blogs of their experiences. Tracking their activities and observations would provide rich information for review. Several of the student participants were offered permanent positions with their parent companies, and some of them were able to advance more rapidly in the first years of employment. Documenting those findings provides objective evidence for the value of creating inter-sourcing relationships.

7. ACKNOWLEDGMENTS

Personal thanks to the reviewers who provided excellent feedback on an earlier version of this paper.

8. REFERENCES

[1] Buche, M.W. and Scillitoe, J.L. 2007. Influence of Gender and Social Networks on Organizational Learning within Technology Incubators. *Mid-American Journal of Business*, 22, 1, 59-67.

[2] Carpenter, D.A. 2003. Meaningful Information Systems Internships. *Journal of Information Systems Education*, 14, 2, 201-207.

[3] Covey, S.R. 2004. *The 7 Habits of Highly Effective People*. Free Press, New York, NY.

[4] Dibbern, J., Winkler, J., and Heinzl, A. 2008. Explaining Variations in Client Extra Costs between Software Products Offshored to India. *MIS Quart.*, 32, 2, 333-366.

[5] Eisenhardt, K.M. 1989. Building Theories from Case Study Research. *Acad. Manage. Rev.*, 14, 4, 532-550.

[6] Heikkilä, J. and Cordon, C. 2002. Outsourcing: a core or non-core strategic management decision? *Strategic Change*, 11, 183-193.

[7] Hirschheim, R., Dibbern, J., and Heinzl, A. 2008. Foreword to the special issue on IS sourcing. *Inform. Syst. Front.*, 10, 125-127.

[8] Klaas, B.S., McClendon, J., and Gainey, T.W. 1999. HR Outsourcing and its Impact: The Role of Transaction Costs. *Pers. Psychol.*, 52, 1, 113-136.

[9] Kosnik, T., Wong-MingJi, D.J., and Hoover, K. 2006. Outsourcing vs. insourcing in the human resource supply chain: a comparison of five generic models. *Pers. Rev.*, 35, 6, 671-683.

[10] Lacity, M.C., Hirschheim, R., and Willcocks, L.P. 1994. Realizing Outsourcing Expectations: Incredible Expectations, Credible Outcomes. *Journal of Information Systems Management*, 11, 7-18.

[11] Lacity, M.C., Willcocks, L.P., and Feeny, D.F. 1996. The Value of Selective IT Sourcing. *Sloan Manage. Rev.*, 37, 13-25.

[12] Prahalad, C.K., and Hamel, G. 1990. The Core Competence of the Corporation. *Harvard Bus. Rev.*, 63, 79-91.

[13] Schniederjans, M.J. and Zuckweiler, K.M. 2004. A quantitative approach to the outsourcing-insourcing decision in an international context. *Manage. Decis.*, 42, 7/8, 974-986.

[14] Scott, S. 2011. The 5 Benefits of Outsourcing Your Online Business. DOI: http://www.stevescottsite.com/the-5-benefits-of-outsourcing-your-online-business.

[15] Willcocks, L.P. and Feeny, D. 2006. IT Outsourcing and Core Capabilities: Challenges and Lessons at Dupont. *Inform. Syst. Manage.*, 23, 1, 49-56.

[16] Yin, R.K. 1993. *Applications of Case Study Research.* Sage, Newberry Park, CA.

[17] Yin, R.K. 1994. Case Study Research: Design and Methods, Second Edition. Sage, Thousand Oaks, CA.

APPENDIX
Interview Questions

These questions pertain to the sourcing arrangement made between the company, the university, and the student interns. Questions will be tailored minimally based on the role of the person being interviewed (e.g. student intern).

1)   What challenges, if any, were there upon entering into the arrangement?

2)   How much emphasis was placed on (data) security concerns?

3)   How much and what methods of training and socialization were used?

4)   How much individual attention was given to the student interns?

5)   How successful do you think the program was at providing an educational benefit for the student interns?

6)   What metrics were used to document successful achievement?

7)   By those standards, how successful was the arrangement on average?

8)   How much communication was present between the local office and headquarters? With the university?

9)   Could you describe the typical timeline of the process for a student intern, including the type of work the intern was tasked with?

10)   How often was a permanent position offered to the interns? How often was it accepted?

11)   How did you feel about the arrangement overall and why?

12) Any other comments?

How Visible is Scholarly Research on IT Personnel? A Funny Thing Happened on the Way to Publishing in JAIS

Monica Adya	Mike Gallivan	Gaetan Mourmant	Fred Niederman
Marquette University	Robinson Coll. of Business	Visiting Prof., IESEG	St. Louis University
Department of Management	George State University	President, XLerateur Inc.	Operations and ITM
College of Business	Atlanta, GA, USA	Vancouver, Canada	Cook School of Business
(414) 288-7526	(404) 413-7363	(604) 781-9698	(314) 315-0941
monica.adya@mu.edu	mgallivan@gsu.edu	gmourmant@gmail.com	niederfa@slu.edu

ABSTRACT

This panel will discuss the visibility of IS research beyond the immediate community of SIG MIS scholars and propose actions that IS academics and educators can take to raise its visibility.

Categories and Subject Descriptors

H.0 Management of IS, IS discipline

Keywords

IS personnel research, citations, inter-disciplinary research, knowledge dissemination, research visibility

1. INTRODUCTION

IS personnel research addresses at least three distinct constituent groups: IS colleagues (those who conduct or do not conduct IS personnel research); IT practitioners, and scholars in other academic fields such as management, accounting information systems, entrepreneurship and computer science. Recent research (Gallivan [2]) suggests that the visibility of IS personnel research lags behind that of other IS topics, in the view of non-IS scholars.

Triggering this discussion are findings pertaining to the degree to which IS papers appearing in the IS "Basket of Six" journals recognized as exemplary by the AIS Senior Scholars. These findings show that papers on IS personnel were rarely cited in other academic disciplines; in fact this topic category of IT personnel research was associated with the lowest citation rates among outside scholars among the 13 general IS research topics identified in a key review paper by Sidrova, et al [3].

The overall goal of this panel is to discuss the degree to which lower citation rates than other IS sub-fields is problematic; what some of the causes for such a finding might be; and what some responses might be taken to increase the number of citations outside the IS field pertaining to IS personnel research.

2. FACTORS LIMITING DISSEMINATION

Factors identified as limiting to the disbursement of our research ranged from institutional to personal factors. We present these below as outcomes from our collective brainstorming efforts.

2.1 Insular Focus on IS Journals

One can argue that we are responsible for the limited dissemination of our research by only focusing on IS journals. Some contributing factors might be:

Promotion and tenure requirements - Do our promotion and tenure processes discourage faculty from submitting research to other related reference disciplines? Perhaps there is less incentive to publish in HR journals for IS personnel researchers than for other IS scholars to publish in strategy, economics, and other areas. Perhaps there are fewer "crossover" journals that publish both IS and related field material in HR than in other areas such as communications and organizational strategy.

Scope of reference disciplines that we choose – Do we focus overly much on organizational behavior and HR as possible publication outlets rather than exploring a broader swath of outside fields? Are there other disciplines such as engineering management and human factors that would present a welcome home for our research?

2.2 Relevance to Other Disciplines

Are all IT Personnel Phenomena Unique to IS? Much of the writing in IS personnel pertains to workers who specialize in computing within organizations. Perhaps there is a market for considering these employees as examples of general phenomenon where the sample happens to come from IS. For example, gender research may pertain to specific IS jobs and environments, but may also exemplify broader phenomena across related areas.

Are We Prescriptive? Extending the above example on gender, what can we tell other disciplines about how we have analyzed and addressed these practical problems? Certain areas, such as the career choices made by men and women, we have conducted many intervention studies to be able to offer solutions.

How Welcoming are We to Reference Disciplines? If we expect reference journals to open doors for us, we must reciprocate. How often do our calls for papers go to reference journals? How often do we scout and encourage IT personnel research from non-IS colleagues?

3. POTENTIAL SOLUTONS

3.1 Long-Term Solutions

Find Common Problems: Shared problems are often the foundation for knowledge generation. For instance, if other business disciplines share the same concerns with lower representation of women in their majors, we have an opportunity to enrich our own research by engaging in cross-disciplinary collaboration that understands the phenomena in a more holistic manner.

SIGMIS-CPR'13, May 30–June 1, 2013, Cincinnati, Ohio, USA.
ACM 978-1-4503-1975-1/13/05.

Bridge with Reference Journals: Could we identify a set of non-IS journals where our community can build a case for publishing IT personnel research – our equivalent of a "Basket of Six" non-IS journals? Could these reference journals be engaged to publish at least one impactful IT personnel-focused paper a year, subject to their editorial rigor? What can we offer as reciprocity from IS?

Evolve Institutional Culture: Like-minded faculty can demonstrate success in successful collaborative outcomes through publishing in cross-disciplinary research. Given time, there may be change that one can hope for.

Success Stories. We may need to develop methodologies to specifically expand and generalize our IT personnel findings to other disciplines. Maybe some cases that demonstrate successful expansion to other disciplines would be helpful in encouraging other IS researchers to do the same. One of us is currently in the process of publishing such an instance of successful expansion.

Power Structures. Clearly, power structures must be considered, if we want to reach these goals. This is a not something that all scholars are aware of – or even skilled at doing, but often, this is necessary to effect change. For instance, it may be critical for us to attend non-IS conference (Academy of Management or ones dealing with Accounting IS) in order to raise awareness of our field, as well as the quality of our research and leading journals.

3.2 Short-Term Solutions

Branding and Dissemination: For areas where the community has developed a great deal of knowledge, we can improve our branding and dissemination Specific areas to upgrade include:

1. *Online Repository of IT Personnel Research*: With concerted effort, an online repository of research needs to be created where researchers, practitioners, and doctoral students at minimum could turn to.

2. *Electronic Newsletter*: In addition to the online resource, a quarterly electronic newsletter could summarize key IT personnel research produced in recent months and inform opportunities for collaborative research.

3. *Books? Textbooks?* The CIO panel at SIGMIS 2012 in Milwaukee revealed interesting and specific IT HR issues. Addressing those through a book could be a fruitful way to increase our visibility

Institutional-level Research Promotion: Through some recent experiences at our own institutions, we propose the following:

1. *E-Publications*: At one of our universities, our library is using e-publications to promote our research via the university website. They obtain authorization from various journals to post our full articles online. This has resulted in a significant increase in paper downloads.

2. *Newsletters and Website Promotion*: Each quarter, one of our institutions features a recently published article by faculty on the college website and also in an electronic newsletter. This increases the visibility of our research.

3. *Changing P&T Policies*: One of our institutions created a cross-disciplinary list of accepted journal rankings counting faculty publication in any area journal as equivalent.

4. PANEL MEMBER BIOGRAPHIES

Monica Adya is Associate Professor of Management, Marquette University. She received her PhD in Management Information Systems from Case Western Reserve University. Monica works in the area of IT and people, offshoring practices, and decision/knowledge systems. She was the conference co-chair for SIGMIS CPR 2012 and serves on editorial boards of several journals.

Mike Gallivan is Associate Professor of CIS at Georgia State University in Atlanta. He received his PhD from MIT Sloan School of Management, as well as MBA and MPH degrees from University of California, Berkeley. He has published on a range of behavioral and organizational IS research topics. He served as SIGMIS Conference Chair in 2005 and 2010, ICIS Track Chair in 2005 and 2011 and on editorial boards of leading IS journals.

Gaetan Mourmant is Visiting Professor at IESEG, France, and President of XLerateur Inc. in Vancouver, Canada. He received his PhD degree in Information Systems from the joint PhD program between Paris Dauphine University and Georgia State University. He has experience as a Marketing Database Analyst for a global financial institution. His research interests are IT entrepreneurship, computer-mediated communication, crowdsourcing, and grounded theory.

Fred Niederman is the Shaughnessy Endowed Professor of MIS at Saint Louis University. He holds the PhD and MBA degrees from University of Minnesota, plus a BA degree in English literature from University of California, Santa Barbara. His research interests include global IS management, IS personnel, and using IT to support teams and groups. Recently he has been studying IT integration issues following corporate mergers and acquisitions.

5. REFERENCES

[1] Beath, C.; Berente, N.; Gallivan, M.; and Lyytinen, K. "Special Issue: Expanding the Frontiers of IS Research," forthcoming, *Journal of the Association for Information Systems*, April 2013.

[2] Gallivan, M. "When is IS Research a Reference Discipline? An Analysis of Citations to IS Research in Other Fields," working paper, Georgia State University, Atlanta, GA, 2013.

[3] Sidorova, A., Evangelopoulos, N., Valacich, J. and Ramakrishnan, T. "Uncovering the Intellectual Core of the Information Systems Discipline," *MIS Quarterly*, 32, 2008, 467-482.

Success is More Than a Resumé: The Role of Social and Psychological Capital in Compensation for Offshore BPO Professionals

Violet Ho
University of Richmond
Robins School of Business
1 Gateway Road
Richmond, VA 23173
vho@richmond.edu

Jonathan Whitaker
University of Richmond
Robins School of Business
1 Gateway Road
Richmond, VA 23173
jwhitaker@richmond.edu

Sunil Mithas
University of Maryland
Robert H. Smith School of Business
4357 Van Munching Hall
College Park, MD 20742
smithas@rhsmith.umd.edu

Prasanto K. Roy
Cybermedia
Cyber House
B35 Sector 32
Gurgaon 122001, India
pkr@cybermedia.co.in

ABSTRACT

Multi-national corporations (MNCs) are increasingly using offshore business process outsourcing (BPO) to manage their primary and support functions and achieve their strategic objectives. Though India is regarded as the "undisputed leader in offshore services," the Indian BPO industry is plagued by high employee turnover and labor shortages. Indian BPO firms will need effective employee selection and retention strategies to sustain their growth. While compensation is an important mechanism to attract and retain employees, and competencies such as "practical intelligence" are important to the performance of technical professionals, research has not yet examined how offshore BPO firms price these competencies and determine compensation for their professionals. This paper addresses the research gap by developing theory on the role of social and psychological capital in employee compensation, and tests the theory using data from 3,900 Indian BPO professionals over the 2006–2008 time period.

Categories and Subject Descriptors

H.0 **[Information Systems]**: General

General Terms

Economics, Management, Theory

Keywords

BPO, compensation, information systems, offshore, outsourcing, professionals, psychological capital, social capital.

1. INTRODUCTION

Multi-national corporations (MNCs) are under growing pressure to simultaneously increase quality, reduce costs and decrease cycle time. In one effort to respond to this pressure, MNCs are reevaluating and reconfiguring their vendor and geographic platforms [1; 2]. In particular, MNCs are increasingly using offshore business process outsourcing (BPO) to manage their primary and support functions and achieve their strategic objectives [3; 4; 5].

India is regarded as the "undisputed leader in offshore services" [6], accounting for 50% of the offshore BPO market [7; 8]. Employment at global services firms in India grew at a double-digit rate from the mid-1990s to the mid-2000s [9], India service exports averaged 35% growth from 2000-2005 [10], and the India offshore service industry tripled from $4 billion in 2000 to almost $13 billion in 2004 [8]. However, because the Indian BPO industry is plagued by high employee turnover and labor shortages [11], Indian BPO firms will need effective employee selection and retention strategies to sustain their growth.

While employee compensation is an important mechanism to attract and retain workers [12], and competencies such as "practical intelligence" are important to the performance of technical employees [13], research has not yet examined how offshore BPO firms price these types of competencies and determine compensation for employees. This paper addresses the research gap by developing theory on the role of social and psychological capital in employee compensation, and testing the theory using data from 3,900 Indian BPO professionals over the 2006–2008 time period.

This paper makes two contributions. First, this is one of the first studies to examine compensation practices in Indian BPO firms, which constitute a major player in a growing industry [14]. While compensation practices and determinants have been the subject of some research in the IS literature [15; 16], the BPO industry is sufficiently different that a focused examination of these issues among BPO professionals is warranted. For example, the BPO industry is less than ten years old and remains relatively new compared to the more mature IT industry [11; 17]. As such, compensation strategies in BPO firms may not parallel those in IT organizations. Further, the nature of work carried out by BPO professionals is considerably different from that done by professionals in IT and other conventional industries. For instance, while IT jobs have been described as encompassing "complex, technical assignments that require originality, independent judgment, and analytical skills" [15, p. 1428], BPO jobs such as those carried out in call centers can be highly regimented and standardized, with coercive and normative controls to deter employees from deviating from prescribed work procedures and exercising independent judgment [18].

More broadly, the unique nature of work in BPO firms makes the examination of social and psychological capital even more critical in predicting BPO employees' compensation. BPO jobs are often characterized as extremely taxing and stressful, with BPO professionals working in environments that expose them to elevated levels of stress and abuse that exceed those of experienced in typical professional jobs [11; 18]. There are multiple sources of stress for BPO professionals, including atypical work schedules requiring long and irregular hours (such as overnight shifts) to cater to an international clientele in different time zones. Such stress is exacerbated by limited vacation time (typically one week per year), specific log-in times, and even timed bathroom breaks [19].

A second stressor is the demanding performance metrics imposed on BPO professionals. For example, BPO workers in call centers can respond to as many as 100 telephone calls in one shift, and are required to abide by prescribed scripts in each call [20]. In order to achieve cost efficiencies and customer service quality, BPO professionals are given strict deadlines and targets, and are subject to multiple quality control mechanisms including constant monitoring and remote call listening-in by supervisors [19].

Third, the nature of BPO work, which often involves interacting with and displaying positive emotions to clients, puts additional pressures on BPO professionals, as demonstrated by research showing that emotional labor demands contribute to emotional exhaustion and decreased psychological well-being [21; 22; 23]. The cross-cultural nature of interactions with clients also places additional stress on BPO professionals, arising from the requirement to speak in a different accent and even adopt a different name and persona when interacting with foreign clients, resulting in a loss of personal identity and exposing them to racial abuse from clients [11; 18]. These demanding job requirements have resulted in BPO firms being labeled as "new-age sweatshops" and BPO professionals as "cyber coolies" [19], setting BPO professionals apart from other professional jobs.

We contend that coping with these challenges requires a different set of skills than technical competencies and human capital, which do not necessarily prepare workers to deal with these work conditions. Specifically, we argue that in the BPO industry, social and psychological capital would play a particularly critical role, over and above that of human capital, to help BPO workers cope with the industry's unique job challenges and, consequently, enjoy greater compensation rewards.

India offers an excellent opportunity to test predictions based on our extension of human, social and psychological capital to the context of BPO services. India has made substantial investments in national education to support science and engineering human

capital [7], and enabled the creation of university-affiliated software-engineering schools to further increase the number of technical graduates [24]. As a result of these human capital investments, India ranked 5th in the 2011 IMD World Competitiveness Yearbook in skilled and experienced ICT workforce, with the 2nd highest number of engineering graduates [25]. It is increasingly recognized that beyond human capital, firms can also harness social and psychological capital to achieve competitive advantage [26]. Supportive relationships and psychological resources are necessary for human resources to achieve sustainable growth and performance [27].

Thus, to the extent that social and psychological resources enable employees to overcome work challenges and perform their jobs well, it is likely that having them will translate into higher compensation. This paper goes beyond examining human capital as a predictor of compensation for BPO professionals, to include the roles of social and psychological capital. Specifically, we investigate social capital in the form of social support from supervisors and co-workers, and psychological capital in the form of psychological energy and excitement toward one's work. We introduce new determinants of compensation to the BPO literature, and also inform BPO professionals' decisions on the types of resources they can invest in to augment their compensation.

2. DETERMINANTS OF COMPENSATION
2.1 Human Capital
Human capital has conventionally included a professional's education and length of work experience, and human capital theory contends that professionals with higher education and more work experience will be better compensated [28]. With higher education, professionals acquire more knowledge, skills, and competencies which they bring to their jobs. To the extent that these capabilities translate into higher productivity and work performance, organizations will offer higher compensation in return. In particular, in the context of Indian BPO firms, the key source of competitive advantage is young employees who are graduates and computer literate [11; 18]. To attract employees who have made the human capital investments to meet these criteria, labor economics dictate that firms will provide higher compensation to these employees than to employees who do not meet these criteria and consequently make lesser contributions to the firm's strategy.

Signaling theory provides another explanation for the positive link between education and compensation [29; 30; 31]. Information asymmetry exists in the labor market, in that while potential employees are aware of their own skills and abilities, the hiring organization does not have access to such intangible attributes. As such, an educational credential serves as a signal to the firm about the potential employees' abilities and "credentiates them as more productive" [32, p. 175], independent of whether they are actually more productive. Thus, those who are better able at signaling their value to the firm will be better paid by the firm. Consistent with this argument, research demonstrates that holding constant the number of years of education, professionals with a degree earn more than those without a degree [32].

Work experience is another element of human capital for which BPO firms will offer higher compensation. The Indian BPO industry has been experiencing recent labor shortages in trained professionals, and this trend is forecasted to continue in the near future [11; 33]. As a result, BPO firms do not have the time or resources to invest in training new employees, and instead prefer professionals with some previous BPO experience [18]. Professionals with such experience are expected to spend less time learning the job and are able to more quickly contribute to the firm's strategy, commanding a higher salary premium.

The theory of firm-specific human capital also predicts that professionals with longer tenure at a specific BPO firm will receive higher compensation from that firm. Professionals with more experience at a firm tend to develop firm-specific skills and knowledge over time, and these skills enhance the professional's productivity and contribution, for which the firm is willing to pay a premium. For example, over time BPO professionals may become more familiar with the firm's work procedures, such as standardized scripts, and develop greater efficiency in carrying out their work. Thus, BPO firms are inclined to offer higher wages to retain these professionals, particularly with the high turnover and shortage of trained professionals in the industry.

2.2 Social Capital

While the link between compensation and human capital has been the subject of research in the economics and management literatures, the role of other types of individual resources as determinants of employee compensation has not been considered. Beyond cognitive abilities and knowledge, professionals can possess other strengths and resources that enhance their contribution to the firm and command a higher salary. For example, theories of intelligence have acknowledged that in addition to the traditional concept of cognitive intelligence (IQ), other forms of intelligence exist such as social and emotional intelligence [34; 35; 36; 37]. Research in applied psychology and organizational behavior has demonstrated that individuals with social and psychological resources enjoy a performance advantage [38; 39], which we argue will translate into higher compensation.

In this study, we focus on social support from supervisors and co-workers as a form of social capital. Employees with supervisors and/or co-workers who value their contributions and care about their well-being [40; 41] can tap these relationships to help enhance their productivity and in turn their compensation. The performance benefits of workplace social capital have been documented in several studies [38; 42; 43], and two arguments have been advanced to explain the positive link between social capital and work performance.

The first argument hinges on the role of social capital to help professionals cope with work stress and job demands [44; 45; 46], such that professionals with more social capital are better able to garner these resources to help deal with stressful job demands and report higher performance outcomes. Specifically, social support has been found to be especially valuable where one experiences high stress (and less valuable at low levels of stress), suggesting that social capital would be critical for BPO professionals given the high stress characteristic of their jobs. Further, many BPO workers move away from their families to live by themselves after entering the BPO profession [20], and combined with the lack of interactions with friends due to atypical work hours, this loss of familial and friendship-based support underscores the need for workplace support to help cope with stressful job demands and realize compensation rewards.

A second argument linking social capital to job performance draws from social exchange theory and the norm of reciprocity, which dictates that in an exchange relationship such as employment, receiving some form of benefit obligates the recipient to reciprocate in some way [47; 48]. This argument is most commonly advanced to explain the role of supervisor social capital in predicting work performance, and contends that professionals who have supportive supervisors will reciprocate the support by putting in extra effort to achieve the firm's strategy, because supervisors act as agents for the firm [49]. Extending from these two arguments, we expect that productivity benefits from having social capital in the workplace will translate into higher compensation, and this study offers the first empirical look at the previously untested link between social capital and employee compensation.

> *H1: Compensation for BPO professionals is positively related to supervisor social capital.*

> *H2: Compensation for BPO professionals is positively related to co-worker social capital.*

2.3 Psychological Capital

A third type of individual resource is psychological capital, which encapsulates an employee's positive psychological capacities that can be harnessed for performance improvement. Recent work in positive psychology and positive organizational behavior have confirmed the notion that individuals vary in their character strengths [50] and positive psychological states [51], and employees who can harness their psychological capital to overcome negative aspects of their work report greater job satisfaction and better work performance [39]. In particular, a recent study conducted in an Indian BPO firm confirmed that BPO workers who had higher levels of hope (a form of positive psychological capacity) performed better at their jobs, establishing the relevance of psychological capital to the BPO context [52]. In this paper, we examine another type of work-based psychological resource, in the form of employee psychological energy and excitement for their jobs, and contend that professionals with higher levels of energy will enjoy greater performance benefits and command a higher salary premium.

Human energy can be conceptualized as a resource that helps individuals regulate their behaviors and emotions in compliance with organizational or group norms and expectations [53; 54]. Such energy has been defined as an affective experience that encompasses a sense of positive arousal and vitality, and individuals with high levels of such resource feel energized and enthusiastic [55; 56]. While this energy is important for high performance [57], it is also a limited resource that gets depleted at work. This is especially so in jobs when employees engage in deliberate behaviors and acts of volition requiring self-control and regulation [58], elements that are highly characteristic of the emotional labor commonly performed by BPO professionals [23]. Additionally, other job characteristics that closely parallel those in the BPO industry have been shown to contribute to the depletion of such energy, including long work hours, lack of benefits and perks such as vacation days, standardized work routines, and a high degree of interpersonal interaction [53; 58]. As such, we argue that psychological energy is a particularly critical resource to help BPO professionals deal with the taxing nature of their jobs and, in turn, translate into higher work productivity and compensation.

Our rationale for expecting professionals who approach their work with higher levels of psychological energy and excitement to receive higher compensation is premised on the ego depletion hypothesis in social psychology [58; 59]. Research experiments have consistently shown that individuals who engaged in effortful, deliberate acts such as clerical tasks subsequently perform worse on tasks requiring self-control and self-regulation [60]. When the nature of the task is tedious, involves multiple rules, and requires a high degree of self-control (typical of BPO jobs that take on the form of emotional labor and are performed in a highly-scripted manner), individuals' psychological energy and ego become depleted, and their performance and persistence in subsequent tasks are compromised [58; 61]. Thus, we expect that individuals who are endowed with higher levels of this psychological resource should be better able to sustain their performance despite working under such conditions, enjoying higher financial compensation as a result.

While the performance implications of psychological energy depletion have been replicated in multiple experiments, no study has yet extended this concept to the field setting with professionals performing their regular job functions. Further, while existing research on psychological energy has focused primarily on how to build or restore this psychological capital, the financial benefits of possessing psychological capital have yet to be established. This is the first study to examine the role of psychological energy in an organizational setting, and we argue that professionals who possess such a resource will not only be less prone to suffer performance deficits from ego depletion, but also display greater persistence when doing their jobs, enjoying higher compensation.

H3: Compensation for BPO professionals is positively related to psychological capital.

3. DATA AND METHODOLOGY

Our data on BPO professionals in India comes from three national surveys conducted by a leading Indian market research firm from 2006-2008. The research firm conducted the surveys in two phases each year. Using 2006 as an example, in the first phase the research firm sent out a detailed HR questionnaire to 120 BPO companies in India. These companies included the BPO subsidiaries of Indian firms such as TCS and Wipro, and multi-national firms with a presence in India such as IBM Daksh. The research firm then selected the top 19 firms based on firm size and growth for a second phase employee survey. The research firm worked to obtain an unbiased sample by taking steps to ensure that management did not influence the selection of respondents or their responses, and by promising confidentiality to respondents. Continuing with 2006 as an example, 1,367 BPO professionals from 19 firms provide complete responses for the variables of interest in this study.

The research firm followed a similar strategy in 2006 and 2008. The surveys for 2006-2008 included a total of 3,923 Indian BPO professionals with complete responses for the variables of interest in this study. We believe the respondent profile in these surveys is a reasonable representation of BPO professionals in India. Because of the large number of participating firms and the large number of employees at those firms, along with the study design that randomly picks employees from participating firms, we expect a negligible amount of overlap in respondents across years. The data includes measures related to human capital (education and experience), social capital, psychological capital, and compensation. To measure supervisor social capital, five items were developed to capture the various forms of resources that supervisors provide as part of their supervisory role, including advice, feedback, recognition, and concern [40; 62]. To measure peer social capital, two items that assessed a broader, more global form of peer support were developed, in view of the fact that peer support can take on many more different forms and are often informal and discretionary in nature [63]. To measure psychological capital, four items were developed to capture respondents' level of energy and excitement for various facets of their jobs, including the growth opportunities, the work itself, and how work contributes to the firm.

The dependent variable in our study is as follows:

Compensation. Natural log of bracketed variable for annual gross compensation in Rupees.

Independent variables in our study are as follows:

Supervisor social capital. Extent to which a professional perceives support from their supervisors (five items).

Peer social capital. Extent to which a professional perceives support from their co-workers (five items).

Psychological capital. Extent to which a professional perceives psychological capital.

Firm-specific experience. Months of BPO experience at current firm.

General experience. Months of BPO experience at other firms.

Total experience. Months of total work experience.

MBA. Highest education is Master's degree in Business.

Bachelor's Engineering. Highest education is Bachelor's degree in Engineering.

Control variables in our study are as follows:

Male. Gender (1=male, 0=female).

Married. Marital status (1=married, 0=single).

Age. Bracketed variable for respondent age.

Hours per week. Hours worked per week.

Year. Dummy variables for years 2007 and 2008.

Factor loadings of the items measuring social and psychological capital were all above the 0.4 threshold that is conventionally accepted as meaningful [64]. The fact that the items loaded onto three distinct factors also provides evidence of discriminant validity. Alpha coefficients for the scales measuring supervisor social capital, peer social capital, and psychological capital were 0.945, 0.877, and 0.874 respectively, indicating that the scales are reliable [65].

For our data on BPO professionals in India, the median level of total compensation is 1.75 million Rupees (equivalent to \$US 35,000 at an exchange rate of US\$ 1 = Rs 50). Compensation includes take home pay plus other allowances, and does not include stock options and other non-monetary benefits. Fourteen percent of respondents in our data attained a Bachelor of Engineering degree (four-year degree), 15% attained an MBA degree, and the remaining 71% attained another degree such as a three-year Bachelor of Arts or Bachelor of Business degree. The average length of BPO experience at the current firm is 1.9 years, the average length of BPO experience at previous firms is 0.6 years, and the average length of non-BPO experience is 1.2 years, for a total average work experience length of 3.7 years. The average age of BPO professionals in our data is 28 years old, and 70% of the BPO professionals are male. Compensation is positively correlated with an MBA education (0.15), BPO experience at the current firm (0.28), BPO experience at previous firms (0.26), and total experience (0.50). The consistency of these correlations with prior research on the compensation of IT professionals [66] provides added confidence in our data.

Following previous research in labor economics [67; 68; 69] and IS [66; 70; 71; 72; 73], we specify standard cross-sectional log-linear earnings models suggested by the Mincerian earnings function and subsequent extensions used by Krueger and other researchers. Let W represent annual compensation of the respondent, X_1 a vector of education- and experience-related endowments for the respondent, X_2 a vector of demographic characteristics for the respondent, and Z a vector of observed characteristics for the firm, respectively.

$$ln\ W_i = \alpha\ X_{1i} + \beta\ X_{2i} + \gamma\ Z_i + \delta\ X_{1i}\ Z_i + \varepsilon_i, \qquad (1)$$

where α, β, γ, and δ are parameters to be estimated, and ε is the error term associated with observation i. We estimate Equation 1 by ordinary least squares. The average of variance inflation factors (VIF) in our model is 2.33, with a maximum VIF of 6.36, which suggests that multi-collinearity is not a serious concern in this study.

Our analysis considers the human capital and productive competencies of professionals using multiple variables related to education and experience [16]. Our use of variables for education and experience to represent human capital is consistent with over 75% of papers in a recent meta-analytic review of human capital research [74]. We also respond to the call to go further than most prior research by including fine measures of education and experience to represent a broader range and gradation of skill levels [75]. We test the relationship of compensation with an MBA degree (indicator of managerial skills) and a Bachelor's in Engineering degree (indicator of technical skills). We also test the relationship of compensation with multiple forms of experience-related human capital, including firm-specific BPO experience, general BPO experience, and other work experience. It is important to analyze various forms of experience-related human capital, because some forms of experience represent technical skills that are specific to a particular firm (firm-specific BPO experience), and other forms of experience represent technical skills that may be transferrable to other firms (general BPO experience) [76].

We control for other non-BPO work experience that may not represent technical skills. We control for individual-level demographic variables to account for variables that influence compensation for technical professionals, including age and gender [77]. Consistent with prior research in labor economics, we control for squared terms of firms-specific BPO experience, general BPO experience, and other work experience [67]. We also include a variable for each year to control for general unemployment levels and other labor market demand factors [78].

4. RESULTS AND DISCUSSION

Hypothesis 1 predicted that compensation for offshore BPO professionals is positively related to supervisor social capital. This hypothesis is supported by the results of equation 1 ($\beta = 0.020$, $p<0.000$). The result is consistent with theory that employees with supervisors who value their contributions and care about their well-being can tap these relationships to enhance their productivity [40], and earn higher compensation for their higher level of productivity.

Interestingly, Hypothesis 2, which predicted that compensation for offshore BPO professionals is positively related to co-worker social capital, is not supported ($\beta = -0.031$, $p<0.000$). In fact, the coefficient is negative and statistically significant. We can think of two potential explanations for this contrary finding. One potential explanation is that professionals who have social capital with co-workers may attempt to rely on their co-workers to cover for their own performance deficiencies, and that firms may award lower compensation to professionals with these performance deficiencies. A second potential explanation is that some professionals may enjoy social relationships with co-workers so much that they are distracted from their own work, with lower performance as a result.

Hypothesis 3 predicted that compensation for offshore BPO professionals is positively related to psychological capital. This hypothesis is supported by the results of equation 1 ($\beta = 0.018$, $p<0.000$). The result is consistent with theory that individuals with high levels of such psychological capital feel energized and enthusiastic, and are able to apply this energy to sustain their motivation and performance even in repetitive BPO tasks that may drain professionals with lower levels of psychological capital.

Our results for human capital variables on education and experience provide added confidence in our model. Consistent with recent research [66], we find that all forms of human capital are positively associated with compensation, including work experience at the current firm, work experience at other firms in the BPO industry, total work experience, managerial education in the form of an MBA, and technical education in the form of a Bachelor's in Engineering degree.

The results of control variables also provide useful information about the labor market for BPO professionals in India. Male BPO professionals earn more than female IT professionals, similar to findings for other fields in India [79]. Older IT professionals earn more than younger IT professionals, suggesting that allegations of age discrimination in the U.S. [see 80] may not apply in India. The fact that our main study variables on supervisor social capital and psychological capital are positive and significant even in the presence of human capital variables and control variables reinforces the importance of theory developed in this paper.

We also conducted supplementary analyses to examine the relative effects of the different forms of capital. While our objective was to examine the role of social and psychological capital in shaping BPO professionals' compensation, an ancillary question is how much does each form of capital contribute to explaining the total criterion variance (i.e., R-squared value). To address this question, we conducted a relative weight analysis [81], and results indicate that the entire set of human capital predictors accounted for 60% of total R-squared value, while social capital accounted for 4.5% and psychological capital 2.3%

of the R-squared value. These results further underscore the importance of social and psychological capital, over and above the effect of human capital in predicting BPO professionals' compensation.

4.1 Research and Practical Implications

From a research perspective, this paper makes two contributions. First, we study compensation practices in Indian BPO firms, which constitute a major player in a relatively new and growing industry. The Indian BPO industry faces challenges of high employee turnover and labor shortages [12], and firms in this industry need effective employee selection and retention strategies to sustain their growth. Second, we extend prior IS research that develops theory on the role of human capital in compensation for IT professionals [66], and we develop theory on the role of social and psychological capital in compensation for BPO professionals. We test the theory using data from 3,900 BPO professionals in an emerging economy over the 2006–2008 time period.

From a research perspective, our findings demonstrate that competencies such as "practical intelligence" [13] have important implications for the performance and compensation of technical professionals. Practical intelligence, defined as the managerial, intrapersonal, and interpersonal skills and resources that individuals possess to resolve work problems, are argued to be instrumental in helping workers manage not just others but also themselves, their tasks, and their careers, and the present findings support this contention. Specifically, the social capital examined in the present study constitutes one such "intelligence" or resource that can help BPO professionals manage their tasks, by facilitating them to obtain technical help, advice, and/or social support from workplace colleagues to deal with work challenges, and is ultimately manifested in higher compensation. Similarly, psychological capital is another type of intelligence that can be particularly useful for BPO professionals to manage themselves, and those with higher levels of psychological energy and excitement can ignite this resource to stimulate and sustain work efforts in the face of demanding and stressful job conditions. While it may be more challenging for IS researchers to define and document these "soft" skills, it is important to consider these competencies in future research, alongside more measurable "hard" skills indicated by education and experience, and the present study takes a first step in defining two possible forms of such "soft" skills.

From a managerial perspective, this paper contributes to an improved understanding of how firms price competencies and experience of BPO professionals in emerging economies, because compensation practices play an important role in employee acquisition and retention [82]. Our findings suggest that BPO firms must focus on personal characteristics in addition to professional characteristics as they hire and develop their employees. While BPO firms can evaluate education and work experience from applications for potential employees and internal records for existing employees, firms must use their interview and performance evaluation processes to also evaluate the social and psychological capital of potential and existing employees. Further, once employees are hired and promoted, BPO firms must encourage a positive supervisor culture to maximize employee performance. Professionals who feel supported by their supervisors have better performance than equally-talented professionals who do not have supervisor social capital.

While it is helpful for BPO firms to have a collegial atmosphere, BPO firms must also recognize that a social environment does not equate to improved performance for all employees. Some professionals may try to use their relationships with co-workers to cover for their own performance deficiencies, and some professionals may actually be distracted from their work by their relationships with co-workers.

Finally, this study offers implications for scholars and practitioners seeking to understand the drivers of BPO professionals' compensation in countries other than India. While cross-national differences in political, legal, and HR systems exist and contribute to the uniqueness of compensation drivers in each country, similarities and differences in key cultural values can also determine whether the present findings are generalizable to other countries. For instance, the level of collectivism in India is comparable to that in several other countries in which BPO organizations commonly operate, including Mexico, China, and the Philippines [83]. Consequently, the influence of peer social capital is likely to be somewhat comparable in these countries where social interdependence is similarly emphasized and where individuals are integrated into strong, cohesive groups [84]. Likewise, the similarity between India's and each of these countries' high power-distance orientation suggests that the present findings on the influence of supervisor social capital on India's BPO professionals would also extend to BPO professionals in these three countries [83]. In contrast, countries such as Northern Ireland, which also has a sizable BPO industry but is comparatively less collectivistic, may find a weaker role of peer social capital in influencing BPO employees' compensation.

4.2 Limitations and Future Research

There are two important limitations in this study, both of which can be addressed by future research. One limitation is that this paper tests theory using data from employees in one emerging economy. Firms and employees in India may have unique cultural considerations and business practices compared with other countries [85], and therefore the findings in our study may not be generalizable to firms in other countries. This limitation can be addressed in future research by studying the role of social and psychological capital in compensation across countries, as has been done for other factors in prior research [86].

While our survey data was collected over a three-year period, a second limitation is that data on human capital, social capital, psychological capital, and compensation for each employee was collected at a single point-in-time (during either 2006, 2007 or 2008). In future research, it would be useful to collect longitudinal data on each employee over time, so researchers can study changes in compensation based on changes in human, social and psychological capital.

In a related point, while this paper studies supervisor and co-worker social capital from the perspective of the individual professional, it would also be useful for future research to study the interventions firms can make to increase supervisor and co-worker social capital. For example, what types of management practices can firms implement for supervisors to help professionals feel more supported?

Another area for future research would be to capture other performance evaluation data, in addition to compensation data, to measure employee performance. While this paper uses compensation as a measure of employee performance, it would be useful for researchers and practitioners to know more about the specific mechanisms through which performance improves based on increases in supervisor social capital and psychological capital.

To conclude, this study investigates the effect of social capital and psychological capital on the compensation of BPO professionals in India. We find that BPO professionals in India with supervisor social capital and psychological capital are compensated relatively more highly than employees without these forms of social and psychological capital. Contrary to our expectations, we find that co-worker social capital may not lead to higher compensation, because professionals may try to use their relationships with co-workers to cover for their own performance deficiencies, or their relationships with co-workers may distract them from their own work. Our findings suggest that Indian BPO firms should focus on both professional and personal competencies as they hire and develop their employees. Because the Indian BPO industry is a critical business partner for many MNCs, these findings have important implications for for the broader global economy.

5. ACKNOWLEDGEMENTS

We thank CyberMedia Research, and in particular Anirban Banerjee (Associate Vice President, Research and Advisory Services) and Suman Dutta (Senior Manager, User Research) for their help with the data for this research.

REFERENCES

[1] Mithas, S. and Whitaker, J. 2007. Is the World Flat or Spiky? Information Intensity, Skills and Global Service Disaggregation. *Information Systems Research 18*, 237-259.

[2] Tanriverdi, H., Konana, P. and Ge, L. 2007. The Choice of Sourcing Mechanisms for Business Processes. *Information Systems Research 18*, 280-299.

[3] Lacity, M.C., Willcocks, L.P. and Rottman, J. 2008. Global Outsourcing of Back Office Services: Lessons, Trends, and Enduring Challenges. *Strategic Outsourcing 1*, 13-34.

[4] Mani, D., Barua, A. and Whinston, A.B. 2010. An Empirical Analysis of the Impact of Information Capabilities Design on Business Process Outsourcing Performance. *MIS Quarterly 34*, 39-62.

[5] Whitaker, J., Mithas, S. and Krishnan, M.S. 2011. Organizational learning and capabilities for onshore and offshore business process outsourcing. *Journal of Management Information Systems 27*, 11-42.

[6] Marriott, I. 2010. Gartner's 30 Leading Locations for Offshore Services, 2010-11 Gartner, Stamford, CT, 1-11.

[7] Manning, S., Massini, S. and Lewin, A.Y. 2008. A Dynamic Perspective on Next-Generation Offshoring: The Global Sourcing of Science and Engineering Talent. *Academy of Management Perspectives 22*, 35-54.

[8] NASSCOM-McKinsey 2005. NASSCOM-McKinsey Report 2005: Extending India's Leadership of the Global IT and BPO Industries National Association of Software and Service Companies, New Delhi.

[9] Dossani, R. and Kenney, M. 2006. Reflections upon "Sizing the Emerging Global Labor Market". *Academy of Management Perspectives 20*, 35-41.

[10] Dossani, R. and Kenney, M. 2007. The Next Wave of Globalization: Relocating Service Provision to India. *World Development 35*, 772-791.

[11] Kuruvilla, S. and Ranganathan, A. 2010. Globalisation and Outsoucing: Confronting New Human Resources Channges

in India's Business Process Outsourcing Industry. *Industrial Relations Journal 41*, 136-153.

[12] Joseph, D., Ng, K.Y., Koh, C. and Ang, S. 2007. Turnover of Information Technology Professionals: A Narrative Review, Meta-Analytic Structural Equation Modeling, and Model Development. *MIS Quarterly 31*, 547-577.

[13] Joseph, D., Ang, S., Chang, R.H.L. and Slaughter, S.A. 2010. Practical Intelligence in IT: Assessing Soft Skills of IT Professionals. *Communications of the ACM 53*, 149-154.

[14] Nadkarni, S. and Herrmann, P. 2010. CEO Personality, Strategic Flexibility, and Firm Performance: The Case of the Indian Business Process Outsourcing Industry. *Academy of Management Journal 53*, 1050-1073.

[15] Ang, S., Slaughter, S.A. and Ng, K.Y. 2002. Human Capital and Institutional Determinants of Information Technology Compensation: Modeling Multilevel and Cross-Level Interactions. *Management Science 48*, 1427-1445.

[16] Slaughter, S.A., Ang, S. and Boh, W.F. 2007. Firm-Specific Human Capital and Compensation-Organizational Tenure Profiles: An Archival Analysis of Salary Data for IT Professionals. *Human Resource Management 46*, 373-394.

[17] Baruah, A. 2011. Indian BPO industry Sees Silver Lining in US Slowdown In *InformationWeek*.

[18] Remesh, B.P. 2004. Cyber Coolies in BPO: Insecurities and Vulnerabilities of Non-Standard Work. *Economic & Political Weekly 39*, 492-497.

[19] Budhwar, P.S., Luthar, H.K. and Bhatnagar, J. 2006. The Dynamics of HRM Systems in Indian BPO Firms. *Journal of Labor Research 27*, 339-360.

[20] Vaid, M. 2009. Exploring the Lives of Youth in the BPO Sector: Findings from a Study in Gurgaon. In *Health and Population Innovation Fellowship Program Working Paper, No. 10* Population Council, New Delhi, India.

[21] Hochschild, A.R. 1983. *The Managed Heart: Commericalization of Human Feeling*. University of California Press, Berkeley, CA.

[22] Morris, J.A. and Feldman, D.C. 1996. The Dimensions, Antecedents, and Consequences of Emotional Labor. *Academy of Management Review 21*, 986-1010.

[23] Witt, L.A., Andrews, M.C. and Carlson, D.S. 2004. When Conscientiousness Isn't Enough: Emotional Exhaustion and Performance Among Call Center Customer Service Representatives. *Journal of Management 30*, 149-160.

[24] Farrell, D., Laboissière, M.A. and Rosenfeld, J. 2006. Sizing the Emerging Global Labor Market: Rational Behavior from Both Companies and Countries Can Help It Work More Efficiently. *Academy of Management Perspectives 20*, 23-34.

[25] Roy, A. and Marriott, I. 2011. Analysis of India as an Offshore Services Location Gartner, Stamford, CT, 1-11.

[26] Luthans, F. and Youssef, C.M. 2004. Human, Social and Now Positive Psychological Capital Management: Investing in People for Competitive Advance. *Organizational Dynamics 33*, 143-160.

[27] Luthans, F., Norman, S., Avolio, B.J. and Avey, J.B. 2008. The Mediating Role of Psychological Capital in the Supportive Organizational Climate-Employee Performance Relationship. *Journal of Organizational Behavior 29*, 219-238.

[28] Becker, G.S. 1975. *Human Capital: A Theoretical and Empirical Analysis, with Special Reference to Education*. National Bureau of Economic Research, Cambridge, MA.

[29] Spence, M. 1973. Job Market Signaling. *Quarterly Journal of Economics 87*, 355-374.

[30] Connelly, B.L., Certo, S.T., Ireland, R.D. and Reutzel, C.R. 2011. Signalling Theory: A Review and Assessment. *Journal of Management 37*, 39-67.

[31] Weiss, A. 1995. Human Capital vs. Signalling Explanation of Wages. *Journal of Economic Perspectives 9*, 133-154.

[32] Hungerford, T. and Solon, G. 1987. Sheepskin Effects in the Returns to Education. *The Review of Economics and Statistics 69*, 175-177.

[33] NASSCOM 2008. Roadmap 2012 - Capitalizing on the Expanding BPO Landscape NASSCOM-Everest Group, New Delhi, India.

[34] Gardner, H. 1999. *Intelligence Reframed: Multiple Intelligences for the 21st Century*. Basic Books, New York.

[35] Gardner, H. 2006. *Multiple Intelligences: New Horizons*. Basic Books, New York.

[36] Goleman, D. 1995. *Emotional Intelligence: Why It Can Matter More than IQ*. Bantam, New York, NY.

[37] Goleman, D. 2006. *Social Intelligence: The New Science of Human Relationships*. Bantam, New York, NY.

[38] Baruch-Feldman, C., Brondolo, E., Ben-Dayan, D. and Schwartz, J. 2002. Sources of Social Support and Burnout, Job Satisfaction, and Productivity. *Journal of Occupational Health Psychology 7*, 84-93.

[39] Luthans, F., Avolio, B.J., Avey, J.B. and Norman, S. 2007. Positive Psychological Capital: Measurement and Relationship with Performance and Satisfaction. *Personnel Psychology 60*, 541-572.

[40] Eisenberger, R., Stinglhamber, F., Vandenberghe, C., Sucharski, I.L. and Rhoads, L. 2002. Perceived Supervisor Support: Contributions to Perceived Organizational Support and Employee Retention. *Journal of Applied Psychology 87*, 565-573.

[41] Kottke, J.L. and Sharafinski, C.E. 1988. Measuring Perceived Supervisory and Organizational Support. *Educational and Psychological Measurement 48*, 1075-1079.

[42] Fisher, C.T. 1985. Social Support and Adjustment to Work: A Longitudinal Study. *Journal of Management 11*, 39-53.

[43] Osca, A., Urien, B., González-Camino, G., Martínez-Pérez, M.D. and Martínez-Pérez, N. 2005. Organisational Support and Group Efficacy: A Longitudinal Study of Main and Buffer Effects. *Journal of Managerial Psychology 20*, 292-311.

[44] Cohen, S. and Wills, T.A. 1985. Stress, Social Support, and the Buffering Hypothesis. *Psychological Bulletin 98*, 310-357.

[45] House, J.S. 1981. *Work Stress and Social Support*. Addison-Wesley, Reading, MA.

[46] Seers, A., Mcgee, G.W., Serey, T.T. and Graen, G.B. 1983. The Interaction of Job Stress and Social Support: A Strong Inference Investigation. *Academy of Management Journal 26*, 273-284.

[47] Blau, P.M. 1964. *Exchange and Power in Social Life*. Transaction Publishers, Piscataway, NJ.

[48] Gouldner, A.W. 1960. The Norm of Reciprocity: A Preliminary Statement. *American Sociological Review 25*, 161-178.

[49] Organ, D.W. 1988. *Organizational Citizenship Behavior: The Good Soldier Syndrome*. Lexington Books, Lexington, MA.

[50] Peterson, C. and Seligman, M.E.P. 2004. *Character Strengths and Virtues: A Handbook and Classification*. American Psychological Association, Washington, DC.

[51] Luthans, F. 2002. The Need for and Meaning of Positive Organizational Behavior. *Journal of Organizational Behavior 23*, 695-706.

[52] Combs, G.M., Clapp-Smith, R. and Nadkarni, S. 2010. Managing BPO Service Workers in India: Examining Hope on Performance Outcomes. *Human Resource Management 49*, 457-476.

[53] Fritz, C., Lam, C.F. and Spreitzer, G.M. 2011. It's the Little Things that Matter: An Examination of Knowledge Workers' Energy Management. *Academy of Management Perspectives 25*, 28-39.

[54] Hobfoll, S.E. 1989. Conservation of Resources: A New Attempt at Conceptualizing Stress. *American Psychologist 44*, 513-524.

[55] Quinn, R.W. and Dutton, J.E. 2005. Coordination as Energy-in-Conservation. *Academy of Management Review 30*, 36-57.

[56] Ryan, R.M. and Frederick, C. 1997. On Energy, Personality and Health: Subjective Vitality as a Dynamic Reflection of Well-Being. *Journal of Personality 65*, 529-565.

[57] Dutton, J.E. 2003. *Energize Your Workplace: How to Build and Sustain High-Quality Connections at Work*. Jossey-Bass, San Francisco, CA.

[58] Baumeister, R.F., Bratslavsky, E., Muraven, M. and Tice, D.M. 1998. Ego Depletion: Is the Active Self a Limited Resource? *Journal of Personality and Social Psychology 74*, 1252-1265.

[59] Baumeister, R.F., Muraven, M. and Tice, D.M. 2000. Ego Depletion: A Resource Model of Volition, Self-Regulation and Controlled Processing. *Social Cognition 18*, 130-150.

[60] Vohs, K.D., Baumeister, R.F., Schmeichel, B., Twenge, J.M., Nelson, N.M. and Tice, D.M. 2008. Making Choices Impairs Self-Control: A Limited-Resource Account of Decision Making, Self-Regulation, and Active Initiative. *Journal of Personality and Social Psychology 94*, 883-898.

[61] Wan, E.W. and Sternthal, B. 2008. Regulating the Effects of Depletion through Monitoring. *Personality and Social Psychology Bulletin 34*, 32-46.

[62] Morrison, E.W. 2002. Newcomers' Relationships: The Role of Social Network Ties During Socialization. *Academy of Management Journal 45*, 1149-1160.

[63] Settoon, R.P. and Mossholder, K.W. 2002. Relationship Quality and Relationship Context as Antecedents of Person- and Task-Focused Interpersonal Citizenship Behavior. *Journal of Applied Psychology 87*, 255-267.

[64] Hair, J.F.J., Anderson, R.E., Tatham, R.L. and Black, W.C. 1998. *Multivariate Data Analysis*. Prentice Hall, Upper Saddle River, NJ.

[65] Nunnally, J.C. and Bernstein, I.H. 1994. *Psychometric Theory*. McGraw-Hill, New York.

[66] Mithas, S. and Krishnan, M.S. 2008. Human Capital and Institutional Effects in the Compensation of Information Technology Professionals in the United States. *Management Science 54*, 415-428.

[67] Krueger, A.B. 1993. How Computers Have Changed the Wage Structure: Evidence from Microdata, 1984-1989. *Quarterly Journal of Economics 108*, 33-60.

[68] Mincer, J. 1974. *Schooling, Experience, and Earnings*. Columbia University Press, New York.

[69] Mincer, J. 1958. Investments in human capital and personal income distribution. *Journal of Political Economy 66*, 281-302.

[70] Heckman, J.J., Lochner, L.J. and Todd, P.E. 2003. Fifty years of Mincer earnings regression (NBER paper 9732). In *Working paper*.

[71] Mithas, S. and Krishnan, M.S. 2009. From Association to Causation via a Potential Outcomes Approach. *Information Systems Research 20*, 295-313.

[72] Mithas, S. and Lucas, H.C. 2010. Are Foreign IT Workers Cheaper? U.S. Visa Policies and Compensation of Information Technology Professionals. *Management Science 56*, 745-765.

[73] Levina, N. and Xin, M. 2007. Comparing IT Workers' Compensation Across Country Contexts: Demographic, Human Capital, and Institutional Factors. *Information System Research 18*, 193-210.

[74] Ng, T.W.H., Eby, L., Sorensen, K.L. and Feldman, D.C. 2005. Predictors of Objective and Subjective Career Success: A Meta-Analysis. *Personnel Psychology 58*, 367-408.

[75] Crino, R. 2008. Offshoring, Multinationals and Labour Market: A Review of the Empirical Literature. *Journal of Economic Surveys 23*, 197-249.

[76] Sturman, M.C., Walsh, K. and Cheramie, R.A. 2008. The Value of Human Capital Specificity Versus Transferability. *Journal of Management 34*, 290-316.

[77] Joseph, D., Ang, S. and Slaughter, S.A. 2008. Relative Wage Differences and the Career Transitions of IT Professionals. In *Academy of Management Annual Meeting Proceedings*, Anaheim, CA, 1-5.

[78] Granovetter, M.S. 1981. Toward a Sociological Theory of Income Differences. In *Sociological Perspectives on Labor Markets* Academic Press, New York, 11-47.

[79] Kingdon, G.G. 1998. Does the Labour Market Explain Lower Female Schooling in India? *Journal of Development Studies 35*, 39-65.

[80] Matloff, N. 2003. On the Need for Reform of the H-1B Non-Immigrant Work Visa in Computer-Related Occupations. *University of Michigan Journal of Law Reform 36*, 815-914.

[81] Johnson, J.W. 2000. A Heuristic Method for Estimating the Relative Weights of Predictor Variables in Multiple Regression. *Multivariate Behavioral Research 35*, 1-19.

[82] Ferratt, T.W., Agarwal, R., Brown, C.V. and Moore, J.E. 2005. IT Human Resource Management Configurations and IT Turnover: Theoretical Synthesis and Empirical Analysis. *Information Systems Research 16*, 237-255.

[83] House, R.J., Hanges, P.J., Javidan, M., Dorfman, P.W. and Gupta, V. 2004. *Culture, Leadership, and Organizations*. SAGE Publications, Thousand Oaks, CA.

[84] Hofstede, G. 1991. *Cultures and Organizations: Software of the Mind*. McGraw-Hill, Maidenhead, UK.

[85] Black, J.S. and Morrison, A.J. 2010. A Cautionary Tale for Emerging Market Giants. *Harvard Business Review 88*, 99-103.

[86] Morgeson, F.V., Mithas, S., Keiningham, T.L. and Aksoy, L. 2011. An Investigation of the Cross-National Determinants of Customer Satisfaction. *Journal of the Academy of Marketing Science 39*, 198-215.

Getting Work Done:
Evaluating the Potential of Crowdsourcing as a Model for Business Process Outsourcing Service Delivery

Lee B. Erickson
The Pennsylvania State University
College of Information Sciences and Technology
330B Information Sciences and Technology Building
University Park, PA 16802
703-625-7966

lbe108@psu.edu

Eileen M. Trauth
The Pennsylvania State University
College of Information Sciences and Technology
330C Information Sciences and Technology Building
University Park, PA 16802
814-865-6457

etrauth@ist.psu.edu

ABSTRACT

Crowdsourcing is the use of large groups of individuals to perform tasks traditionally performed by employees or designated agents. For business process outsourcing (BPO) service providers, the crowd may represent a new way to reduce costs and increase efficiencies associated with labor-intensive services. The ability to connect with the crowd to get work done may also open up new possibilities for workers in rural or economically depressed areas, and those within emerging markets. It is unclear, however, what challenges a crowdsourced services business model creates for organizations. An exploratory case study examining the potential of the crowd as a source of on-demand labor for delivering labor-intensive BPO services reveals the key role of information technology in overcoming economic, technical, and social challenges. Five key challenges were identified and are discussed: 1) protecting sensitive data, 2) ensuring quality of work, 3) ensuring timely completion of tasks, 4) managing increased workload, and 5) ensuring the sustainability of the model.

Categories and Subject Descriptors

D.2.9 [**Management**]: Productivity
K.6.1 [**People and People Management**]: Staffing

General Terms

Management, Performance, Economics, Experimentation

Keywords

crowdsourcing, innovation, business process outsourcing, business process crowdsourcing

1. INTRODUCTION

The on-going worldwide economic recession is impacting businesses, both large and small, forcing them to reexamine their business models for getting work done. Information technology (IT) and IT professionals are playing a strategic role in this process by developing new models that reduce costs, increase

efficiencies, add value, and facilitate change [8]. One such business model is the use of IT to connect with large groups of individuals to perform tasks typically performed by employees or designated agents. Commonly referred to as crowdsourcing [7], companies are leveraging the crowd to meet a variety of organizational needs including product/service innovation, marketing/branding, knowledge capture, and cost reduction/productivity [4]. With regard to the latter, this new business model opens up the possibility of connecting with significantly more workers at reduced cost. It also holds the potential to create new opportunities for rural workers in economically depressed areas and within emerging markets. For those who have access to the Internet, crowdsourcing may make it easier to find work thus reducing the need to relocate to larger urban areas.

While not all crowdsourcing tasks are paid, the focus of this paper is the paid use of the crowd to complete labor-intensive business tasks. Specifically, we discuss the challenges associated with a crowdsourced business model designed to reduce costs associated with business process outsourcing (BPO) services.

We begin with a brief overview of BPO services and the growing use of workers in emerging markets. This is followed by our research question and methodology. Next, an overview of the case and specific challenges faced by the company is presented. We end with a discussion of the role IT and IT professionals play in overcoming specific challenges associated with this new service delivery model.

2. LITERATURE REVIEW

BPO includes both the outsourcing of routine business tasks and critical business functions [19]. The value of BPO to the contracting company includes the ability to: 1) reduce costs, 2) improve experiences for customers, 3) improve service quality, and 3) increase competitive advantage through new innovative approaches and processes [2, 3]. Additionally, by outsourcing business process, companies can focus their attention and resources on core offerings instead of building infrastructure, developing processes, and hiring resources to perform common business tasks.

As the global economic recession continues, BPO service providers are under growing pressure to identify ways to reduce costs and increase speed of service delivery, while maintaining the quality of the work completed [9, 11, 16]. This is especially critical for tasks that are difficult to automate and therefore require humans to complete (e.g., language translation).

Specifically, BPO service providers are struggling to: 1) identify ways to reduce costs associated with labor-intensive tasks, 2) diversify their geographic bases to reduce risks associated with high-attrition rates of workers in large cities, and 3) identify higher-skilled workers to complete critical business processes.

The Internet opens up the possibility of connecting with workers around the globe to reduce cost through an on-demand BPO workforce. This use of the crowd has been referred to as Business Process Crowdsourcing [12]. Business Process Crowdsourcing represents a new service delivery model that may benefit BPO service providers, as well as marginalized or underprivileged rural workers in emerging markets.

For BPO service providers, Business Process Crowdsouring may provide an alternative model to the current fixed cost model (i.e., off-shore outsourcing facilities and paid in-house staff). By turning to the crowd, service providers may be able to reduce overall costs by lowering wages, eliminating physical facilities, and reducing support costs [18]. Further, a crowdsourced services model creates the potential for a 24 x 7 workweek that may help to increase productivity. Finally, such a model may allow service providers to locate individuals with specific or unique skills more easily and engage these individuals at reduced cost.

For example, India represents approximately 35% of the BPO market with nearly $11 billion in export revenues and 700,000 workers [15]. As such, BPO service providers represent significant employment opportunities for Indian workers [17]. India is particularly competitive due to the relatively inexpensive cost of labor, the size of the labor pool, the stability of the government, and the recent governmental investments in infrastructure, especially in rural areas [11, 16].

As current investments in education, training, and infrastructure reach more and more rural areas of India, BPO service providers are beginning to build delivery centers outside large cities in the hopes of lowering costs and connecting with a more stable workforce [11]. Such investments also open up the potential for individual workers with access to computers to leverage existing infrastructure to connect with service providers who may be looking to expand their on-demand workforce.

While a number of studies have been conducted to examine the benefits and working conditions of employees in traditional BPO centers [9,13, 17], currently there is limited research investigating the challenges of a crowdsourced services delivery model. This paper presents findings from a case study examining the challenges a crowdsourced services delivery model may create for organizations. Findings reveal technical, economic, and social challenges. Specifically, five key challenges were identified: 1) protecting sensitive data, 2) ensuring the quality of the work, 3) ensuring timely completion of the work, 4) managing a virtual labor pool, and 5) ensuring the sustainability of the model.

3. METHODOLOGY

The case described here is part of a grounded theory research study designed to identify trends and patterns associated with crowdsourcing by established organizations. Specifically, the research question to be addressed was: *What challenges do organizations face when leveraging crowdsourcing to complete labor-intensive BPO tasks?*

As crowdsourcing is an emergent phenomenon with limited empirical work and existing theory, a grounded theory approach to data collection and analysis was used [1]. The research method used was an embedded single case study design with two levels of analysis: 1) the organization and 2) the specific crowdsourcing

initiative. Interviews were the primary means of interpretive data collection and were used to build in-context understanding of the phenomenon from the viewpoints of individuals engaged in the phenomenon [6, 10, 14, 21].

Prior to conducting interviews, an interview guide was created to elicit data at both levels of analysis [21]. To address the organizational level of analysis, interview questions focused on the company's goals for the initiative, organizational structure, and current processes. To gather information at the initiative level, questions focused on the purpose of the initiative, the tasks being completed, and who was invited to participate (i.e., the make-up of the crowd). A number of questions were also included that spanned both levels of analysis, thus providing insights into the organization and the initiative. Specifically, questions addressed processes for integrating the crowd's input into current BPO offerings, facilitators of and barriers to implementation, and unexpected outcomes or issues.

3.1 Data Collection and Analysis

Individuals at multiple levels within the organization who had first-hand experience with the crowdsourcing initiative were recruited. Because individuals within the organization studied came with differing experiences and understanding, it was important to gather a wide range of perspectives [21]. Moreover, because organizations often compartmentalize information, individuals at different levels within the organization were desirable to expose potential differences in understanding of organizational goals, as well as different understandings regarding the potential challenges associated with the initiative.

A total of six semi-structured interviews lasting 30 to 90 minutes each were conducted with seven employees. Interviewees held positions at multiple levels including Director, research scientist, and postdoctoral researcher. Interviews were held over a two-day period in the fall of 2011. Four individuals were interviewed in one-on-one face-to-face sessions, and three were interviewed remotely via phone. One follow up interview was conducted via phone approximately one year after the initial interviews to obtain information on the progress of the initiative. Interviews were recorded and transcribed, and then analyzed using grounded methods with the objective of uncovering key themes related to challenges associated with a crowdsourced services delivery model.

In line with grounded methods, no a priori categories were created. Instead, open coding was used to extract key characteristics and create logical descriptive categories [5, 20]. Themes were identified based on two criteria. First, a theme was identified if more than one interviewee mentioned a similar concern, issue, or topic. Second, a theme was created when one interviewee described a situation, activity, or event that would help to explain or account for a comment by another interviewee. As patterns emerged around specific themes, categories were combined, reconfigured, or eliminated based on this criteria. A detailed case write-up outlining: 1) an overview of the organization, 2) the data collected, 3) a description of the initiative, including goals, implementation, participants, tasks to be completed, and success metrics, 4) impacts to the organization, both positive and negative, 5) facilitators, 6) challenges, and 7) a discussion of findings was also created. Member checking was used to establish the credibility of the findings by allowing interviewees to review the case write-up to ensure it was free of factual errors and "rang true" with the participants' experiences [20].

4. OVERVIEW OF CASE

DocCorp[1] is a global document management and BPO service company headquartered in the U.S. with over 100,000 employees in more than 160 countries. DocCorp offers a variety of BPO services including outsourced call centers and digital document management services. Like many service providers, DocCorp formally defines terms of service with customers using service level agreements (SLAs) that stipulate performance standards and delivery times for specified services, as well as penalties for failing to meet defined service levels.

To address the rising costs associated with hiring employees and managing outsourced labor overseas, DocCorp was examining the use of a crowdsourcing business model to deliver labor-intensive BPO services to its customers. While multiple sources of on-demand labor were being considered, the focus here is on the application of such a model to labor forces in emerging markets.

5. FINDINGS

A dedicated research team at DocCorp was tasked with the job of exploring, developing, and incubating new innovative approaches to delivering digital document services and solutions for customers. The goal of the initiative was to reduce costs associated with the completion of labor-intensive business processes such as digitization of forms, data entry, and translation of documents. One option under consideration was leveraging a crowdsourced on-demand workforce to replace or supplement more costly resources (i.e., full-time employees, contract employees, and off-shore outsourcing facilities). Key to the use of a crowdsourced model was demonstrating significant reduction in costs while maintaining quality and time commitments as defined in customer SLAs. In short, the goal was to indentify a more flexible and cost effective way to get work done for customers.

5.1 The Work and the Crowd

Tasks to be completed varied from simple verification of data across multiple documents (e.g., have numbers been transferred correctly) to more complex translation of documents from one language to another (e.g., from Spanish to English). Furthermore, tasks typically had a defined answer (e.g., the numbers match), or an acceptable range of answers (e.g., one of a number of appropriate words). Finally, the crowd might be asked to complete the entire task (e.g., translate this entire document), or smaller parts of a task (e.g., translate this paragraph). In addition to completing tasks such as translating a sentence, additional tasks might include verifying work completed by others, for example rating the accuracy of a translated sentence.

The use of online technologies meant that the crowd could be located potentially anywhere in the world, assuming there was access. Depending on the nature of the task to be completed, the crowd could be anonymous or would need to be prequalified to ensure they had the necessary skills and knowledge to complete the work at the quality required. Furthermore, different tasks might require individuals in the crowd to have different knowledge and skills. For example, tasks such as verification of data (e.g., are these two numbers the same) would require only basic English and typing skills. Other tasks, however, such as translation of documents from one language to another, would require specialized language skills.

---

[1] A pseudonym is being used to protect the identity of the participating organization.

Ideally, by having many more options, DocCorp hoped to automatically match the task to be completed to the best resource for the job. For example, non-sensitive data that required only basic skills (e.g., matching numbers) could be completed by anyone in the crowd. Non-sensitive data that required specialized skills (e.g., language translation) could be completed by pre-qualified individuals within the crowd. Finally, highly sensitive data, regardless of the task, could be forwarded to a certified facility that could guarantee data security. Such a model held the potential to significantly reduce infrastructure and management costs associated with hiring employees and overseeing outsourced contracts. In the words of one interviewee, "In the case of outsourcing we only have one organization. Instead, DocCorp could divvy up the jobs, giving the right job to the right crowd. Here we have a choice and we can select from them. That is the major difference."

5.2 Challenges

While only in the initial stages of evaluation, DocCorp's efforts shed light on the challenges Business Processing Crowdsourcing creates for companies. Furthermore, analysis revealed that IT played a critical role in connecting DocCorp with workers, as well as managing and evaluating the work completed by the crowd. As one interviewee explained, the goal was to be "ahead of the curve" in terms of advancement of technology to support the "next generation of work." This included: 1) connecting directly with workers with computers at home, 2) placing kiosks in centralized areas for workers without computers, and 3) building timesharing models where multiple individuals shared time on one computer.

To examine the potential of this new model, different researchers within the group were exploring how technology could be leveraged to find solutions for different aspects of service delivery. Multiple efforts were underway to determine whether complex processes could be broken down into smaller parts that could be completed independently. Efforts included attempting to identify which parts of the process could be successfully crowdsourced and which could not.

All interviewees reported significant challenges in identifying whether technology could be used to ensure the crowd met contractual obligations of SLAs. Specific concerns centered around three areas: 1) protecting sensitive data, 2) ensuring quality of work, and 3) completing tasks within the required timeframe. Additionally, assuming that these challenges could be successfully addressed, proof was required that such an approach would be more cost effective than DocCorp's current model. Finally, DocCorp also faced challenges in ensuring that such a model would be sustainable. Each of these challenge is discussed in more detail next.

5.2.1 Data Security: Ensuring The Crowd Can Be Trusted

Currently, a number of DocCorp's customers required protection of sensitive personal and corporate information. Additionally, for some jobs, federal regulations and laws mandated data security procedures. As such, ensuring the security of sensitive data was crucial to the success of the initiative.

While DocCorp had processes in place to ensure the security of customer data within physical data centers, a virtual and unknown workforce presented new challenges. With physical facilities, workers were co-located in secure buildings and processes were put in place to ensure workers were who they said they were (i.e., photo ID badges, background checks). Further, processes were in place to ensure sensitive data would not be compromised (e.g., leaving bags at the door, taking nothing in or out). However, physical checks and balances would not be possible with a virtual labor pool. Instead, technical approaches to ensuring security would be required.

While a number of automated technology options were under consideration, interviewees expressed concerns that such potential approaches might extend the time required to complete tasks and/or increase the resources needed to manage the process. This, in turn, might negate costs savings or even potentially increase overall costs.

5.2.2 Quality: Ensuring The Crowd Meets Defined Standards

Interviewees also reported concerns over relying on unknown workers with varying levels of skill to consistently produce quality work. In the words of one interviewee, "It's hard to guarantee how fast or how good the work will be." Preliminary experimentation with sample data on publically available crowdsourced Internet marketplaces[2] resulted in varying levels of quality. Specifically, quality decreased as tasks became more complex. Researchers were attempting to assess whether poor quality was a result of the crowd not having the right skills or the crowd not being reliable even when tasks were relatively simple. Regardless, unless some level of quality could be guaranteed the crowd would not be an acceptable alternative to current resources.

To address this issue, researchers were attempting to identify technological approaches and processes for ensuring that individuals working on tasks had the necessary level of skills to complete the desired task. As with ensuring security of sensitive data, a critical component was demonstrating that additional costs to qualify workers would not negate potential costs savings.

5.2.3 Turnaround Time: Ensuring The Crowd Completes the Job When Needed

In addition to ensuring data security and quality, interviewees reported challenges in ensuring the timely delivery of services. Assuming quality and security issues could be overcome, there was no guarantee the crowd would complete the job when needed.

Contractual turnaround times outlined in SLAs required that DocCorp get the job done in the time specified. In the words of one interviewee, "If I have to get these hundred thousand forms digitized and sent back to this customer today, I need to be able to make sure that somebody picks it up and delivers." Further, even when there were no contractual time requirements, DocCorp could not simply hope that the crowd would work on the job. As one interviewee commented, "You could post a job, but nobody might pick it up."

In additional, even if individuals in the crowd did complete the work in a timely manner, there was no guarantee that these specific individuals would return to take on additional work. Incentivizing the crowd was problematic because the make-up of the crowd would not be stable over time. Interests, commitment, and motivations would vary from day to day making it difficult to identify appropriate incentives for encouraging participation and ensuring the best workers would return. In short, a crowdsourced

model came with no guarantees that jobs would be completed at all, much less in a timely manner or at the required quality.

5.2.4 Increased Workload: Managing Crowd Labor

An on-demand 24 x 7 crowdsourced workforce held the potential to complete significantly more work than DocCorp's current resources. While a virtual workforce would reduce overhead costs related to physical facilities and contract management, an increase in the volume of work would present new challenges related to workflow and workforce management. As such, interviewees were concerned with how best to manage the increased volume of work that could be completed. To address this issue, DocCorp was looking at technical solutions to common supervisory and workflow issues such as how best to organize large teams of workers who would not know each other or be co-located.

5.2.5 Longevity: Ensuring the Sustainability of the Model

Finally, interviewees expressed concerns over the sustainability of a crowdsourced business model. The ability to tap into a crowdsourced workforce, held the benefit of reducing overhead and management costs. Additionally, it provided DocCorp with the potential of connecting to a workforce who would complete tasks at lower wages. While many different on-demand workforces were being explored, with respect to workers in emerging markets, the model also held the potential of creating additional employment options for workers in rural areas. Those with computers could work from home on a flexible schedule. Those without computers could travel daily to local centers equipped with kiosks or timeshare computers to complete tasks. Rural centers could help to keep families together, reducing the numbers of people living in poverty in cities, and helping to fuel rural economies. However, to encourage workers to return to take on additional work, DocCorp needed to ensure workers were satisfied and did not feel exploited. Therefore, efforts were underway to create a social and organizational model that would provide benefits to both workers and the employer. Key to such a model was the crowd viewing DocCorp as a fair and predictable source of wages.

In addition to the sustainability of a virtual workforce, interviewees expressed concerns related to the application of labor laws to a crowdsourced labor pool. While online crowdsouring is not currently subject to such laws, one interviewee commented that there were concerns regarding potential "minefields" related to how to manage things like minimum wage when workers are not employees. Critical to the sustainability of the model was avoiding potential costly legal issues that might arise in the future should such laws be applied to crowdsourced labor.

6. DISCUSSION

The case presented here illustrates the strategic role that IT is playing in DocCorp's ability to determine if a crowdsourced service delivery model can deliver quality services at reduced costs. While a crowdsourced on-demand workforce theoretically has the potential to lower costs associated with BPO service, it presented considerable technical, economic, and social challenges. A number of business units within DocCorp had shown interest in the levering technologies to support a crowdsourcing model, however, before any business unit would adopt or integrate the crowd into their processes empirical proof was needed that such a model would reduce costs yet maintain quality. Because the nature of the tasks to be completed was relatively simple, DocCorp was able to create use cases that tested and demonstrated value to the company. A follow-up interview one year after initial

---

2 Internet marketplaces allow anyone to post work to be completed by the crowd. Workers are paid a fee (typically nominal) for work completed (e.g., MechanicalTurk).

interviews revealed that DocCorp had generated a number of promising uses cases related to this new business model. In fact, for certain tasks such as digitization of forms, use cases showed that workers on large crowdsourcing sites could deliver the quality needed at no more cost than currently incurred when hiring workers in lower wage countries (e.g., India). While only working with sample data, researchers were optimistic about the use of a crowdsourced services model for delivery of simple routine tasks. With regard to more complex tasks, use cases continued to show that quality was an issue.

From an economic perspective, the use of the crowd represented a process innovation designed to deliver quantifiable economic benefits. Key to achieving these economic gains is DocCorp's ability to identify new cutting edge technologies, interfaces, and algorithms that could be used to 1) protect sensitive data, 2) identify the best worker(s) in the crowd, 3) ensure the quality and timely completion of the work product, 4) create an efficient workflow, and 4) better manage the workflow process. Further, DocCorp's approach of locating IT kiosks and timesharing centers in rural locations could facilitate connections to on-demand sources of labor previously out of reach or only accessible through more costly outsourcing organizations. These rural centers could also open up new opportunities for rural workers in emerging markets.

While researchers at DocCorp were experimenting with the potential of a crowdsourced delivery model, before this new model would be considered or implemented, business unit managers needed to be confident that it would reduce costs without compromising SLAs. As such, the researcher team was attempting to identify the conditions under which alternative resources would reduce costs without increasing risk. That is, implementation of a crowdsourced services model would be a business decision based on hard evidence.

In examining this new business model for getting work done, DocCorp has realized that focusing on the technical and economic challenges alone will not ensure success. The use of the crowd also creates social challenges. The sustainability of a crowdsource service delivery model will be directly tied to the crowd's willingness to do the work. Key to sustaining a crowdsourced workforce is finding solutions that ensure the crowd feels they are being treated fairly. Success requires the creation of an organizational and socially focused model that benefits both employers and workers in the crowd.

7. CONCLUSIONS

The case presented here shows that the ability to connect with the crowd to get work done may create new opportunities for IT professionals to identify, build, and manage new platforms and processes that allow companies to extract value from the crowd. Such initiatives, however, require more than technical solutions. IT professionals must also take into account the social issues that may impact success. This suggests a new and expanded role for IT professionals developing solutions that connect their organizations to the crowd to get work done. This new role requires IT professionals be sensitive to the impacts of technology on the crowd and the ramifications of those impacts on their organizations. Such initiatives may not only benefit companies attempting to lower costs of labor-intensive services, but they may also open up new possibilities for workers in remote or economically depressed areas. However, the sustainability of crowdsourced labor requires the ability to manage and attend to the needs of a virtual and ever changing workforce.

It is worth noting a few limitations of this study. While this case does shed light on a new potential business model for delivery of BPO services, more cases are needed to build substantive theory and understanding related to this new phenomenon. At this early stage of inquiry, companies are only beginning to experiment with new crowdsourced service delivery models. More research is needed to determine whether such a model is feasible and beneficial to both companies and workers. Additionally, researchers should examine the role government will play in ensuring critical infrastructure is available in remote areas. As without the ability to connect, workers will be forced to relocate to more urban areas.

8. REFERENCES

[1] Byrant, A. & Charmaz, K. (2007). *The SAGE Handbook of Grounded Theory*. London: SAGE Publications.

[2] Campbell, C. S., Maglio, P. P., & Davis, M. M. (2011). From self-service to super-service: A resource mapping framework for co-creating value by shifting the boundary between provider and customer. *Information System and E-Business. Management Journal*, 9(2), 173–191.

[3] Davis, M., Spohrer, J., & Maglio, P. (2011). Guest editorial: How technology is changing the design and delivery of services. *Operations Management Research*, 4(1), 1–5.

[4] Erickson, L. B., Petrick, I., & Trauth, E. M. (2012). Hanging with the right crowd: Matching crowdsourcing need to crowd characteristics. Proceedings of the *Eighteenth Americas Conference on Information Systems*, Seattle, WA.

[5] Glaser, B. G., & Strauss, A. L. (1967). *The discovery of grounded theory*. New York: Aldine de Gruyter.

[6] Gregor, S. (2006). The nature of theory in information systems. *Management Information Systems Quarterly*, 30(3), 611.

[7] Howe, J. (2006). *Crowdsourcing*: A definition. Retrieved November 30, 2009 from http://www.crowdsourcing.typepad.com/cs/2006/06/crowdsourcing_a.html.

[8] IBM Global Business Services. (2009). *The New Voice of the CIO: Insights from the Global Chief Information Officer Study*. Somers, NY: IBM.

[9] Joshi, U. (2010, June). Antecedents of employee attrition in BPO industry. *Indian Journal of Economics and Business*, 9(2), 361(8).

[10] Klein, H. K. & Meyers, M. D. (1999, March). A set of principles for conducting and evaluating interpretive field studies in information systems. *MIS Quarterly*, 23(1), 67-94.

[11] Lacity, M., Carmel, E., & Rottman, J. (2011). Rural Outsourcing: Delivering ITO and BPO Services from Remote Domestic Locations. *Computer*, 44(12), 55 –62.

[12] La Vecchia, G., & Cisternino, A. (2010). Collaborative workforce, business process crowdsourcing as an alternative of BPO. Proceedings of the 10th international conference on Current trends in web engineering, *ICWE'10* (pp. 425–430). Berlin, Heidelberg: Springer-Verlag.

[13] Mehta, Dhermendra, Jitendra K. Sharma, and Naveen K. Mehta. 2011. An empirical study on job prospects in BPO: Indian perspective. *UTMS Journal of Economics*, 2(1), 29–35.

[14] Myers, M. D. (2009). *Qualitative research in business & management*. SAGE.

[15] NASSCOM-EVEREST (2012). *Indian BPO Study: Roadmapping 2012 - Capitalizing on the expanding BPO landscape* (Report). New Delhi, India: NASSCOM.

[16] PricewaterhouseCoopers. (2005, April). *The Evolution of BPO in India (Research report)*. New York, NY: PricewaterhousCoopers.

[17] Sengupta, S. (2011). An exploratory study on job and demographic attributes affecting employee satisfaction in the Indian BPO industry. *Strategic Outsourcing: An International Journal*, 4(3), 248–273.

[18] Simonson, E., & Brahma, S. (2011). *Every crowd has a silver lining: Crowdsourcing is gaining traction despite inherent challenges* (Report). Everest Global, Inc.

[19] Strauss, B. & Jedrassczyk, M. (2008, July). Business Process Outsourcing (BPO): Value creation through external service partners.

[20] Trauth, E. M. & Jessup, L. M. (2000). Understanding Computer-Mediated Discussions: Positivist and Interpretive Analyses of Group Support System Use. *MIS Quarterly*, 24(1), 43–79.

[21] Yin, R. K. (2009). *Case Study Research: Design and Methods. Applied Social Research Methods Series* (Fourth Ed. Vol. 5). Los Angeles: SAGE Publications.

The Meaning of IT Work

Guorong Lim
Nanyang Technological
University
50 Nanyang Avenue S3-
01C-96
Singapore 639789
+65 67906153
glim3@ntu.edu.sg

Sing Hwa Yeh
Nanyang Technological
University
50 Nanyang Avenue S3-
01C-96
Singapore 639789
+65 67906153
shyeh1@ntu.edu.sg

Christine Koh
Nanyang Technological
University
50 Nanyang Avenue S3-
01C-96
Singapore 639789
+65 67906153
askkoh@ntu.edu.sg

Damien Joseph
Nanyang Technological
University
50 Nanyang Avenue S3-
B2C-99
Singapore 639789
+65 67904831
adjoseph@ntu.edu.sg

ABSTRACT

Research has consistently highlighted the importance of meaning of work. Yet, the meaning of IT work remains unexamined in the IT literature. This study fills this gap by reporting on a study that aims to identify themes describing the meaning of IT work. This study adopts a qualitative grounded approach to identify a set of fifteen (15) themes that represent three types of meanings of work, i.e. Self, Others and Context. A large-scale field study was conducted to validate the meanings of IT work. The results of the field study indicate that the 15 themes identified have face validity. Self-related themes were selected more by IT professionals as describing the meaning of IT work compared to Others or Context. The top four themes describing the meaning of IT work concerned the opportunity to learn and develop oneself; deriving a sense of achievement from work; leveraging knowledge and skills; and creating something of value through work that impacts the company and its clients. We conclude this study with implications for research and the practice of IT.

Categories and Subject Descriptors

K.7.1 [**Occupations**]

Keywords

Information Technology, Meaning, Meaningfulness, Professionals

1. INTRODUCTION

The Computer and People Research (CPR) Conference has conducted half a century research on IT professionals and their work. The scope of CPR research encompasses work attitudes, values, motivations, competencies, careers and behaviors [1]. Yet, as far as we are aware, IT research has not examined what IT work means to IT professionals. Understanding the meaning of work is important because it is fundamental to how IT professionals approach, enact, and experience their work and workplaces [16]. The meaning one ascribes to work is an important source of work values, attitudes and motivation [8]. It is unclear what work means for IT professionals and how meaningful work is related to work values, attitudes and motivations.

As IT research has not yet examined the meaning of IT work, we draw from an extensive body of research in organizational behavior and psychology that has examined the meaning of work in various professions such as nursing [7], zookeeping [3] and teaching [4]. Across occupations, there are commonalities in meanings of work and subtle differences in the descriptors or themes of meanings [9].

We, therefore, take the opportunity to identify the themes that describe the meaning of IT work; and to validate the themes as describing the meaning of IT work. We sought to meet these two objectives by conducting a study in two phases. The first phase adopts a qualitative grounded approach to identify the themes IT professionals associate with meaningful IT work. The second phase adopts a field study to validate these themes by assessing the extent to which IT professionals describe meaningful IT work along the themes identified.

2. LITERATURE REVIEW

The concept of "meaning of work", while intuitively simple, is difficult to define because it signifies different things to different people. The meanings of work are inherently subjective, "rooted in individuals' subjective interpretations of work experiences and interactions" [20 p. 94]. These meanings may be constructed from individual perceptions; and/or from social norms and shared perceptions. Prior research, too, has conceptualized and defined the "meaning of work" in various ways ranging from general beliefs about work to work-related values and attitudes [2, 20].

As far as we are aware, this study is the first to explore the meaning of IT work. As such, it is important that this study clarify the definitions and conceptualizations of terms. Specifically, this study differentiates the "meaning of IT work" from related concepts such as "meaningful" or "meaningfulness".

In this study, "meaning of IT work" refers to the *type* of meaning IT professionals make of their work. "Meaning" here refers to the output of having made sense of work, or of *what* work signifies within the context of an individual's life [18, 20]. The meaning of work typically holds a positive connotation, although research acknowledges that meanings may also be neutral or negative.

The "meaning of IT work" is to be distinguished from the terms "meaningful IT work" and "meaningfulness of IT work". The terms "meaningful work" and "meaningfulness of work" refer to the *amount* of significance work holds for an individual [18, 20]. As such, "meaningful IT work" and "meaningfulness of IT work" is work experienced as significant and holding positive meaning for IT professionals.

A recent review [20] of the meaning of work literature in psychology and organizational behavior has surfaced three types of meanings: Self, Others and the Context. The empirical evidence supports that individuals characterize the meaning of work along these types. But, the actual descriptors of each type, what we label in this paper as themes, differ across sample characteristics [20].

Self-related themes describe the meaning of work in terms of personal values, personal beliefs and intrinsic work motivations. Values refer to the "end states" individuals aspire to through work [10]. Personal beliefs about work refer to the role and function of work in one's life. Intrinsic work motivations refers to one's desire to conduct work because of one's ethic [3], enjoyment of doing so [19], or interest in conducting that work [14, 22]. A study of knowledge workers provides an exemplar of a Self theme of meaningful work - "experiencing personal awareness and growth" [4].

Others-related themes describe meaning of work in terms of interactions and relationships with other individuals within and outside the workplace. Other individuals provide cues on work related cognitions and behaviors that influence the construction and development of the individual's own attitudes [21, 24]. Essentially, the object of meaning tends to be a known or close social group such as a work team, colleagues, organization or family[24]. A study of knowledge workers lists "contributing to the successful relations with others" as an exemplar of a Others theme of meaningful work [4].

Context-related themes describe meaning of work in terms of interactions with workplace and non-workplace environments. The environments within which individuals operate provide cues for the development and trigger of cognitions, attitudes and behaviors. A study of public service employees provides an exemplar of a Context-related theme of meaningful work - "working towards a brighter future" [23]. Another study of knowledge workers lists "making the world a better place" as a Context descriptor of meaningful work [4].

3. METHOD

The key objectives of this paper are to identify the themes that describe the meaning of IT work; and to validate the themes as describing the meaning of IT work. Accordingly, we conducted this study in two phases. The first phase adopts a qualitative grounded approach to identify the themes IT professionals associate with meaningful IT work. The second phase adopts a field study to validate the themes representing the meaning of IT work.

3.1 Identifying Themes of Meanings

In collaboration with the local computer society, we posed an open-ended question - "What does meaningful IT work represent for you?" to its members, through the society's official website. The 6,183 members (as at December 2011) of the computer society are IT professionals working in the IT industry (74%, other industries 26%) holding a range of jobs such as mid-level IT managers (37%), IT consultant (20%), senior IT managers (13%), systems analyst and programmers (8%), and other IT job roles (22%). The modal age of these members is 31-40 years (40%) with 36% of members between 41-50 years old. IT males dominate with 70% of members.

The unit of analysis in this phase is the themes that describe the meaning of IT work. A total of 271 responses (4.4%) were received from a membership base of 6,183 IT professionals. The responses obtained formed the data for subsequent analyses. A response to the question posed to IT professionals could contain one or more statements describing the meaning of IT work. We identified 345 statements describing the meaning of IT work from the 271 responses of IT professionals.

We followed the approach prescribed by Miles and Huberman [15] to code and analyze the statements. One of the authors examined the statements in detail, discussed them with the co-authors, collated and categorized them into themes. Each statement was coded as representing one theme. The themes were, in turn, categorized as representing one of the three types of meanings of IT work – Self, Others and Context.

As a further check for definitional clarity and reliability [15], two other authors independently read the responses and coded the statements into the identified themes. The final Cohen's Kappa was 0.73, above the conventional 0.70 threshold for interrater reliability [13].

Following the coding of statements into themes, the list of themes was presented to a committee of senior IT executives from the local computer society. The senior IT executives reviewed and provided feedback on the themes. The committee and authors finalized a list of fifteen (15) themes representing the three types of meanings of IT work. This coding and independent review process lends additional credence to the validity of the themes surfaced from IT professionals' responses.

3.2 Validating the Themes

Again in collaboration with the local computer society, we asked members to select five (5) out of the fifteen (15) themes that best described the meaning of IT work. This information was sought as part of a larger field study commissioned by the computer society. The field study was conducted between November 2011 and January 2012.

We obtained responses from 824 IT professionals. The responding IT professionals worked in the IT industry (47%), public sector (12%) and education (11%); with the remaining working in other industries. The respondents held a range of jobs in IT project management (27%), IT management (17%), IT services (15%), systems development (13%), sales and marketing (6%); with the remaining in other IT job roles. The sample comprised equal numbers of IT professionals working as in-house IT expertise (53%) and as IT vendors (47%).

The sample comprised 21% of respondents between the ages of 21 to 30; 40% between 31 and 40; 28% between 41 to 50 years and the remaining 11% were 50 years and older. IT males dominate with 76% of members; 24% females. Most IT professionals in our sample had attained at least a bachelors degree (94%) with non-degree holders comprising 6% of the sample.

4. RESULTS AND DISCUSSION
4.1 Themes of Meanings

The qualitative analysis of the 345 statements describing the meaning of IT work resulted in fifteen (15) themes (Table 1). Consistent with the extant literature, we were able to classify these themes into three types of meanings: Self, Others, and Context.

As noted above, Self-related themes describe the meaning of work in terms of personal values, personal beliefs and intrinsic work motivations. Consistent with this definition, we find that IT professionals describe the meaning of IT work as, e.g. having many opportunities to learn and develop oneself; deriving a great sense of achievement from one's work; and work that can leverage on one's knowledge and skills.

Recall that Others-related themes describe meaning of work in terms of interactions and relationships with other individuals within and outside the workplace. Consistent with this definition, IT professionals describe the meaning of IT work as, e.g. creating something of value through one's work that impacts the company and its clients; inspiring, mentoring and developing other IT professionals; and developing close relationships with the varied people one works with.

That IT professionals describe the meaning of IT work in terms of Others is interesting. The existence of this set of themes debunk the stereotype that IT professionals "define themselves and their value in terms of the number and difficulty of the technical skills they have mastered" [5, p. 108]. Rather, this finding suggests that IT professionals define their value in terms of the social impact of their contributions.

Finally, Context-related themes describe meaning of work in terms of interactions with workplace and non-workplace environments. Consistent with the themes on social impact, IT professionals describe the meaning of IT as, e.g. receiving good financial rewards for the effort put in; efforts and contributions to the organization are recognized by supervisors/co-workers; and work is appreciated by others. This finding corroborates prior research conducted in non-IT occupations where employees also conceptualize their work in terms rewards and recognition by society [20].

We also note the greater variation in Self-related meanings (7 themes) compared to Others (4 themes) and Context (4 themes). The higher number of Self-related themes compared to Others and Context suggests IT professionals may have developed a more differentiated meaning of IT work with regard to the self-concept [3, 24].

4.2 Validating the Themes

The results of the field study survey data indicate that the 15 themes identified above have face validity; as evidenced by themes being selected by at least 19% of the sample (Table 1).

Self-related themes were selected more by IT professionals as describing the meaning of IT work compared to Others or Context. Each of the Self-related themes was selected by at least 30% of the sample. The top three Self-related meaning selected by IT professionals concerned the opportunity to learn and develop oneself (49.6%), followed by deriving a sense of achievement from work (45.0%), and leveraging knowledge and skills (43.6%). These three themes were among the overall top four most selected meanings of IT work.

Departing from the Self-oriented themes, the overall third most selected theme describing IT work is an Others-related theme - creating something of value through work that impacts the company and its clients (44.5%). Each of the remaining Others-

related and Context-related themes were selected by less than 35% of the respondents.

Overall, the results suggest that IT professionals see their work in terms of professional development [12], as a profession where achievement is valued over advancement [25] and where IT professionals apply information technologies to solve business problems. This is consistent with the work context within which IT professionals operate; one characterized by a turbulent technological environment driven by innovations and intense competition.

Sub-group analyses revealed some interesting differences by gender, age, and education. Males are more likely to describe meaning of IT work as working with new/latest technologies ($\chi^2 = 13.79$, $df = 1$, $p < 0.001$); making a difference to society ($\chi^2 = 12.93$, $df = 1$, $p < 0.001$) and working on things they are passionate about ($\chi^2 = 6.16$, $df = 1$, $p < 0.05$). Females, on the other hand, are more likely to look for the opportunity to learn and develop ($\chi^2 = 3.60$, $df = 1$, $p < 0.100$).

Younger IT professionals, compared to older IT professionals, are more likely to describe the meaning of IT work in terms of appreciation by others ($\chi^2 = 18.16$, $df = 7$, $p < 0.05$). This theme was endorsed more by IT professionals under the age of 25 years than by IT professionals over the age of 45 years. In contrast, older IT professionals emphasize the sense of achievement more ($\chi^2 = 16.60$, $df = 7$, $p < 0.05$). Of the IT professionals who chose this theme, most were over the age of 45 years and least by those between 26-30 years.

Educational attainment also appears to influence IT professionals' descriptions of the meaning of IT work. Postgraduate degree holders, compared to lower educational attainment, were more likely to describe the meaning of work as making a difference to society ($\chi^2 = 6.33$, $df = 2$, $p < 0.05$) and creating something of value that impacts the company and its clients ($\chi^2 = 7.04$, $df = 2$, $p < 0.05$). Comparatively, bachelors degree holders, compared to the other two groups, were more likely to describe the meaning of IT work as receiving good financial rewards for effort ($\chi^2 = 7.28$, $df = 2$, $p < 0.05$). IT professionals with non-degree attainment described the meaning of IT work as developing close relationships with others they work with ($\chi^2 = 8.61$, $df = 2$, $p < 0.05$); recognition of effort and contributions by supervisors/coworkers ($\chi^2 = 5.63$, $df = 2$, $p < 0.10$).

That the themes describing the meaning of IT work vary by age, gender and educational attainment need further work teasing out the implicit theories held by these sub-groups.

5. CONCLUSION

The key objectives of this paper are to identify the themes that describe the meaning of IT work; and to validate the themes as describing the meaning of IT work. To that end, we leveraged on the strengths of both qualitative grounded data and large-scale field survey data, of IT professionals in Singapore. As far as we are aware, this study is the first to identify the themes describing the meaning of IT work.

Through a combination of qualitative grounded approach and large-scale field survey, our results identified a list of fifteen themes specific to the IT profession. IT professionals describe the meaning of IT work in Self-related themes more than in terms of Others or the Context.

The results of our study have several theoretical and practical implications. First, the introduction of a new theoretical perspective – meaning of work – helps understand what motivates IT professionals. As noted above, the meaning one ascribes to work is an important source of work values, attitudes and motivation [8]. Second, recent research has suggested that vocational calling [3, 11] and personality [6, 17] are lenses through which individuals describe the meaning of work. Future research could extend this paper to examine the role of antecedents to the meaning of IT work.

Third, future research could examine the meaningfulness of IT work, i.e. the extent of significance of IT work. Examining the significance of IT work would be a natural extension of the work started in this paper.

Finally, we encourage the replication of this study in other work settings and in other cultures. The replication of this study would help establish the generalizability of the themes of meanings pertaining to IT work as well as surface differences.

These initial results also have implications for practice. Human resource practitioners and IT managers should consider providing ample opportunities for continual self-development and tasks for which IT professionals are able to leverage their knowledge and skills. Further, recognition systems may emphasize achievements and value creation. These recommendations are made because specific job characteristics are known to influence individuals' sense-making of what work means and what it signifies [7].

6. REFERENCES

[1] Adya, M. and R. Horton. *Proceedings of the 50th Annual Conference on Computers and People Research*. 2012. Milwaukee, Wisconsin, USA: ACM.

[2] Brief, A.P., et al., *Inferring the Meaning of Work from the Effects of Unemployment*. Journal of Applied Social Psychology, 1995. **25**(8): p. 693-711.

[3] Bunderson, J.S. and J.A. Thompson, *The Call of the Wild: Zookeepers, Callings, and the Double-Edged Sword of Deeply Meaningful Work*. Administrative Science Quarterly, 2009. **54**(1): p. 32-57.

[4] Chen, G.A., *The Meaning of Meaningful Work: The Subjective-Objective Meaningfulness in Knowledge Work*, in *Stephen A. Ross Business School*2007, University of Michigan: Ann Arbor, MI.

[5] Enns, H.G., T.W. Ferratt, and J. Prasad, *Beyond Stereotypes of IT Professionals: Implications for IT Hr Practices*. Communications of the ACM, 2006. **49**(4): p. 105-109.

[6] Funder, D.C., *Personality*. Annual Review of Psychology, 2001. **52**: p. 197-221.

[7] Grant, D., A. Morales, and J. Sallaz, *Pathways to Meaning: A New Approach to Studying Emotions at Work*. American Journal of Sociology, 2009. **115**(2): p. 327-364.

[8] Guion, R.M. and F.J. Landy, *Meaning of Work and Motivation to Work*. Organizational Behavior and Human Performance, 1972. **7**(2): p. 308-339.

[9] Harpaz, I., *Meaning of Working Profiles of Various Occupational Groups*. Journal of Vocational Behavior, 1985. **26**(1): p. 25-40.

[10] Harpaz, I. and X.N. Fu, *The Structure of the Meaning of Work: A Relative Stability Amidst Change*. Human Relations, 2002. **55**(6): p. 639-667.

[11] Hirschi, A., *Callings and Work Engagement: Moderated Mediation Model of Work Meaningfulness, Occupational Identity, and Occupational Self-Efficacy*. Journal of Counseling Psychology, 2012. **59**(3): p. 479-485.

[12] Joseph, D., M.L. Tan, and S. Ang, *Is Updating Play or Work? The Mediating Role of Updating Orientations in the Threat of Professional Obsolescence – Mobility Intentions Link*. International Journal of Social and Organizational Dynamics, 2012. **1**(437-47).

[13] Landis, J.R. and G.G. Koch, *The Measurement of Observer Agreement for Categorical Data*. Biometrics, 1977. **33**(1): p. 159-174.

[14] Lust, J.A., *Rewards and Intrinsic Motivation: Resolving the Controversy*. Personnel Psychology, 2004. **57**(1): p. 259-261.

[15] Miles, M.B. and A.M. Huberman, *Qualitative Data Analysis: An Expanded Sourcebook*1994, Thousand Oaks, CA: Sage Publications, Inc.

[16] Morse, N.C. and R.S. Weiss, *The Function and Meaning of Work and the Job*. American Sociological Review, 1955. **20**(2): p. 191-+.

[17] Parks, L. and R.P. Guay, *Personality, Values, and Motivation*. Personality and Individual Differences, 2009. **47**(7): p. 675-684.

[18] Pratt, M.G. and B.E. Ashforth, *Fostering Meaningfulness in Working and at Work*, in *Positive Organizational Scholarship*, K.S. Cameron, J.E. Dutton, and R.E. Quinn, Editors. 2003, Berrett-Koehler Publishers, Inc.: San Francisco. p. 309–327.

[19] Ros, M., S.H. Schwartz, and S. Surkiss, *Basic Individual Values, Work Values, and the Meaning of Work*. Applied Psychology-an International Review-Psychologie Appliquee-Revue Internationale, 1999. **48**(1): p. 49-71.

[20] Rosso, B.D., K.H. Dekas, and A. Wrzesniewski, *On the Meaning of Work: A Theoretical Integration and Review*, in *Research in Organizational Behavior: An Annual Series of Analytical Essays and Critical Reviews, Vol 30*, A.P. Brief and B.M. Staw, Editors. 2010. p. 91-127.

[21] Salanick, G.R. and J. Pfeffer, *A Social Information Processing Approach to Job Attitudes and Task Design*. Administrative Science Quarterly, 1978. **23**: p. 224-253.

[22] Thatcher, J.B., Y.M. Liu, and L.P. Stepina. *The Role of the Work Itself: An Emprirical Examination of Intrinsic Motivation's Influence on IT Workers' Attitudes and Intentions*. in *Special Interest Group Computer Personnel Research Annual Conference*. 2002. Kristianland, Norway: Association for Computing Machinery.

[23] Worts, D., B. Fox, and P. McDonough, *'Doing Something Meaningful': Gender and Public Service During Municipal Government Restructuring*. Gender, Work and Organization, 2007. **14**(2): p. 162-184.

[24] Wrzesniewski, A.C., J.E. Dutton, and G. Debebe, *Interpersonal Sensemaking and the Meaning of Work*. Research in Organizational Behavior, Vol 25, 2003. **25**: p. 93-135.

[25] Zabusky, S.E. and S.R. Barley, *Redefining Success: Ethnographic Observations on the Careers of Technicians*, in *Broken Ladders: Managerial Careers in the New Economy*, P. Osterman, Editor 1996, Oxford University Press: New York, NY. p. 185-214.

Table 1: The Meaning of IT Work for IT Professionals [a]

Type of Meaning	Themes In Each Type	% Endorsed	Rank by %
Self	(3) I have many opportunities to learn and develop myself.	49.6%	1
	(5) I derive a great sense of achievement from my work.	45.0%	2
	(14) I can leverage on my knowledge and skills.	43.6%	4
	(11) I get to work on things I am passionate about.	35.2%	5
	(15) I can work with new / the latest technologies.	33.8%	7
	(12) I can exercise my own judgments and decisions on how I do my work.	30.5%	8
	(9) I can meet with new and different challenges every day.	30.2%	9
Others	(4) I can create something of value through my work, that impacts my company and its clients.	44.5%	3
	(8) I can inspire, mentor and develop other IT professionals.	27.2%	12
	(6) I develop close relationships with the varied people I work with.	25.5%	13
	(7) My work benefits my colleagues and users by making their work easier.	24.6%	14
Context	(2) I receive good financial rewards for the effort I have put in.	34.1%	6
	(10) My efforts and contributions to the organization are recognized by supervisors/co-workers	28.7%	10
	(13) My work is appreciated by others.	28.1%	11
	(1) I can make a difference to society.	19.4%	15

[a] N=824 IT professionals

Attitudes towards Online Communication:
An Exploratory Factor Analysis

Nicola Marsden
Heilbronn University
Max-Planck-Str. 39
74081 Heilbronn, Germany
+49-(0)7131-504-565
nicola.marsden@hs-heilbronn.de

ABSTRACT

This paper presents the results of an exploratory factor analysis exploring attitudes of professionals towards online communication. Using items based on the theoretical approaches to scientific study of online communication identified by Walther and Parks [20], an attitude survey was conducted with N=100 professionals regarding their approach to online and face to face communication. The factor analysis yielded three approaches focusing on 1.) media choice, 2.) the hyperpersonal options of online communication, and 3.) social cues in online communication. These can help understand the use of information technology by today's workforce.

Categories and Subject Descriptors

H.1.2 [**Models and Principles**]: User/Machine systems – *human factors, human information processing, software psychology*; H.5.3 [**Information Interfaces and Presentation (e.g. HCI)**]: Group and Organization Interfaces – *asynchronous interaction, collaborative computing, computer-supported cooperative work, evaluation/methodology, synchronous interaction, theory and models, web-based interaction*; K.4.3 [**Computers and Society**]: Organizational Impacts – *computer-supported collaborative work;* K.7.0 [**The Computing Profession**]: General

General Terms

Management, Measurement, Experimentation, Human Factors.

Keywords

attitudes, factor analysis, online collaboration, computer-mediated communication.

1. INTRODUCTION

Communicating online has become normality for today's workforce. Working in the same building or at remote locations and connected through the internet, collaborators cope with numerous challenges. The way people face and cope with these challenges is to some extend influenced by their attitudes towards communicating online. A person's attitude represents the approach he or she takes towards something: Attitudes have affective, cognitive, and behavioral components, they imply feelings, beliefs, and actions.

Take, for example, that someone worries about not being able to establish a friendly relationship if she does not see a person face to face. In this case, "worrying" is the affective component of the attitude, the belief that you have to see somebody face to face to establish a friendly relationship represents the cognitive component, and avoiding having only online communication with a co-worker would be the behavioral component. Thus people's attitudes are a relevant factor in guiding actions, and eliciting attitudes can help understand the use of information technology by today's workforce.

These attitudes do not exist isolated from other attitudes and the overall personality, rather, they are interconnected with an inner logic, offering orientation in the world and continuously integrating the experiences a person makes. They are a basis for everyday understanding, serving functions of explanation and prediction – and can be conceptualized as intuitive or 'subjective' theories [7].

These subjective theories are shaped by a person's experience. But they also shape the experiences a person makes. For example: A person might have the belief that online communication cannot be as personal and close as face-to-face communication. This person will probably try to have face-to-face communication whenever he or she is intending to establish a good relationship with someone. And be cautious when communicating online. This might then lead to this person having better relationships when communicating face-to-face and less personal relationships when communicating online. So in the sense that attitudes guide people's action and their conceptual framework constrains how they make sense of new evidence, subjective theories may lead to self-fulfilling prophecies (cf. [19]). Or, in consequence, choice of media, mode of communication, preferences in collaboration platforms etc. can only be understood if the worker's attitudes are taking into consideration.

To elicit the subjective theories of the workforce towards communicating online, the existing research on computer-mediated communication can provide the groundwork for conceptual exploration. Over the past 30 years, research on communication via computers has developed dramatically and scientific research has taken different approaches to explaining the dynamics of online communication and personal connection [1]. Walther and Parks [20] categorized the different scientific theories which served as a basis for researching computer-mediated communication. Although the number of scientific studies done in the different research traditions has changed over the years, their classification of the different approaches still holds up and yields a fertile ground for exploring subjective theories about online communication.

Their classification is rooted in basic communication constructs, dealing with the way in which communicative cues available in online settings affect communication. Based on this focus of communicative cues, five clusters of theoretical approaches were identified and labeled "cues filtered out", "cues to choose by", "cues filtered in", "cues about us", and "cues bent and twisted".

In eliciting the subjective theories of people collaborating online, these scientific theories are used as a basis. Since the attitudinal structure of laypeople is not expected to be as differentiated as scientific approaches, the two approaches "cues filtered in" and "cues about us, not you and me" shown by Walther and Parks [20] are considered to be too similar to be differentiated by laypersons' subjective theories and will not be differentiated for the purpose of this study. Hence, four approaches have been focused to identify attitudes in users of online communication which are related to scientific theories [6]: cues filtered out; cues to choose by; cues filtered in/cues about us, not you and me; cues bent and twisted. These four approaches are characterized as follows.

Cues filtered out

The basic assumption is that online communication has a deficit compared to face to face communication because nonverbal cues in a face to face conversation cannot be replicated in an online environment. Cues filtered out approaches [2] focus on the cues which are not being transmitted in computer-mediated communication. The basic assumption is that there are certain communicative functions which cannot be accomplished without the signals that accompany physical copresence and proximity. It is thus assumed that face to face interaction is necessary to relate and work together effectively [11]. The ability to monitor one another's attention and availability are critical processes which cannot take place in computer-mediated communication, the exchange is missing social presence [14] and lacking social context cues [8].

Cues to choose by

This approach is based on the notion that there has to be a match between information richness and media richness [4, 5]. The basic assumption is that people choose a medium according to the cues they need. Some types of messages might be conveyed more efficiently in one medium than in another – thus it is important to match the message and the medium. A cue system or bandwidth is taken as a causal property: As bandwidth gets lower, certain aspects of communication are assumed to change. These differences include a decline in civility, coordination, empathy, and friendliness. There is assumed to be an optimal match between the message equivocality or uncertainty and the chosen media such that efficiency and effectiveness is optimal.

Cues filtered in/Cues about us, not you and me

These approaches focus on the fact that online communication brings in new cues which are not available in face to face communication – thus offering more or other ways to communicate. For example, communicators can exchange social information through style (spelling, signature, emoticons etc.) and timing (e.g. night versus day time) of verbal messages online. This line of research has shown that the absence of certain cues can enhance communication because cues present in face to face interaction might actually have negative effects: Physical appearance can lead to negative attitudes towards a person based on the physical attractiveness, markers of taste, age, habitus, signs of out-group-membership etc. Thus the absence of cues in online communication can, under certain circumstances, forge stronger group identities than face to face interaction [15, 16]. Based on the theories of social identity and self-categorization (e.g., [17]) individuals are conceptualized to have multiple layers of self that become relevant depending on which social identity is salient. When personal identities are salient, the person behaves according to the norms, beliefs and standards which correspond to his or her unique identi-ty. When social identities are salient, the behavior is based on the norms of the group with which one is identified. This process is enhanced by online communication that lacks multimedia cues and renders the partners visually anonymous: Under conditions of visual anonymity, people act in ways more normative to the salient group [12, 13, 15]. When pictures or videos are added, these effects diminish: Individuating information conveyed through physical appearance leads to the individuals being evaluated independently and with less group bias [9, 10]. Based on this approach, online communication makes group memberships and social identity more salient and promotes greater group identification.

Cues bent and twisted

Online communication can be even more personal that face to face communication („hyperpersonal"), because in an asynchronous online setting, sender, receiver, channel, and feedback can work together to promote more socially desirable levels of interaction than face to face communication [18]: In online communication, individualizing cues such as appearance, which are necessarily available in face to face interaction are not readily available. The cues available can be manipulated by the sender to customize his or her self-presentation. In asynchronous interactions, the sender can mindfully compose the message, edit and review the content before sending it to the receiver. The focus of all cognitive resources can be on the message construction and the cognitive load can be divided over a longer time than in face to face communication. In combination with these identity optimizing effects, the receiver tends to formulate idealized perceptions of the sender, interpreting the information available in terms of a common identity with the sender. Thus a positive feedback loop can lead to an interaction which is more positive than a face to face interaction might have been.

2. RESEARCH QUESTION

The research question that guided this investigation is: Based on a factor analysis, is there evidence that the attitudinal structure of professionals towards online communication is similar to the scientific theoretical approaches differentiated in this field.

3. METHOD

3.1 Participants and Procedures

The research was conducted in Germany, the questionnaire was completed online by N=100 participants which were professionals in the fields media, public relations, and pedagogy. 631 individual emails had been sent out by the author asking the addressee to participate in the survey, i.e. the response rate was 15,8 %. Data for the current study were collected in the spring of 2012 via online surveys. The online surveys were constructed using web-based data collection software. For the online data collection, possible participants were identified, emailed a link to the survey, and urged to respond.

3.2 Measure

The questionnaire comprised 16 attitudinal items (see appendix). They were constructed based on the four different approaches to computer-mediated communication in order to develop a measurement which reflects attitudes towards online communication based on the four theoretical approaches. For each approach there were four items. All of the measures utilized were Likert-type scales that contained positively- and negatively-formulated items. Participant responses were converted to numerical scores and ranged from 1, indicating "strongly disagree" to 5, indicating "strongly agree". The questionnaire included four questions regarding the participants' online experience and four demographic questions.

3.3 Analysis

Responses to the questionnaire were converted to numerical scores. Negatively phrased questions were inverted such that a positive response always corresponded to a higher numerical value. Underlying dimensions in the attitudes towards online communication were evaluated with exploratory factor analysis. Following principal-components extraction, factors were rotated with Kaiser's varimax criterion. Factor extraction was specified for eigenvalues larger than 1.00.

4. RESULTS

This section begins with a description of the participating population. This is followed by the results of the factor analysis on attitudes towards online and face to face communication.

4.1 Description of the Sample

A total of 100 participants had answered. Of these 42 were female, 53 were male (in the numbers reported here, the difference to 100 always represents the missing data due to the fact that respondents chose to not answer a question). Regarding their age, 11 respondents were 21-30 years old, 16 were 31-40 years old, 34 were 41-50 years old, 27 were 51-60 years old and 10 were older than 60 years.

Of the respondents, 18 had a vocational training, 78 had a University degree. The professional branches represented in the sample are shown in table 1.

Table 1. Respondents' Professional Backgrounds

Professional Background	No. of respondents	%
Business	26	26 %
Social Science/Arts	11	11 %
IT	4	4 %
Pedagogics	26	26 %
Engineering	4	4 %
interdisciplinary	8	8 %
other/no answer	21	21 %

Regarding the items dealing with online communication the results showed that 81 respondents were online every day, 14 were online several times a week. In terms of mobile devices, 49 respondents had a mobile phone which did not allow them to access their emails, 43 had a mobile phone which did allow them to access their emails and 5 did not have a mobile phone at all.

Table 2. Results of the Factor Analysis

Item	extracted communalities	factor		
		1	2	3
D2 Communication via mail or online has many disadvantages compared to face to face communication.	.528			-.644
D3 The main problem regarding online communication is that so much information gets lost – because there is no voice, body language, etc.	.581	.659		
D4 I see quite a few advantages in online communication compared to face to face communication. (inverted)	.579		-.681	
M1 Problems with online communication usually occur when the technology does not match the task – e.g. when you try to brainstorm using email.	.445	.653		
M2 The key to successful online communication: Deciding, whether it is necessary to see one another to solve an issue – and the either call for a meeting or solve the issue online.	.695	.670		
M4 The greater the danger of a misunderstanding, the more important is a face to face talk.	.499	.682		
S1 One of the major problems of online communication is that the social aspects of collaboration get neglected. (inverted)	.577	-.629		
S2 People working together find appropriate ways to socialize, even in online communication.	.611			.760
S3 Online communication in a professional setting offers many options to build up a positive relationship with someone.	.638			.691
S4 When trying to establish a positive relationship with someone online you have to watch out for different things than in face to face communication.	.485	.650		
H1 In international teams, a face to face meeting can actually be negative. It might make sense to only communicate online.	.764		.799	
H2 Online communication can lead to a better understanding and better collaboration than seeing one another face-to-face.	.556		.647	
H3 Online communication can actually improve collaboration in virtual international teams: Because you do not hear and see one another, many problems of face to face meetings take a back seat, e.g. non-stop talkers, misunderstandings due to accents and dialects, being influenced by how someone looks.	.590		.755	
H4 Face to face contact is important for collaboration, because only face to face can you develop a common identity as a team and a true team spirit. (inverted)	.436	-.558		

Letters in front of the item number represent the scientific approach that this item was based on, see "sources" in Appendix.

Regarding the experience with online communication, 8 respondents reported they had no or little experience collaborating online, 84 reported the communication with their colleagues was partially online and partially face to face and 5 reported the majority of their professional communication took place online.

4.2 Factors yielded regarding Attitudes

In constructing the questionnaire the attempt was made to test whether the four different theoretical approaches classified by Walther and Parks [20] can also be found as attitudes towards online communication.

The exploratory factor analysis showed that based on the eigenvalue a solution with four factors had the best fit. Yet these factors did not correspond to the four theoretical approaches to computer-mediated communication. With a cut-off at 0.4 the fourth factor had only one item loading on it: Item M3 "Even with team-member distributed all over the world, you should have face to face meetings to work on complex tasks – the advantage of a face to face meeting justifies the high travel expenses which result from this."

Attempts to find a suitable solution with two, three or five factors did not fulfill the eigenvalue criterion. These analyses showed that two items did not differentiate between the factors: Item M3 had communalities below 0.2 in the two- and three-factor solution and represented a separate factor in the four- and five-factor solution (see above). Item D1 "In general, face to face communication is better than online communication." had communalities below 0.5 in all solutions.

Consequently, items M3 and D1 were excluded from the analysis. The best fit yielded a three-factor solution which is presented in table 2. Considering factor loadings above 0.5 to be salient, each of the remaining 14 items loads on one of the three factors. The rotation was converged in five iterations.

4.3 Correlation of Age and Gender

For age and gender, analyses of variance were used to analyze differences regarding the three factors. The analyses did not yield any significant results.

5. DISCUSSION

The exploratory factor analysis conducted to investigate the structure of professionals attitudes towards online communication showed a three-factor solution having the best fit after items that worked poorly had been removed. In interpreting the factors, it seems they represent the following focus on certain aspects of online communication:

- Factor 1 represents an attitude which focuses on the necessity to make the right choice of media: The loss of (social) information is considered crucial and face to face has a decisive lead over online communication that can not be replicated (item D3, S1, H4). Thus it is important to choose an appropriate mode of communication for the task at hand (item M1, M2, M4) and watch out for different things online and face to face (item S4).

- Factor 2 represents an attitude which focuses on the new chances and advantages of online communication: Face to face communication is considered as something that can actually be negative (H1, D4) and online communication is taken to offer possibilities for communication which are even better than face to face communication (item H2) and can improve communication (item H3).

- Factor 3 represents an attitude which focuses on relationships to others: It is assumed that people working together find appropriate ways to socialize, even in online communication (item S2), that online communication offers many options to build up positive relationships with others (item S3) and the idea that communication via mail or online has many disadvantages is rejected.

While the factors only partially represent the way the items were parceled in sub-scales, they can still be interpreted as representing the theoretical approaches differentiated by Walther and Parks [20]:

- "Cues to choose by" in factor 1, with the attitude which focuses on deficits of online communication and the necessity to make the right choice of media,

- "Cues bent and twisted" in factor 2, with the attitude which focuses on the new chances and advantages of online communication,

- "Cues filtered in"/"Cues about us, not you and me" in factor 3, with the attitude which focuses on relationships to others.

For each factor, the majority of the items loading on it were also developed to describe this attitude. Yet there were also items loading unexpectedly. The subscale developed to represent the "cues filtered out" attitude (item D1-D4) did not yield an independent factor at all, i.e. it seems that the "cues filtered out" approach, which simply focuses on the deficits of online communication, is not one of the participants' attitudinal dimension: Item D1 was left out of the analysis since it did not differentiate between the factors at all. Item D2 loads negatively on factor 3 "cues filtered in"/"cues about us, not you and me" and can be interpreted as challenging the notion that negative communication originates in the media rather than the relationship itself. Item D3 loads on factor 1 "cues to choose by", suggesting that the loss of information like body language or voice seems to be taken as an issue which can be dealt with in terms of media choice. Item D4 was developed as a negatively formulated item representing the attitude that "cues-filtered out" is a problem in online communication. Rather, it turned out to be a building block of the "cues bent and twisted" factor.

The fact that the dimension "cues filtered out" does not directly correspond to a factor in this exploratory factor analysis suggests that the simplistic deficit approach to online communication is not part of the attitudinal structure of professionals. This is interesting because it has been argued that the cues filtered out model has a high face validity and "still rings true for many" [1, p. 57; 5] and thus should be popular as a basis for subjective theories. But it seems there is another parallel between the subjective theories and the scientific approaches: The cues filtered out theories, which were the first ones to attempt to explain computer-mediated communication, have been eclipsed by the other approaches in the scientific literature. Likewise, the attitudinal structure discovered in this study shows that the participants who focused on the deficits always considered these relative to the message being conveyed: Based on the "Cues to choose by" approach represented in factor 1, the deficits of online communication are only considered an issue if there is a mismatch between the complexity of the message and the media richness. The simplistic deficit approach does not seem prevalent in today's workforce's attitudes about online communication any more.

Overall, the attitudinal structures found in this study show that individuals using the same media might differ in the perception of these media. Drawing on the idea that these attitudinal approaches represent subjective theories, they frame the experiences a person has with online communication and guide his or her sensemaking [22] regarding the experiences made communicating online. These approaches can turn into self-fulfilling prophecies, thus they are highly relevant for online communication, e.g. by individuals obtruding their choice of media upon others, withdrawing from online communication or building impressions of others based on their personal approach to online communication rather than other attributes they might have.

6. CONCLUSIONS AND FUTURE WORK

The findings from the exploratory factor analysis with 100 participants show that there are three different attitudinal approaches which people take to online communication: First, a focus on media choice, second, a focus on the hyperpersonal options of online communication, and third, a focus on social cues in online communication. These subjective approaches roughly mirror the scientific approaches that have been used to explain the dynamics of online communication. In employing and designing online communication, these attitudes should be considered: As a basis for sensemaking these attitudinal approaches can influence the communication itself, having an impact on the use and the quality of online communication.

This exploratory factor analysis can only give a first hint at which attitudes might be relevant for successful online communication. Further work needs to be done to confirm these factors and develop an instrument for diagnosing attitudes towards online communication. A valid, reliable and objective measure can serve a basis for researching the correspondence to diversity criteria such as gender, experience or professional background. Further work could also elicit the subjective theories represented by these attitudinal dimensions and implications for the actual online communication could be examined.

7. REFERENCES

[1] Baym, N. K. (2010). *Personal Connection in the Digital Age*. Malden, MA: Polity Press.

[2] Culnan, M. J. & Markus, M. L. (1987). Information technologies, in F.M. Jablin, L.L. Putnam, K.H. Roberts & L.W. Porter (Eds), *Handbook of Organizational Computing: An Interdisciplinary Perspective*. Newbury Park, CA: Sage. 420–43.

[3] Daft, R. L., & Lengel, R. H. (1986). Organizational information requirements, media richness, and structural determinants. *Management Science*, Vol. 32, 554–571.

[4] Daft, R. L., Lengel, R. H., & Trevino, L. K. (1987). Message equivocality, media selection, and manager performance: Implications for information systems. *MIS Quarterly*, Vol. 11, 355–368.

[5] Duthler, K. W. (2006). The Politeness of Requests Made Via Email and Voicemail: Support for the Hyperpersonal Model. *Journal of Computer-Mediated Communication*, Vol. 11, 500-521.

[6] Götz, K. & Marsden, N. (2010). *Soziale Interaktionen im Netz*. In: R. Holten & D. Nittel (Eds.): Theorie und Empirie von E-Learning. Einsatzchancen in Hochschule und Weiterbildung. Bielefeld: Bertelsmann, 81-94.

[7] Groeben, N. & Scheele, B. (2000). Dialogue-hermeneutic Method and the "Research Program Subjective Theories".

[8] Kiesler, S., & Sproull, L. (1992). Group decision making and communication technology. *Organizational Behavior and Human Decision Processes*, Vol. 52, 96-123.

[9] Lea, M., & Spears, R. (1995). Love at first byte? Building personal relationships over computer networks. In J. T. Wood & S. Duck (Eds.), *Under-studied relationships: Off the beaten track*. Thousand Oaks, CA: Sage, 197-233.

[10] Lea, M., Spears, R., & de Groot, D. (2001). Knowing me, knowing you: Anonymity effects on social identity processes within groups. *Personality & Social Psychology Bulletin*, Vol. 27, 526–537.

[11] Nardi, B and Whittaker, S. (2002). *The place of face to face communication in distributed work*. In: Distributed Work: New Research on Working Across Distance Using Technology, P. Hinds and S. Kiesler, Eds. Cambridge, MA: MIT Press, 83-110.

[12] Postmes, T., Spears, R., & Lea, M. (1998). Breaching or building social boundaries? SIDE effects of computer-mediated communication. *Communication Research*, Vol. 25, 689–715.

[13] Postmes, T., Spears, R., Sakhel, K., & de Groot, D. (2001). Social influence in computer-mediated communication: The effects of anonymity on group behavior. *Personality and Social Psychology Bulletin*, Vol. 27, 1243–1254.

[14] Rice, R. E., & Case, D. (1983). Electronic message systems in the university: A description of use and utility. *Journal of Communication*, Vol. 33, No. 4, 131–154.

[15] Spears, R., & Lea, M. (1992). Social influence and the influence of the 'social' in computer-mediated communication. In M. Lea (Ed.), *Contexts of computer-mediated communication*. New York, NY: Harvester Wheatsheaf, 30–65.

[16] Spears, R., & Lea, M. (1994). Panacea or panopticum? The hidden power of computer-mediated communication. *Communication Research*, 21, 427–459.

[17] Turner, J. C., Hogg, M. A., Oakes, P. J., Reicher, S. D., & Wetherell, M. S. (1987). *Rediscovering the social group: A self-categorization theory*. Oxford, UK: Blackwell.

[18] Walther, J. B. (1996) Computer-Mediated Communication: Impersonal, Interpersonal, and Hyperpersonal Interaction. *Communication Research*, Vol. 23, 3-43.

[19] Walther, J. B. & Bazarova, N. N. (2007), Misattribution in Virtual Groups: The Effects of Member Distribution on Self-Serving Bias and Partner Blame. *Human Communication Research*, Vol. 33, 1-26.

[20] Walther, J. B. & Parks, M. R. (2002). Cues filtered out, cues filtered in computer-mediated communication and relationships. In M. L. Knapp & J. A. Daly (Eds.), *Handbook of interpersonal communication* (3rd edition). Thousand Oaks, CA: Sage, 529-563.

[21] Walther, J. B., Gay, G. & Hancock, J. T. (2005). How Do Communication and Technology Researchers Study the Internet? *Journal of Communication*, Vol. 55, No. 3, 632–657.

[22] Weick, Karl (1995). *Sensemaking in Organizations*. Thousand Oaks: Sage.

Forum Qualitative Social Research, Vol. 1., No. 2, Art. 10. http://nbn-resolving.de/urn:nbn:de:0114-fqs0002105.

APPENDIX

Items were administered in German, translated by the author.

	Item	Sources
D1	In general, face to face communication is better than online communication.	Self-developed items based on the "Cues filtered-out" approach by Walther and Parks [20] - "D" in front of item number is short for "deficit approach"
D2	Communication via mail or online has many disadvantages compared to face to face communication.	
D3	The main problem regarding online communication is that so much information gets lost – because there is no voice, body language etc.	
D4neg	I see quite a few advantages in online communication compared to face to face communication.	
M1	Problem with online communication usually occur when the technology does not match the task – e.g. when you try to brainstorm using email.	Self-developed based on the "Cues to choose by" approach by Walther and Parks [20] – "M" in front of item number is short for "media choice approach"
M2	The key to successful online communication: Deciding, whether it is necessary to see one another to solve an issue – and the either call for a meeting or solve the issue online.	
M3	Even with team-member distributed all over the world, you should have face to face meetings to work on complex tasks – the advantage of a face to face meeting justifies the high travel expenses which result from this.	
M4	The greater the danger of a misunderstanding, the more important is a face to face talk.	
S1neg	One of the major problems of online communication is that the social aspects of collaboration get neglected.	Self-developed based on the "Cues filtered in" and "Cues about us, not you and me" approaches by Walther and Parks [20] – "S" in front of item number is short for "social information processing approach"
S2	People working together find appropriate ways to socialize, even in online communication.	
S3	Online communication in a professional setting offers many options to build up a positive relationship with someone.	
S4	When trying to establish a positive relationship with someone online you have to watch out for different things than in face to face communication.	
H1	In international teams, a face to face meeting can actually be negative. It might make sense to only communicate online.	Self-developed based on the "Cues bent and twisted" approach by Walther and Parks [20] – "H" in front of item number is short for "hyperpersonal perspective"
H2	Online communication can lead to a better understanding and better collaboration than seeing one another face-to-face.	
H3	Online communication can actually improve collaboration in virtual international teams: Because you do not hear and see one another, many problems of face to face meetings take a back seat, e.g. non-stop talkers, misunderstandings due to accents and dialects, being influenced by how someone looks.	
H4neg	Face to face contact is important for collaboration, because only face to face can you develop a common identity as a team and a true team spirit.	

Letters in front of the item number represent the scientific approach that this item was based on, see last column.
"neg" means that this item is formulated negatively.

An Online Recommendation System for E-commerce Based on Apache Mahout Framework

Mr. Sachin Walunj
Information Technology Department
Sinhgad College of engineering, vadgaon, pune, India
[1]sachinwalunj2008@gmail.com

Mr.Kishor Sadafale
Information Technology Department
Sinhgad College of engineering, vadgaon, pune, India
[2]kishor_sadafale@yahoo.com

ABSTRACT

Selecting a foundational platform is an important step in developing recommender systems for personal, research, or commercial purposes. This can be done in many different ways the platform may be developed from the ground up, an existing recommender engine may be contracted (OracleAS Personalization), code libraries can be adapted, or a platform may be selected and tailored to suit (LensKit, MymediaLite, Apache Mahout, etc.). In some cases, a combination of these approaches will be employed. For E-commerce projects, and particularly in the E-commerce website t, the ideal situation is to find an open-source platform with many active contributors that provides a rich and varied set of recommender system functions that meets all or most of the baseline development requirements. Short of finding this ideal solution, some minor customization to an already existing system may be the best approach to meet the specific development requirements. Various libraries have been released to support the development of recommender systems for some time, but it is only relatively recently that larger scale, open-source platforms have become readily available. In the context of such platforms, evaluation tools are important both to verify and validate baseline platform functionality, as well as to provide support for testing new techniques and approaches developed on top of the platform. Apache Mahout as an enabling platform for research and have faced both of these issues in employing it as part of work in collaborative filtering recommenders.

Categories and Subject Descriptors

H.3.3 [**Information Storage and Retrieval**]: Information Search and Retrieval - *Information Filtering*

General Terms

Algorithms, Performance, Experimentation

Keywords

Personalized recommendation, apache mahout framework, recommendation system, collaborative filtering.

1. INTRODUCTION

In everyday life, people rely on recommendations from other people by spoken words, reference letters, and news reports from news media, general surveys, travel guides, and so forth. Recommender systems assist and augment this natural social process to help people sift through available books, articles, webpages, movies, music, restaurants, jokes, grocery products, and so forth to find the most interesting and valuable information for them[1][2]. The developers of one of the first recommender systems, Tapestry (other earlier recommendation systems include rule-based recommenders and user-customization), coined the phrase "collaborative filtering (CF)," which has been widely adopted regardless of the facts that recommenders may not explicitly collaborate with recipients and recommendations may suggest particularly interesting items, in addition to indicating those that should be filtered out.

Collaborative Filtering

Collaborative filtering (CF) is a technique, popularized by Amazon and others, that uses user information such as ratings, clicks, and purchases to provide recommendations to other site users. CF is often used to recommend consumer items such as books, music, and movies, but it is also used in other applications where multiple actors need to collaborate to narrow down data. CF in action on Amazon[3], as shown in Fig.1

Figure 1. Example of collaborative filter on Amazon

1. **User-based**: Recommend items by finding similar users. This is often harder to scale because of the dynamic nature of users.
2. **Item-based**: Calculate similarity between items and make recommendations. Items usually don't change much, so this often can be computed offline.
3. **Slope-One**: A very fast and simple item-based recommendation approach applicable when users have given ratings (and not just Boolean preferences).
4. **Model-based**: Provide recommendations based on developing a model of users and their ratings.

All CF approaches end up calculating a notion of similarity between users and their rated items. There are many ways to compute similarity, and most CF systems allow you to plug in different measures so that you can determine which one works best for your data [3].

Collaborative Filtering algorithm is a classic personalized recommendation algorithm; it's widely used in many commercial recommender systems. Collaborative filtering algorithm is an algorithm based on the following assumptions idea, People have similar preferences and interests their preferences and interests are stable we can predict their choice according to their past preferences. Because of the above assumptions, the collaborative filtering algorithm is based on the comparison of one user's behavior with other user's behavior, to find his nearest neighbors, and according to his neighbor's interests or preferences to predict his interests or preferences.

The first step of collaborative filtering algorithm is to obtain the users history profile, which can be represented as a ratings matrix with each entry the rate of a user given to an item. A ratings matrix consists of a table where each row represents a user, each column represents a specific product, and the number at the intersection of a row and a column represents the user's rating value. The absence of a rating score at this intersection indicates that user has not yet rated the item. Owing to the existence problem of sparse scoring, use the list to replace the matrix. The second step is to calculate the similarity between users and find their nearest neighbors. There are many similarity measure methods. The Pearson correlation coefficient is the most widely used and served as a benchmark for CF. Generally use the Cosine similarity measure method[4][5].

2. CHARACTERISTICS AND CHALLENGES OF COLLABORATIVE FILTERING

2.1 Data Sparsity

In practice, many commercial recommender systems are based on large datasets. As a result, the user-item matrix used for collaborative filtering could be extremely large and sparse, which brings about the challenges in the performances of the recommendation.

One typical problem caused by the data sparsity is the cold start problem. As collaborative filtering methods recommend items based on users' past preferences, new users will need to rate sufficient number of items to enable the system to capture their preferences accurately and thus provides reliable recommendations.

Similarly, new items also have the same problem. When new items are added to system, they need to be rated by substantial number of users before they could be recommended to users who have similar tastes with the ones rated them. The new item problem does not limit the content-based recommendation, because the recommendation of an item is based on its discrete set of descriptive qualities rather than its ratings[5].

2.2 Scalability

When numbers of existing users and items grow tremendously, traditional CF algorithms will suffer serious scalability problems, with computational resources going beyond practical or acceptable levels. For example, with tens of millions of customer and millions of distinct catalog items, a CF algorithm with the complexity is already too large. As well, many systems need to react immediately to online requirements and make recommendations for all users regardless of their purchases and ratings history, which demands a high scalability of a CF system.

2.3 Synonyms

Synonymy refers to the tendency of a number of the same or very similar items to have different names or entries. Most recommender systems are unable to discover this latent association and thus treat these products differently For example, the seemingly different items "children movie" and "children film" are actually referring to the same item. Indeed, the degree of variability in descriptive term usage is greater than commonly suspected. The prevalence of synonyms decreases the recommendation performance of CF systems. Topic modeling (like the Latent Dirichlet Allocation technique) could solve this by group different words belonging to the same topic.

2.4 Grey Sheep

Grey sheep refers to the users whose opinions do not consistently agree or disagree with any group of people and thus do not benefit from collaborative filtering. Black sheep are the opposite group whose idiosyncratic tastes make recommendations nearly impossible. Although this is a failure of the recommender system, non-electronic recommenders also have great problems in these cases, so black sheep is an acceptable failure.

2.5 Shilling attacks

In a recommendation system where everyone can give the ratings, people may give lots of positive ratings for their own items and negative ratings for their competitors. It is often necessary for the collaborative filtering systems to introduce precautions to discourage such kind of manipulations.

2.6 Diversity

Collaborative filters are expected to increase diversity because they help us discover new products among myriad choices. Some algorithms, however, may unintentionally do the opposite. Because collaborative filters recommend products based on sales or ratings, they cannot usually recommend products with limited historical data. This creates a rich-get-richer effect for popular products, leading to less diversity. A Wharton study details this phenomenon and several ideas which may promote diversity in collaborative filtering recommendations.

3. APACHE MAHOUT SOLUTION

To support research in collaborative filtering, several recommender system platforms were surveyed, including LensKit, easyrec5, and MymediaLite. Apache Mahout provides many of the desired characteristics required for a recommender development workbench platform. Mahout is a production-level, open-source, system and consists of a wide range of applications that are useful for a recommender system developer collaborative filtering algorithms, data clustering, and data classification. Mahout is also highly scalable and is able to support distributed processing of large data sets across clusters of computers using Hadoop. Mahout recommenders support various similarity and neighborhood formation calculations, recommendation prediction algorithms include user-based, item-based, Slope-One and Singular Value Decomposition (SVD), and it also incorporates Root Mean Squared Error (RMSE) and Mean Absolute Error (MAE) evaluation methods. Mahout is readily extensible and provides a wide range of Java classes for customization. As an open-source project, the Mahout developer/contributor community is very active; the Mahout wiki also provides a list of developers and a list of websites that have implemented Mahout[4][7].

3.1 Taste Architecture:

Taste is the Recommender System part of Mahout and it provides a very consistent and flexible collaborative filtering engine. It supports the user-based, item-based and Slope-one recommender systems. It can be easily modified in due to its well-structured modules abstractions. The package defines the following interfaces:
1. DataModel
2. UserSimilarity and ItemSimilarity
3. UserNeighborhood
4. Recommender

With these interfaces, it's possible to adapt the framework to read different types of data, personalize your recommendation or even create new recommendation methods. Below is presented a figure with Taste's architecture.

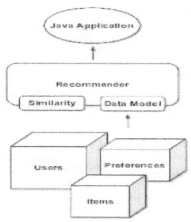

Figure 2. Taste Architecture

The User Similarity and Item Similarity abstractions are here represented by the box named "Similarity". These interfaces are responsible for calculating the similarity between a pair of users or items. Their function usually returns a value from 0 to 1 indicating the level of resemblance, being 1 the most similar possible. Through the DataModel interface is made the access to the data set. It is possible to retrieve and store the data from databases or from filesystems (MySQLJDBCDataModel and FileDataModel respectively). The functions developed in this interface are used by the Similarity abstraction to help computing the similarity.

The main interface in Taste is Recommender. It is responsible for actually making the recommendations to the user by comparing items or by determining users with similar taste (item-based and user-based techniques). The Recommenderaccess the similarity interface and uses its functions to compare a pair of users or items. It then collect the highest similarity values to offer as recommendations.

The UserNeighborhood is an assistant interface to help defining the neighborhood into the User-Based recommendation technique.

It is known that for greater data sets the item-based technique provides better results. For that, many companies choose to use this approach, such as Amazon. With the Mahout framework it's not different; the item-based method generally runs faster and provides more accurate recommendation.

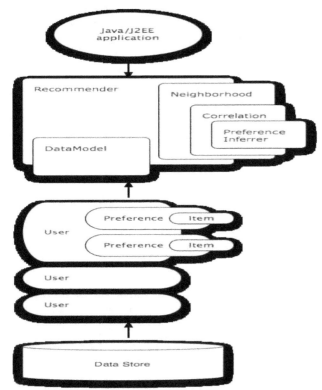

Figure 3. Mahout Architecture

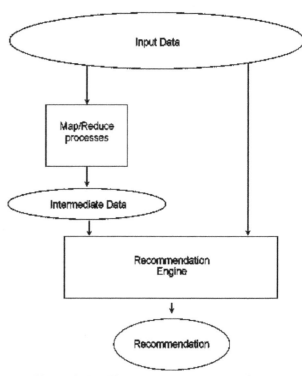

Figure 4. Intelligent Recommendation System

4. AN INTELLIGENT RECOMMENDATION SYSTEM

The main purpose of a recommendation engine is to make inferences on existing data to show relationships between objects. Objects can be many things, including users, items, products, and so on. Relationships provide a degree of likeness or belonging between objects. For example, relationships can represent ratings of how much a user likes an item (scalar), or indicate if a user bookmarked a particular page (binary).

To make a recommendation, recommendation engines perform several steps to mine the data. Initially, begin with input data that represents the objects as well as their relationships. Input data consists of object identifiers and the relationships to other objects. Figure shows this at a high level.

Consider the ratings users give to items. Using this input data, a recommendation engine computes a similarity between objects. Computing the similarity between objects can take a great deal of time depending on the size of the data or the particular algorithm. Distributed algorithms such as Apache Hadoop can be used to parallelize the computation of the similarities. There are different types of algorithms to compute similarities. Finally, using the similarity information, the recommendation engine can make recommendation requests based on the parameters requested.

It could be that believed recommendation engines were helpful, but stayed away because thought they were too complicated to try. The recommendation engine domain is in fact large and can be very complex.

Collaborative filtering is an easy and popular technique. It's easy because customers do the important work they drive the criteria of what to highlight. Collaborative filtering analyzes ratings from other users or items to make recommendations. There are two approaches within collaborative filtering: the main difference between them lies in the ability of each to scale as the number of users in the system grows

4.1 User-based recommendation

This type of recommendation builds similarities between users by looking at the commonalities of the items rated by each user.

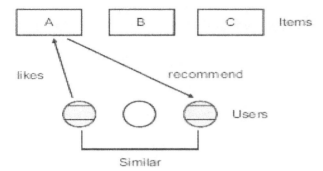

Figure 5. User –based recommendation

If a user likes item A, then the same item can be recommended to other users who are similar to user A. For example, if the items are courses, two users could be considered very similar if they both took the same courses. In the other extreme, their similarity would be low if they did not take any similar course. To make recommendations, the algorithms rely on the ratings that similar users gave to those courses not taken by the user. This recommendation is the most basic one however, its main limitation is that in order to generate the similarities, it needs to compare each user to every other user. This is acceptable for an application with a low number of users, but if the number of users increases, the time to perform this evaluation increases exponentially[9].

4.2 Item-based recommendation

Item-based recommendation, on the other hand, begins by looking at the items that are associated with the user.

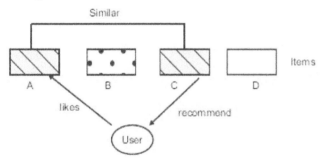

Figure 6. Item-based recommendation

If items A and C are highly similar and a user likes item A, then item C is recommended to the user. For each item associated with the user, the algorithm computes how similar it is to the other items in the collection to build the list of recommendations. In order to determine how likely the user is to like a recommended item, the algorithm looks at the ratings that the user has given to the item and gives a weighted rating to each recommended item. The main issue with item-based recommendation is that it needs to build a similarity index for every available item. Changes in the items, however, are less frequent than changes in users and, therefore, it is feasible with this type of recommendation to pre-compute similarities offline and update them at specific periods [9].

5. BUILDING A RECOMMENDATION ENGINE

Mahout currently provides tools for building a recommendation engine through the Taste library a fast and flexible engine for CF. Taste supports both user-based and item-based recommendations and comes with many choices for making recommendations, as well as interfaces for your own. Taste consists of five primary components that work with Users, Items and Preferences:

1. DataModel: Storage for Users, Items, and Preferences
2. UserSimilarity:Interface defining the similarity between two users
3. ItemSimilarity: Interface defining the similarity between two items
4. Recommender:Interface for providing recommendations
5. UserNeighborhood:Interface for computing a neighborhood of similar users that can then be used by the Recommenders

These components and their implementations make it possible to build out complex recommendation systems for either real-time-based recommendations or offline recommendations. Real-time-based recommendations often can handle only a few thousand users, whereas offline recommendations can scale much higher. Taste even comes with tools for leveraging Hadoop to calculate recommendations offline. In many cases, this is a reasonable approach that allows to meet the demands of a large system with a lot of users, items, and preferences[4][8].

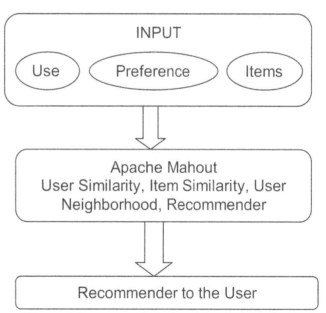

Figure 7. Recommendation engine using apache Mahout

7. CONCLUSION

Online businesses are working very hard to increase their customer bases by providing competitive prices, products and services. In this effort, recommendation systems can be an important means of increasing sales and information awareness among customers. Item based recommendation provides the better result than the user based recommendation. The successful implementation of a mahout framework provided flexibility in using pre-existing algorithms. It solved the problem of scalability by using the hadoop platform because it is built on the hadoop framework. Apache mahout offers testimony that a recommendation system provides customizable recommendations enable online companies to perform business more effectively.

8. REFERENCES

[1] Carlos E. Seminario,DavidC.Wilson. "Case study evaluation of mahout as a recommender platform".ACM 2012.

[2] Zhi-Dan Zhao, Ming-Sheng Shang."User-based Collaborative-Filtering Recommendation Algorithm on Hadoop". third International conference on knowledge Discovery and data mining 2012.

[3] Greg Linden, Brent Smith, and Jeremy York," Amazon.com Recommendations Item-to-Item Collaborative Filtering"Published by the IEEE Computer Society 1089-7801/03/$17.00©2003.

[4] RuiMaximoEsteves, ChunmingRong."Using Mahout for clustering Wikipedia's latest articles- A comparison between k-means and fuzzy c-means" third international conference on cloud computing Technology and science 'In the cloud 2011.

[5] C. Desrosiers and G. Karypis. "A comprehensive survey of neighborhood-based recommendations methods". In F. Ricci, L. Rokach, B. Shapira, and P. B. Kantor,editors, Recommender Systems Handbook. Springer, 2011.

[6] M. D. Ekstrand, M. Ludwig, J. A. Konnstan, and J. T. Riedl. "Rethinking the recommender research ecosystem: Reproducibility, openness, and lenskit". In Proceedings of the 5th ACM Recommender Systems Conference (RecSys '11), October 2011.

[7] M. Ge, C. Delgado-Battenfeld, and D. Jannach. "Beyond accuracy: Evaluating recommender systems by coverage and serendipity". In Proceedings of the 4th ACM Recommender Systems Conference (RecSys '10), September 2010.

[8] https://cwiki.apache.org/MAHOUT/recommender-documentation.html

[9] SatnamAlag, "Collective Intelligence In Action", Manning Publications Co., first edition, 2009.

[10] Shine Ge, Xinyang Gen "An SVD-based Collaborative Filtering Approach toAlleviate Cold-Start Problems",In 2012 9th International Conference on Fuzzy Systems and Knowledge Discovery (FSKD 2012)

[11] Min Xiao, BingjieYan,"Collaborative filtering recommendation algorithm based on shift of users' preferences" IEEE 2010.

[12] SutheeraPuntheeranurak, ThanutChaiwitooanukool,"An Item-based Collaborative Filtering Method using Item-based Hybrid Similarity"IEEE 2011.

Team Leaders' Perceptions in the Renewing of Software Production Process

Pasi Virtanen
Tampere University of Technology
Po Box 541
FIN-33101 Tampere, Finland
+358-50-3366400
pasi.virtanen@tut.fi

ABSTRACT

A contemporary software company is often based on mergers and acquisitions resulting in a number of organizational cultures and ways of working within the mother company. The inconsistencies between teams cause friction and ineffectiveness adding to the need of improve one's competitiveness in the ever toughening competitive situation. The streamlining of the operation is often felt the strongest on the operative level. The aim of this paper is to identify the roles and functions of team leaders in implementing a procedural change in software producing business enterprise. The study offers some solutions to the challenges that team leaders face when implementing change in their teams. Here change means new ways of working, including a change of used programming language. This study is a qualitative case study of a large software company that is renewing its software development processes towards component-based-software-engineering (CBSE). The research observes the phenomenon from a software engineering management point of view, and thus combines management with leadership issues.

Categories and Subject Descriptors

D.2.9 [**Productivity; Programming teams**]

General Terms

Management, Human Factors, Standardization.

Keywords

Organizational change, team leaders, software production development

1. INTRODUCTION

Some organizations still use the same approach to working that was used when the IT sector was first formed. The approach was derived from the then prevailing conditions, i. e. based on the way an industrial enterprise was managed [26]. In order to maintain their sustainability, IT businesses need to rethink their practices [23, 39]. In contemporary business, software companies are often the result of the merger of two or more companies [22, 27, 46]. Mergers take place for a number of reasons: to acquire the products of a company, to acquire channels through which a

company operates, or to acquire the technology of a company, to name just three. Despite the change in ownership, the operations acquired often remain the same, as do the teams. As a result, the management of the company will face many future challenges, especially when making changes at an organizational level.

Management in the IT sector has to deal with a shift in the business logic. The majority of software companies are currently leveraging their operations towards a service-centered ideology from the old product-oriented approach [3]. The organizations need to draw more from innovation and creative uses of information technology to create holistic solutions for their customers' needs. This is a positive development from the customer's and market's point of view [10]. These developments, however, present the challenge of how to renew the processes and business models of the companies. The challenges vary from implications for the career paths of the IT workforce and skills and knowledge, to human resource strategies.

Input from teams and team leaders is essential for the success of the change process [8]. The team leaders are both the object and the subject of the change. The team leaders must balance the needs and requirements of their superiors with those of their subordinates. Top management expects obedience and the swift implementation of the renewals according to their instructions, but at the same time they also expect the performance and the level of operation with the projects to be maintained. The team members, on the other hand, want improvements in the way tasks are carried out and in the working environment. The team leaders are between the rock and a hard place trying to comply with both parties.

The research question: "What is the role of team leaders in the renewal of a software production process?" is studied through answering the questions: what does the management expect from team leaders? What does the team expect from its leader? How do team leaders place themselves into the equation?

This paper is a case-based qualitative study that identifies the challenges team leaders face during the change process of a software company. The case is a multi-site software and services producing company. The study was carried out in one of the divisions of the company that comprised multiple business units. In total, 44 interviews were carried out in the study. By mirroring these challenges with the literature, suggestions can be drawn on how to cope with the challenges. The paper contributes to both information system development and software process improvement field by bringing together personnel-related challenges in a technical research context.

The next chapter presents the theoretical background. The blurry borders between the context and the phenomenon itself are highlighted by the paper's order of discussion. The case study and the research methods are presented in section three. The paper concludes with the results of the study and a summary of the points raised.

2. THE RESEARCH CONTEXT AND THEORETICAL INSIGHTS

2.1 Component Based Software Engineering

An IT company's productivity is based on the effectiveness of its software (SW) development teams and processes. In several studies, component based software engineering (CBSE) has been acknowledged to be a way to increase the effectiveness of SW development, as it decreases the amount of overlapping work and procedural redundancy [see e.g. 35]. The overlap is caused by the fact that each team programs more or less similar features in their products. In CBSE, the software features are components that are connected to each other through different kinds of interfaces.

The components are stored in a repository by their maker. The components are freely sought and acquired from the repository according to the needs of SW design and production.

CBSE is organized into centralized and decentralized component production. Centralized component production means that component creation and its use are two separate things [16, 25]. In centralized component production, a specialized unit is responsible for the creation and production of components for SW-teams to use. In decentralized component production, anyone can be a component creator, producer, or user. The organization of component production can, however, also be a hybrid of both centralized and decentralized component production, having features from both modes [25]. Interaction and communication between the people developing and using reusable software are crucial factors in enabling the componentization in any chosen model [40].

CBSE is more easily adopted in companies that are involved in the SW product business where the production process remains largely the same as opposed to enterprise solutions where the product is tailored according to the needs of the customer [31]. The change towards CBSE is not only a technical problem; it is also a managerial problem, as it involves the sharing of one's own code and the use of the code of others. On the technical side, the definition of what makes a component and the repository are relatively easy to accomplish. To alter the mindset of the people involved may prove to be trickier. Team leaders are in the position to make this change happen [9, 17, 49].

CBSE is a challenging organizational change: a third of all CBSE cases fail [36]. CBSE requires proper planning and adjustments according to the objectives set to the initiative and to the needs of teams involved [36]. Sometimes, CBSE projects fail because the projects are made to fit with existing structures without enough motivation and technical training [18]. At other times, pressure from customers and projects with financial objectives take attention away from the CBSE initiative and the project fails.

2.2 Change Management

Change management, as a subject, is a well-studied field [6, 7, 38, 42]. There are those who claim that the phenomenon should be studied as a transformation rather than as a mere change in

ways of working [2]. Kotter [28] describes eight reasons for the failure of change (Figure 1). Their negations, the avoidance of mentioned features, show how to avoid the failure. The list of features is used here to illuminate the complexity of change.

1.	Satisfaction to prevailing situation
2.	Under-powered change sponsors
3.	Vision underestimated
4.	Vision not sufficiently communicated
5.	Obstacles in the vision's way
6.	No short term successes
7.	Change gets claimed a success too soon
8.	Change not embedded in the organizational culture

Figure 1. Kotter's Eight Change Preventing Factors

According to Kotter [28], management needs to first make the organization understand and accept the necessity of the change. The are many managerial skills needed in successful change management [5]. Management must make the rest of the organization see a better future with the advanced change. Management must point out the threats caused by an ill-prepared future and show that, with precautions, these risks can be avoided.

To plan countermeasures for side effects such as self-interests or a lack of willingness, the change promoters should first assess the resistance they are likely to meet [30]. The organization then needs a counterweight against any resistance to change. The team promoting the change must be powerful enough to make decisions and must be supported by top management [28].

Management must have a vision of the new operation, and this vision must be communicated repeatedly and effectively to the organization. The vision gives the change a goal. Without a vision, the change amounts to merely a set of separate actions that are all pulling the operation in multiple directions. These separate actions create confusion and disorder. When the whole organization agrees to the vision, the change is easier to direct and control. A lack of vision, therefore, is a threat to successful change [29, 41], and the power of a well-formulated vision should not be underestimated.

Even the best visions are no good if the employees cannot see them [33]. Communication of the vision must, therefore, be delivered to employees via multiple channels and at multiple levels. One common communication-related problem is that different individuals interpret the communication differently. The human mind makes its own interpretation and assumptions of the communications it receives [50].

If the organizational structure of the organization hinders the development, it must be renewed. The obstacles to development may be psychological or physical. Structures are the easiest obstacles to deal with. To deal with mental obstacles, more time and effort are required [34].

Change needs short-term motivation. Successes are needed to show that the change is do-able. Successful pilot projects can be used as testimonials to motivate the rest of the organization. At the same time, these success stories can also be used to silence opposition to the change. A pilot project must have three features: it must be known, it must be true, and it must be related to the change. However important the short-term successes are, it is crucial that the final success is not declared prematurely. The closest thing to last phase of the change is when "business as usual" is the new way of doing things.

2.3 The Role of Middle Management

The team leaders are the middle managers, and as such they are the interface where the strategic level converges with the operational level [15]. One of the tasks of team leaders is to implement strategy [9]. The team leaders are responsible for four types of activity: committing to the change, assisting others through the change, implementing change related procedures in their teams, and keeping the business going [4]. Despite the importance of middle management, there seems to be little research concerning their role [4].

One of the tasks of the team leaders is to implement the strategy in the teams in order to meet the required objectives. This places the team leaders into the role of change intermediaries. They are the subject implementing the change onto their subordinates but also the object for the change as far as they themselves are concerned [4]. The team leaders, knowing their teams' potential, assess the capabilities of their teams. Team leaders know their peers, and thus they operate as informants of the organizational knowledge. The team leaders encourage and promote an attitude of wisdom (willingness to search for and share knowledge) that is required to succeed [19]. This responds to the requirement of having experienced staff implementing the change [37], as experience means insightfulness and wisdom. Social interaction enhances knowledge sharing between units [43]. Social interaction that promotes trust and reduces uncertainty is needed when creating an attitude of wisdom. Social interaction is vital when introducing CBSE, as it gets people to share knowledge and components. Well-executed, inter-unit information flows benefit innovativeness [44] and efficiency in project completion times [18]. The opposite of this may exist when teams are overly independent or physically dispersed. In such cases, they may compete with each other [Lynex & Layzell according to 32]. This may lead to a proprietary view of the components and the code.

If the team leaders were included in the strategy formation, their expertise would aid achieving the goals [47]. This is in contradiction to the arguments that claim that if the strategy is exposed to managers whose work will be affected negatively, it may cause conflicts [47]. The mind-set suggesting that the strategy should be kept vague fits better with the more traditional way of managing. In such bureaucratic environments, middle management is more dissatisfied with the operation [45]. Individual situations are to be assessed case-specifically, but in general it seems that benefits of including the middle management in strategy work outweigh possible negative outcomes. Increased visibility is advocated widely in the management literature. Managers that are skilled in a participative management style are less likely to resist the change, as they feel more assured in the situation [13]. This is, however, a culture-related issue.

Knowledge is appreciated as a critical element for a successful organization [see e. g. 18]. It is often a problem when employees are not aware of the knowledge of an organization. The creation of new ideas would be easier if existing knowledge could be applied and iterated onward [20, 21]. Considering the objectives for information flows, the team leaders have a central role in achieving the goals and making the change happen. Their role is to guide and monitor the actual process improvement.

3. THE CASE COMPANY AND THE RESEARCH METHODS

3.1 The Case Company

The case company is a large software company operating in business-to-business markets [24, 27]. It is a supplier of complex ICT solutions. Due to the company's acquisitions and mergers, the operation is based on 50 - 60 independent teams located at eight sites. The teams differ in many ways: organizational backgrounds and culture, procedures and processes, technologies used, products and customers.

Each team is responsible for its own software development, production, and sales. Thus, the teams are doing overlapping work that causes extra costs. The company reviewed its software development process to eliminate redundancies and to improve productivity. To accomplish this, the full use of the organizational knowledge is needed. The information flows must be improved and closer collaboration between teams and individuals throughout the organization is a necessity. The key persons to accomplish these tasks are the team leaders.

The case company made a decision to harmonize its software production and to improve the software development processes. They aimed to tackle the problem by implementing decentralized CBSE. This meant that in addition to their routines, teams were required to identify potential components, i.e. products or features that could be used by other teams. As the team leaders have the best overview of what is really going on, they are in a centric role in scouting for suitable component candidates. For support, the management formed a team, the architect group, of professionals to act as change agents and promoters. When approved as a component, a feature is stored in a component repository on the company's intranet. In the repository, components are accessible for the whole organization.

The organizational structure did not support the interactions componentization requires, as the company had earlier been a project-based one. The main challenge was to transform the organization into a more holistic thinking SW development oriented process. The products had been programmed on Java, Progress, VB6, X-language (own design) and Microsoft tools, on platforms including Java/Oracle. To make component making easier in the division, the management decided to use unified technology which was .NET and C#. The technology chosen was already used by a few of the teams, but for most it was new.

3.2 Research Methods

The object of this qualitative case study [12, 48] is a software company. Theme interviews were used to study the renewal of the software production processes of the company. The interviews were recorded and transcribed as detailed interview data. The interview data were then analyzed by thematization to form a picture of the events. The themes were created by using both theoretically driven categories and categories generated from the data [1]. The themes under which the data were classified were identified from the success factors listed in the literature [14, 37]. The themes included phrases such as *software development*, *project management*, and *resource allocation*. Having found confirmation or falsification for the success factors, the contents of the findings were assessed. Based on the assessments, interpretations of their meaning were made.

The organization appointed the interviewees; 44 interviews were conducted. Because the focus of the study was on the team leaders' role, the majority of the interviewees were from this group. Top managers and the whole architect team were among the interviewees in order to lift the interviews off the operational level and also to shed light onto the expectations laid upon the team leaders (see Table 1). The interviewees were from various hierarchical levels that also included programmers and sales persons in addition to the previously mentioned groups, to give a comprehensive picture of the phenomenon and to triangulate the findings. The interviewees were assured of their anonymity for reasons of confidentiality.

Table 1. Summary of the interview data

Interviewees	Architects	Management	Team leaders	Programmers	Other	Total
Site A		2	2		1	5
Site B	3	1	4	1	1	10
Site C			4	4		8
Site D		1	2			3
Site E	2	1	1	4	2	10
Site F	1		1			2
Site G	2		1		1	4
Site H			2			2
Total	8	5	17	9	5	44

The architect team that comprised six persons and top management were interviewed to record their views on and their expectations of the change process. Seventeen team/unit leaders were also interviewed. Some were interviewed twice with temporal intervals. Furthermore, nine programmers and sales persons were interviewed to get more insight but also to see whether their views would support the findings.

4. EMPIRICAL FINDINGS

4.1 Expectations of the Management

The team leaders get their instructions from the branch manager who is second in seniority only to the managing director. The team leaders have the responsibility of organizing the work of their team. Most of the time, the task in hand is a specific-customer project based on a certain type of technology. The management expected the team leaders to carry out their plans and to also carry on with the projects that were on going:

> [..] basically, they [team leaders] work as they have worked up until now, they just have to implement it. It just has to be prioritized high. [..] our highest BU-executive said that this is so important, that it will be coerced if nothing else works. (Architect 1)

The management's instructions to the team leaders were clear: a said number of components must be produced according to the specific guidelines, in the given time. The team leaders were to suggest components from their team to the architect group that approved the components entered in the repository. Later the components were to be added to the repository in a more independent manner. The team leaders should regularly check the repository for components that they could use in their projects. The objectives were shared throughout the organization, and the objectives were expected to be met. Management support for the change remained minimal.

> [..] there is no extra motivation or resources [..] the target number of components is recorded in the team leaders' objectives for the year and they are considered achievable. [..] is not combined to sanctions nor rewards. (Branch manager)

The team leader is a communicator of the change whose task is to inform the team about the expectations of the management. Sometimes, there was a conflict of interest that needed to be dealt with. The architect team was optimistic about solving the conflicting situation because the team leaders were regarded as professionals with an understanding of the proceedings. However, sometimes there was still a choice that had to be made between the customer project and the change initiative.

> [..] componentization is a standard issue in the team meetings. Its meaning is communicated from the team's point of view [..] Problem is that they have another model embedded in their minds [..] intelligent people understand the justifications [..] the short term choice of rather make the money [..] (Architect 2)

The real motivation, besides learning opportunities, was discussed. For example, are compensations needed? In addition to contemplating the obvious monetary gratification for the compliant, the architect group had to also take reluctance into account. The feelings were, however, positive and coercion was seen only as the last resort.

> [..] contemplated rewarding both component engineers and users thereof [..] more important to spur the individuals wanting to reuse [..] Our ambition is strong, so strong we may have to adopt coercing if nothing else works [..] (Architect 3)

According to the architect team members, the communication of the project was well planned and executed. The management expected the team leaders to encourage their teams to adopt the new set of working methods. The trust in SW quality was not seen to present a problem. Furthermore, no problems were anticipated over the ownership of the code. According to the plan, there would be no problems for the teams to search, find, and use components made by other teams or in releasing one's own components to be used by others. All the questions that might have risen in these areas were seen as the responsibility of the team leaders to answer.

4.2 Team Members' Expectations Concerning the Role of Team Leaders

The team members regarded their leaders as information channels. The team members needed information about the trainings but also about the change as a whole. The team leader had to find the answers. However, there were some remnants of the times when the teams still belonged to individual companies.

> [..] you can develop yourself and your skills, but don't know exactly how [..] (Programmer 5)

> [..] he's the only way to get to know what's going on [..] (Programmer 1)

> [..] if they've been competitors, the chemistries don't work and the information doesn't get shared [..] some politicking might be there too [..] (Programmer 2)

Team members are in close relationship with the team's leader. It is in the corporate culture that the team leaders have intimate knowledge of the skills and interests of their team members. According to the task at hand, team leaders then allocate team members based on their skills and interests. There is mutual respect and understanding between the two parties. Team members trust the team leader to decide how their workload is best shared, according to their competencies.

> [..] it should be decided already when defining [the product] what resources are required and also allocated if we were to do a component (Programmer 3)

The team members acknowledged that there are overlaps and redundancies. The CBSE was recognized as a possible solution. The team members were sceptical about how they were supposed to become familiar with CBSE and still meet the set objectives. They put pressure on their team leader to solve the problems. A major obstacle was the unified programming language. If a team was without prior knowledge of this particular language, it had to be acquired. The acquisition of know-how was to be done either by training the existing personnel or lending a member from another team.

> [..] we cannot afford to change the programming environment [..] if we have to use [the chosen technology] the four preliminary components will die instantly, we simply don't have the time [..] (Programmer 4)

Team members expected the team leader to improve the working conditions and lead the team to complete the projects. The team spirit was strong and the members shared and expressed their concern about how their results were affected by the change.

> [..] team's result is rubbish if the team is ordered to do components for six months instead of doing projects they may charge [..] (Programmer 6)

The team leaders operate as filters and as support for their subordinates, but they also represent the organization to the team. Sometimes, this task is thankless and places the individuals under contradictory pressure from both sides.

4.3 The Team Leaders' Thoughts

The team leaders appreciated the need for change. A logical step in improving the processes was the reduction of the overlaps and redundancy. This meant extra work, in addition to the normal routines. The team leaders had also to monitor the company's intranet for any changes in the status of the component repository. The workload piled up.

> [..] the documentation [of components] takes more time [..] up to 50% [..] who are incredibly busy, everyone else is also working at nights [..] (Team leader P)

> [..] on average somewhat under 20 hours overtime a week [..] (Programmer R)

As a result, not all the team leaders could take part in all the meetings. The architect team reported that they had communicated the change project throughout the company. Still, there were feelings of uncertainty among the team leaders about the why's and how's.

> [..] in general our team is not that well aware of how the components should be made, so we continued our old practice [..] Team leader Y

The imbalance in the objectives and the thoughts concerning the resource allocation made the team leaders take sides, and, as a result, the goal-achieving measures were not enforced to the fullest. The concern of how the team members managed to cope was uttered.

> [..] the team is up to their ears with work, I didn't want to overburden them [..] (Team leader J)

> [..] we've had our share of problematic projects that have consumed people's time and coping [..] Team leader N

> [..] it should be systematically pointed out from where the extra 50% of time should be taken from [..] it is hard to find both the resource and the money [..] (Team leader P)

Motivation is affected because it is not rewarded. But even so, the workload was the feature that most concerned the team leaders. The team leaders saw themselves in the way the parties described them. They had to make a choice of how to respond to the call from both sides.

5. DISCUSSION

The idea behind the implementation of CBSE was to eliminate overlapping work and to use knowledge across teams and over project boundaries. The role of team leaders was to act as a two-way informant and effectively share the knowledge of their teams, also in form of components, as stated by Conway and Monks [8]. However, the technological uncertainties concerning the programming language and knowledge management–related challenges, such as communicating about the initiative and workload sharing within the teams, should have been considered more carefully and extra resources allocated to overcome them in accordance to Morisio et al. [35]. By recognizing the obstacles at the beginning of the change process, the change to CBSE could have happened more smoothly. The technical implementation of CBSE--the definition of components and the repository--was performed well as their definitions were to be found on the intranet.

The systematic implementation of the change is critical. The teams have their own ways of conducting everyday business they need to renew. Change must first happen on the mental level. Individuals need to adjust their thinking to the changing operation and future technology. They require solid and plausible justification for the need for change, as Kotter [27] describes. In this case, the hardening competitive situation provided the justification. The architect group operated under the mandate of the managing director, and thus the required support was also provided at least on some level.

The vision-related issues failed. The vision was formulated, but it was not excellent. The communication of the vision was adequate from the architect group's point of view. This was not the case, however, among those whom it affected most, the teams. The data shows uncertainty and a lack of clarity therein. The obstacles were removed as far as they could have been. There were components produced showing that they could be done. Sadly, there were again some miscommunications and the message remained somewhat blurred. The change was still under way when the study finished, and thus this paper cannot take a stand on how the last two issues on Kotter's [27] list were addressed.

The team leaders are presented with a tall order. The pressure comes from both sides, from hierarchically above and below. The management requires completion of their customer projects and they are required to trim their teams to produce components for the whole organization. The team leaders appreciate the beneficial objectives of the change, but feel let down when it comes to how they are supposed to accomplish it.

This kind of change needs promotion through well-executed and organization-wide communication. The chosen technology should be agile enough to meet the needs of individual teams. Another alternative is to make compromises in the way the new way of working and the technology is implemented and also in the length of the transition period. The change can be achieved only if management creates the right circumstances and provides the necessary resources. This supports the findings in the previously published literature saying that without means or time reuse typically fails. Leadership in this kind of undertaking is crucial for a successful outcome. Skilled change management is needed for a successful harmonization initiative and especially if the new way is to actually become the "regular way" of working. In such a situation, it is typical that the procedural change may take years or may even be continuous.

As this paper is based on a highly culture-related case study, the outcomes are not directly generalizable in other contexts. The more democratic approach to middle management's use fits poorly in the authoritarian management culture. However, some features, for example the need for management support and the importance of middle management, are applicable over the contextual boundaries.

6. CONCLUSIONS

This paper has discussed the role of team leaders in organizational change. The management made strategic decisions and gave the team leaders the task to implement them. The expectations laid upon the team leaders were twofold: the expectations of management and the expectations of team members. The theoretical view of how to deal with the change is compared with the observed proceedings in the case company. This paper also suggests some solutions for the inconsistencies found.

The theoretical contribution is primarily meant to fortify the theories of change management but also to add the notion of the importance of communication. Further study, where the cultural aspect is dealt with more closely, is recommended.

The empirical contribution aims to illustrate theory through a practical case. The centric and knowledgeable position of the team leaders gives them a view of the operation that is hard to match or replace. Software businesses that are renewing their software production processes towards CBSE would benefit a great deal from appointing and empowering team leaders during the design and preparation phases of the renewal process. When implementing the guidelines, it is worth remembering that this cannot be done without the involvement of the team leaders. However, commitment is not enough; the change must be resourced adequately. Top management supported the initiative, but was not fully aware of the actual requirements. Money is needed, but most of all time. This is something that can only be assessed by the team leaders.

Another significant issue to be brought up is that both technological and human perspectives must be taken into account in the harmonization of a software development process. Technology is needed for making things easy and efficient. Still, it is more important to have the right attitude towards knowledge sharing, and in this, the team leaders are the key players.

Such a change process bears significant managerial implications. The features and qualifications required from leaders in this kind of situation are not necessarily easy to meet. These challenges are not only technological matters nor are they purely questions of a more human nature. It is a unique combination that suits each situation. To be able to master the technological side of the whole harmonization process is challenging, but the human challenges are surely no less challenging. The core of this study is summed up according to Desouza et al. [11] who state that: "The biggest obstacle to effective knowledge management is not implementing a cutting-edge IT solution, but getting people to talk and share their know-how."

7. REFERENCES

[1] Alasuutari, P. 1995. *Researching culture: Qualitative method and cultural studies*. Sage Publications Limited.

[2] Anderson, D. and Ackerman-Anderson, L. 2010. *Beyond change management: Advanced strategies for today's transformational leaders*. Pfeiffer.

[3] Babaie, E. et al. 2006. *Forecast: IT services, worldwide, 2003–2010*. Gartner Forecast, Gartner Group.

[4] Balogun, J. 2003. From blaming the middle to harnessing its potential: Creating change intermediaries. *British Journal of Management*. 14, 1 (2003), 69–83.

[5] Bass, B.M. and Riggio, R.E. 2005. *Transformational leadership*. Lawrence Erlbaum.

[6] Beitler, M.A. 2006. *Strategic organizational change: a practitioner's guide for managers and consultants*. Ppi.

[7] Boonstra, J. 2004. *Dynamics of organizational change and learning*. Wiley.

[8] Conway, E. and Monks, K. 2010. Change from below: the role of middle managers in mediating paradoxical change. *Human Resource Management Journal*. 21, 2 (2010), 190–203.

[9] Currie, G. 2002. The influence of middle managers in the business planning process: a case study in the UK NHS. *British Journal of Management*. 10, 2 (2002), 141–155.

[10] Demirkan, H. et al. 2009. Service-oriented technology and management: Perspectives on research and practice for the coming decade. *Electronic Commerce Research and Applications*. 7, 4 (2009), 356–376.

[11] Desouza, K.C. et al. 2006. Four dynamics for bringing use back into software reuse. *Communications of the ACM*. 49, 1 (2006), 96–100.

[12] Eisenhardt, K.M. 1989. Building theories from case study research. *Academy of management review*. (1989), 532–550.

[13] Fenton-O'Creevy, M. 1998. Employee involvement and the middle manager: evidence from a survey of organizations. *Journal of Organizational Behavior*. 19, 1 (1998), 67–84.

[14] Fitzgerald, B. 1998. An empirically-grounded framework for the information systems development process. *Proceedings*

of the international conference on Information systems (1998), 103–114.

[15] Floyd, S.W. and Wooldridge, B. 2003. Middle management's strategic influence and organizational performance. *Journal of Management Studies*. 34, 3 (2003), 465–485.

[16] Frakes, W.B. and Kang, K. 2005. Software reuse research: Status and future. *Software Engineering, IEEE Transactions on*. 31, 7 (2005), 529–536.

[17] Galpin, T. 1996. Connecting culture to organizational change. *HR MAGAZINE*. 41, (1996), 84–93.

[18] Grant, R.M. 1996. Toward a knowledge-based theory of the firm. *Strategic management journal*. 17, (1996), 109–122.

[19] Hansen, M.T. 1999. The search-transfer problem: The role of weak ties in sharing knowledge across organization subunits. *Administrative science quarterly*. 44, 1 (1999), 82–111.

[20] Hargadon, A. and Sutton, R.I. 1997. Technology brokering and innovation in a product development firm. *Administrative science quarterly*. (1997), 716–749.

[21] Hargadon, A.B. 2002. Brokering knowledge: Linking learning and innovation. *Research in Organizational behavior*. 24, (2002), 41–86.

[22] Herbsleb, J.D. and Moitra, D. 2001. Global software development. *Software, IEEE*. 18, 2 (2001), 16–20.

[23] Hester, A.J. 2010. Increasing collaborative knowledge management in your organization: characteristics of wiki technology and wiki users. *Proceedings of the 2010 Special Interest Group on Management Information System's 48th annual conference on Computer personnel research on Computer personnel research* (2010), 158–164.

[24] Hoch, D.J. et al. 2000. *Secrets of software success: Management insights from 100 software firms around the world*. Harvard Business Press.

[25] Jacobson, I. et al. 1997. *Software reuse: architecture, process and organization for business success*. acm Press.

[26] Jalava, J. and Pohjola, M. 2007. ICT as a source of output and productivity growth in Finland. *Telecommunications Policy*. 31, 8 (2007), 463–472.

[27] Kakola, T. 2003. Software business models and contexts for software innovation: key areas software business research. *System Sciences, 2003. Proceedings of the 36th Annual Hawaii International Conference on* (2003), 8–pp.

[28] Kotter, J.P. 1996. *Leading change*. Harvard Business Press.

[29] Kotter, J.P. 2007. Leading change: Why transformation efforts fail. *Harvard Business Review*. 85, 1 (2007), 96.

[30] Kotter, J.P. and Schlesinger, L.A. 2008. Choosing strategies for change. *Harvard business review*. 86, 7/8 (2008), 130.

[31] Kukko, M. et al. 2008. Knowledge management in renewing software development processes. *Hawaii International Conference on System Sciences, Proceedings of the 41st Annual* (2008), 332–332.

[32] Kunda, D. and Brooks, L. 2000. Assessing organisational obstacles to component-based development: a case study

approach. *Information and Software Technology*. 42, 10 (2000), 715–725.

[33] Larkin, S. and Larkin, T.J. 1996. Reaching and Changing Front Line Employees. *Harvard Business Review*. 74, 3 (1996), 95–104.

[34] Messerschmitt, D.G. and Szyperski, C. 2003. Software ecosystem: understanding an indispensable technology and industry. *MIT Press Books*. 1, (2003).

[35] Meyers, B.C. and Oberndorf, P. 2001. Managing software acquisition: Open systems and COTS products. *Recherche*. 67, (2001), 02.

[36] Morisio, M. et al. 2002. Success and failure factors in software reuse. *Software Engineering, IEEE Transactions on*. 28, 4 (2002), 340–357.

[37] Niazi, M. et al. 2006. Critical success factors for software process improvement implementation: an empirical study. *Software Process: Improvement and Practice*. 11, 2 (2006), 193–211.

[38] Randall, J. 2004. *Managing change/changing managers*. Routledge.

[39] Saetang, S. and Haider, A. 2011. Conceptual aspects of IT governance in enterprise environment. *Proceedings of the 49th SIGMIS annual conference on Computer personnel research* (2011), 79–82.

[40] Sherif, K. et al. 2006. Resources and incentives for the adoption of systematic software reuse. *International Journal of Information Management*. 26, 1 (2006), 70–80.

[41] Strebel, P. 1996. Why do employees resist change. *Harvard business review*. 74, (1996), 86–94.

[42] Trompenaars, F. and Prud'homme, P. 2004. *Managing change across corporate cultures*. Capstone Chichester.

[43] Tsai, W. 2002. Social structure of "coopetition" within a multiunit organization: Coordination, competition, and intraorganizational knowledge sharing. *Organization science*. 13, 2 (2002), 179–190.

[44] Tsai, W. and Ghoshal, S. 1998. Social capital and value creation: The role of intrafirm networks. *Academy of management Journal*. 41, 4 (1998), 464–476.

[45] Westley, F.R. 2006. Middle managers and strategy: Microdynamics of inclusion. *Strategic Management Journal*. 11, 5 (2006), 337–351.

[46] Wijnhoven, F. et al. 2006. Post-merger IT integration strategies: An IT alignment perspective. *The Journal of Strategic Information Systems*. 15, 1 (2006), 5–28.

[47] Wooldridge, B. and Floyd, S.W. 2006. The strategy process, middle management involvement, and organizational performance. *Strategic Management Journal*. 11, 3 (2006), 231–241.

[48] Yin, R.K. 2008. *Case study research: Design and methods*. Sage Publications, Incorporated.

[49] Yukl, G. 1981. *Leadership in organizations*. Simon & Schuster Trade.

[50] Åberg, L. 2002. *Esimiehen viestintäopas: riemua johtamiseen!* Inforviestintä.

Together but Apart – How Spatial, Temporal and Cultural Distances affect FLOSS Developers' Project Retention

Andreas Schilling
Centre of Human Resources Information Systems
University of Bamberg, Germany
+49 951 8632873
andreas.schilling@uni-bamberg.de

Sven Laumer
Centre of Human Resources Information Systems
University of Bamberg, Germany
+49 951 8632873
sven.laumer@uni-bamberg.de

Tim Weitzel
Centre of Human Resources Information Systems
University of Bamberg, Germany
+49 951 8632871
tim.weitzel@uni-bamberg.de

ABSTRACT

Companies rely more and more on virtual teams which consist of globally dispersed members. Unfortunately, members' separation can raise considerable interpersonal challenges. In order to prevent conflicts from deescalating and ensure effective teamwork, companies pay careful attention to the management of members' spatial, temporal and cultural distances. While initiatives developing Free Libre Open Source Software (FLOSS) similarly combine a worldwide distributed workforce, relatively little is known about how members' separation affects their collaboration. However, without such an understanding no adequate advice can be derived for managers of FLOSS initiatives on how to foster members' collaboration and retention. Building on lessons learned from the organizational domain this research hypothesizes that spatial, temporal and cultural distances are key factors for FLOSS developers' team integration and project retention. To evaluate our research hypotheses, we study FLOSS developers' contribution and conversation behavior and extract objective figures on their spatial, temporal and cultural distances to each other.

Categories and Subject Descriptors

K.6.1 [**Management of Computing and Information Systems**]: Project and People Management - Staffing

General Terms

Management, Measurement, Human Factors

Keywords

Free Libre Open Source Software, Cultural Distance, Spatial Distance, Temporal Distance, Retention

1. INTRODUCTION

Globalization and recent advances in Internet Communication Technology (ICT) fundamentally changed the image of todays' workplaces. According to a recent study, nearly 90% of white collar employees are part of teams whose members are distributed around the world [27]. Regularly, this is because many organizations launch global teamwork initiatives to increase efficiency. However, the very same initiatives often produce enormous interpersonal challenges for the members involved [12]. The consequences of weak social relationships between team members are grave. Not only can they cause decreases in working motivations, but also reduce the overall performance of the team [21]. Examining the formed relationships in globally dispersed teams, existing studies highlight the relevance of project members' context. Based on their lessons learned, organizations train project leaders of global teams on how to react and manage members' spatial, temporal and cultural distances [36]. In contrast to the organizational domain, the consideration of spatial, temporal and cultural distances has been neglected so far in understanding the failure and success of initiatives developing Free Libre Open Source Software (FLOSS). FLOSS projects are of high importance to organizations and private households. Nearly three quarters of companies rely on FLOSS for their mission essential tasks [15] and most people around the world use FLOSS for browsing the internet [33]. Despite this relevance, the vast majority of FLOSS initiatives fail, most commonly due to a lack of sustained developers [4]. While existing evaluations support the key role of project members' interpersonal ties for ensuring their continuance, only little is known about the factors which constitute these social ties. However, without an understanding of the underlying processes which facilitate members' team integration, no adequate managerial advice can be derived on how to facilitate the retention of the contributor base.

This research examines how FLOSS developers' separation from each other negatively affects their team integration and project retention. With respect to organizational literature in [8, 11, 21, 35], we define and analyze team members' distance as a three-dimensional construct. The first dimension of this construct refers to team members' spatial distance. Studying projects in the organizational context Cramton and Webber conclude that close spatial distances between team members stimulate their social relationships through enabling face-to-face meetings [5]. Considering these findings, we expect that spatial distances between FLOSS developers' similarly constrain their interpersonal relationships. Another dimension of members' separation is temporal distance. Organizational evaluations recommend overlapping working hours among project members for enhancing teamwork processes [8]. Inspired by these findings, we evaluate whether FLOSS developers' temporal distances have a negative effect on their social relationships. The third dimension of team members' distance that we evaluate is their cultural distance. For this dimension, we build on the theoretical foundation proposed by Hofstede [17]. As in the case of organizations, we expect cultural differences among FLOSS developers to complicate their collaboration and interaction. As a consequence, we examine the research question:

Do spatial, temporal and cultural distances between FLOSS developers negatively affect their social relationships with each other and their project continuance?

This research has implications for research and practice. By evaluating the effects of project members' distances on their interpersonal relationships, we extend existing FLOSS literature which neglected so far the role of contextual factors. Beyond the FLOSS domain, this evaluation enriches organizational literature, which recommends considering knowledge workers as volunteers [9]. In complement to these theoretical contributions, this research provides a basis for deriving practicable advice. Through understanding how team members' distances affect their relationships with each other, project managers can adequately intervene and enhance the collaboration and retention of their contributor base. In addition, the derivation of practicable measures assists managers of organizational projects in bridging members' distances.

To present the underlying concepts of our evaluation and derive our research hypotheses, this paper is structured as follows. The following section summarizes existing FLOSS research on project members' interpersonal relationships. Combining existing FLOSS literature with experiences from the organizational domain, we present in section three the hypothesized links between members' distances and their formed interpersonal relationships, which in turn foster project continuance. Section four details our chosen research methodology and the used measures. Finally, we outline the expected results of our evaluation and present a conclusion of our research.

2. FLOSS RESEARCH

Existing literature approaches the development of interpersonal relationships in FLOSS projects in two ways. Studies employing a structural perspective repeatedly highlight FLOSS developers' conversational behavior as an indication for their team integration. According to Qureshi and Fang, FLOSS developers socialize into the project's community through participating in mailing-list conversations. In addition, the researchers provide evidence that members' conversation behavior follows interaction trajectories, so that their previous participation is indicative for their future actions [26]. Singh et al. support the relevance of project members' mailing-list interactions. Using Hidden Markov Models, the researchers demonstrate that FLOSS developers' mailing-list interactions influence their progression within the project [32]. Based on the evaluation of former Google Summer of Code students, Schilling et al. provide further support to the assumption that members' interaction on the projects' mailing-list is indicative for their compatibility to each other and for their project continuance [29]. Moreover, FLOSS literature supports

the relevance of personal similarities between team members. Research results by Singh et al. suggest that shared project experiences among project members are a strong stimulus for their interpersonal relationships [31].

Relatively few studies examined the relational factors which facilitate members' team integration. The few studies which examine the development of social relationships from a relational perspective highlight the role of members' social context. Based on their detailed analysis, Fang and Neufeld conclude that FLOSS developers have to comply with norms and values of the existing project community in order to become long-term contributors [13]. Stewart and Gosain come to a similar conclusion. The researchers provide evidence that it is necessary for members of a FLOSS project to share norms, beliefs and values in order to develop interpersonal relationships with each other, which in turn leads them to continue in the project [34].

Although we know relatively little about contextual factors in the FLOSS domain, they are important for understanding social relationships between project members. This is because contextual factors are the underlying fundament which constitutes project members' interactions with each other. Therefore they should be considered by the management of FLOSS initiatives. This research regards FLOSS developers' distance to each other as a key contextual element for understanding their social relationship. Consistent with organizational literature, we define distance as a multifaceted construct which affects the formation of social relationships among team members in various ways. Based on study results from the organizational domain the following section presents our research hypotheses.

3. THEORY DEVELOPMENT

In order to distinguish the different dimensions of FLOSS developers' separation and their effect on team integration and retention, we draw from lessons learned in the organizational domain. Previous evaluations of virtual teams in organizations highlight the important influence of spatial, temporal and cultural distances on members' team integration [8, 11, 21, 35]. While there are important differences between virtual teams in organizations and FLOSS projects in regard of remuneration and exerting formal control, both collaboration initiatives also have important similarities with each other. As in the context of FLOSS, members of virtual teams in organizations often are free in allocating their efforts towards achieving a specified goal [6]. Moreover, the success of collaboration initiatives in both domains depends considerably on members' interpersonal relationships with each other [19, 31]. With respect to these similarities in members' collaboration behavior we hypothesize that spatial, temporal and cultural distances also have an effect on FLOSS developers' level of team integration. In addition, we hypothesize that FLOSS developers with high levels of team integration remain longer at the project. Figure 1 illustrates our research model.

Most studies in the organizational context examine the effects of team members' dispersion in terms of spatial distances [24]. While organizational studies at first only differentiated dichotomously between co-located and dispersed team members, more recent studies note the nuanced effects of members' spatial separation [24]. A direct consequence of team members' geographic distance is their ability to engage in spontaneous face-to-face meetings. Such meetings facilitate team members' social relationships. According to Wiesenfeld et al. face-to-face conversations convey much stronger social context cues than purely virtual communication means. As the authors point out, this is because people can transfer a social context much better when interacting with each other in person [38]. While FLOSS projects are characterized through the absence of any proximity constraints, Crowston et al. show that FLOSS developers indeed engage in face-to-face meetings if possible [7]. Developers can meet in person through official project meetings like Linux User Groups (LUG) or spontaneous arrangements. Either way, FLOSS developers' geographic distance considerably constrains their ability to interact with other members face-to-face. Research results by Hu et al. suggest positive consequences of FLOSS developers' co-location. In particular, the researchers point out that FLOSS developers who belong to the same city are more likely to evaluate one another positively [20]. With respect to previous evaluations, we expect, therefore, that members' face-to-face meetings with each other facilitate their integration process. Consequently, we expect that FLOSS developers who are in terms of spatial distance closer located to other members integrate faster with the existing developer team and hypothesize that:

H1: The shorter a developer's spatial distance to the existing members of a FLOSS initiative, the faster she integrates into the project team.

Another kind of proximity, which affects the ways in which project members' interact with each other, is temporal distance. Working on a project at different hours can cause considerable challenges for members' coordination. Espinosa and Pickering show that team members' temporal dispersion creates high coordination costs [12]. According to Cummings et al., current communication means are no help for temporally dispersed teams. The authors show in their evaluation that both synchronous and asynchronous communication forms only assist project members with overlapping working hours. As the authors point out, it seems to be the case that members who work temporally apart from each other cause high coordination and interaction costs for the project [8]. As a result of the inability to communicate in real-time, relational conflicts and misunderstandings can occur [12]. Kankanhalli et al. as well as Elliott and Scacchi even warn that projects whose members work temporally apart from each other are more likely to experience a deescalation of interpersonal conflicts [10, 21]. As in the organizational context, temporal dispersion is highly present in FLOSS projects. Given that members of FLOSS initiatives contribute primarily in their spare time, they naturally vary in the times they work for the project. While existing research results suggest that members' temporal dispersion overall benefits FLOSS projects' code development activity [3], there are also study results which indicate negative consequences on interpersonal relationships. Bagozzi and Dholakia stress the advantages of synchronous project communication. The authors conclude that project members who communicate with other team members in real time develop much stronger interpersonal relationships [1]. Combining organizational experiences and existing FLOSS literature we hypothesize that:

H2: The shorter a developer's temporal distance to the existing members of a FLOSS initiative, the faster she integrates into the project team.

In addition to spatial and temporal distances, cultural differences negatively affect organizational software development [2]. Hofstede defines culture as "the collective programming of the mind, that distinguishes members of one human group from

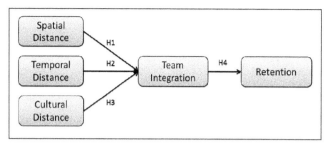

Figure 1: Research Model

another" [16, p.26]. Based on comprehensive empirical studies, Hofstede identified five key cultural characteristics which affect individuals' behavior [16, 17]. These five characteristics are: individuals' level of power distance (the acceptance of unequal power distribution), the acceptance of uncertainty, the dominance of either masculine or feminine values and the orientation on long-term vs. short-term goals. Evaluations of projects with culturally diverse members show lower levels of team identification and cohesion [37]. The reasons for this are various. One reason is that members with different cultural backgrounds differ in the way they accept low levels of performance [35]. Moreover, cultural differences can complicate team members' communication. Espinosa et al. show that cultural differences can cause misinterpretations among team members [11]. Existing research supports the relevance of cultural influences in the virtual domain. Shen et al. show that national similarities affect individuals' virtual interactions [30]. In the context of FLOSS development, Padmanabha supports the relevance of project members' cultural characteristics as defined by Hofstede to explain their attachment to a project [25]. In addition, Stewart and Gosain point out that sharing personal characteristics stimulates FLOSS developers' interpersonal relationships. Based on their evaluation, the authors conclude that team members who share values, norms and beliefs build strong trust relationships with each other [34]. Hence, as in the case of organizations, we hypothesize that project members' cultural differences affect their integration into the FLOSS development:

H3: The shorter a developer's cultural distance to the existing members of a FLOSS initiative, the faster she integrates into the project team.

Existing FLOSS literature suggests that team members' level of project integration is a key element for understanding their ongoing commitment. Qureshi and Fang point out that FLOSS developers need to build strong interpersonal relationships with the existing project team to become long-term contributors [26]. Singh et al. support this. Based on an examination of FLOSS developers' project behavior, the authors point out that new members' engagement in conversations with existing developers is a key element for understanding their continuance [32]. Studying project retention from a relational perspective, Fang and Neufeld show that FLOSS developers identify with the projects' community through their interactions [13]. This identification in turn stimulates them to continue in the project. Research findings by Ke and Zhang support the role of members' interpersonal relationships for their continuance [22]. The authors show that project members who identify with the community are more likely to continue in the project. Moreover, study results by Bagozzi and Dholakia highlight members' socialization with the project team in order to explain their ongoing commitment [1]. Based on existing FLOSS literature, which highlights the influence of members' team integration for their ongoing project retention, we hypothesize that:

H4: Developers with a high level of team integration remain longer in a FLOSS project.

4. RESEARCH METHODOLOGY

To evaluate how spatial, temporal, and cultural distances affect FLOSS developers' team integration and continuance, we rely on various objective measures. In the case of FLOSS development, data on developers' communication and contribution behavior are publicly available. On the one hand, mailing-lists record FLOSS project members' conversations with each other. On the other hand, FLOSS projects' code versioning systems log every code contribution of their developers. In contrast with subjective measures, the use of objective data provides us with two important advantages. First, the extracted data visualizes a much more comprehensive picture of the underlying interpersonal processes. In comparison, the use of survey data depends not only on members' accurate memories of their past interactions and code contributions but also on achieving a reliable response rate. Moreover, the used dataset enables us to evaluate our research hypotheses on longitudinal base over multiple FLOSS projects without interviewing developers repeatedly.

Combining a rich developer base with a diverse FLOSS project spectrum, KDE provides an appropriate research context for our evaluation. KDE is a popular desktop environment for UNIX systems. It consists of a rich variety of subprojects to which developers can contribute. With over 1000 registered developers, it has one of the largest contributor bases worldwide. Starting in early 2013 we will launch a survey in which we will ask KDE developers about their current place of residence. Next, we approach from a project perspective and identify those KDE projects of which most developers participated in our survey. Based on this project selection, we determine the various dimensions of members' separation with respect to existing research by evaluating the following measures.

In order to assess team members' **spatial distance**, we will rely on a measure proposed by Scellato et al. [28]. With "node locality" the authors define a metric which measures the degree of team members' spatial separation. The formula of this metric is listed in Table 1. In addition to the distance $(d_{i,j})$ between the two project members i and j it considers the factor β for smoothing very long and very short distances. In order to apply this metric, we transform members' place of residence in geographic coordinates. Based on this decoding process, we apply in a second step the Haversine formula which calculates the spatial distance between two coordinates on a sphere [14]. Although the earth is not a perfect sphere, the Haversine formula is a very efficient and accurate estimation for the spatial distance between two coordinates on earth.

For determining members' **temporal dispersion**, we examine how their actual working hours overlap at the FLOSS project. To do so, we modify a metric presented in [3]. In their examination, Colazo and Fang use the variance of team members' starting time at the FLOSS project to determine their temporal separation. However, this measure does not consider that team members' working time may vary. In order to consider this aspect, we measure members' temporal distance using the variance of overlapping working hours with other developers. To determine members' working hours $(wh_{i,t})$ at the FLOSS project, we

Table 1: Measurement Model

Spatial distance	
Formula	Description
$$sd_i = \sum_{j=1}^{N} e^{\frac{-d_{i,j}}{\beta}}$$	Adopted measure from [28] for the total distance of developer i to all other project members $(j..N)$.

Temporal distance	
Formula	Description
$$td_i = \frac{1}{n}\sum_{j=1}^{N}\sum_{t=1}^{T}\left(wh_{i,t} - \overline{wh_t}\right)^2$$	Measures the variance of overlapping daily working hours between developer i and the other members $(j..N)$ summed up over all time periods $(1..T)$.

Cultural distance	
Formula	Description
$$cd_i = \sum_{j=1}^{N} CD_{ij}$$ $$CD_{ij} = (PDI_i - PDI_j) + (UAI_i - UAI_j)$$ $$+ (MAS_i - MAS_j) + (LTO_i - LTO_j)$$ $$+ (IDV_i - IDV_j)$$	This measure captures members' cultural diversity. The used index scores are adopted from Hofstede's evaluation results [17].

Team integration	
Formula	Description
$$integ_i = \sum_{t=1}^{T} MP_{i,t}$$	Count for all mailing list posts written by developer i over all examined time periods $(1..T)$.

Retention	
Formula	Description
$$T_i = T_{C_{i,1}} - T_{C_{i,n}}$$	Timespan in days between a project members' first $(T_{C_{i,1}})$ and most recent code commit $(T_{C_{i,n}})$.

calculate the timespan between their first and last project commit on a daily basis. Comparing with other measures, which use static time-zone differences [24], our metric considers members' dynamically varying working times.

As for the design of our research hypotheses, we build on Hofstede's research for the measurement of members' **cultural diversity**. In particular, we rely on the national index scores compiled by Hofstede in order to measure project members' cultural distance. Corresponding with the dimensions which constitute cultural differences, Hofstede derived, based on a comprehensive evaluation of more than 116,000 employees, national scores for Power Distance Index (*PDI*), Uncertainty Index (*UI*), Masculine (*MAS*), Long Term Orientation (*LTO*), and

Individuality Index (*IDV*) [16, 17]. Since their compilation, these index scores have been supported by various cultural studies and most recently been refined by the author himself [18]. To apply Hofstede's national index scores in our evaluation, we first derive KDE members' country of residence based on their provided address details. Then, in a second step, we calculate a cumulative index (*cd*) which sums up all of a member's cultural differences with the rest of the team.

Finally, we draw on extant FLOSS literature to derive objective measures for FLOSS developers' **team identification** and **project retention**. Following research in [26], we consider FLOSS developers' engagement in mailing-list conversations with other project members as an indicator for the degree to which they integrate into the project team. To do so, we count each of the members' exchanged mailing-list posts with other members of the FLOSS team. In line with research in [4], we use the contribution log file to measure members' project permanence. In particular, we extract the timestamps of members' first ($T_{C_{i,1}}$) and most recent commit ($T_{C_{i,n}}$). Then, in a second step, we calculate the time difference in days (T_i) between these two dates.

5. EXPECTED RESULTS

Considering the lessons learned in the organizational context, we expect that spatial, temporal and cultural distances play an important role for FLOSS developers' team integration and their project continuance. Existing studies on online social networks point to members' geographic co-location as a key element for understanding their sharing and interaction behavior [23, 28]. In line with these findings, we expect that spatial distance plays a similar important role for FLOSS developers' team integration and project continuance. Considering the collaborative spirit in FLOSS projects, it remains to be seen whether temporal and cultural distances have a less severe effect than in the organizational domain. Existing study results, however, suggest that FLOSS projects are also vulnerable to members' different temporal and cultural background [1, 34]. Overall, our evaluation helps to understand how project members' context influences their integration and retention. With this understanding, managers of FLOSS projects can control relevant levers and reason for concrete actions such as launching regional meetings to improve the retention of their contributor base. In addition to the FLOSS context, the derived controls and advice can benefit project managers in the organizational domain.

6. CONCLUSION

FLOSS projects are a pervasive part in our daily life. Enterprises rely for their mission critical tasks on FLOSS [15] and most private consumers use FLOSS for browsing the Internet [33]. Despite the relevance for companies and private households, the majority of all FLOSS initiatives fail. According to Colazo and Fang, this is due to a lack sustained developers [4]. While various FLOSS studies stress the relevance of project members' interpersonal relationships in order to facilitate their retention, relatively few of these evaluations looked at the influence of contextual factors. Based on organizational literature this research considers FLOSS developers' spatial, temporal, and cultural distance as key elements for understanding their team integration and project retention. With respect to organizational literature, we develop our research model and derive the corresponding research hypotheses. To evaluate our research model, we examine the actual communication and contribution behavior of FLOSS developers. Based on a developer survey at the KDE project we evaluate objective figures for project members' spatial, temporal

and cultural distances to each other. With this evaluation we contribute not only to a comprehensive understanding for FLOSS developers' relationships but also in deriving adequate advice for managers of FLOSS initiatives.

7. REFERENCES

[1] Bagozzi, R. P. and Dholakia, U. M. 2006. Open Source Software User Communities: A Study of Participation in Linux User Groups. *Management Science* 52, 7, 1099–1115.

[2] Barrett, M. and Oborn, E. 2007. *Knowledge sharing in cross-cultural software teams*. Judge Business School Working Papers, Cambridge, University of Cambridge.

[3] Colazo, J. A. and Fang, Y. 2010. Following the Sun: Temporal Dispersion and Performance in Open Source Software Project Teams. *Journal of the Association for Information Systems* 11, 12, 684–707.

[4] Colazo, J. and Fang, Y. 2009. Impact of license choice on Open Source Software development activity. *Journal of the American Society for Information Science & Technology* 60, 5, 997–1011.

[5] Cramton, C. and Webber, S. 2005. Relationships among geographic dispersion, team processes, and effectiveness in software development work teams. *Journal of Business Research* 58, 6, 758–765.

[6] Crowston, K., Heckman, R., and Misiolek, N. 2010. *Leadership in self-managing virtual teams*.

[7] Crowston, K., Howison, J., Masango, C., and Eseryel, U. 2007. The Role of Face-to-Face Meetings in Technology-Supported Self-Organizing Distributed Teams. *IEEE Transactions on Professional Communication* 50, 3, 185–203.

[8] Cummings, J. N., Espinosa, J. A., and Pickering, C. K. 2009. Crossing Spatial and Temporal Boundaries in Globally Distributed Projects: A Relational Model of Coordination Delay. *Information Systems Research* 20, 3, 420–439.

[9] Drucker, P. F. 2002. They're not Employees, They're People. *Harvard Business Review* 80, 2, 70–77.

[10] Elliott, M. S. and Scacchi, W. 2004. Free Software Development: Cooperation and Conflict in a Virtual Organizational Culture. In *Free/Open Source Software Development*, 152–173.

[11] Espinosa, J. A., DeLone, W., and Lee, G. 2006. Global boundaries, task processes and IS project success: a field study. *Information Technology & People* 19, 4, 345–370.

[12] Espinosa, J. and Pickering, C. 2006. The Effect of Time Separation on Coordination Processes and Outcomes: A Case Study. In *Proceedings of the 39th Annual Hawaii International Conference on System Sciences (HICSS'06)*.

[13] Fang, Y. and Neufeld, D. 2009. Understanding Sustained Participation in Open Source Software Projects. *Journal of Management Information Systems* 25, 4, 9–50.

[14] Gellert, W., Gottwald, S., Hellwich, M., Kästner, H., and Küstner, H. 1989. *The VNR concise encyclopedia of mathematics*. Van Nostrand Reinhold, New York.

[15] Gold, A. 2007. *Open Source Solutions: Seek Value Beyond Cost*. Accessed 1 May 2011.

[16] Hofstede, G. 1980. *Culture's consequences: International differences in work-related values*.

[17] Hofstede, G. 2001. *Culture's consequences: Comparing values, behaviors, institutions and organizations across nations*.

[18] Hofstede, G. J. and Minkov, M. 2010. *Cultures and organizations. Software of the mind ; intercultural cooperation and its importance for survival*. McGraw-Hill, New York, NY.

[19] Hollenbeck, J. R., DeRue, D. S., and Guzzo, R. 2004. Bridging the Gap between I/O Research and HR Practice: Improving Team Composition, Team Training, and Team Task Design. *Human Resource Management* 43, 4, 353–366.

[20] Hu, D., Zhao, J. L., and Chen Jiesi. 2012. Reputation Management in an Open Source Developer Social Network: An Empirical Study on Determinants of Positive Evaluations. *Decision Support Systems* 53, 3, 526–533.

[21] Kankanhalli, A., Tan, B. C., and Wei, K.-K. 2007. Conflict and Performance in Global Virtual Teams. *Journal of Management Information Systems* 23, 3, 237–274.

[22] Ke, W. and Zhang, P. 2010. The Effects of Extrinsic Motivations and Satisfaction in Open Source Software Development. *Journal of the Association for Information Systems* 11, 12, 785–808.

[23] Liben-Nowell, D., Novak, J., Kumar, R., Raghavan, P., and Tomkins, A. 2005. Geographic routing in social networks. *Proceedings of the National Academy of Sciences* 102, 33, 11623–11628.

[24] O'Leary, M. B. and Cummings, J. N. 2007. The Spatial, Temporal, and Configurational Characteristics of Geographic Dispersion in Teams. *MIS Quarterly* 31, 3, 433–452.

[25] Padmanabha, R. 2007. *FLOSS (Free/Libre Open Source Software): A Theme for Cultural Differences Study,* Jindal Global University (JGU).

[26] Qureshi, I. and Fang, Y. 2010. Socialization in Open Source Software Projects: A Growth Mixture Modeling Approach. *Organizational Research Methods* 14, 1, 208–238.

[27] RW3. October 15th. *Survey Reveals Global Employees Not Prepared for Virtual Teamwork*. http://rw-3.com/2012/05/survey-reveals-global-employees-not-prepared-for-virtual-teamwork/.

[28] Scellato, S., Mascolo, C., Musolesi, M., and Latora, V. 2010. Distance matters: geo-social metrics for online social networks. In *Proceedings of the 3rd conference on Online social networks*.

[29] Schilling, A., Laumer, S., and Weitzel, T. 2012. Who Will Remain? An Evaluation of Actual Person-Job and Person-Team Fit to Predict Developer Retention in FLOSS Projects. In *45th Hawaii International Conference 2012 (HICSS'12)*, 3446–3455.

[30] Shen, C., Monge, P., and Williams, D. 2011. The Evolving Virtual Relationships: A Longitudinal Analysis of Player Social Networks in a Large MMOG. In *A Decade in Internet Time*.

[31] Singh, P. V., Tan, Y., and Mookerjee, V. 2011. Network Effects: The Influence of Structural Social Capital on Open Source Project Success. *MIS Quarterly* 35, 4, 813-A7.

[32] Singh, P. V., Tan, Y., and Youn, N. 2011. A Hidden Markov Model of Developer Learning Dynamics in Open Source Software Projects. *Information Systems Research* 22, 4, 790–807.

[33] Statcounter Inc. *Statcounter Global Stats*. http://gs.statcounter.com/#browser-ww-monthly-201107-2012009. Accessed October 15th.

[34] Stewart, K. J. and Gosain, S. 2006. The Impact of Ideology on Effectiveness in Open Source Software Development Teams. *MIS Quarterly* 30, 2, 291–314.

[35] Sturman, M. C., Shao, L., and Katz, J. H. 2012. The effect of culture on the curvilinear relationship between performance and turnover. *Journal of Applied Psychology* 97, 1, 46–62.

[36] Symons, J. and Stenzel, C. 2007. Virtually borderless an examination of culture in virtual teaming. *Journal of General Management* 32, 3, 1-17-17.

[37] Watson, W. E., Kumar, K., and Michaelsen, L. K. 1993. Cultural Diversity's Impact on Interaction Process and Performance: Comparing Homogeneous and Diverse Task Groups. *Academy of Management Journal* 36, 3, 590-602-602.

[38] Wiesenfeld, B. M., Raghuram, S., and Garud, R. 1998. Communication Patterns as Determinants of Organizational Identification in a Virtual Organization. *Journal of Computer-Mediated Communication* 3, 4, 0.

Determinants of Success in Crowdsourcing Software Development

Hamed Tajedin
Schulich School of Business
4700 Keele St.,
Toronto, Ontario, Canada, M3J 1P3
(647) 774-4657
Hamed.tajedin@gmail.com

Dorit Nevo
Schulich School of Business
4700 Keele St.,
Toronto, Ontario, Canada, M3J 1P3
(416) 736-2100
dnevo@schulich.yorku.ca

ABSTRACT

With the advent of digitization, recent years have witnessed a surge toward collective undertaking of production process different from traditional ways of organizing. In this vein, crowdsourcing has lent itself into a successful emerging mode of organizing and firms are increasingly using it in their value creation activities. However, despite popularity in practice, crowdsourcing has received little attention from IS scholars. Specifically, what the determinants of success in this model are remains an unexplored area of research that we strive to address in this paper. We focus on software development via crowdsourcing and drawing on studies from IS success, OSS and software development, we build a model of success that has three determinants: the characteristics of the project, the composition of the crowd and the relationship among key players. Finally, we describe our research methodology and conclude with potential contributions of our work.

Categories and Subject Descriptors

H.0 [General]

Keywords

Crowdsourcing, outsourcing, opensource software, software development

1. INTRODUCTION

With the advent of digitization, recent years have witnessed a surge toward collective undertaking of production process different from traditional ways of organizing in which required collocation of individuals. Opensource software movement (OSS) has shown that production of software can happen outside firm boundaries through contribution of talents who are globally spread. The success of this model has attracted managers' attention to crowdsourcing model through which firms can harness the power of a crowd of interested individuals who can virtually gather around a production goal. As crowdsourcing has lent itself into an efficient mode of organizing, a growing number of firms have been using it. An estimate of the amount of money paid to the crowd of over 2 million people for a sample of crowdsourcing service providers is about $750 million in 2009. More recent estimates show that the number of crowd workers is growing in excess of 100% a year while Nearly 77% of all workers have a primary job. In terms of revenue for service providers, crowdsourcing demonstrated a 50% growth in 2010 and 75% in 2011. Despite this popularity growth in practice, crowdsourcing has received little attention from IS scholars. Specifically, what the determinants of success in this model are remains an unexplored area of research that we strive to address in this paper.

Firms have been using crowdsourcing for a diverse set of purposes, from problem solving [1] to accomplishing part of their operation [2], to harnessing the external knowledge of individuals beyond their boundaries in order to come up with new ideas for business development [3]. While there are numerous applications for crowdsourcing, software development is one with special importance to IS scholars since it bears the IT artifact that shapes the core of our research domain [4]. However as an emerging phenomenon, successful accomplishment of such method of software development is a challenge for practitioners [5]. Software development via crowdsourcing can happen directly, i.e. a firm reaches out to the crowd of individuals through an open call, or it can happen indirectly via an intermediary in which the intermediary bridges the crowd to the firm. The latter is more popular in practice since the intermediary has the advantage of possessing a crowd of coders over time that participates in various projects. This is the instance of crowdsourcing that we have focused on and we would like to study the determinants of success in such setting. More specifically, we try to answer the question of what are the key success factors of crowdsourcing software development with the existence of an intermediary.

We find three areas of research in IS to be relevant to our work and can help us in framing our research direction. First, given that crowdsourcing counts as a form of sourcing arrangement [6] the findings from strong body of knowledge on information technology outsourcing (ITO) can shed light on different aspects of our setting that has been explored in a more general context. In spite of the fact that ITO is a well explored area in IS, there is a dearth of research on emerging sourcing arrangements; with a few exceptions, e.g. [7], the literature is mainly focused on a dyad level, i.e. client and vendor. In our setting, which an intermediary or 'middleman' acts as a service provider to both client and vendor, the whole structure of the relationship is changed and further research is required to determine the extent to which the findings of traditional sourcing arrangements apply to these settings.

Second, the similarities that opensource software (OSS) and crowdsourcing share make the former an apt area from which inferences about the latter can be drawn. However, we believe the existence of the firm at the focal point of crowdsourcing has several consequences that translate into the differences between this model and OSS. First, unlike the opensource spirit of non-proprietary use of software and General Public License (GPL), the firm appropriates the outcome of crowdsourcing through developing legal frame-works that address issues of transferring intellectual property [8]. Second, projects in opensource are defined arbitrarily by interested developers and receive contribution through self-selection mechanisms. This, in turn, results in uneven distribution of developers' attention and their contribution among projects. SourceForge.net, for example, had only 60,642 projects with more than one release, and 23,754 with more than one member, out of the a pool of 201,494 software projects in 2009 [9]. It has been estimated that no more than 6% of the projects on SourceForge.net are able to attract a noticeable community of users and developers [9]. In crowdsourcing, however, the firm has a proactive role in attracting contribution from the crowd by anchoring monetary rewards that do not exist in opensource. Hence the subtle difference between the OSS and crowdsourced software requires further investigation of the latter, albeit by drawing on the findings of OSS research.

Finally, with our focus on determinants of success, our work fits within the broader literature of IS success which is widely accepted throughout IS research as the principal criterion for evaluating information systems. Since the seminal work of DeLone and McLean in 1992, there have been a number of studies which apply this model to different domains of IS such as e-commerc [10, 11], e-government [12], knowledge management [13, 14], health-care [15], system implementation [16, 17], opensource [18] and many more. However, as new phenomena emerge within the scope of IS research, so does the issue of defining success and its determinants. In this vein, the literature lacks studies that focus on crowdsourcing and provide a model of success for it.

In sum, our work at the intersection of the three aforementioned areas of IS research focuses on crowdsourcing as a new phenomenon that provides an excellent opportunity to address the gaps that was reviewed and by doing so, furthers our knowledge on success of emerging sourcing arrangements.

2. Crowdsourcing: What do we know?

Crowdsourcing represents "the act of a company or institution taking a function once performed by employees and outsourcing it to an undefined (and generally large) network of people in the form of an open call" [19]. Although this definition comes from non-academic world and there is not a generally agreed-upon definition for crowdsourcing in literature, it basically reflects the basic concepts of crowdsourcing; the existence of a focal entity, outsourcing, crowd, and open call.

As an emerging phenomenon, most of the studies on crowdsourcing are descriptive and try to explain the phenomenon by showing successful cases [3, 5, 20, 21] or classifying existing models [22-25]. Besides these, there are a few conceptual works that look at the phenomenon from various perspectives. For example, Proulx et al [26] take a perspective of information capitalism in defining crowdsourcing and argue that paradoxically the crowdsourcing can give both a sense of empowerment and alienation to the crowd. Moreover, Wexler [8] looks at crowdsourcing from a sociological perspective and explains how

the crowd has transformed from an irrational entity, which causes problems, to a collectively intelligent entity that can, when managed, solve problems. And finally, Afuah and Tucci [27] look at crowdsourcing from a problem solving perspective and argue that that under certain circumstances crowdsourcing transforms an organization's search for knowledge by spanning its boundaries and enabling access to external resources. However, there is also a growing number of empirical works on crowdsourcing. For example Leimeister et al [28], look at the design issues of competition-based crowdsourcing and Brabham [2] looks at the motivation of participants in a crowdsourcing instance.

As the quick review above indicates, crowdsourcing is the root phenomenon that seeds the research in various disciplines and the literature around it is expanding around various topics. Yet the number of studies in IS that have aspects of crowdsourcing as a focal research question is limited. This might partly be due to difficulty of knitting crowdsourcing instances to the nomological network of IS discipline [4]. In addition, we believe crowdsourcing provides an excellent opportunity for conducting transformational research that delineates the role of technology in transforming organizations and environment [29]. Therefore, we focused on software development via crowdsourcing, which has the IT artifact in its core and we are interested in determinants of success in this method of software development.

In the model of software development with crowdsourcing that we have focused on, there are three key players; the crowdsourcer, i.e. project sponsor or client, the intermediary that acts as a service provider to the client, and the crowd, i.e. the community of developers. The project sponsor defines the project and uses the service of the intermediary to reach out the community of participants in order to have the project accomplished. There are two ways that a project can be accomplished with submissions of individuals from the community. The first way is that each person that participates in the project accomplishes a small task different from that of others and the final outcome is achieved via cooperation and collaboration of these small chunks of work. For example consider the development of Wikipedia in which the submissions of people from the crowd are accumulated above each other to shape the output (See [2] for another example). On the other hand, instead of working collaboratively on tasks, individuals can compete against each other for these small tasks so that the best submission is selected for each part of the broken down project (this is similar to ideas competition case, see [28]). The model of crowdsourced software development that we have chosen and is more common in practice is of the latter form in which participants compete against each other by submitting pieces of work (design, architecture, code, bug report, etc.). The collaborative form of software development is more similar to open-source method. However as was explained, even though crowdsourcing and open source have a lot in common, in contrast to opensource, crowdsourcing entails both a focal entity, which appropriates the outcome and monetary incentivizing mechanisms. It has been shown that the intervention of extrinsic incentives such as monetary rewards can have undermining impacts on intrinsic motivations [30]. This, in turn, can reduce the sample of developers who take part in crowdsourcing projects to those who are more motivated by monetary rewards, compared to contributors to broader set of OSS projects. This attrition in the population of developers can be easier to imagine by considering what Raymond describes as the motivations of developers in opensource movement: "[t]he 'utility function' Linux hackers are maximizing is not classically economic, but is the intangible of their own ego satisfaction and reputation among other hackers" [31](p. 41).

In the following section we propose a model of success for this method of software development that is based on ideas from IS success and software development areas.

3. Success of Crowdsourcing Software Development

The first step in having a success model is to define success and clarify what it refers to in software development by crowdsourcing. An Information System has many stakeholders that each can bring different definition of success into play. Software development with crowdsourcing is process that leads to an IT artifact, i.e. the developed software and in this sense it is subject to evaluation by comprehensive models of IS success that exist in the literature (e.g. [32, 33]). With this approach, the unit of analysis is the crowdsourced software and its success reflects how much the output of crowdsourcing has been successful that can be distinguished in terms of net benefits it can provide. However, we can also focus on the development phase of crowdsourcing and assess how much the development has been successful in yielding the intended deliverables to stakeholders. In this approach, success should be defined for different set of stakeholders than the former approach and different set of criteria should be used to assess the development process. For example in crowdsourcing context, success of a project can be defined as how much the project is completed on time from a manager's view or it can be as how much it has helped developers to find better jobs from participants' view. Moreover, as we focus on software development, success should be defined within the limited scope of initiation to release. The model of success should reflect how effective and efficient the whole process has been. At this phase the process should be the unit of analysis and the IT-artifact acts as the glue that binds different players to the process. At post-development phase, on the other hand, the focus of analysis is the IT artifact that is available to users. Hence, we define the success from the perspective of the main stakeholder, i.e. the project sponsor or crowdsourcer.

The success of a software development by crowdsourcing from the perspective of project sponsor is basically the extent to which the process has met the requirements within the desired time frame, cost and quality scope. This concept definition, however, can be operationalized and measured by second order factors. To this aim, we draw on the work of Crownston et al [34] and DeLone and McLean [32] as the basis of our operationalization. At the technical level, success measures can be code quality and documentation quality. These measures are quite applicable to the context of crowdsourcing as developers compete based on code quality. In existing methods of crowdsourcing via intermediaries, through a peer review process, experts and experienced developers evaluate submissions from the crowd. Accordingly, the outcome of this evaluation can be a proxy for user satisfaction as another dimension of success.

After a piece of code is developed by crowdsourcing, the project sponsor has to integrate the code to its existing systems, review the code for security issues, and keep the code up-to-date as the system changes over time [5]. So the use dimension of success can be measured in this sense and it can reflect the amount of rework that is needed for a code to be integrated in the project

sponsor's system. The last dimension of success can reflect the net benefits in terms of economic gains, or speed of project completion that are realized by crowdsourcing. For the next step, we focus on determinants of success.

The first set of factors that influence the success of development process emanates from project characteristics. We posit that certain project characteristics can enhance success in crowdsourcing method of software development. The characteristics such as modular architecture allow parallel contribution of individuals to be integrated for the single whole. It has been suggested that sophisticated coding problems that make the task challenging can contribute to success of OSS [35]. This can hold true for crowdsourcing as well, since in both methods of development, developers voluntarily select projects to participate and anecdotal evidences suggest that technical sizzle can motivate developers [31]. Moreover, companies who have used crowdsourcing service have claimed that finding the right type of problem and providing appropriate amount of problem detail for developer community have been an issue for them. As Lakhani and his colleagues [5] narrate "...clients discovered that contest participation decreased if they were unclear about what problems they wanted to solve or presented problems that were too complex or vast in scope; in those cases, the TopCoder community struggled to produce an acceptable solution" (p. 10). Since the contributions of the crowd of developers are to build a single whole, projects that can be broken down to small modules that are clear in requirement and have limited interdependencies seem to contribute to success.

Similar to OSS licensing, another important issue in crowdsourcing is that of legal considerations [3]. However, OSS tenets are against proprietary ownership of software code and hence, restrictive licenses have shown to be ineffective in pulling developers, e.g. [18]. In crowdsourcing, on the other hand, the crowdsourcer seeks intellectual property right for its developed software and might see their benefits at risk due to crowdsourcing [5]. Hence, the choice of appropriate type of license for projects and keeping the community informed can be crucial in attracting developers and achieving success. Considering all this, we can infer that:

Proposition 1: Project characteristics affect success of crowdsourcing software development where projects with modular, challenging but not complex structure, and clear scope and license type have greater influence on success.

For any given crowdsourcing provider, there are large numbers of projects that will be in need of contributions from the community. Contrary to traditional managerial methods in which resources are allocated to each project contingently, in crowdsourcing, projects should virtually attract resources themselves. Proposition one suggests that certain project characteristics are necessary to attract resources. Moreover, the composition of community plays a critical role in a project fate. The more people are attracted to a project, the more diversity will shape and newer viewpoints and methods are applied to the project. This is one of the strength points of crowdsourcing that the crowd can even provide the client with a better understanding of the problem or potential solutions [3, 5]. The effect of diversity on success of software project has also been shown in literature [36]. For a team of software developer, diversity can play a crucial role for emergence of new ideas and opinions as well as new ways of doing the task and solving the problems. This, in turn, can positively affect the success of the project. But one can imagine a maximum point for this after which not only with the increase of diversity the performance does not improve but also it deteriorates due to problems that emerge because of coordination and communication.

Besides diversity, the community should also have the competencies that the project requires. Use of popular languages has been shown to be an effective factor for success since there are readily more developers who can accomplish tasks with common coding languages. Moreover, although the community may be composed of a large number of people, there is a huge variance in terms of expertise among members. The size of community at a crowdsourcing service provider, for example, is large, but the number of people within that community who actively participate in projects is much smaller; the talent pool of this community that can stand at global rankings accounts for 0.5% of the total population [5]. The chance of success will rise if lesser skilled members are cultivated and more professional contributors take part in projects, hence:

Proposition 2: Crowd composition affects success and this effect is higher for diverse crowds with more number of developers who are competent at software development.

In addition, crowdsourcing happens in a social context where individuals interact and communicate to get new information and share knowledge. The importance of relationship management in outsourcing settings is well emphasized, e.g. [6, 37-40]. Relations among developers and between crowdsourcer and community are of utter importance. Cohesion among project team members would lead to more effective communication and learning [41]. On the other hand, trust formation, communication quality, and identification with the project team are factors that have been associated with success of OSS [42] and due to similarity of the development methods we can expect the same to hold true for crowdsourcing.

Another form of relations that count is the one between project sponsors and the community. This has been particularly emphasized in the work of Ågerfalk and Fitzgerald [43] who focus on firms who use OSS as a method of developing their software, which is quite similar to crowdsourcing. They contend that openness, trust, tact, professionalism, transparency, and complementariness are key success factors in opensourcing. As they put it: "...opensourcing is not primarily about commissioning software development to a third party, but rather about engaging in long-term collaborative activities leading to a sustainable ecosystem. Since many of the collaborators in this ecosystem are likely to be the customer's competitors, the collaboration is necessarily done in a spirit of co-opetition... Both customer and community members have a shared responsibility to actively contribute to the development and sustainability of the ecosystem" (p. 404). The collaborative interaction of community and sponsor can also lead to better understanding of problem and enhanced designs. Hence:

Proposition 3: Retention of collaborative relations among developers and between community and project sponsor positively affects success.

So to sum up, we propose that three factors affect the success of crowdsourced projects in software development. The first stem from the characteristics of the project and we posit that certain kind of projects are more appropriate for crowdsourcing and that task technology fit plays an important role here [44]. The second factor is the crowd composition and how diverse and competent the community of developers is. Since the projects are accomplished by submissions from the crowd, the more readily the it has the knowledge and skill sets that are required for a given project, the more number of submissions with better quality would be expected. Finally the last factor is the relationship among the actors in play. Both studies from outsourcing and from opensource software development underscore the importance of maintaining a collaborative relationship among actors in order to achieve success and hence we posit the same would hold for a crowdsourcing instance.

4. Research Method

Associate As previously mentioned, in the model of crowdsourcing that we focused on, there is an intermediary that acts as the service provider to various clients, which want to accomplish their projects via crowdsourcing. TopCoder.com is one of those service providers that have established a community of hundreds of thousands of developers. We have chosen TopCoder because it is a successful example of crowdsourcing platform. It has been founded in 2001 and now it offers crowdsourcing service for software development to various clients across numerous projects.

We chose a mixed method to conduct our research project. The first part is qualitative and we intend to collect primary data via interviews from individuals representing all three aspects of the model, i.e. the community, the service provider, and the clients. This will enable us to see the phenomenon from different aspects and analyze it from the viewpoint of each stakeholder involved. We are now in the phase of data collection and analysis. We have conducted 13 interviews; 7 interviews with community members and 6 interviews with TopCoder managers. The interviews have been semi-structured (the complete interview protocol can be provided upon request) and there have been minor modifications to some questions during data collection phase. All interviews have been conducted during a three-day period at the site of an event held by TopCoder and they have been audio recorded. The interviews are from 29 to 122 minutes (with an average of 45 minutes) are now in phase of transcription. We have a model in mind but our strategy is to be open to our data letting it guide us further along the way to shape our model. We still have five interviews in our plan with clients of TopCoder that will be added to our collected data.

The second phase of our research is a quantitative test of our model on the same-targeted sample. We will test our model with a questionnaire that will be answered by subjects from the three perspectives of community, service provider, and clients. As we pass phase one, we can more specifically design this part of our research in details.

5. Potential Contribution

Crowdsourcing literature is the focal phenomenon in studies from different disciplines from sociology, e.g. [8, 26], economics, e.g. [45], management, e.g. [27] to IS, e.g. [24]. Yet we believe that as an emerging concept, there is a lot to be explored in this area of research especially in information systems domain.

We have focused on software development via crowdsourcing. In essence, when a company is considering crowdsourcing for developing a piece of code, it is making the make/buy decision but if two decades ago buy decision would be translated to outsourcing, nowadays there is another option of crowdsourcing on the table for the same chosen strategy. We have a strong body of research in information technology outsourcing in IS. While the finding of such studies can be illuminating for traditional outsourcing arrangement, the new setting of crowdsourcing bears new structure and dynamism that make it dramatically different from outsourcing. In a traditional outsourcing arrangement there are always two key players, client and vendor, and the literature in information technology outsourcing (ITO) or business process outsourcing (BPO) looked at the relationship between these dyads of organizations. For example a stream of research on ITO looks at determinants of success in a sourcing arrangements by assessing the effects of contractual, e.g. [46, 47] and relational, e.g. [37, 48] forms of governance between client and vendor. In a few studies, the relationship that is being studied goes beyond this dyad and the role of intermediaries are considered, e.g. [7]. But, in line with other studies at this area, the focus remains at the organizational level of analysis. In all these studies, the structure of IOR that is being studied is comprised of collective entities at organizational level.

However, in a crowdsourcing model of software development with the existence of an intermediary, not only individuals as single developers come into play, but also another collective entity emerges, the crowd, that is more of a sociological entity. The existence of individuals, organizations, and the community (or the crowd) in this model, makes this model of interorganizational relationship (IOR) a unique one that has not yet received enough attention in the literature. The structure of this IOR is a complex combination of relationships consisting of three forms: 1) the relationship between the client and the intermediary; 2) the relationship between individuals as single developers with both intermediary and the client; 3) the relationship between the intermediary and the community of developers. While the studies of ITO can cover the organization to organization relationship that exists in this model, there are relationships in this model that go beyond what has been covered by ITO and we believe the findings from this study can shed light on how this relationship works. While the studies of ITO can cover the organization to organization relationship that exists in this model, there are relationships in this model that go beyond what has been covered by ITO and we believe the findings from this study can shed light on how this relationship works.

In addition to structural differences between crowdsourcing and outsourcing, there are differences in what is required to have a sourcing arrangement in the two setting. Simply talking, outsourcing arrangement requires searching, assessing the supplier capabilities, contracting, and monitoring. In this setting, the firm goes beyond its boundary for a specific service or product but after the process of finding the supplier, it will settle down with an option (or multiple options) of a supplier(s), prospecting that it (they) will provide the requirement. In a crowdsourcing arrangement, however, the scenario is changed even though the same thing is sought; when a firm reaches out to the crowd, it does not go through the same process of searching for suppliers, assessing their capabilities, arranging the best legal contracts so that other party is held accountable if it does not provide what it has claimed, and continuously putting resources on monitoring the performance of the supplier. Instead, the crowd provides the service or product that the firm seeks, and the firm

puts some effort into choosing the best option out of what is available. For example consider the case that an R&D problem is outsourced to a scientific lab versus being crowdsourced. In the first case, the firm first seeks the best lab that has the potential to solve the problem, and then the firm goes through a process after which the lab provides the solution. But in case of crowdsourcing, the crowd provides answers to the question and the firm selects the best one from the set of submitted solutions. This is not to say that the latter process is easier or simpler, but it is obviously different from that of an outsourcing arrangement, and the difference lies at the focus of the selection efforts that the firm puts resources on. Hence, although similar, the determinants of success are different in the two settings. We believe that our study can shed light on the determinants of success in this new setting, thus can further our understanding of the broader concept of outsourcing.

Moreover, our study has a software development context that is similar to that of OSS. While there are similarities between the two, there are also subtle differences that make crowdsourcing a unique setting. The findings of crowdsourcing can also feed back the OSS where the role of community comes into play. However, this should happen cautiously as the drivers of community participations may not necessarily be the same in the two settings.

6. REFERENCES

[1] Sieg, J.H., M.W. Wallin, and G. Von Krogh, "Managerial challenges in open innovation: a study of innovation intermediation in the chemical industry". R&d Management, 2010. 40(3): p. 281-291.

[2] Brabham, D.C., "Moving the crowd at threadless". Information, Communication & Society, 2010. 13(8): p. 1122-1145.

[3] Jouret, G., "Inside Cisco's search for the next big idea". Harvard business review, 2009. 87(9): p. 43-45.

[4] Benbasat, I. and R.W. Zmud, "The identity crisis within the IS discipline: Defining and communicating the discipline's core properties". Mis Quarterly, 2003: p. 183-194.

[5] Lakhani, K., D. Garvin, and E. Lonstein, "TopCoder (A): Developing software through crowdsourcing". Harvard Business School General Management Unit case, 2010(610-032).

[6] Oshri, I., J. Kotlarsky, and L.P. Willcocks, The handbook of global outsourcing and offshoring 2011: Palgrave Macmillan.

[7] Mahnke, V., J. Wareham, and N. Bjorn-Andersen, "Offshore middlemen: transnational intermediation in technology sourcing". Journal of Information Technology, 2008. 23(1): p. 18-30.

[8] Wexler, M.N., "Reconfiguring the sociology of the crowd: exploring crowdsourcing". International Journal of Sociology and Social Policy, 2011. 31(1/2): p. 6-20.

[9] Meirelles, P., et al. A study of the relationships between source code metrics and attractiveness in free software projects. in Software Engineering (SBES), 2010 Brazilian Symposium on. 2010. IEEE.

[10] De Wulf, K., et al., "The role of pleasure in web site success". Information & Management, 2006. 43(4): p. 434-446.

[11] Soh, C., M.L. Markus, and K.H. Goh, "Electronic marketplaces and price transparency: Strategy, information

technology, and success". Mis Quarterly, 2006. 30(3): p. 705-723.

[12] Gil-García, J.R. and T.A. Pardo, "E-government success factors: Mapping practical tools to theoretical foundations". Government Information Quarterly, 2005. 22(2): p. 187-216.

[13] Markus, M.L., "Toward a theory of knowledge reuse: Types of knowledge reuse situations and factors in reuse success". Journal of Management Information Systems, 2001. 18(1): p. 57-94.

[14] Wu, J.-H. and Y.-M. Wang, "Measuring KMS success: A respecification of the DeLone and McLean's model". Information & Management, 2006. 43(6): p. 728-739.

[15] Häyrinen, K., K. Saranto, and P. Nykänen, "Definition, structure, content, use and impacts of electronic health records: a review of the research literature". International journal of medical informatics, 2008. 77(5): p. 291.

[16] Sharma, R. and P. Yetton, "The contingent effects of training, technical complexity, and task interdependence on successful information systems implementation". Mis Quarterly, 2007. 31(2): p. 219-238.

[17] Wixom, B.H. and H.J. Watson, "An empirical investigation of the factors affecting data warehousing success". Mis Quarterly, 2001. 25(1): p. 17-32.

[18] Subramaniam, C., R. Sen, and M.L. Nelson, "Determinants of open source software project success: A longitudinal study". Decision Support Systems, 2009. 46(2): p. 576-585.

[19] Howe, J. The rise of crowdsourcing. Wired Magazine, 2006. 14, 1-4.

[20] Greengard, S., "Following the crowd". Communications of the ACM, 2011. 54(2): p. 20-22.

[21] Huston, L. and N. Sakkab, "Connect and develop". Harvard business review, 2006. 84(3): p. 58-66.

[22] Bonabeau, E., "Decisions 2.0: the power of collective intelligence". Mit Sloan Management Review, 2009. 50(2): p. 45-52.

[23] Cook, S., "The contribution revolution". Harvard business review, 2008. 86(10): p. 60-69.

[24] Doan, A., R. Ramakrishnan, and A.Y. Halevy, "Crowdsourcing systems on the World-Wide Web". Communications of the ACM, 2011. 54(4): p. 86-96.

[25] Haythornthwaite, C. Crowds and communities: Light and heavyweight models of peer production. 2009. IEEE Computer Society.

[26] Proulx, S., et al., "Paradoxical empowerment of produsers in the context of informational capitalism". New Review of Hypermedia and Multimedia, 2011. 17(1): p. 9-29.

[27] Afuah, A. and C.L. Tucci, "Crowdsourcing As a Solution to Distant Search". Academy of Management review, 2012. 37(3): p. 355-375.

[28] Leimeister, J., et al., "Leveraging crowdsourcing: activation-supporting components for IT-based ideas competition". Journal of Management Information Systems, 2009. 26(1): p. 197-224.

[29] Agarwal, R. and H.C. Lucas Jr, "The information systems identity crisis: Focusing on high-visibility and high-impact research". Mis Quarterly, 2005: p. 381-398.

[30] Frey, B.S. and R. Jegen, "Motivation crowding theory". Journal of economic surveys, 2001. 15(5): p. 589-611.

[31] Raymond, E., "The cathedral and the bazaar". Knowledge, Technology & Policy, 1999. 12(3): p. 23-49.

[32] DeLone, W.H. and E.R. McLean, "Information systems success: The quest for the dependent variable". Information systems research, 1992. 3(1): p. 60-95.

[33] Seddon, P.B., "A respecification and extension of the DeLone and McLean model of IS success". Information systems research, 1997. 8(3): p. 240-53.

[34] Crowston, K., H. Annabi, and J. Howison, "Defining open source software project success". Former Departments, Centers, Institutes and Projects, 2003: p. 4.

[35] Comino, S., F.M. Manenti, and M.L. Parisi, "From planning to mature: On the success of open source projects". Research Policy, 2007. 36(10): p. 1575-1586.

[36] Liang, T.P., et al., "Effect of team diversity on software project performance". Industrial Management & Data Systems, 2007. 107(5): p. 636-653.

[37] Kotlarsky, J. and I. Oshri, "Social ties, knowledge sharing and successful collaboration in globally distributed system development projects". European Journal of Information Systems, 2005. 14(1): p. 37-48.

[38] Kotlarsky, J., P.C. Van Fenema, and L.P. Willcocks, "Developing a knowledge-based perspective on coordination: The case of global software projects". Information & Management, 2008. 45(2): p. 96-108.

[39] Rottman, J.W. and M.C. Lacity, "Proven Practices for Effectively Offshoring Proven Practices for Effectively Offshoring IT Work". Mit Sloan Management Review, 2006. 47(3): p. 56-63.

[40] Srikanth, K. and P. Puranam, "Integrating distributed work: comparing task design, communication, and tacit coordination mechanisms". Strategic Management Journal, 2011. 32(8): p. 849-875.

[41] Singh, P.V., Y. Tan, and V. Mookerjee, "Network effects: The influence of structural social capital on open source project success". SSRN eLibrary, 2008.

[42] Stewart, K.J. and S. Gosain, "The impact of ideology on effectiveness in open source software development teams". Mis Quarterly, 2006: p. 291-314.

[43] Agerfalk, P.J. and B. Fitzgerald, "" Outsourcing to an Unknown Workforce: Exploring Opensourcing as a Global Sourcing Strategy". Management Information Systems Quarterly, 2008. 32(2): p. 385-409.

[44] Zigurs, I. and B.K. Buckland, "A theory of task/technology fit and group support systems effectiveness". Mis Quarterly, 1998: p. 313-334.

[45] Horton, J.J. and L.B. Chilton. The labor economics of paid crowdsourcing. 2010. ACM.

[46] Gopal, A. and B.R. Koka, "The Role of Contracts on Quality and Returns to Quality in Offshore Software Development Outsourcing". Decision Sciences, 2010. 41(3): p. 491-516.

[47] Gopal, A., et al., "Contracts in offshore software development: An empirical analysis". Management Science, 2003: p. 1671-1683.

[48] Liker, J.K. and T.Y. Choi, "Building deep supplier relationships". Harvard business review, 2004. 82(12): p. 104-113.

Applying the Job Demand-Resource Theoretical Framework to Better Understand the Stress Inducing and Reducing Aspects of IT in Jobs

Jignya Patel
PhD Student
FCBE 363, Fogelman College of
Business and Economics
University of Memphis
Memphis, TN 38152
+1 (901) 678 4547
jmpatel@memphis.edu

William. J. Kettinger
FedEx Endowed Chair & Professor
FAB 346, Fogelman College of
Business and Economics
University of Memphis
Memphis, TN 38152
+1 (901) 678 4547
bill.kettinger@memphis.edu

Sung Yul Ryoo
Assistant Professor
Department of Business
Administration
Daejin University
Gyeonggi-do 487-711, Korea
+82 (31) 539-1752
syryoo@daejin.ac.kr

ABSTRACT

While past literature in information systems (IS) has noted the stress inducing effect of information technology (IT) on employee well-being, little research has focused on the stress reducing potential of IT. This paper is the first in IS to makes use of the Job Demand-Resource theoretical framework to examine the concurrent stress inducing and stress reducing impact of IT on employee's work exhaustion, job satisfaction and turnover intention. In particular, we hypothesize that stress induced due to having to learn IT and being monitored by IT can cause work exhaustion while informational, communicational and usability support available by IT can cause job satisfaction. We further hypothesize that IT's stress reducing potential moderates the effect of general job demands on work exhaustion. The research can help managers identify the source of employee turnover and the appropriate interventions needed to reduce turnover when IT is introduced into a job.

Categories and Subject Descriptors

K.4.3 Employment

General Terms

Human Factors, Management, Performance.

Keywords

Technostress, Turnover, Job Demand-Resource Theory, IT Support.

1. INTRODUCTION

Stress in the workplace has been a topic of considerable research in organizational behavior (OB). Studies have provided evidence that job related stressors such as work overload, physical environment, and social stressors cause stress.

Technostress research in information systems (IS) has focused on information technology (IT) induced stress on individuals and organizational outcomes [2; 12; 14; 15]. However, little research in IS has integrated the findings from the OB and the IS Technostress literatures, the lack of which, may have limited the predictability of stress on organizational outcomes such as turnover intention. We believe these two streams need to be integrated because stress experienced by end users of IT at workplace is a function of both stress due to IT used and stress due to workplace factors. Therefore to obtain a more holistic view and to continue advancing knowledge on technostress in workplace, the first objective of this study is to explore simultaneously the effects of stress due to both IT and innate job characteristics.

While literature in IS has recognized that IT adds value to employee and their jobs, surprisingly little research has looked at IT's potential for reducing workplace stress. Examining IT related stressors as well as IT's potential to reduce stress presents scholars with a more holistic view of how work place stress affects employees. Thus, with the intent of enhancing an understanding of technostress in workplace, the second aim of this study is to investigate the effects of IT's stress reducing factors on individual outcomes. In light of the above discussion, the main research questions addressed by the paper are (1) what are the potential stress reducing factors of IT related to technostress? (2) How do these factors in conjunction with other well-recognized job and IT related stress inducing and stress reducing factors affect employee's work exhaustion, job satisfaction and turnover intention?

We use the Job Demand-Resource (JDR) theory to help us position the stress inducing and stress reducing aspects of IT and other job related stressors in relation to work exhaustion and turnover intention of employees. Our results show that general job demands [resources] do indeed exists separately from IT specific demands [resources] and the imbalance between stress inducing and the stress reducing effects can actually increase the likelihood of an employee to leave the job. This is an important result for practitioners since it implies that managing the balance between both IT specific and general job resources and demands might be the key to retaining employees in an organization.

2. Theory: Job Demand-Resource Model

The Job Demand-Resource (JDR) model is based on three premises. First, every occupation has its own risk factors associated with stress and these risk factors can be categorized into demands and resources. Job demands refer to those physical, psychological, social, or organizational aspects of the job that require sustained physical and/or psychological (cognitive and emotional) effort or skills and are therefore associated with certain physiological and/or psychological costs [3]. Job resources refer to those physical, psychological, social, or organizational aspects of the job that are either functional in achieving work goals, reduce job demands and the associated physiological and psychological costs or stimulate personal growth, learning, and development [3]. Second, two different underlying psychological processes cause the development of job strain and motivation. Job demands exhaust employees of their mental and physical resources therefore leading to a deterioration of their psychological or physiological health. On the other hand, job resources play an extrinsic motivational role by helping individuals achieve their work goals or an intrinsic motivational role by fostering employees' growth, learning and development which in turn leads to high work engagement or job performance [3]. Third, in addition to the main effects, job resources also buffer the effect of job demands on strain by reducing the tendency of organizational properties to generate specific stressors, alter the perceptions and cognitions of individuals evoked by demands, moderate responses that follow the appraisal process, or reduce the health-damaging consequences of such responses [9]. Therefore, the reason why resources moderate the effect of demands on strain is different for different resources.

3. Hypotheses Development

3.1 General Job Demands

We study our research model in the context of a transportation industry. This is a particularly meaningful context because diffusion of IT in the trucking industry has forced truck drivers to adapt to the new environment thereby adding IT as an potential stressor to the already existing stressors e.g. work overload, social stressors and physical environment stressors, and IT may also have the potential to reduce stress by providing useful information and communication capabilities to both managers and truck drivers to complete their job more effectively and efficiently.

Past literature in transportation have recognized work overload, physical environment demands and social demands to be the most prominent stressors among truck drivers [5]. Work overload stressor refers to conditions under which individuals are required to do more than they are able because of time limitation available for performance [13]. Most studies examining the positive effect of work overload on burnout give empirical evidences that heavy workload translates into higher job demand leading to elevated stress and reduced efficiency. Social demands are the stressors experienced by an employee due to the interactions in social and professional work relationships. Poor or unsupportive relationships, lack of respect, unfair treatment and isolation from

colleagues and/or supervisors can be a potential source of stress because it may lead to distress and frustration, hence causing burnout [8]. Physical environment stressor is the physical characteristics of the job environment that may evoke stress in an individual e.g. bad weather, traffic, etc. because such variables have the capability to interfere with optimum human functioning, thereby inducing burnout, and eventually reducing job performance and job satisfaction [8]. Thus we propose,

H1: General job demands are positively related to work exhaustion.

3.2 IT Specific Job Demands

Our study extends the JDR literature by including IT learning stressor and IT monitoring stressor as two additional job demands that are induced due to certain characteristics of IT [2]. IT learning stressor refers to the stress associated with learning to use IT. They result from those characteristics of IT that interfere with the worker's ability to use IT because of its complexity or hassle involved in its operation. This may make employees feel inadequate with regard to their computer skills and therefore force them to spend time and effort in learning and understanding IT [12; 15]. IT monitoring stressor refers to the stress experienced by individuals due to the obtrusive nature of technology. Research on electronic monitoring provides evidence that workers experience more stress when employees are electronically monitored than when they are not monitored. IT monitoring can be seen as intrusive to users and may induce tension, anxiety, depression and anger among employees. Constant electronic monitoring can lead to stress due to constant fear of losing the job [14]. Over time such emotions can decrease intrinsic motivation of a worker thus leading to burnout. Thus, we propose

H2: IT specific demands are positively related to work exhaustion

3.3 General Job Resources

Previous transportation literature has recognized job autonomy and fairness of rewards to be the most important factors in predicting a driver's job satisfaction. Job autonomy is the degree to which the job provides substantial freedom, independence and discretion in scheduling the work and in determining the procedures to be used in carrying it out. The more the worker feels he has control over what goes on, the more he feels his job allows him to be creative and is appropriate to his abilities. This leads to positive feelings of accomplishment and growth which in turn leads to higher levels of satisfaction. Fairness of rewards is the extent to which the worker perceives his treatment by others at work is unprejudiced and impartial. Such perceptions inform employees that the organization warrants their wellbeing by safeguarding them against any injustice or unfairness. Therefore it is reasonable to predict that perceptions of the extent to which the organization offers supportive resources like fairness of rewards are likely to act as a motivator thereby influencing a worker's attitude towards his job. Thus we propose

H3: General job resources are positively related to job satisfaction.

3.4 IT Specific Job Resources

In addition to general job resources, we extend the motivational potential of job resources to include IT specific resources. IT possesses structural features that are designed to overcome human weaknesses and once applied, the technology should bring productivity, efficiency and satisfaction to individuals and organizations [7]. Structural features are specific types of rules and resources, or capabilities, offered by the system. Numerous dimensions for describing structures have been proposed [7], nonetheless it is possible to categorize these structures by looking at their fundamental capabilities in assisting individuals to complete their task. Dennis et. al., [6] proposed three dimensions of IT structures, namely (1) IT information support- IT's capability in providing information to users (2) IT communication support-IT's capability in assisting users to communicate with peers and (3) IT usability support- IT's capability in allowing users to easily use IT in their daily routines. According to Self Determination Theory (SDT), humans have a strong inner desire to fulfill basic psychological needs, including the need to feel competent in what they do and the need to feel related to others. SDT suggests that work contextual variables allow for satisfaction of these needs which in turn facilitate psychological well-being like job satisfaction.

Information support is the capability of IT to gather, share, aggregate, structure, or evaluate information. This kind of support includes conditions in which IT organizes and displays information to the worker to make better choices and decisions thus reducing task related uncertainties. Information in empowers workers to act more wisely and sensibly thereby enabling them to make better choices and decisions thereby allowing employees to feel competent in performing their job effectively. IT communication support can be defined as any aspect of IT that supports, enhances, or defines the capability of a worker to communicate and co-ordinate with others [6]. It includes aspects of IT that enhance information exchange and access to other employees. In doing so, it can help satisfy the need for relatedness by providing employees with a sense of communion. Lastly, IT usability support refers to its capability in allowing users to adopt, adapt and technology in their as easily as possible. Such support can relieve the employees with the cognitive load of understanding and using the technology thereby satisfying the need to be competent in using IT. This helps workers gain confidence in appropriating IT in a faithful manner to accomplish their task as efficiently as possible thus leading to job satisfaction.

H4: IT specific job resources are positively related to job satisfaction

3.5 Interaction Effects

Based on the third premise of the JDR model, we further propose that general job resources and IT specific job resources moderate the effect of general job demands on work exhaustion[1]. Job autonomy can moderate effect of work overload because employees have the capability to decide for themselves when and how to complete their work thereby reducing the stress felt due to work overload. Fairness of rewards will also moderate the effect of social stressors because an awareness of unprejudiced and impartial treatment can alter the negative emotions resulting from isolation and disrespect into a more positive emotions. Thus we propose

H5a: General job resources will negatively moderate the relationship between general job demands and work exhaustion.

IT Communication support may moderate the effect of social stressors because it can provide social support that protects employees from the pathological effects of demands [4]. IT Usability support can moderate the effect of work overload because competence in the tool may help workers in completing their work in the time allotted and therefore completing the work may not seem as challenging. Furthermore, the ease of use of IT can help drivers feel less challenged in operating IT and as a result drivers are more capable of using IT to complete their work. Information support from IT can moderate the effect of physical environment stressor and work overload on work exhaustion because information can provide employees some control over uncertainties in their job. This allows employees to be able to plan ahead, find alternatives or solve unexpected occurrences resulting in reduced work exhaustion. The extent to which drivers see the information from IT as an important factor for their safety and timely accomplishment of work can mask the coercive perception of IT monitoring. Thus, we propose

H5b: IT specific Resources will negatively moderate the relationship between general job demands and work exhaustion.

H6b: IT specific Resources will negatively moderate the relationship between IT specific demands and work exhaustion.

3.6 Antecedents of Turnover Intention

Turnover intention is defined as a voluntary intention of employees to quit their organizations [1; 11]. Previous literature on turnover has demonstrated that employees with high level of strain are more likely to voluntarily quit from their jobs than employees with low strain levels. For example, [1] showed that work exhaustion has a significant effect on IT professionals' turnover intension. Furthermore, a review of the literature on the relationship between employee turnover and job satisfaction has reported a consistent negative relationship between the constructs [10; 16]. Higher job satisfaction is generally believed to be associated with increased productivity, lower absenteeism, and lower employee turnover [10]. Lastly, we propose that job satisfaction has a negative effect on employee's work exhaustion in the context of our study because truck drivers are more likely to feel exhausted if they are not motivated enough due to unavailability of sufficient resources.

H6: Job satisfaction is negatively related to turnover intention.

H7: Job satisfaction is negatively related to turnover intention

H8: Work exhaustion is positively related to turnover intention.

---

[1] The theoretical logic of the moderating role of general job resources on the relationship between IT specific demands and work exhaustion (H6a) could not be argued and therefore was not hypothesized.

3.7 Research Model

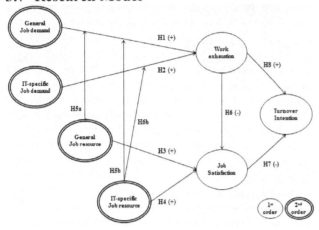

Figure 1. Research model

4. Research Method

Interviews were first conducted with two managers, five dispatchers and two truck drivers of a large Trucking company in the Southern US to establish content validity of our survey measures. We then developed a refined survey instrument and test it with a pilot sample of 26 drivers. Participants were asked to provide feedback on the clarity of questions, response options, and the length of time it took them to complete the survey. Based on their feedback, adjustments were made to the survey items before implementing the final scale on a large-scale sample[2]. A $15 Wal-Mart gift card was given as an incentive to every driver who completed the survey. Appendix A contains the confirmatory factor analysis for data collected from 205 drivers.

5. Results

6. Discussion

The contributions of our paper are three folds. First, the findings of this study explicitly identifies IT's capability in reducing stress, thereby significantly extending the present understanding of technostress in IS literature. At the same time, this study extends the organizational behavior literature by identifying IT related stress inducing and stress reducing factors thereby significantly extending the Job Demand Resource Theory. Lastly, IT's stress reducing conceptualization in the proposed model is based on theoretical arguments that could be generalized to other occupations (e.g. software professionals) as well as other technologies (e.g. Smartphones and tablets).

7. Practical and Managerial Implications

This study has several important implications for managers. First, IT-specific job resource can not only help increase job satisfaction but also help reduce the stressful impacts of general job demand. Thus, managers should then discuss the potential IT value for adjusting the work environment to the needs and abilities of individual employees and need to improve the perceptions of IT support by selecting and/or implementing systems that are more sophisticated. Second, it is worth mentioning to managers IT can have a dual impact in terms of inducing and reducing stress. Recognizing this finding enables managers to address the central

operational challenge of employee stress and turnover by developing a tool to assess the levels of stress.

Our research has important implications for technostress research in the IS field. First, past technostress studies have examined attributes that capture only one side of a double-edged sword of IT with regard to stress. This study complements technostress literature in explaining how IT can lessen or enhance stress in the work environment. In doing so, we significantly contribute to the JDR theory by including the IT component in addition to the well-researched job demands and job resources constructs. Second, future research can explore the specific characteristics of IT that show the potential to reduce stress so that future technologies can be designed in a way where the stress inducing potential of IT is mitigated while the stress reducing potential of IT is promoted.

8. Limitations

Our study has a number of limitations that should be addressed in future work. First, our use of trucking firms in a physically labor-intensive industry in this study may limit the generalizability of the current results. Future studies should test these relationships in both information-intensive and labor-intensive industries. Such studies could confirm the generalizability of our results and/or yield some implacable differences between the two contexts. Second, past studies suggested that personal resources could moderate the relationships between detrimental working conditions and employee wellbeing [17]. Examining this moderation would be another future research direction.

9. ACKNOWLEDGMENTS

The authors would like to express their sincere gratitude to the intermodal trucking company for providing access to truck drivers who kindly responded to our survey to provide valuable data. We greatly appreciate the support of the University of Memphis' The Intermodal Freight Transportation Institute.

REFERENCES

[1] Ahuja, M.K., Chudoba, K.M., Kacmar, C.J., Mcknight, D.H., and George, J.F., 2007. It road warriors: Balancing work-family conflict, job autonomy, and work overload to mitigate turnover intentions. *MIS Quart. 31*, 1, 1-17.

[2] Ayyagari, R., Grover, V., and Purvis, R., 2011. Technostress: Technical antecedents and implications. *MIS Quart. 35*, 4, 831-858.

[3] Bakker, A.B. and Demerouti, E., 2007. The job demands-resources model: State of the art. *Journal of Managerial Psychology 22*, 3, 309.

[4] Cohen, S. and Wills, T.A., 1985. Stress, social support, and the buffering hypothesis. *Psychological Bulletin 98*, 2, 310-357.

[5] De Croon, E.M., Sluiter, J.K., and Frings-Dresen, M.H.W., 2003. Need for recovery after work predicts sickness absence: A 2-year prospective cohort study in truck drivers. *J. Psychosomatic Res. 55*, 4, 331-339.

[6] Dennis, A.R., Wixom, B.H., and Vandenberg, R.J., 2001. Understanding fit and appropriation effects in group support systems via meta-analysis. *MIS Quart. 25*, 2, 167-193.

[7] Desanctis, G. and Poole, M.S., 1994. Capturing the complexity in advanced technology use: Adaptive structuration theory. *Organ. Sci. 5*, 2, 121-147.

[8] Judge, T.A., Thoreson, C.J., Bono, J.E., and Patton, G.K., 2001. The job satisfaction-job performance relationship: A qualitative and quantitative review. *Psychological Bulletin 127*, 3, 376-407.

---

[2] The final survey instrument is available from the authors upon request.

[9] Kahn, R.L. and Byosserie, P., 1992. Stress in organizations. In *Handbook of industrial and organizational psychology* M.D. Dunette and L.M. Hough Eds. Consulting Psychologist Press, Palo Alto, CA.

[10] Mobley, W.H., Griffeth, R.W., Hand, H.H., and Meglino, B.M., 1979. Review and conceptual analysis of the employee turnover process. *Psychological Bulletin 86*, 3, 493-522.

[11] Moore, J.E., 2000. One road to turnover: An examination of work exhaustion in technology professionals. *MIS Quart. 24*, 1, 141-168.

[12] Ragu-Nathan, T.S., Tarafdar, M., and Ragu-Nathan, B.S., 2008. The consequences of technostress for end users in organizations: Conceptual development and empirical validation. *Inform. Systems Res. 19*, 4, 417-433.

[13] Shaw, J. and Weekley, J., 1985. The effects of objective work-load variations of psychological strain and post-work-load performance. *J. Management 11*, 1, 87-98.

[14] Tarafdar, M., Qiang, T.U., Ragu-Nathan, B.S., and Ragu-Nathan, T.S., 2007. The impact of technostress on role stress and productivity. *J. Management Inform. Systems 24*, 1 (Summer2007), 301-328.

[15] Tarafdar, M., Tu, Q., and Ragu-Nathan, T.S., 2010. Impact of technostress on end-user satisfaction and performance. *J. Management Inform. Systems 27*, 3 (Winter2010), 303-334.

[16] Thatcher, J.B. and Perrewe, P.L., 2002. An empirical examination of individual traits as antecedents to computer anxiety and computer self-efficacy. *MIS Quart. 26*, 4, 381-396.

[17] Xanthopoulou, D., Bakker, A.B., Demerouti, E., and Schaufeli, W.B., 2007. The role of personal resources in the job demands-resources model. *International Journal of Stress Management 14*, 2, 121-141.

Appendix A

	LS	MS	PE	SS	WO	WE	JA	IS	AS	CS	FOR	TO	SAT
LS1	0.87	0.29	0.16	0.20	0.20	0.17	-0.09	0.12	0.11	0.04	0.02	0.06	0.03
LS2	0.90	0.29	0.19	0.22	0.26	0.21	-0.10	0.09	0.14	0.00	-0.03	0.16	-0.09
LS3	0.90	0.19	0.15	0.16	0.21	0.25	-0.11	0.04	0.01	-0.02	0.00	0.13	-0.04
LS4	0.88	0.27	0.16	0.16	0.28	0.30	-0.15	-0.01	-0.07	-0.05	-0.11	0.23	-0.15
MS1	0.32	0.86	0.23	0.47	0.50	0.39	-0.17	-0.08	-0.14	-0.16	-0.21	0.36	-0.23
MS2	0.25	0.93	0.26	0.50	0.50	0.38	-0.18	-0.16	-0.20	-0.14	-0.24	0.34	-0.25
MS3	0.20	0.92	0.27	0.56	0.50	0.36	-0.14	-0.19	-0.12	-0.12	-0.25	0.35	-0.27
MS4	0.29	0.95	0.27	0.53	0.53	0.40	-0.17	-0.12	-0.15	-0.16	-0.23	0.36	-0.27
PE1	0.14	0.21	0.81	0.28	0.21	0.13	0.00	-0.02	0.05	0.09	-0.07	0.07	-0.05
PE2	0.10	0.19	0.78	0.25	0.21	0.17	0.05	-0.12	-0.03	0.09	-0.06	0.10	-0.12
PE3	0.22	0.28	0.85	0.31	0.32	0.26	-0.03	0.03	0.07	0.12	-0.08	0.15	-0.13
PE4	0.12	0.26	0.84	0.28	0.27	0.24	0.04	-0.03	0.01	0.08	-0.06	0.15	-0.10
PE5	0.17	0.20	0.76	0.23	0.27	0.20	0.01	0.04	0.03	0.12	0.02	0.09	-0.08
SS1	0.23	0.55	0.32	0.84	0.46	0.30	-0.24	-0.16	-0.15	-0.11	-0.29	0.27	-0.21
SS2	0.20	0.55	0.33	0.94	0.51	0.37	-0.26	-0.10	-0.09	-0.16	-0.25	0.29	-0.26
SS3	0.14	0.50	0.28	0.94	0.46	0.30	-0.26	-0.15	-0.08	-0.21	-0.24	0.30	-0.25
SS4	0.20	0.46	0.30	0.93	0.48	0.36	-0.28	-0.15	-0.09	-0.21	-0.28	0.31	-0.29
WO1	0.25	0.52	0.31	0.49	0.90	0.40	-0.35	-0.19	-0.24	-0.13	-0.41	0.40	-0.38
WO2	0.26	0.53	0.28	0.50	0.94	0.38	-0.42	-0.20	-0.19	-0.15	-0.42	0.37	-0.39
WO3	0.25	0.55	0.32	0.49	0.95	0.43	-0.40	-0.16	-0.24	-0.13	-0.39	0.40	-0.37
WO4	0.23	0.43	0.28	0.45	0.88	0.37	-0.39	-0.09	-0.11	-0.09	-0.34	0.29	-0.32

	LS	MS	PE	SS	WO	WE	JA	IS	AS	CS	FOR	TO	SAT
WE1	0.31	0.36	0.28	0.28	0.40	0.85	-0.30	-0.16	-0.21	-0.09	-0.32	0.35	-0.39
WE2	0.20	0.30	0.16	0.34	0.31	0.81	-0.34	-0.01	-0.14	-0.13	-0.30	0.25	-0.31
WE3	0.19	0.37	0.19	0.34	0.37	0.89	-0.38	-0.10	-0.28	-0.16	-0.33	0.32	-0.39
WE4	0.20	0.41	0.21	0.32	0.41	0.91	-0.35	-0.13	-0.25	-0.18	-0.37	0.37	-0.34
JA1	-0.08	-0.16	0.05	-0.26	-0.42	-0.42	0.89	0.22	0.43	0.31	0.57	-0.42	0.53
JA2	-0.14	-0.16	0.01	-0.23	-0.36	-0.35	0.91	0.11	0.30	0.24	0.57	-0.35	0.46
JA3	-0.13	-0.18	-0.01	-0.22	-0.38	-0.31	0.88	0.09	0.26	0.20	0.52	-0.35	0.48
JA4	-0.10	-0.12	-0.01	-0.30	-0.33	-0.29	0.83	0.12	0.23	0.20	0.50	-0.27	0.38
IS1	0.05	-0.13	-0.05	-0.13	-0.22	-0.10	0.08	0.86	0.46	0.30	0.19	-0.16	0.23
IS2	0.04	-0.15	-0.03	-0.16	-0.18	-0.15	0.19	0.89	0.48	0.38	0.28	-0.21	0.38
IS3	0.08	-0.17	-0.06	-0.18	-0.15	-0.13	0.17	0.95	0.51	0.39	0.25	-0.23	0.37
IS4	0.05	-0.04	0.09	-0.03	-0.03	-0.03	0.08	0.71	0.38	0.17	0.22	-0.03	0.25
AS1	0.02	-0.20	0.04	-0.13	-0.24	-0.25	0.36	0.57	0.91	0.42	0.40	-0.28	0.34
AS2	0.06	-0.11	0.06	-0.09	-0.19	-0.21	0.34	0.49	0.95	0.42	0.36	-0.27	0.32
AS3	0.08	-0.12	0.01	-0.11	-0.14	-0.25	0.31	0.46	0.94	0.46	0.36	-0.23	0.27
AS4	0.05	-0.18	0.01	-0.10	-0.21	-0.25	0.30	0.50	0.94	0.42	0.33	-0.26	0.30
CS1	-0.02	-0.10	0.14	-0.12	-0.07	-0.12	0.25	0.22	0.32	0.82	0.11	-0.09	0.12
CS2	-0.02	-0.17	0.10	-0.24	-0.17	-0.17	0.25	0.31	0.44	0.88	0.19	-0.11	0.17
CS3	0.04	-0.10	0.14	-0.15	-0.08	-0.14	0.23	0.38	0.43	0.92	0.22	-0.19	0.25
CS4	-0.03	-0.17	0.06	-0.16	-0.17	-0.14	0.23	0.38	0.43	0.89	0.28	-0.19	0.24
FOR1	-0.03	-0.23	-0.08	-0.28	-0.38	-0.36	0.61	0.21	0.34	0.20	0.94	-0.41	0.53
FOR2	-0.05	-0.28	-0.09	-0.31	-0.42	-0.38	0.61	0.24	0.37	0.22	0.97	-0.46	0.57
FOR3	-0.01	-0.24	-0.07	-0.27	-0.42	-0.36	0.59	0.30	0.40	0.27	0.96	-0.42	0.57
FOR4	-0.03	-0.21	0.01	-0.23	-0.37	-0.34	0.53	0.30	0.37	0.19	0.90	-0.39	0.52
TO1	0.23	0.37	0.17	0.27	0.35	0.30	-0.34	-0.14	-0.24	-0.13	-0.40	0.83	-0.48
TO2	0.09	0.27	0.07	0.26	0.28	0.31	-0.32	-0.21	-0.26	-0.17	-0.35	0.86	-0.56
TO3	0.07	0.30	0.07	0.29	0.33	0.34	-0.34	-0.22	-0.28	-0.19	-0.37	0.90	-0.59
TO4	0.18	0.37	0.18	0.27	0.40	0.34	-0.38	-0.09	-0.15	-0.08	-0.39	0.81	-0.48
SAT1	-0.07	-0.27	-0.14	-0.26	-0.42	-0.44	0.54	0.34	0.35	0.23	0.58	-0.55	0.91
SAT2	-0.06	-0.26	-0.11	-0.26	-0.40	-0.42	0.52	0.34	0.31	0.23	0.52	-0.64	0.95
SAT3	-0.06	-0.26	-0.08	-0.26	-0.31	-0.31	0.43	0.34	0.29	0.19	0.51	-0.53	0.93
SAT4	-0.08	-0.27	-0.11	-0.24	-0.35	-0.38	0.46	0.33	0.28	0.19	0.54	-0.60	0.94

Note: LS - Learning Stressor, MS - Monitoring Stressor, PE - Physical Environment Stressor, SS - Social Stressor, WO - Work Overload, WE - Work Exhaustion, JA - Job Autonomy, IS - Information Support, AS - Appropriation Support, CS - Communication Support, FOR - Fairness of Rewards, TO - Turnover Intention, SAT - Job Satisfaction

Improving E-Learning Motivation Using Social Software

Thomas Wirtky
Otto Friedrich University Bamberg,
Germany
Department of
Information Systems and Services
thomas.wirtky@uni-bamberg.de

ABSTRACT

Trained personnel are crucial for success in a knowledge society. Unsurprisingly, e-learning is expected to provide more than operational efficiency in organizations, which it did in the academic context, but did not in the corporate context. This research proposal argues that human motivation is the key difference between the two contexts. Social software seems to positively impact motivation, but how and which social software features to implement in a corporate e-learning context is still unknown. Hence, this research hypothesizes and analyzes the impact of social software features on user motivation to participate. It develops a model explaining why social software impacts motivation and ultimately uses experiments embedded in a design science approach to explain how and which social software features to implement in a given context. This proposal details this approach and provides intermediate findings in the quest for personnel motivation and corporate e-learning success.

Categories and Subject Descriptors

H.1.2 [**Models and principles**]: User/Machine Systems; K.3.1 [**Computers and education**]: Computer Uses in Education

General Terms

Management, Design, Human Factors

Keywords

HRIS, e-learning, motivation, social software

1. INTRODUCTION

Trained human resources are most critical in a knowledge society [15]. IT-enabled training (e-learning) was thought to be one of the fastest growing sectors [35], to revolutionize education [28], and to provide more to organizations than just operational efficiency [50]. It struggled in the beginning [34,52], but later enjoyed considerable success in academia [49]. However, success is limited in the corporate context [20].

The reason for this lack of success is unlikely to be the e-learning technology, content or pedagogical design principles as these factors hardly differ between the academic and the corporate contexts. DeRouin et al. even found in their literature review that those organizational employees who participated in e-learning

reacted favorably [14], which implies that technology, content and design are appropriate. Instead, the environmental conditions are more likely to affect corporate employees differently than students in academia. In the corporate context, programs need to be shorter, directly applicable and more self-directed than instructor-led [7,14]. While a student's short-term success is measured in academic grades, which are sometimes even directly dependent on e-learning participation, short-term success of a corporate employee is usually not directly connected with training and e-learning participation. Thus, motivation of the learner is different and more critical for corporate employees to participate [17,43].

Social software is expected to increase motivation [9,46,48]. The term social software is used synonymously with web 2.0, which basically refers to web-based software allowing users to not only consume information, but also to generate information and to socially interact with each other [18,39]. The combination of e-learning and social software is termed e-learning 2.0, which promises a new era in technology enabled learning, potentially providing the means for life-long learning even in dynamic environments [6,31,51]. Unfortunately, it is not often implemented in the corporate e-learning context yet [3], which is probably why there is no research explaining which and how individual social software features impact motivation in this context. As a result, there is no guidance for practitioners designing, delivering, and implementing e-learning [14], which calls for the research question. ***How do social software features impact the motivation for corporate e-learning participation?*** The answer could lead to corporate e-learning becoming successful and to life-long learning becoming more than a popular phrase.

We use a narrow definition of e-learning to only include asynchronous technologies, i.e., technologies that provide electronic, time and place-independent access to knowledge, which is preprocessed for educational purposes. By contrast, synchronous technologies such as online conferencing and collaboration tools, which facilitate real-time distance trainings, are not included. This is due to the fact that social human interaction is already part of the definition of synchronous e-learning limiting the potential impact of additional social features on motivation.

This proposal contains three main sections, which (i) discuss the related literature regarding the research questions, (ii) outline the proposed research approach, and (iii) provide a preview of intermediate results. A summary of the expected contributions and limitations complete this paper.

2. RELATED RESEARCH

Figure 1 illustrates three related research areas, which this section briefly discusses in the following.

2.1 E-learning and motivation

The motivation to participate in e-learning does not significantly differ from motivation to participate in any training activity. Thus, we conducted an extended literature review on training motivation. Since motivation research has a long history and cuts "across all subareas within psychology" [40], it is not surprising to find a diversity of corporate training motivation models in reputable journals of the last 20 years. Despite the models' differences, they also share common findings and constructs, which can be associated with more abstract motivational facets [12]. Figure 2 illustrates an adapted motivational overview from Heckhausen and Heckhasuen and identifies nine motivational facets [25]. A discussion of each model listed in Table 1 would go beyond the scope of this paper. It is important to note that Hurtz and Williams provided the most comprehensive model [30], which is why it serves as a basis for our research model as outlined below in chapter 3.1.2.

2.2 Social software and motivation

The ability of social software to facilitate collaboration is one commonly mentioned advantage. Thus, there is a research stream concerning human motivation to contribute and to collaborate that focused on the question why human voluntarily use social software technology and share their knowledge with others [e.g., 5,8,19]. Although the findings might be relevant when setting up an experiment at a later stage of this research, they do not answer the question how social software impacts motivation.

Research regarding the impact of social software on motivation exists, but not at the required level of detail as three exemplary research contributions illustrate in the following. In the first contribution, the authors of a research-in-progress publication opted against using an empirically supported research model and in favor of a more general Person-Environment Fit based approach trying to explain the impact of web 2.0 on system use in general [42]. Unfortunately, this ambitious attempt did not yield any findings yet, which could be relevant for the context of corporate e-learning. Empirical data of a second contribution supports the hypothesis that a website's socialness increases perceived usefulness, perceived ease of use, perceived enjoyment and the intention to visit a website [46]. The authors define socialness as the extent of a website's ability to allow for human social interaction, and they use video-based user interaction in an online shop for testing their hypothesis. Although these findings are consistent with earlier finding regarding the usage of interactive videos in an e-learning environment, it is unlikely that these findings are applicable to an asynchronous, non-interactive e-learning context since non-interactive videos do not improve e-learning effectiveness [53]. The third contribution provides evidence for social factors to indirectly impact e-learning participation [9]. Unfortunately, the author defined social factors not as social software features, but as interpersonal and external influences.

Summing it up, despite the mentioned concerns regarding the applicability of the findings to the asynchronous e-learning context, we generally conclude that social factors have a positive impact on motivation [9,48], in some cases even on more than one motivational facet [46], but the question which social software features to implement in order to maximize motivation in the corporate asynchronous e-learning context is still unanswered. This leaves practitioners without guidance for e-learning implementations and widens the already existing gap between them and academics in the area of e-learning [14].

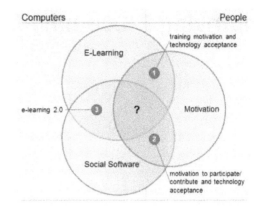

Figure 1: Research question and related research areas

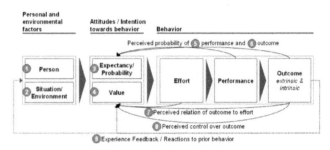

Figure 2: Overview of abstract motivational facets

Table 1: Comparison of training motivation models by nine abstract motivational facets

	(1) Person	(2) Environment	(3) Expectancy	(4) Valence	(5) Probability of performance	(6) Probability of outcome	(7) Inequity / Relation of outcome to effort	(8) Control over outcome	(9) Reactions to prior behavior
Birdi et al. [4]	●	●	●	-	●	●	-	-	-
Cheng [9]	●	-	●	-	●	●	-	-	-
Chiu et al. [10]	-	-	●	-	-	-	●	-	●
Clark et al. [11]	-	●	●	●	-	●	-	-	-
Garavan et al. [22]	-	●	●	●	-	●	-	-	-
Hurtz and Williams [30]	●	●	●	●	●	●	●	-	●
Maurer and Tarulli [36]	●	●	●	●	●	●	-	-	-
Noe and Wilk [37]	●	●	●	-	●	●	-	-	-
Tharenou [44]	●	●	●	●	-	●	-	-	-
Venkatesh [45]	●	-	●	●	●	●	-	-	-

2.3 E-learning and social software

Social software features are expected to significantly improve e-learning as mentioned earlier. Unfortunately, research on social software in e-learning primarily focuses on technical possibilities or the impact on the learning process or learning outcome [e.g., 6,31,33,51]. Unfortunately, it is not yet concerned with the motivation to participate.

3. PROPOSED RESEARCH APPROACH

As illustrated in Figure 3 we propose to approach the research question in two steps. Step 1 - the theoretical foundation – is important in order to provide the currently missing guidance for design and implementation work [14] and offer explanations as to *why* social software features impact motivation. In step 2 – the design research process, we will directly address the research question as to *how* social software features impact the motivation to participate in corporate e-learning.

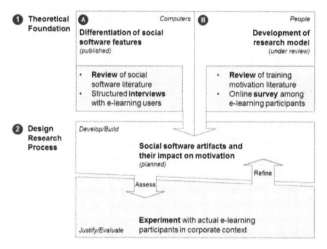

Figure 3: Outline of proposed research approach (adapted from Hevner et al. 2004)

3.1 Theoretical Foundation

As argued above, motivation is critical for e-learning participation, the usage of social software is an emerging trend, and a model explaining the impact of social software features on motivation to participate in e-learning activities is missing. We propose to approach this gap from two perspectives. Firstly, we differentiate social software features from a technology point of view, and we secondly develop a model from a human motivation point of view, which includes the impact of social software.

3.1.1 Differentiation of social software features

Existing models suggest that social factors do have a positive impact on motivation do not differentiate individual social software features [9,46,48]. Due to a lack of theory, deductively deriving a differentiation is unsatisfactory. Thus, this research interviews corporate e-learning users who are familiar with social software for their hypothetical opinion on the potential inclusion of social software features in their e-learning environments. After neglecting unfavorable features, it applies the inductive approach of an exploratory factor analysis to the gathered data on the remaining favorable features in order to uncover differentiated use of social software features. We opt for personal interviews in case participants have questions regarding individual features. The interviews are structured because social software features are known for nearly ten years [18], and motivation theory is known since Aristotle [24].

3.1.2 Development of research model

According to the results of a literature review illustrated in Table 1 above, the model of Hurtz and Williams is the most comprehensive training motivation model and serves as a basis for this research [30]. We intend to modify the model for two reasons. First, the original model is longitudinal and sometimes contradicts the previously established research, and second, the impact of social software needs to be included. We intend to empirically support any modification by surveying corporate e-learning participants, and comparing the modified model with the unmodified one.

3.2 Design research process

To our knowledge, there is no corporate e-learning platform with social features available for research purposes yet. We therefore do not follow a behavioral science approach, but the design science approach as it is ideal to extend boundaries to unknown research areas such as e-learning 2.0 [16,23,27,47]. We thereby follow other academics calling for more design research in the e-learning space [26,32]. In search for a satisfactory design [41], the experimental setting requires the implementation of the previously identified social factors as artifacts, which are then evaluated in an iterative trial-and-error approach [27]. The previously defined research model will become part of the design research in form of "Justificatory Knowledge", which explains not only how to improve motivation, but also why it is improving [23].

We envision an experiment comparing two groups of e-learning participants while providing only one of them with the experimental social software features. The contextual focus is on the user's decision to participate in e-learning. Hence, the focus is on the decision to launch an e-learning module out of a list of many available corporate e-learning modules, which a typical corporate learning management system (LMS) presents.

4. INTERMEDIATE RESULTS

There are results concerning the first part of this research – the theoretical foundation – that we briefly outline in the following.

4.1 Differentiation of social software features

We conducted structured interviews on social software features listed in Table 2 in Germany with 39 young IS employees of a well-known international IT services company. The participants work in different departments of the organization with each department having the freedom to use different e-learning platforms. They work in different locations across Germany, cover a wide range of functions. The average age of the sample is 22 years, and it contains 15% females. This sample not only has a high need for flexible ways of learning given the high pace of the IT industry, but also comprises the IS enthusiasm required to be most suitable for providing hypothetical opinions on social software features. These opinions were captured in 7-point Likert-scales ranging from 1 (very unfavorable) to 7 (very favorable) with 4 being neutral.

The findings confirm first of all that users generally have a favorable view on social software features in the context of corporate e-learning, but these features are seldom implemented in the different e-learning platforms that the participants had exposure to. There are a few features that have mean and median values smaller or equal to zero, which are considered unfavorable in the context. These features are as illustrated in Table 2 personal forums of peers and supervisors as well as status messages and newsfeeds. A satisfactory Kaiser-Meyer-Olkin value of 0.673 and a significant Bartlett test of sphericity allowed for an exploratory factor analysis on the remaining favorable features. A supplementary parallel analysis [29,38] revealed three main components. Table 2 contains the resulting factor loadings of favorable social software features after Varimax rotation if they are greater than 0.5. The components appear to represent distinguishable user needs. The first component (Factor A) seems to combine features that meet the need of e-learning users to receive additional opinions and meta-information about e-learning modules e.g., ratings or comments of peers and trainers. The components two and three (Factors B and C) appear to represent the need for two distinct learning methods, which are learning from experts and learning from peers.

4.2 Development of research model

The primary focus and purpose of the research model is to serve as an explanation of why certain social software features impact e-learning motivation. More specifically, we are focusing on the context of a LMS, which provides a user with a list of e-learning modules and where the user finally decides whether to participate and launch a certain module or not. As mentioned earlier, the base model of Hurtz and Williams needs to be modified to account for contradictions with previous research and to account for the impact of social software features. As all modifications are outlined in a paper under review, this section continues with a brief description of the resulting model illustrated in Figure 4 and of the hypotheses regarding the impact of social software.

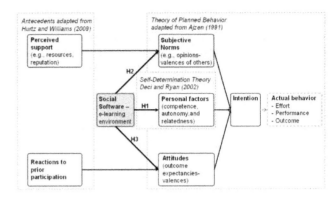

Figure 4: Research model

The main part of the research model is clearly based on the theory of planned behavior [1]. Hurtz and Williams extended it with the antecedents 'Perceived Support' and 'Reactions to prior participation' as these factors are especially relevant in the training motivation context [30].

This research argues that the motivational factor relatedness, which is based on the human need for social belonging, has a high probability in explaining the impact of social software on training motivation. Research in child development found that security of attachment i.e., relatedness explains exploratory learning

Table 2: Descriptive statistics and factor loadings of social software features

	Usefulness in e-learning					Factor loadings[c]		
	N[a]	Mean	SD	Min/ Max	Me- dian	A	B	C
Personal forums - text based (blog)								
of peers[b]	38	3.87	(1.73)	1/7	4	-	-	-
of trainers	38	4.61	(1.65)	1/7	5		0.72	
of supervisors[b]	38	3.82	(1.67)	1/7	4	-	-	-
Comments on modules								
from peers	39	5.05	(1.69)	1/7	5	0.60		
from trainers	39	5.18	(1.48)	2/7	5	0.54	0.58	
from supervisors	39	4.62	(1.68)	1/7	5		0.67	
Ratings of modules								
from peers	39	5.41	(1.57)	1/7	6	0.80		
from trainers	39	4.85	(1.57)	2/7	5	0.82		
from supervisors	39	4.38	(1.70)	1/7	5	0.64		
Asynchronous communication (chat)								
with peers	39	4.67	(1.54)	1/7	5			0.78
with trainers	39	5.10	(1.37)	2/7	5			0.80
with supervisors	39	4.10	(1.59)	1/7	4		0.80	
Comments on items	39	4.64	(1.74)	1/7	5	0.74		
Sharing of items with others	39	4.44	(1.80)	1/7	5	0.78		
Collaborative forum (wiki)	39	5.13	(1.61)	1/7	5		0.66	
Earmarking of items (tagging)	39	4.79	(1.47)	2/7	5	0.57		0.58
Search content by person	39	4.13	(1.66)	1/7	4			0.62
Status messages (micro blogs)[b]	38	4.00	(2.00)	1/7	4	-	-	-
Newsfeed on trainings (RSS)[b]	38	3.82	(1.75)	1/7	4	-	-	-

a) N varies due to missing data   b) excluded from factor analysis since mean and media ≤ 4   c) Factor loadings <0.5 are not displayed behaviors [21], which could also hold to some degree for adults. Furthermore, we suggest replacing the construct 'behavioral control' in the theory of planned behavior with relatedness and the other two factors of the self-determination theory [13], which are competence and autonomy. Ajzen clarified the definition of 'behavioral control' to be a reflection 'perceived self-efficacy' and 'perceived controllability' [2], which are in fact equivalents to competence and autonomy as defined by Deci and Ryan [13]. As the self-determination theory is an intrinsic motivation theory, the new construct 'Personal factors' including competence, autonomy and relatedness resembles a person's expectation of a behavior to be intrinsically motivating.

H1: *Given our context of an LMS, we hypothesize that the availability of social software features associated with previously identified factor A (see Table 2)such as module ratings and opinions of peers will allow for social interaction and will therefore positively impact 'Personal factors'.*

According to Ajzen, Subjective Norms "are concerned with the likelihood that important referent individuals or groups approve or disapprove of performing a given behavior" [1].

H2: *As social software features in an LMS, allows a user to better know the opinion of potentially important referents, we further hypothesize a positive impact of social software on 'Subjective Norms'.*

After completion of an e-learning module, participants can expect to have the opportunity to provide their own opinions, rakings and comments to others in the LMS using social software features. The theory of planned behavior captures these kind of outcome expectancies in the 'Attitudes' construct [1].

H3: *We also hypothesize that social software features will positively impact 'Attitudes'*

Future research steps include the empirical validation of the model containing self-determination theory instead of 'behavioral control', and the experimental evaluation of the three hypotheses.

5. POTENTIAL CONTRIBUTIONS AND LIMITATIONS

This research potentially contributes to both researchers and practitioners. The former will have their call for more design research in the e-learning area answered [e.g., 26,32], and they will benefit from a deeper understanding on how and why social software impacts motivation. We also expect to contribute further insights about the technologies' impact on the participants' development and performance. Furthermore, the proposed research model could be generalized to other contexts where the subject of research is the impact of social technology on user motivation. Practitioners will benefit from the guidance that this research provides regarding which social software features to implement in a corporate e-learning context with the goal to maximize user motivation. This way, it will also contribute to the closure of the gap between e-learning research and practice [14]. Ultimately, if corporate e-learning becomes successful, the research's contribution will exceed its research scope and contribute to life-long learning and to a higher availability of trained personnel which is crucial for any organization's success [15].

The primary limitation of this research stems from its practical orientation. Findings gained from the experiment are bound to the implementation context of corporate asynchronous e-learning. Their validity e.g., academic context or synchronous e-learning context would require further research as social software features are likely to play a different role.

6. REFERENCES

[1] Ajzen, I. The theory of planned behavior. *Organizational Behavior and Human Decision Processes 50*, 2 (1991), 179–211.

[2] Ajzen, I. Perceived Behavioral Control, Self-Efficacy, Locus of Control, and the Theory of Planned Behavior. *Journal of Applied Social Psychology 32*, 4 (2002), 665–683.

[3] Andriole, S.J. Business impact of Web 2.0 Technologies. *Communications of the ACM 53*, 12 (2010), 67–79.

[4] Birdi, K., Allan, C., and Warr, P. Correlates and perceived outcomes of four types of employee development activity. *Journal of Applied Psychology 82*, 6 (1997), 845–857.

[5] Boateng, R., Malik, A., and Mbarika, V. Web 2.0 and Organizational Learning: Conceptualizing the Link Conceptualizing the Link. *Americas Conference on Information Systems (AMCIS) Proceedings*, (2009).

[6] Brown, J.S. and Adler, R.P. Minds on Fire: Open Education, the Long Tail, and Learning 2.0. *Educause Review*, January/February (2008), 16–32.

[7] Brown, K.G. and Ford, J.K. Using computer technology in training: Building an infrastructure for active learning. In K. Kraiger, ed., *Creating, implementing, and managing effective training and development*. Jossey-Bass, San Francisco, CA, 2002, 192–233.

[8] Brown, S. A., Dennis, A.R., and Venkatesh, V. Predicting Collaboration Technology Use: Integrating Technology Adoption and Collaboration Research. *Journal of Management Information Systems 27*, 2 (2010), 9–54.

[9] Cheng, Y.-M. Antecedents and consequences of e-learning acceptance. *Information Systems Journal 21*, 3 (2011), 269–299.

[10] Chiu, C.-M., Chiu, C.-S., and Chang, H.-C. Examining the integrated influence of fairness and quality on learners' satisfaction and Web-based learning continuance intention. *Information Systems Journal 17*, 3 (2007), 271–287.

[11] Clark, C.S., Dobbins, G.H., and Ladd, R.T. Exploratory Field Study of Training Motivation: Infiluence of Involvement, Credibility, and Transfer Climate. *Group & Organization Management 18*, 3 (1993), 292–307.

[12] Colquitt, J.A., LePine, J.A., and Noe, R.A. Toward an integrative theory of training motivation: A meta-analytic path analysis of 20 years of research. *Journal of Applied Psychology 85*, 5 (2000), 678–707.

[13] Deci, E.L. and Ryan, R.M. *Handbook of self-determination research*. University of Rochester Press, 2002.

[14] DeRouin, R.E., Fritzsche, B.A., and Sales, E. E-Learning in Organizations. *Journal of Management 31*, 6 (2005), 920–940.

[15] Drucker, P.F. The New Society of Organizations. In R. Howard, ed., *The Learning Imperative: Managing people for continuous innovation*. Harvard Business Press, 1993, 3–17.

[16] Dubin, R. *Theory Building*. Free Press, London, 1978.

[17] Dublin, L. If You Only Look Under the Street Lamps…or Nine e-Learning myths. *The e-Learning Developer's Journal*, June (2003), 1–7.

[18] Ebersbach, A., Glaser, M., and Heigl, R. *Social Web*. UVK Verlagsgesellschaft mbH, Konstanz, 2011.

[19] Ekweozor, U. and Theodoulidis, B. Who owns the knowledge that I share? *Americas Conference on Information Systems (AMCIS) Proceedings*, (2010).

[20] Fee, K. *Delivering E-Learning: A complete strategy for design, application and assessment*. Kogan Page Limited, 2009.

[21] Frodi, A., Bridges, L., and Grolnick, W. Correlates of Mastery-Related Behavior: A Short-Term Longitudinal Study of Infants in Their Second Year. *Child Development 56*, 5 (1985), 1291–1298.

[22] Garavan, T.N., Carbery, R., Malley, G.O., and Donnell, D.O. Understanding participation in e-learning in organizations: a large- scale empirical study of employees. *International Journal of Training and Development 14*, 3 (2010), 155–168.

[23] Gregor, S. and Jones, D. The Anatomy of a Design Theory. *Journal of the Association for Information Systems 8*, 5 (2007), 312–335.

[24] Hardie, W.F.R. *Aristotle's ethical theory*. Clarendon Press, Oxford, 1980.

[25] Heckhausen, J. and Heckhausen, H. *Motivation and Action*. Cambridge University Press, Cambridge, UK, 2010.

[26] Herrington, J., Reeves, T.C., and Oliver, R. *A guide to authentic e-learning*. Routledge Chapman & Hall, 2010.

[27] Hevner, B.A.R., March, S.T., Park, J., and Ram, S. Design Science in information systems research. *MIS Quarterly 28*, 1 (2004), 75–105.

[28] Hiltz, S.R. and Turoff, M. Education goes digital - The Evolution of Online Learning and the Revolution in Higher Education. *Communications of the ACM 48*, 10 (2005), 59 – 64.

[29] Horn, J.L. A rationale and test for the number of factors in factor analysis. *Psychometrika 30*, 2 (1965), 179–185.

[30] Hurtz, G.M. and Williams, K.J. Attitudinal and motivational antecedents of participation in voluntary employee development activities. *Journal of Applied Psychology 94*, 3 (2009), 635–53.

[31] Joint-Research-Center. *Learning 2.0: The Impact of Web 2.0 Innovations on Education and Training in Europe*. Dictus Publishing, 2011.

[32] Kelly, A.E. Research as Design. *Educational Researcher 32*, 1 (2003), 3–4.

[33] London, M. and Hall, M. Unlocking the value of web 2.0 technologies for training and development: The shift from instructor-controlled, adaptive learning to learner-driven generative learning. *Human Resource Management 50*, 6 (2011), 757–775.

[34] Lytras, M. and Pouloudi, A. E-Learning: Just a Waste of Time. *Americas Conference on Information Systems (AMCIS) Proceedings*, (2001).

[35] Martin, G., Massy, J., and Clarke, T. When absorptive capacity meets institutions and (e)learners: adopting, diffusing and exploiting e-learning in organizations. *International Journal of Training and Development 7*, 4 (2003), 228–244.

[36] Maurer, T.J. and Tarulli, B.A. Investigation of perceived environment, perceived outcome, and person variables in relationship to voluntary development activity by employees. *Journal of Applied Psychology 79*, 1 (1994), 3–14.

[37] Noe, R.A. and Wilk, S.L. Investigation of the factors that influence employees' participation in development activities. *Journal of Applied Psychology 78*, 2 (1993), 291–302.

[38] O'Connor, B.P. SPSS and SAS programs for determining the number of components using parallel analysis and velicer's MAP test. *Behavior research methods, instruments, & computers: a journal of the Psychonomic Society, Inc 32*, 3 (2000), 396–402.

[39] O'Reilly, T. What Is Web 2.0. *Pattern Recognition 30*, 2005, 0–48. http://oreilly.com/web2/archive/what-is-web-20.html.

[40] Petri, H.L. and Govern, J.M. *Motivation - Theory, Research, and Applications*. Wadsworth Publishing, 2003.

[41] Simon, H.A. *The Sciences of the Artificial*. MIT Press, Cambridge, MA, 1969.

[42] Soliman, M.A. and Beaudry, A. Undertanding individual adoption and use of social computing: A user-system fit model. *International Conference on Information Systems (ICIS) Proceedings*, (2010).

[43] Tai, L. *Corporate E-Learning: An Inside View of IBM's Solutions*. Oxford University Press, New York, NY, USA, 2008.

[44] Tharenou, P. The relationship of training motivation to participation in training and development. *Journal of Occupational & Organizational Psychology 74*, 5 (2001), 599–621.

[45] Venkatesh, V. Creation of Favorable User Perceptions: Exploring the Role of Intrinsic Motivation. *MIS Quarterly 23*, 2 (1999), 239.

[46] Wakefield, R.L., Wakefield, K.L., Baker, J., and Wang, L.C. How website socialness leads to website use. *European Journal of Information Systems 20*, 1 (2010), 118–132.

[47] Walls, J., Widemeyer, G., and El Sawy, O. Building an Information System Design theory for Vigilant EIS. *Information Systems Research 3*, 1 (1992), 36–59.

[48] Wang, M., Vogel, D., and Ran, W. Creating a performance-oriented e-learning environment: A design science approach. *Information & Management 48*, 7 (2011), 260–269.

[49] Wirt, S., Choy, S., Rooney, P., Provasnik, S., Sen, A., and Tobin, R. *The condition of Education 2004 (NECS 2004-077)*. Washington, D.C., 2004.

[50] Wirtky, T., Eckhardt, A., Laumer, S., Wild, U., and Weitzel, T. Going beyond operational efficiency in HR using IT - A Literature Review of Human Resources Information Systems. *Americas Conference on Information Systems (AMCIS) Proceedings*, (2011).

[51] Yang, H.H. and Yuen, S.C.-Y. *Collective intelligence and e-learning 2.0*. Information Science Reference, 2009.

[52] Zemsky, R. and Massey, W. Why the E-Learning Boom Went Bust. *The Chronicle of Higher Education 50*, July 9 (2004).

[53] Zhang, D., Zhou, L., Briggs, R.O., and Nunamaker, J.F. Instructional video in e-learning: Assessing the impact of interactive video on learning effectiveness. *Information & Management 43*, (2006), 15–27.

Psychological Contract in the Information Systems Profession

René Moquin
Doctoral Student
One Bear Place
Waco, TX 76798
(254)710-6503
Rene_moquin@baylor.edu

Cindy Riemenschneider
Professor/Associate Dean
One Bear Place
Waco, TX 76798
(254)710-4061
C_Riemenschneider@baylor.edu

ABSTRACT

The past decade has ushered in challenging events for the IS profession such as economic instabilities, outsourcing/offshoring IS projects, and cloud computing. These eventualities present a stressful environment for emerging and tenured IS professionals. Firms are typically pressured to reduce costs by reducing IS staff only to revisit rehiring the same IS professionals. We investigated the phenomenon of IS professional career commitment to the IS profession using psychological contract theory (PCT) and affective events theory (AET). We present a model that examines the psychological contract in the IS profession (PCP), psychological contract breach in the profession (PCBP) and psychological contract violation in the profession (PCVP). We interviewed twenty-six IS professionals having experienced negative attributions in the IS profession where they reassessed their commitment to the profession (turnover intention) or left the field (turnover). Our results show that all interviewees remained in the field, suggesting the amount of negative conditions in the IS profession may be less significant to turnover. A deeper analysis of the qualitative data indicates that certain elements contribute to interest and commitment to the IS profession such as positive learning opportunities, challenges, and flexibility, such as profession specificity (programmer, CIO, analyst, and database administration). The vastness of the IS profession enables IS professionals to enter another capacity and still experience challenges and accomplishment. We present our implications of the results from a theoretical and practical position.

Categories and Subject Descriptors: H.1.1 [Models and Principles]: Systems Information Theory - information theory

Keywords

Psychological Contact Theory, Affective Events Theory, IS Profession, IS Professionals, Expectations, Promises

1. INTRODUCTION

The last decade has been unstable for the Information Systems (IS)/Information Technology (IT) professional. In the early 2000's, an increased demand for ecommerce systems appeared in part because information and communication technologies (ICT) were being used by a majority of firms. The escalating need for IS/IT professionals was a positive event in the IS profession. The consensus for a steady and long lasting injection of IS/IT

SIGMIS-CPR'13, May 30 - June 1, 2013, Cincinnati, Ohio, USA.
Copyright 2013 ACM 978-1-4503-1975-1/13/05...$15.00

professionals in the field was perceived as anything but transitory [1]. However, in a span of approximately two years, interest in ICT began to wane as investors reduced their spending, IS/IT was downsized, economic instability created fear in ICT investors [2], and portions of the IS/IT profession were outsourced; in many respects, the value adding IS/IT professional seemed like a passing fad. Presently, IS professionals are often asked to do more with less [3], do less with less [4], work in highly complex environments often spanning into other functional areas [5], and address complex business and user requirements [6]. The dot-com bust saw IS/IT jobs outsourced as a possible reaction to recoup high investment losses [1]. In the years following the bust, firms continued to reduce IS//IT overhead by retaining enough staff to keep operational costs low. This event possibly supports the notion of the migration of some IS professionals toward transactional-type engagements. A possible side effect of this migration reduces the number of previously full time IS personnel (Chiang, et al., 2012). An additional side effect of such adaptive reactions may be evident by increases in employee resentment and stress, eliciting concerns over job security, pay, and the intrinsic value of the profession [7]. Therefore, stability in the IS profession is somewhat mythical. Weber (2004) suggests that although outsourcing and offshoring has existed for the past two decades, recent investments in offshoring engagements reduced the need for U.S.-based IS professionals. However, and quite paradoxically, recent research suggests that IS/IT professionals with ICT domain knowledge, interpersonal communication, and professional experience are important and available domestically, necessitating an increased demand for these skills [8].

Recruiting, retaining, and developing competent IS professionals are important concerns among top management [5]. The turbulent IS profession has seen unfairly treated IS professionals experiencing negative side effects during such common events as mass layoffs and the speed of technology change [3]. As the need for IS professionals increases, recently laid-off IS professionals cautiously approach contractual engagements [2]. Employees and organizations exist together in a work relationship rooted in social exchange. Each expects specific obligations or promises from the other. Firms expect their employees to work hard and exhibit organizational commit. Employees expect to receive a paycheck for their work and, in some conditions, a performance bonus. The objectiveness of this relationship is mostly identifiable and largely simple to satisfy. However, a more abstract and subjective contract that exists between the employee and firm is the psychological contract. A psychological contract (PC), founded largely in social exchange theory, is the subjective and implied exchange or expectation of promises, written or spoken between an employee and employer [9]. This contract is separate from the traditional official and legally acknowledged work contract. Psychological contracts are mostly subjective and often unidentifiable by both parties. Often, the PC is broken as employees invest significant physical and mental energy with little or no perceived reciprocation of organizational promises [10]. Two important facets of the psychological contract are breach and violation. A breach is the cognitive awareness of unmet expectations [11]. Contract violation appears as the application of an emotion or affect that represents the degree of the breach [11].

This qualitative research will explore psychological contract violation in the IS/IT profession by introducing a new set of constructs derived from our foundational research of Rousseau (1987), and Robinson & Morrison (2000). These new constructs are psychological contract with the profession (PCP), psychological contract breach in the profession (PCBP), and psychological contract violation in the profession (PCVP). The intent of our research is three-fold. First, this research seeks to discover previously unexplored factors influencing PCVP experienced by IS professionals as relating to their profession. Second, this study will create a foundation to provide sufficient evidence to enable us to conduct future quantitative research on the discovered concepts. Finally, this study extends current research by presenting, defining, and explicating PCVP by focusing on the experiences between the IS professional and the IS profession. This focus is in opposition to the traditional means of a dyadic relation between two or more individuals or entities. Thus, our study contributes to psychological contract research in one important way: we extend PC theory beyond the employee and organization situation to the IS professional and the IS profession. Our research removes the tangible dyadic interactional component between two agents to an introspective condition. This condition places the burden of PC success or failure in the hands of the IS professional.

Given the importance of retaining IS professionals, we examine the phenomenon of IS professional's attitudes of PCP by drawing upon two theories: psychological contract theory and affective events theory. We begin by presenting a literature review on psychological contract, contract breach, contract violation, and affective events theory. Following the literature review, we present the formal theoretical discourse used in our study. Following the theory section is the qualitative research methodology, data analysis, and the detail results of our qualitative study.

2. THEORY
2.1 Psychological Contract Theory
The psychological contract (PC) theory exists as a perceptual and subjective internalization of promises and their reciprocation between two or more agents [9], [12], [13], [14]. Perception and subjectivity present a reciprocation complexity because some PC's can contain thousands of items, with only a discrete set being accessible at any one time [15]. In addition, some promises are largely unknown between agents. The existence of two or more agents highlights a relational element. Generally, an agent (employee) internalizes a set of promises owed to him/her from a second agent in return for their effort and commitment. A reciprocation failure can deteriorate the agent relationship and diminish effort and commitment. A major distinguishing characteristic of the psychological contract is perception [12, p. 6]. Two key elements in its formation are subjectivity and nomology; it is likely agents have different views of the contract [12]. For example, in a job recruitment event, an organization and potential employee discuss benefits such as job security, job opportunities, prestige, and other advantages, in exchange for hard

work and dedicated service. Each agent can potentially interpret the discussion differently. The employee may believe the benefits will come within a short timeframe whereas the firm may expect five or more years of service before reciprocation ensues. Psychological contract subjectivity involves an ontological construction of expectations within the agent and thus is (1) largely inaccessible to external agents, and (2) susceptible to synchronicity issues with the organizational agent [16].

2.1.1 Psychological Contract Breach
The psychological contract breach (PCB) is a complex cognitive and subjective phenomenon whereby an individual is aware of unmet promises [11]. The complexity of PCB exists in determining which promises were unmet [11, p.526] and their salience to the individual. Extant research supports the outcome of missed promises as a reduction of employee performance, trust, satisfaction, and organizational commitment [11]. In addition, conditions of violation are associated to feelings of betrayal and injustice [10]. However, it is also reasonable to assume a nominal reaction.

A perceived missed promise can exist as the reneging or inadvertent failure to uphold obligations. Reneging is a purposeful failing to reciprocate obligations whereas unavoidable circumstances such as a poor performing organization or an economic downturn, inadvertently squelches reciprocation of promises [10]. Incongruence is the schemata divergence of promises and their salience between the employee and organization. If the reasons for reneging are not communicated to the employee, it is likely perceived as such [12]. A key cognitive process in a breach is the mental assessment of the condition. Since employees are most likely to assume that a promise was reneged [10, p.247], an important issue for researchers and practitioners is enabling employees and managers to recognize the appearance of PCB as incongruence such as a poor economy or corporate takeover. This awareness can potentially change their interpretation of the breach. Examples of PCB exist in the relationship between supervisors and subordinates, and the employee and the organization. At the base of this definition is an emotional outcome: how one responds to the event. However, prior to an emotional response is a situation assessment or PCB. Therefore, PCB is first a cognitive process [10]. It is important, though not always followed, that the incumbent determine the nature of the breach, and the salience of the missed obligation before an emotional outcome is presented.

2.1.2 Affective Events Theory
Addressing emotions and affect in decision making, Weiss and Cropanzano (1996, p.11) address AET as "a focus on the structure, causes, and consequences of affective experiences at work" and additionally "directs attention away from features of the environment and toward events as proximal causes of affective reactions." The establishment of affect research focused on job satisfaction as and its commonly accepted view of emotions driven [17].Weiss and Cropanzano (1996) suggest that affect and satisfaction are separate entities such that satisfaction exists as a unitary construct and affect encompasses deeper variations of descriptive power. Thus, an individual's feelings about his/her job are likely a contextual aggregation of emotions *and* judgments. The concept of time is included in this study where it is largely overlooked in previous research. Weiss and Cropanzano (1996) argue that time is an important factor in determining job satisfaction. Specifically, emotions and moods vary on a number of distal influences such as environment and

personal disposition. In short, how one feels about his or her job may be contextually bounded to the day, week, month, or year.

Emotion is an outcome of a cognitive assessment of conscious or subconscious object, has limited duration, and fits into a discrete set of categories such as fear (wide eyes, trembling), anger (furrowed brow, frowning or showing of teeth), joy/happiness (laughter, smiling), and interest (Fredrickson, 2001;Shaver, Schwartz, Kirson, & O'Conner, 1987). The most subtle nuances of positive and negative emotions build upon the root emotions, measured in degrees of existence. Shaver and colleagues (1987) conducted empirical research into the classification and salience of emotions. In their study, 112 participants rated emotional terms on a four-point scale developing an enumeration of the familiar and unfamiliar groupings. A cluster analysis of 135 emotion names emerged dividing these list of words related to love, joy, surprise, anger, sadness, and fear.

Affect, existing as the multidimensional and overarching entity to emotional linkage and judgment, exists as a situational cognitive assessment at varying levels of job satisfaction. Weiss and Cropanzano (1996) argue that an individual's satisfaction with their job is more a positive or negative judgment than an ephemeral fluctuation of emotional or mood-based evaluation. The element of time acts as a divisor between emotions and affect in that affective assessments and outcomes last longer than emotions. Thus, job satisfaction exists in the following elements: emotion (affect), judgment, proximal influencers, and time. In its initial form, AET "...was intended to provide a roadmap or "macrostructure" to help guide research on emotional experiences at work." [18] We draw from AET since affective events can influence individual job satisfaction to turnover intension or actual turnover.

3. RESEARCH MODEL
3.1 Model
Our model serves as our guiding foundation to this study. Its development emerged from the literature review on psychological contract theory [12] and affective events theory [17]. The purpose of our model is to follow an event from its inception to affect driven behavior and psychological contact violation. We begin with an event, such as an IS professional experiencing expectation incongruence with the IS profession. The effected individual processes the incongruence by comparing it to their internal list of expectations. As Kotter (1973) suggests, saliency of the expectation interacts with job satisfaction. Therefore, the more significant the expectation, the larger negative effect incongruence generates. Thus, it is reasonable that perceived incongruence on significant internal expectation is associated to the existence of contract breach. As a result, this outcome acts as input to another assessment event examining the linkage of the incongruence to affect/emotion. The type of affect/emotion is a key element in this process such that the more salient an expectation the higher the degree of negative emotion and coping mechanisms. Our model notes two outcomes, affect driven behaviors or psychological contract violation. Our model, therefore, addresses the following research question: How do IS professionals remain engaged and committed to the IS profession while in the presence of unmet profession expectations, and negative, stressful, and uncertain environments? We begin by using the theoretical lens of psychological contract and affective events theories as presented in the previous section. We then directed our study to extracting the possible antecedents associated to psychological contract breach, and ultimately to contract violation.

3.2 Methodology
3.2.1 Context and Data Collection
The foundation of this research exists in identifying perturbations between an IT professional and their profession. What keeps an IT professional in the profession? Similarly, what motivates an IT professional to seek another profession? Our goal is to extend the current research by exploring the possibility of contributing antecedents not present in the current literature. Our study extends psychological contract theory to the IS professional and their profession. We integrate affective events theory to examine the role emotions (affect) serve in the assessment of PCB/PCV. Therefore, it was determined that the logical first step was to use the qualitative method to understand the phenomenon. Through these lenses and their relational and interpersonal dyadic function, our research focuses on the complex and frequent occurrence of PCB and PCV in the IS profession. Based on a recent empirical study examining the antecedents to psychological contract violation within the IS profession [3], our hope is to disentangle potentially unexplained antecedents couched in various ontologies, thus providing a deeper explanation of the phenomenon.

Selecting the appropriate participants for our exploratory study required developing qualifying criteria. As such, criteria-based sampling narrowed our selection to those individuals potentially experiencing the same phenomenon [19]. Therefore, sample candidates had at least five or more years' of experience in the IS profession and worked in at least two or more IS sub-fields, such as systems administrator, applications developer, IT/IS manager, Vice President of IT, or Chief Information, Officer, or Chief Technology Officer (CIO/CTO). We focused on those participants that fit these criteria because they would most likely have adequate experience and tenure in the profession to have potentially experienced contract breach or violation since these generally develop after spending time with the profession or organization [20]. Therefore, we believe that criteria-based sampling was the appropriate method for our research.

We then generated a participant list using a customer contact database after receiving appropriate permission from the participating firm. Additional firms, outside the customer database were located and contacted for participants. In all, 335 different organizations were contacted using multiple methods, such as email and phone calls. All organization and participant names have been altered to protect their confidentiality. Addressing affiliation between the interview and participants, the majority of participants (65%) were 'strangers' [21], twenty-six percent were indirectly affiliated (i.e. some prior contact), and the remaining 9% of participants were directly affiliated (i.e. graduate students in the same educational program). To achieve the representation of 'voices' [21], it was paramount to gather different perspectives to achieve triangularity [22], consistency of experience, and reduction of elitist perspectives [23]. In some cases, several IT professionals were interviewed at the same organization. The questions were open-ended, providing interviewees a chance to express their assessments on their membership in the IS/IT profession. As such, the 'interview script' was generally followed. The point of deviation from the script occurred when (1) the participant presented an idea or event that warranted further investigation, and (2) some participants answered 2 or more questions with a single response. Each interview was scheduled to last 45 minutes and the average interview lasted 30 minutes. We attempted to minimize social dissonance by enabling participants to schedule their interview, establishing the identity of the interviewer and interviewee through a series of basic demographic questions (see Appendix C). The interviews took place face-to-face and by phone. Ensuring confidentiality and anonymity, each participant reviewed and signed a consent form explaining the purpose of the study, the method of data collection, and their rights as a participant. All interviews were recorded, transcribed, and reviewed for completeness. The interviews were used as our primary data source.

3.2.2 Data Analysis

We began our coding process by using an open and inductive coding approach [24]. The establishment of our theory base presented a focused coding process from which content analysis was used to satisfy the constant comparative process, supplying instances meeting existent codes and generating new codes. Our purpose was to examine the data for unique characteristics of the IS professional to IS profession relationship necessary to build a contextual but comprehensive schema defining the phenomena. An initial coding process on all interviews was carried out by the primary author to develop a preliminary taxonomy using the open coding method [24]. A three-member research team examined the data for validity, and consistency. With the preliminary taxonomy, each member coded a subset of interviews to address inter-rater reliability. The process began with a debriefing session designed to orient all members to the research topic and phenomena under study. A single interview was then sent to each member of the team to begin the first round of independent coding. As part of the coding process, the unit of analysis represents the interpretation of the data in context. Through the constant comparison of the interview to schema analysis, a valid and parsimonious schema was developed. Once the final taxonomy was in place, each member coded a subset of the interviews.

3.2.3 Demographic and Descriptive Statistics

We conducted 26 semi-structured interviews in various companies. One interview, in written format, was too ambiguous to provide enough value for this research and was thus, discarded. Two interviews did not satisfy our criteria and were omitted. In total, twenty-three interviews were used for our research. The interview process lasted between 19 and 45 minutes with an average time of 30 minutes. Of the twenty-three interviewees, 74% were male and 27% were female. The average number of years of professional IS experience was 23 years, and their average age was 51, reflecting well experienced IS professionals. As for organizational positions, 78% were in management positions, eight percent were front line IS professionals, and the remaining 13% were involved in IS at an academic institution, as shown in table 2. Respondents worked in various industry sectors, as indicated in table 1.

3.3 Qualitative Taxonomy

In this section, we examine the potential antecedents of psychological contract breach. The elements emerged from the data as part of the qualitative process previously described. In addition, as each category emerged, a relevant definition was applied from examining literature where the item was used in previous research. For those items that were somewhat generic, such as 'Learning Opportunities', a comparable definition was applied from the appropriate dictionary text. It is also important to note that some categories contain a sub category that contain a deeper description. Overall, our analysis process produced 27 unique categories. The establishment of the antecedents involved a process of examining the outcome of our qualitative process, and focusing on the number of references for each category, as displayed in our qualitative tool (NVivo version 9). We sorted the

categories and observed the top eight categories most referenced, in both unique interviews and actual references of the condition. Although some interviews had multiple references to a category, only the most relevant were retained. Due to space limitations, we present two qualitative categories: Leaning opportunities and Interpersonal relationships.

3.3.1 Learning Opportunities

Learning opportunities present a way to learn new skills by attending professional or academic education events. It also presents an avenue for IS professionals to increase and keep up-to-date their skillset with the changing technology landscape. There are positive and negative forms of leaning opportunities found in our analysis. A positive learning opportunity, for example, can be new certifications, new technologies, or the ability to become involved in the development of a new software application. Conversely, a negative learning opportunity may be the constant upgrading of technical knowledge and skills (i.e. Learning appears as an advantage and disadvantage). Some IS professionals indicate the quick change of technology is unreasonably frequent.

"Some people might be, "Oh, man I just learned this, and now I have learn something else." **Interview 19**

However, the majority of the responses in this category were largely positive such as the following quote.

"...It's not the money I crave. It's challenge." **Interview 9**

In sum, our analysis suggests learning opportunities are interpreted differently among the IS professionals. Some participants see learning situations as a negative outcome of the profession, choosing to fixate on the fields less appealing aspects. However, the majority of interviewees gravitated toward the fields' fast pace noting that change and challenge are positive and appealing driving attributes on the field.

3.3.2 Interpersonal Relationships

We define Interpersonal relationship (IR) as the positive or negative social interaction between two or more parties. We apply this definition to IS professionals and their users. We consider IR as a critical IS component because of the frequent and dynamic aspects of communication and individual personalities (Heider, 1958). A main function of an IS professional is to ensure accessibility and functioning of user-based systems. Users are dependent, largely, on the responsiveness and skillset of the IS professional. In a system crisis, both the user and IS professional are involved, socially in investigating the problem. In some cases, users are unaware of the issues surrounding the problem, often attempting to resolve their own issues, sometimes unsuccessfully. Some interactions can be tense because of a perceived time crunch and user emotional state. Interpersonal relationships are therefore an important dimension to the IS profession, as in the following quote.

"...there are times, particularly when you are dealing with faculty members that they are unreasonable..." **Interview 22**

Users often perceive IS as a utility (i.e. always 'on'). An outage of any digital equipment residing between services and users falls into the purview of technologists. The unfortunate reality is that in some circumstances, an outage may be beyond IS control, such as a Wide Area Network (WAN) outage. Although the interaction between the WAN provider and IS proceeds, users are unable to get to their services and therefore typically frustrated that the utility is not "on." A typical situation could involve a system outage during fiscal year-end. The resulting interactional relationship between users and IS professionals can be strained because of the criticality of year-end process for most organizations. The example below provides explicates a typical IS perception of how users address a utility outage.

"...if everything's running fine you're doing a good job, but if everything's broken it's your fault." **Interview 13**

Some IS professionals describe the user experience as genuinely positive; a chance to meet new people, as in the following quotes.

"...you get to meet those folks and kind of see what's going on, on the front lines and kind of learn what their life is like." **Interview 2**

In sum, our analysis found support for positive and negative interpersonal relationships with IS professionals and users. Some interviews addressed IR experiences in a more neutral manner, not referring to any specific interactions between people and were not included in this analysis.

4. LIMITATIONS

The concepts of our study are non-trivial in every sense of the word such that further research and development is necessary. The level of analysis in our work is the IS professional group (group level). However, caution must be used when generalizing from our relatively small and somewhat non-randomized dataset. Although there were 33 interviews conducted, only 23 were used in this study because our data collection deadline and budget. Additionally, this study is part of a list of requirements for a doctoral program and, in this instance, is bounded by the limitations of course completion time.

The dataset presented a few issues with our analysis. First, although the sample size is in line with similar work (Sherif, K. and Menon, N. M., 2004; Shim et al., 2002; Geissler, G., Zinkhan, G., Watson, R. T., 2005) the diversity is less than desired as the majority are in the c-store field. Second, the makeup of the dataset was largely male. Extra efforts were made to balance the gender makeup by seeking out female IS leaders since we believe they will have a similar but distinct perspective on the IS profession. A third dataset limitation exists in our sampling method. Access to participants for research is known to be a difficult endeavor. The primary author initially resolved the participant debacle by employing convenience sampling.

5. DISCUSSION

In this section, we discuss the results of our finds and present propositions. In future research, the focus is to operationalize these propositions in quantitative research. For the sake of brevity, only two propositions are considered.

5.1.1 Formation of a Breach in the IS Profession

The goal of this section is to determine the existence of contract inconsistency/reneging by presenting the results of our findings. The opportunity to learn new things appeared in our analysis as one of the more salient aspects of the information systems profession. Although constant learning can be viewed as a disadvantage among some respondents, the majority of our sample base believed learning to be a benefit of the field. Most interviewees indicated that the absence of such an opportunity could change their view of the field as less desirable. Extant research suggests the lack of learning opportunities affects an individual's affective normative commitment [25], including goal achievement, skill development, and satisfaction [26]. The absence or minimization of learning opportunities in the IS profession, could result in a contract breach within the profession.

We defined intrinsic accomplishment is the satisfaction an individual experiences when solving complex issues. It is the positive feeling experienced when attempting and solving an issue

believed to be beyond the capabilities of the individual (challenge). Prior research into the intrinsic concept examined intrinsic motivation *leading* to accomplishment. The tripartite model of intrinsic motivation [27] addresses multiple aspects of intrinsic conditions. Intrinsic accomplishment exists in parallel with motivation where each is considered a necessity of psychological needs, as suggested in self-determination theory [28]: autonomy, competence, and relatedness. Several of our interviewees indicated just such an event in their career. In addition, we believe, both from experience and from our research that IS professionals, sometimes prone to recede from social interaction and ambivalence toward their customers (users), find that resolving a user's issue is satisfying. We therefore propose the following. Many interviewees in our analysis appeared to hold intrinsic accomplishment above even the technical aspects of the profession, in essence, working in the profession to help their users become more productive by reducing their frustrations using computing hardware and software. IS professionals with a high sense of intrinsic accomplishment with the IS procession will be less prone to claiming psychological contract breach with the profession.

6. FUTURE RESEARCH

The research addressed here can contribute much to the field of psychological contract and associated areas involving IS turnover, commitment, and satisfaction with the profession. We attempt to widen our view of the dynamics in the turbulent IS profession by focusing at the group level to understand what motivates an IS professional to experience enough of a violation with the field to absorb the switching costs of changing fields outright. Therefore, future research is aimed at first operationalizing our current work to determine if the stated antecedents associate to the occurrence of psychological contract breach or violation with the IS profession. In a follow up set of future research projects, a focus on a core set of antecedences that can provide explanatory power to the phenomenon in the IS profession and the impact emotion and affect have on IS retention in the profession.

7. CONCLUSION

We present a possible method to examining why IS professionals leave and remain in the profession. The IS profession contains many perturbations when we consider the turnover in technology and the level of skills needed to implement these new solutions. If we also consider the common and unfortunate focus on IS as a cost center juxtaposed with the necessity of IS professionals to constantly advertise their value adding potentials to the firm our study contributes to the IS profession.

8. ACKNOWLEDGMENTS

Our thanks to Dr. Jo Ellen Moore, Ph.D. for her insight and suggestions on this research.

References

[1]   R. Weber, "Some Implications of the Year-2000 Era, Dot-com Era, and Offshoring for Information Systems Pedagogy," *MIS Quarterly,* pp. i-xi, 1 June 2004.

[2]   J. Luftman and T. Ben-Zvi, "Key Issues for IT Executives 2011: Cautious Optimism in Uncertain Economic Times," *MIS Quarterly Executive,* pp. 203-212, 2011.

[3]   C. Riemenschneider and D. Armstrong, "What Influences IT Professional Psychological Contract Violation?," in *2012 45th Hawaii International Conference on System Science (HICSS)*, Grand Wailea, 2012.

[4] K. Potter, "IT Cost Optimization Round 2: Strategic Shifts and Doing Less With Less," 20 August 2010. [Online]. Available: http://my.gartner.com/portal/server.pt?open=512&objID=260&mode=2&PageID=3460702&resId=1425415&ref=QuickSearch&sthkw=%22doing+more+with+less%22+%22information+Technology%22.

[5] J. C. Chiang, C. Liao, J. J.-Y. Jiang and G. Klein, "Consequences of Psychological Contract Violations for IS Personnel," *Journal of Computer Information Systems,* pp. 78-87, 2012.

[6] C. Ranganathan and C. N. Outlay, "Life After IT Outsourcing: Lessons Learned from Resizing the IT workforce," *MIS Quarterly Executive,* pp. 161-173, 2009.

[7] J. A. Thompson and J. S. Bunderson, "Violations of Principle: Ideological Currency in the Psychological Contract," *Academy of Management Review,* pp. 571-586, 2003.

[8] S. Overby, "U.S. Beats India for IT Outsourcing Innovation and Understanding," 24 9 2012. [Online]. Available: http://www.cio.com/article/717067/U.S._Beats_India_for_IT_Outsourcing_Innovation_and_Understanding_. [Accessed 29 9 2012].

[9] D. M. Rousseau, "Psychological and Implied Contracts in Organizations," *Employee Responsibilities and Rights Journal,* pp. 121-139, 1989.

[10] E. W. Morrison and S. L. Robinson, "When Employees Feel Betrayed: A Model of How Psychological Contract Violation Develops," *Academy of Management Review,* pp. 226-256, 1997.

[11] S. L. Robinson and E. W. Morrison, "The development of psychological contract breach and violation: a longitudinal study," *Journal of Organizational Behavior,* pp. 525-546, 2000.

[12] D. M. Rousseau, Psychological Contracts in Organizations: Understanding Witten and Unwritten Agreements, Thousand Oaks: Sage Publications, Inc., 1995.

[13] C. Argyris, Understanding Organizational Behavior, Homewood: The Dorsey Press, Inc., 1960.

[14] H. Levinson, C. Price, K. Munden and C. Solley, Men, management and mental health, Cambridge: Harvard University Press, 1962.

[15] J. P. Kotter, "The Psychological Contract: Managing the Joining-Up Process," *California Management of Review,* pp. 91-99, 1973.

[16] S. L. Robinson, "Trust and Breach of the Psychological Contract," *Administrative Science Quarterly,* pp. 574-599, 1996.

[17] H. M. Weiss and R. Cropanzano, "Affective Events Theory: A Theoretical Discussion of the Structure, Causes, and Consequences of Affective Experiences at Work," *Research in Organizational Behavior,* pp. 1-74, 1996.

[18] H. M. Weiss and D. J. Beal, "Reflections on Affective Events Theory," in *Reseach on Emotion in Organizations: The Effect of Affect in Organizational Settings,* San Diego, Elsevier, 2005, pp. 1-21.

[19] J. W. Creswell, Qualitative Inquiry & Research Design, Los Angeles: Sage Publications, Inc., 2013.

[20] T. W. Ng, D. C. Feldman and S. S. Lam, "Psychological Contract Breaches, Organizational Commitment, and Innovation-Related Behaviors: A Latent Growth Modeling Approach," *Journal of applied Psychology,* pp. 744-751, 2010.

[21] M. D. Myers and M. Newman, "The qualitative interview in IS research: Examining the craft," *Information and Organization,* pp. 2-26, 2007.

[22] H. J. Rubin and I. S. Rubin, Qualitative Interviewing: The art of hearing data (2nd Ed.), Thousand Oaks, CA: Sage, 2005.

[23] M. B. Miles and A. M. Huberman, Qualitative Data Analysis, Thousand Oaks: Sage Publications, Inc., 1994.

[24] J. Corbin and A. Strauss, Basics of Qualitative Research 3rd Edition, Thousand Oaks: Sage, 2008.

[25] M. Bambacas, "Organizational handling of careers influences managers' organizational commitment," *Journal of Management Development,* pp. 807-827, 2010.

[26] M. v. Gelderen, L. v. d. Sluis and P. Jansen, "Learning Opportunities and Learning Behaviours of Small Business Starters: Relations with Goal Achievement, Skill Development and Satisfaction," *Small Business Economics,* pp. 97-108, 2005.

[27] N. Carbonneau, R. J. Vallerand and M.-A. K. Lafrenière, "Toward a Tripartite Model of Intrinsic Motivation," *Journal of Personality,* pp. 1147-1178, 2012.

[28] E. L. R. M. Deci, Intrinsic motivation and self-determination in Human Behavior, New York: Plenum Press, 1985.

[29] J. Y. Hong, "Pre-service and beginning teachers' professional identity and its relation to dropping out of the profession," *Teaching and Teacher Education,* pp. 1530-1543, 2010.

[30] K. Inkson and M. B. Arthur, "How to be a Successful Career Capitalist," *Organizational Dynamics,* pp. 48-61, 2001.

[31] D. Gefen and C. M. Ridings, "IT Acceptance: Managing User – IT Group Boundaries," *The DATA BASE for Advances in Information Systems,* pp. 25-40, 2003.

[32] W. H. Turnley and D. C. Feldman, "Re-examining the effect of psychological contract violations: unmet expectations and job dissatisfaction as mediators," *Journal of Organizational Behavior,* pp. 25-42, 2000.

Author Index

www.ingramcontent.com/pod-product-compliance
Lightning Source LLC
Chambersburg PA
CBHW080410060326
40689CB00019B/4196